THE
GREAT WEEKEND
ESCAPE BOOK

Northeast Edition

THE
GREAT WEEKEND
ESCAPE BOOK

From Williamsburg to Cuttyhunk Island

MICHAEL SPRING

E. P. DUTTON, INC. ▪ NEW YORK

This book is for my mother and father.

Grandma Moses's painting "Covered Bridge with Carriage" seems the perfect introduction to a book that emphasizes the arts and local history, and that encourages readers to slow down and pay attention to the seasons.

Published in the United States by
E. P. Dutton, Inc., 2 Park Avenue, New York, N.Y. 10016
Library of Congress Catalog Card Number 84-72668

ISBN: 0-525-48145-1

Editor: Sandra W. Soule
Designed by Nicola Mazzella

CONTENTS

INTRODUCTION

It's time for a completely revised edition of *The Great Weekend Escape Book*—one that reflects current prices and brings you up to date on the fortunes and misfortunes of restaurants and hotels.

Four new escapes are included: Rehoboth Beach, Delaware; Greene County, New York; Cold Spring, New York; and Litchfield Hills, Connecticut. Litchfield Hills is actually three escapes in one, since you'll need at least three weekends to discover all that this region has to offer.

These new chapters will be of particular interest to those of you who are eager to discover some new weekend retreats. The revised chapter on Bay Head contains some exciting new information on Bay Head guest houses, which have undergone major facelifts since 1981. It also adds the Bird and Bottle Inn in Garrison, New York, to the list of highly recommended inns in the northeast.

One thing has not changed. I wrote this edition, as I wrote the first, as though you were a close friend who sat me down and said, "Tell me about 25 glorious weekends."

Since friends put a premium on honesty, I avoided the usual hyperboles of travel writing. Not every covered bridge or historical society is worth a visit. Not every place is the quaintest, oldest, or most charming.

What I tried to do was help you decide what places are really worth seeing—not just in summer, but year-round—and how best to organize your time. Each chapter consists of one area to visit, and is divided into the following categories (where applicable):

1. Distances
2. Major Attractions
3. Introduction
4. What to See and Do

There are trips for everyone.

Some (Cuttyhunk, Tangier) are to islands; others (Poconos, Skyline Drive, Litchfield Hills) are to mountains, rivers, and lakes. A few weekends (Deerfield, Williamsburg) are journeys back in time, while others (Hershey, Bay Head) require no other guidebook but your senses. Newport and Mystic are well-known destinations. Others (Monadnock, Windham County, Greene County) are for people who love to wander off the beaten track or avoid the crowds.

I won't tell you about many places I visited: the ones I wouldn't send friends to or wouldn't choose to revisit myself.

Since I'm asking you to trust me, I had better say a word about my sensibilities. I'm partial to inns and hotels that capture the spirit of a place; that are one of a kind; that could not be anywhere other than where they are. I hate furnishings that are cute, overdecorated, or deliberately old-fashioned. I love to fall asleep in rooms that are softened by age.

I'm fond of country inns, though too much nonsense has been written about them: age in itself is no guarantee of character or charm. (The Holiday Inn in Culpepper, Virginia, is as warm and comfortable as half the inns you read about in books.) I prefer inns with five to ten rooms—small enough to let you feel part of a family; large enough to allow for some privacy. My ideal innkeeper has the tact and intelligence to know when to be friendly and when to leave you alone.

My lower back appreciates hard mattresses, and I have an aversion to yellow water glasses.

Having lived in Japan, I care as much how food is presented—and in what surroundings—as how it tastes. All chefs have bad nights and nights off; and so I base my judgment of restaurants not only on personal experience but on the opinions of long-time local residents, who can't be fooled as easily.

The inns I most highly recommend are:

The Deerfield Inn (Deerfield)
The Inn at Phillips Mill (New Hope)
The Williamsburg Inn (Williamsburg)
Prospect Hill (Charlottesville)
The Mainstay (Cape May)
Bishopsgate (Essex)
The Inn at Castle Hill (Newport)
Morrill House (Newburyport)
The Essex House Inn (Newburyport)
The Inn at Sawmill Farm (Windham County)
The Bird and Bottle Inn (Cold Spring)
The Hermitage (Windham County)
The Whetstone Inn (Windham County)

If you feel I have been too kind or uncritical, or have overlooked interesting places, please let me know so that I can include the information in a third edition. Write to Michael Spring, *Great Weekend Escape Book*, c/o E. P. Dutton, 2 Park Avenue, New York, NY 10016.

Happy traveling!

Special thanks to my editor, Sandy Soule, for her patience, enthusiasm, and good taste.

THE
GREAT WEEKEND
ESCAPE BOOK

Williamsburg, Virginia

(Zip Code, 23187; Area Code, 804)

1. DISTANCES

BY CAR. *From New York*, 8½ hours; *from Philadelphia*, 5½ hours; *from Washington*, 3 hours.

BY BUS. *From New York*, 10 hours; *from Philadelphia*, 8½ hours; *from Washington*, 4½ hours.

BY TRAIN. *From New York*, 7½ hours; *from Philadelphia*, 6¼ hours; *from Washington*, 3½ hours.

2. MAJOR ATTRACTIONS

▪ An opportunity to return to eighteenth-century America and learn how men and women lived before the Revolution.
▪ A townscape of nearly a hundred early American buildings authentically restored or reconstructed on their original foundations.

▪ More than 200 period rooms with a full range of decorative arts and furnishings, from the elegant silver of English governors to humble household objects.

▪ More than 30 master craftsmen and apprentices exhibiting their trades.

▪ Some 90 acres of gardens, comprising what has been called one of the six great gardens in the Western World.

▪ Programs of early American music, dance, and theater.

▪ One of the country's most elegant inns; some 25 early American houses restored for overnight guests.

▪ The battlefield of Yorktown; the site of Jamestown; some of the South's most lavish plantation houses, all open to the public.

3. INTRODUCTION

Success has not spoiled Colonial Williamsburg. It is a class operation. Its directors have a budget to balance, but they are also committed to quality and good taste.

If you lived in the colonial town, would you recognize it today? The guide attempts an answer:

"[You] would recognize its general plan—broad Duke of Gloucester Street stretching nearly a mile from the College of William and Mary to the Capitol; the spacious Market Square and Palace Greens; the houses set back precisely from the street, and the fences defining each lot. Most of the familiar landmarks would be there, including the Capitol, Gaol, Courthouse, Bruton Parish Church, Governor's Palace, College, and Publick Hospital.

"But the paved streets, the brick sidewalks, the street lights and the fire hydrants would be strange to eighteenth-century eyes, as would the curiously dressed thousands of visitors. The whole town would seem tidier, with houses better painted, greens more smoothly cropped, and gardens spruced up and adorned with more flowers. They would miss the dozens of saddle and draft horses and the two-wheeled riding chairs; the cows, chicken, sheep, and other livestock in every part of town; the streets and paths mired with mud or deep in dust; and the crowds of flies and mosquitoes in summer. Perhaps most of all they would miss the pungent smells of animal manure, rooting hogs, backyard privies, and unwashed humanity."

Despite a few concessions to modern life, the restored town still offers Americans a unique opportunity to understand and appreciate their colonial heritage. No slave quarters or lower class homes have yet been restored; but the craft demonstrations and the strolling characters from every walk of colonial life reinforce the American notion that history is told, not in the pageantry of kings and queens, but in the everyday lives of ordinary people.

The story of Williamsburg begins with the ordinary people who founded Jamestown, six miles to the south, in 1607. The 104 colonists landed May 14 on a wooded peninsula on the north bank of a broad river—about 32 miles from the mouth. They named the river "James" and the settlement "Jamestown," in honor of their king, James I. This was to become the first successful English settlement in the new world—13 years before the pilgrims stepped ashore at Plymouth.

Success was a while in coming. The ships left for England in June and when they returned in autumn, with more colonists and fresh supplies, fewer than 50 of the 105 settlers had survived. Two years later, the colonists were preparing to abandon the settlement when the English colonial governor, De La Warr (Lord Delaware), arrived with more men and supplies. The future of the settlement was secured in 1613 when John Rolfe—who later married Chief Powhatan's daughter, Pocahontas—introduced tobacco as a cash crop for export. The first group of Englishwomen arrived in 1619. That same year Jamestown established the first representative government on the American continent. It also introduced slavery and built the first Anglican church.

Jamestown served as the capital of Virginia from 1607 to 1699. In 1693 the settlers obtained a charter to establish the College of William and Mary, the second college in the New World (after Harvard). Because of an Indian massacre, the site was moved inland from Jamestown to the village of Middle Plantation. Construction began with the College Building, based on designs by Sir Christopher Wren (called the Wren Building today).

Jamestown's fate was sealed in 1698 when the State House burned for the fourth time. The low-lying island was also a breeding ground for disease. And so in 1699 the capital was moved to Middle Plantation, and the village was renamed Williamsburg in honor of the reigning English king, William III. The Assembly met at the College building while the Capitol was under construction.

Williamsburg was one of the first planned cities in America. It was laid out by Francis Nicholson, the lieutenant governor from 1698 to 1705, who envisioned a country town with restful public gardens. An old horse path that ran the length of the settlement was straightened and widened to 99 feet, and renamed Duke of Gloucester Street. The Capitol was built at the east end, facing the College one mile away. A residence for the royal governor, the Crown's representative in the Virginia colony, had been constructed between the College and the Capitol in 1720. Every house on the main street was allotted one-half acre of land—enough room for a garden, a small orchard, and outbuildings such as a stable, smokehouse, dairy, slave quarters, and kitchen. Each house was set back from the road a prescribed distance and each plot was fenced. The word "city" today conjures up images of crowded tenements, but in the eighteenth century, Virginia's capital was more rural than urban and nearly every house had a vegetable garden, a few fruit trees, some berry bushes, and a few domestic animals—a cow, a horse or two, some pigs and chickens.

As the new capital, Williamsburg prospered. A market town—unlike the trading centers of New York, Philadelphia, and Boston—its population probably never exceeded 2,000; yet it was the government seat for the most extensive colony, whose boundaries then reached to the Mississippi and the Great Lakes. Visitors today need only look at the grandeur of the Governor's Palace to understand the colony's importance to the Crown.

For most of the year Williamsburg was a quiet college and market town of about 1,800 people. Its social life centered on the College and the Governor's Palace. But four times a year the town came alive—in April and October, when the Court met, and in June and December, when the General Assembly was in session. Then lawyers and planters came to town with their wives for a taste of city life, and the population more than doubled. The Governor's Palace was the scene of elegant balls and dinners. Wealthy planters crowded into Raleigh Tavern to exchange news on crops and, after 1765, complaints about Parliamentary taxation. They bet on horses, attended fairs, and watched plays performed by itinerant actors. Shops were thronged with women buying the latest fashions imported from England.

The House of Burgesses met in the Capitol building. It was here that Patrick Henry urged adoption of his Stamp Act Resolves. Here, on May 15, 1776, the Virginia Convention passed a resolution urging the Continental Congress to declare the colonies independent and create a national federation. And here, a month later, the same convention adopted George Mason's Virginia Declaration of Rights, which became the basis for the first ten amendments to the Constitution.

During the Revolution, the government of the new Commonwealth moved from Williamsburg to Richmond to escape enemy attacks and be closer to the center of the state's growing population. An era had ended, and Williamsburg began its descent into obscurity.

Many of the city's old landmarks weathered the Civil War and the ravages of the early twentieth century. In 1926 the rector of Bruton Parish Church, W. A. R. Goodwin, spoke to John D. Rockefeller, Jr., about restoring these buildings and preserving the city's past. Rockefeller responded with a $100 million donation. The nonprofit Colonial Williamsburg Foundation was established to purchase property and begin restorations.

The Historic Area today encompasses 173 acres, about 85 percent of the colonial city. It has 88 original buildings, another 50 that have been rebuilt on original sites, and 90 acres of gardens and greens. The current staff exceeds 3,500. Four years ago the cost of operating and maintaining the exhibition buildings reached $17,361,956. The figure rose to about $23 million in 1984.

The current $12 admission fee seems a small price to pay for a trip more than 200 years back in time. The journey is essential for anyone who wants to discover the values and traditions of his country's past.

4. WHAT TO SEE AND DO

▪ First stop is the **Visitor Center,** located one-half mile north of the Historic Area. If you drive into Williamsburg on I-64, take the exit marked "Colonial Williamsburg" and drive west, following the signs. The center is a confusion of boy scouts, lost children, and long lines, but you can't avoid it. Try to arrive near opening time at 8:30 A.M., or just before closing time at 10 P.M. A ticket for admission to 13 properties and free shuttle bus transportation costs $12 for adults, $8 for youths 13 to 17, and $5 for children aged 6 to 12. Tickets do not include admission to Bassett Hall, the Governor's Palace, or Carter's Grove. With your general admission ticket, each of these three properties costs $4 for adults and $2 for children. The free booklet, "The Visitor's Companion," lists all current programs and events. Go to the **Special Events desk** and purchase tickets for tours *(see #7, Tours)*, children's programs *(see #16, For Kids)*, and concerts and theatrical events *(see #5, The Arts)*. The *Official Guide* ($1.50) is a useful companion as you tour the Historic Area. If you arrive in Williamsburg in the evening, pick up your tickets and reading materials immediately and do your homework before you go to bed or at breakfast. With so much to see, it's a good idea to get an early start. (An even better idea is to call or write and have these materials sent to you. *See #22, For Further Information.*)

▪ *Williamsburg: The Story of a Patriot* is an extremely intelligent

37-minute film that helps clarify Williamsburg's role in the American Revolution. Parents with children under ten should come prepared with books, candy, or other pacifiers.

THE HISTORIC AREA

▪ The shuttle bus takes you from the Visitor Center to the Historic Area. In summer, it leaves every five minutes from 8:40 to 5:30 and every ten minutes from 5:30 to 10.

▪ What you see depends, of course, on your interests. You might begin at the Capitol at the eastern end of the Historic Area and walk toward the Governor's Palace and the College of William and Mary. The **Capitol** is politically the most important building in Williamsburg. Begun in 1699, it is a landmark in colonial American architecture because it gave the first evidence of transition from the medieval, Jacobean design of Bacon's Castle *(see below)* to what was to become the classical manner of eighteenth-century Virginia. Virginia's House of Burgesses, the oldest representative assembly in the country, met here from 1704. Visitors can sit on the straight-back benches and imagine Patrick Henry protesting the Stamp Act, or legislators debating George Mason's Declaration of Rights.

▪ Down the hill from the Capitol is **The Old Public Jail** (Gaol), where debtors, criminals, and pirates were imprisoned. Children always seem to be morbidly fascinated with the pillory and stocks.

▪ Heading west on Duke of Gloucester Street, visit one of the two exhibition taverns, **Wetherburn's** or the **Raleigh Tavern.** Furnished with period antiques, they will give you a sense of eighteenth-century tavern life. It was here, in the public rooms, the gaming rooms, and the public dancing areas that most of Williamsburg's socializing took place. Wetherburn's Tavern, unlike the Raleigh Tavern, is an original building, not a reconstruction. Wetherburn's Tavern was the scene of much gambling and carousing, in contrast to the Raleigh Tavern, which attracted a more refined and affluent clientele. Jefferson danced here as a student. Washington dined here often. Lafayette was welcomed at the Raleigh Tavern on his return to the U.S. in 1824. Visitors can step up to the bar and imagine themselves surrounded by wealthy planters with their tankards of ale, voicing their objections to British taxes. For a late morning snack, stop in at the **Bakery,** which sells bread and gingerbread cookies and offers demonstrations of colonial baking.

▪ Heading west again, stop in at the **Magazine,** the arsenal of the Virginia colony, which was important in the days leading up to the Revolution.

▪ Now that you have a sense of public life in Colonial Williamsburg, visit one of the three private homes. The **Peyton Randolph House** is particularly well restored, with most of the original paneling. The **George Wythe House** is a two-story Georgian manor with lovely gardens. The detached kitchen recalls a time when kitchens were separated from the main house to avoid the heat and unpleasant smells. Visitors can come here for daily demonstrations of hearth cooking with old implements. The **Brush-Everard House** is original, with a hand-carved staircase and a 300-book colonial library. Decorated with period antiques, any of these three buildings will give you a sense of upper-middle-class life in eighteenth-century Williamsburg. The elegance of these private residences is not altogether misleading, for Williamsburg was an affluent community; but visitors should not forget that slave quarters and craftsmen's homes also existed in colonial times—though they (except for the Geddy House) are strangely missing from Williamsburg today.

▪ Up and down **Duke of Gloucester Street** are a number of craft shops where costumed artisans practice the trades and crafts of colonial America, using eighteenth-century methods and tools to produce replicas of colonial objects. Shops include the apothecary, baker, bookbinder, cabinetmaker, gunsmith, cooper, blacksmith, wigmaker, miller, carpenter, and music teacher. You will want to stop in at one or two and learn about trades that have a special appeal to you today. If you know nothing about wigmaking, you may not care how wigs were made 200 years ago; but if you are an avid cabinetmaker or musician, you'll be fascinated to learn how chairs or violins were constructed in pre-Revolutionary times.

▪ Next stop is the **Governor's Palace,** which reopened in 1981, fully restored with the furnishings and decorations of the residence of the royal governor from 1760 to 1775. The palace was the political and social center of the colony at a time when its boundaries extended to the Mississippi and the Great Lakes. The representative of England—the symbol of the Crown's power and wealth in the New World—lived here in all his pomp and circumstance. Seven colonial governors resided here between 1720 and 1775. Governor Alexander Spotswood supervised its construction and Lord Dunmore fled from it one June morning in 1775, thus ending for all time British rule in Virginia. The palace later served as the residence of the first two governors of the Commonwealth of Virginia, Patrick Henry and Thomas Jefferson. The royal gardens are as formal and elaborate as the Palace itself. Admission is $4 for adults and $2 for children aged 6 to 12. (The cost is double for visitors without a general admission ticket to Colonial Williamsburg.) Tickets are sold at the Visitor Center or at the Robert Carter Office on the Palace Green.

▪ If it is time for lunch, you have a choice of three taverns that serve meals in the Historic Area: **Josiah Chowning's Tavern, Campbell's Tavern,** and **King's Arms Taverns.** *See #17, Dining,* for details.

▪ An unexpected delight are the characters from Williamsburg's past who pop up in the Historic Area when you least expect them. Children in particular appreciate this opportunity for personal participation in the past. Included are a merchant outside one of the stores, a recruiting officer for the local militia who invites visitors to meet on Market Square for rudimentary drill and possible enlistment, a contemplative young lady, a black preacher, and a midwife.

▪ If your feet are ready for a rest, stop at the **Courthouse of 1770** and purchase tickets for a horse-drawn carriage or stage wagon ride through the Historic Area. Tickets cost $2 for the carriages, $1.50 for the wagons.

▪ **Bruton Parish Church** (Duke of Gloucester Street) is one of America's oldest Episcopal churches, in continuous use since 1715 (the steeple was added in 1769). Most prominent planters and all members of the legislative assembly worshiped here. The baptismal font was brought from an earlier church in Jamestown. A bell in its tower is known as Virginia's Liberty Bell because it rang out the news of the signing of the Declaration of Independence and of Cornwallis' surrender at Yorktown. The interior has been restored to its original appearance. The west gallery was reserved for university students, whose initials, carved in the handrail, are still discernible. Admission is free.

▪ The reconstructed **Publick Hospital** of 1773—the first mental hospital in the New World—opened in January, 1985. Nearby is the new **DeWitt Wallace Gallery of the Decorative Arts,** with exhibits drawn from Williamsburg's reserve collections of eighteenth-century ceramics, furniture, maps, and textiles.

▪ Shoppers will find several stores within the Historic Area that sell crafts made by the artisans and approved reproductions of goods that were available in colonial Williamsburg. **Prentis Store** and **Tarpley's Store** both sell such items as Dutch creamers, salt-glazed stoneware, belts from the harness shop, baskets, and handwoven coverlets. The **Post Office** sells reproductions of eighteenth-century prints, blank books, and broadsides. The **Golden Ball** sells gold and silver jewelry. The **Geddy Shop** sells silver and pewter stemware. Goods can also be ordered from individual craftsmen in their shops.

Violins, for example, can be ordered from the **Instrument Maker's Shop,** and tables and chairs from the **Cabinetmaker's Shop.**

▪ To be transported back in time, return to the Historic Area at dawn or dusk, when the crowds are gone. At no other time will you get such a complete sense of the serenity and openness of this colonial town.

▪ Williamsburg's attractions are not limited to the Historic Area. Near the Williamsburg Inn and Lodge is the **Abby Aldrich Rockefeller Folk Art Center** (Bus Stop #5), which features old toys, weathervanes, tobacconist's figures, and paintings by early American folk artists. Visitors who make a point of avoiding art museums or who dismiss folk art as too esoteric should give this collection a chance. Children in particular should be delighted by the toys and household items. Abby Rockefeller began collecting folk art in the 1920s, at the same time that her husband became involved in the restoration of colonial Williamsburg. She pioneered the discovery of this unappreciated art form and in ten years collected over 400 pieces of folk art, all reflecting aspects of everyday life in America. Included in the collection is Edward Hicks's *The Peaceable Kingdom.* The museum is open daily from 11 to 7. Admission is by contribution.

▪ Those who enjoy peeping into the private lives of the rich, or who simply enjoy sumptuous surroundings, will want to tour **Bassett Hall,** the former residence of Abby and John D. Rockefeller, Jr. The two-story eighteenth-century house stands much as it did when the Rockefellers restored and decorated it in the 1930s. The tasteful eclecticism of furnishings—Chinese, American, and English antiques mixed with modern easy chairs and beds—is in striking contrast to the period interiors in the Historic Area. Rockefeller's idea of a place to live a "relaxed, informal" life includes a museum's worth of folk art, some exquisite nineteenth-century Turkish prayer rugs, and a fine collection of English bone china and ceramic figures. This is not a place to bring children. Tickets are sold at the Visitor Center and at the Hall itself. Reservations may be made by phone (229-1000, ext. 4139). Tickets are $4 for adults and $2 for children. Visitors without general admission tickets to Colonial Williamsburg must pay $8 for adults and $4 for children.

▪ Families who have used up their admission tickets should know that admission is free to the Wren building, Bruton Parish Church, and all gardens (except at the Governor's Palace); and that a small contribution will secure admission to the Abby Rockefeller Folk Art Center. The Craft House and Geddy Silver Shop are also free.

• If you have any interest in shopping, the **Craft House** (Bus Stop #6) is the place to go. Save your visit for afternoons or evenings, for once inside you may never want to leave. Authentic reproductions of the furniture and decorative accessories in the Historic Area are on sale here. Goods are attractively arranged as in a charming old house, with the living room and dining room downstairs and the bedrooms upstairs. You will find homey eighteenth-century objects such as trivets copied in brass, wallpapers derived from fragments found under layers of paint, tavern glasses, and pewter trays. Prices range from $10,000 for secretary bookcases to $28 for brass candlesticks. Open Sunday and Monday from 9 to 5 and Tuesday through Saturday from 9 to 9. Visa and Mastercard are accepted. Craft House goods are also sold in shops adjacent to the Williamsburg Inn and in Merchant's Square.

• **Merchant's Square** is located outside the Historic Area. The brick-enclosed patio at the **Trellis Restaurant** is a lovely place for lunch. Lines form at the store across the street for very fine homemade ice cream cones.

• Near the square is the **College of William and Mary.** George Washington took a degree here in surveying, and Thomas Jefferson went to the school of philosophy. Presidents Monroe and Tyler and Chief Justice John Marshall are also on the alumni rolls. In 1691 the General Assembly petitioned England to secure a charter and an endowment for a university. It was granted by King William III and Queen Mary II in 1693. The **Wren Building,** attributed to designs by Sir Christopher Wren, was the first building on the campus and is today the oldest restored public building in Williamsburg. It was burned and rebuilt three times, and was twice restored, in 1928–31 and 1978. Free escorted tours leave daily from 10 to 6; but you can enter the door marked "Tours Begin Here" at any time, and explore on your own.

THE PLANTATIONS

• Among the most prominent visitors to Williamsburg in colonial times were the plantation owners along the James River. No one can understand the social and economic history of the South without some familiarity with these early plantations. You ought to visit at least one of them. The most accessible, only 6½ miles from the Historic Area, is **Carter's Grove.** Owned by Colonial Williamsburg, it is considered one of the great plantation houses of colonial Virginia. Samuel Chamberlain calls it "the most beautiful house in America." The mansion stands on an estate once owned by Robert "King" Carter—the wealthiest and most influential of all the early

Virginians. His grandson, Carter Burwell, built the house in the 1750s as part of a 1,400-acre tobacco plantation. It was built by slave labor and cost 500 British pounds. Both Jefferson and Washington dined here as planter farmers. The early Georgian house has beautiful pine floors and paneling and a magnificently carved black walnut staircase. Plans are under way to turn Carter's Grove into a working plantation with some of its original furnishings. Unfortunately, today it exudes the somewhat musty air of a museum, and is filled with the late nineteenth- and early twentieth-century furnishings of its last owner. Tickets are sold at the Information Center and the Plantation. Tickets cost $4. Visitors without general admission tickets to Colonial Williamsburg must pay $6. Visitors to Carter's Grove can see the results of one of the most important archeological digs in the U.S. at Wolstenholme Town nearby.

▪ Visitors with a serious interest in early plantation life should drive 35 miles west on Route 5 along the James River, from Williamsburg to Richmond. Most of the great plantations—Sherwood Forest, Westover, Berkeley, and Shirley—lie along this route. Admission tickets are less expensive if purchased in advance at the Information Center. To avoid retracing your steps, cross to the southern shore of the James after visiting Shirley, return along Route 10, and take the ferry back to Jamestown (the ferry trip is discussed below).

▪ The first plantation you come to is **Sherwood Forest** (about 18 miles west of Williamsburg on Route 5; phone: 829-5377). The home of two Presidents, John Tyler and William Harrison, it is 300 feet long—the longest frame house in America—and surrounded by six original outbuildings and more than 80 species of trees. At age 24, Tyler's second wife, Julia Gardiner, was the nation's youngest First Lady. The Tylers raised seven children here after he retired from the Presidency. Their descendants still live on the 1600-acre plantation. The grounds are open daily from 9 to 5. The cost is $2 for adults, 50¢ for children. Entrance to the mansion costs $6.75 per person, for groups of four or more.

▪ The second plantation on the route is **Westover** (about 26 miles west of Williamsburg on Route 5; phone: 829-2882), which sits on a large bluff some 50 yards back from the James. The manor house rivals Berkeley Plantation in splendor, but unfortunately only the gardens are open to the public. The lawns have some fine old tulip poplars, sycamores, and a yew tree reputedly planted by George Washington. The grounds are open from 9 to 5. Admission is $2.

▪ **Berkeley Plantation** (about 30 miles west of Williamsburg on Route 5; phone: 795-2453) is an early Georgian mansion built by Benjamin Harrison, a colonial leader, in 1726. His grandson was the nation's ninth President, William Henry Harrison, who returned to Berkeley to write his inaugural address in the same room where he was born. William's grandson, Benjamin Harrison, was the nation's twenty-third President. Though Berkeley is not as conscientiously restored as Shirley, it is locally important because of the Harrisons, and because it is built on a tract of land where settlers first stepped ashore in 1619 and reputedly held the country's first Thanksgiving, more than a year before the Pilgrims landed in Plymouth. The house is open daily except Christmas. Tours of the home cost $3 for adults and $1.75 for children aged 6 to 12. Tours of both house and grounds cost $5 for adults and $1.75 for children.

▪ The only working plantation is, unfortunately, the farthest away. **Shirley** (35 miles west of Williamsburg on Route 5; phone: 795-2385) is also situated closest to the James and is still owned by descendants of the original owners. The three-story brick manor house was built with lavish disregard for cost. It was the home of Anne Hill Carter, mother of Robert E. Lee, and has no rival in Queen Anne architecture in America. The house was begun in 1723 by Edward Hill III for his daughter Elizabeth when she married John Carter, eldest son of Robert "King" Carter, then the richest man in Virginia. The panels and many of the furnishings are original. Thanks to continuous ownership, the outbuildings are in excellent repair. Shirley is open daily except Christmas from 9 to 5. The 45-minute tour costs $5 for adults, $3 for children aged 13 to 21, and $2 for children 12 and under.

▪ For information on the plantations and other sights outside the Colonial Williamsburg area, contact the **Virginia Attractions Desk** (phone: 229-1000, ext. 2756), located downstairs in the Visitor Center.

JAMESTOWN

▪ **Jamestown Colonial Park** (about six miles south of Williamsburg on the Colonial Parkway; phone: 229-3107) places certain demands on the imagination, for there is little more to see of America's first English settlement than the site itself. The more you read beforehand about Jamestown, the more rewarding your visit will be. The Visitor's Center has a 15-minute film and an exhibit on the town's history. The Wilderness Drive is a scenic three- or five-mile loop trip through the marshes and forests of Jamestown Island. This will give you some sense of the wilderness the settlers encountered in 1607. The flat, wooded terrain is ideal for biking. There are turnoffs along the route with paintings depicting life in the early settlement. Admission to the park is $2 per car.

▪ **Jamestown Festival Park** (phone: 229-1607) was built in 1957 to commemorate the 350th anniversary of the Jamestown landing. Located on the mainland, one mile upriver from the original site, it includes life-size models of the three ships the settlers arrived in. You can step aboard the *Susan Constant* and imagine what it was like to cross the Atlantic in a 110-foot vessel. The triangular Fort James is a life-size reconstruction of the first fort of 1607. Admission to Festival Park is $3 for adults and $1.75 for children aged 6 to 12. A combination ticket is available with the nearby Yorktown Victory Center.

SURRY COUNTY

▪ Few visitors know about the **Jamestown Car Ferry,** which takes you on a lovely 20-minute trip across the James River from Jamestown to the peaceful countryside of Surry County. The trip can be combined with a visit to Jamestown Island, which is only a short distance from the ferry landing. A crossing on a warm summer evening at dusk is one of the loveliest trips imaginable, particularly after a long, busy day in Williamsburg. As Jamestown recedes in the distance, you can get a wonderful sense of how John Smith and his compatriots must have felt as they sailed up the James in 1607. You can park your car on the Jamestown shore and stay aboard for the round trip, or you can bring your car and spend an hour or two exploring the sights of Surry County. The cost is 25¢ for passengers and $1 for cars. The ferry leaves on the half hour from the Jamestown side and on the hour from the Surry side.

▪ As you leave the ferry slip and head south on Route 31, you will pass the entrance to the **Rolfe-Warren House,** also known as Smith's Fort Plantation (phone: 357-5976). The house was built in 1720 on land that was originally a gift from Chief Powhatan to John Rolfe on the occasion of Rolfe's marriage to his daughter, Pocahontas. The house has authentic furnishings and picturesque gardens. You can walk to the site of John Smith's 1609 fort, which gives the plantation its name.

▪ Continue south on Route 31 to the town of Surry and stop for a Smithfield ham roll or a hot fudge peanut sundae at the **Surrey House** *(see #17, Dining).*

▪ At Route 10, turn left (east) for five miles and follow signs to **Chippokes Plantation State Park** (phone: 294-3625). The 1400-acre park has a fine antebellum mansion that dates back to 1856. The 300-year-old plantation is still being farmed, and is the only plantation with its original seventeenth-century borders intact. The grounds here are lovely for walks and picnics. The entrance fee to the park is only 50¢, and includes free admission to the mansion.

▪ East of Chippokes Park is **Bacon's Castle** (phone: 359-0239). This Jacobean brick mansion, built in 1655, may be the oldest brick house in English America and the last surviving manor house in high Jacobean style. It was built in a cruciform design, with two-foot-thick walls, a Tudor dungeon, and an attic with portholes for guns. Tours can be arranged through the Virginia Historic Society. Contact the Virginia Attractions Desk in the Information Center for details.

YORKTOWN

▪ Visitors interested in the American Revolution will want to drive to **Yorktown** (13 miles northeast of Williamsburg on the Colonial Parkway) and tour the grounds where the decisive 1781 battle was fought. In 1781, a British army of 7,500 soldiers under Lord Cornwallis invaded Virginia from the south and began to lay waste its farms and towns. The French and American army marched 500 miles from Newport, Rhode Island, in just four weeks, and in September laid siege to the British forces at Yorktown. A fierce artillery barrage was followed by a daring moonlight attack led by Colonel Alexander Hamilton. Cornwallis's efforts to escape across the York River were foiled by a fortuitous storm. On October 19—a sunny fall day—the British laid down their arms and surrendered. This was the last major battle of the war. Cornwallis's surrender helped mobilize British opinion against the war, and the Treaty of Paris, recognizing the independence of the United States, was signed in 1783.

▪ The **Victory Center** (phone: 887-1776) presents an award-winning documentary on events that led to the allied victory, a fine arts gallery, and sound-and-light displays that follow the Revolutionary era from the Boston Tea Party to the final victory at Yorktown. Costumed interpreters reenact eighteenth-century crafts and activities. Open April through October. Admission is $3.50 for adults and $1.75 for children aged 6 to 12. A combination ticket is available with nearby Jamestown Festival Park.

THE POTTERY

▪ **The Pottery** (Route 60, five miles west of Williamsburg; phone: 564-3326 and 564-3327) has 330,000 square feet—the equivalent of 16 football fields—of merchandise. Children should be brought here to learn what has happened to America since the days of colonial Williamsburg.

5. THE ARTS

▪ Colonial Williamsburg (phone: 229-1000) sponsors a rich assortment of musical and theatrical events. Tickets are sold at the

Special Events desk in the Information Center. Remaining tickets are sold at the door just before the performances. Times and events are subject to change, so check the schedule.

▪ **Palace concerts.** Eighteenth-century chamber music concerts in the elegant ballroom of the Governor's Palace are quite popular, so purchase tickets in advance. Programs begin at 8:45 in the spring and fall. Admission is $8.

▪ **Music at the Capitol.** Enjoy seventeenth- and eighteenth-century madrigals and ballads at 8:30 on Sunday in the spring and fall. Admission is $5.

▪ **Musical diversions.** Light eighteenth-century music is played by small ensembles in the Capitol. Programs begin at 8 on Monday and Friday in July and August. Admission is $4.

▪ **A Capitol evening.** Enter the Legislative Chamber in the Capitol and witness and participate in Patrick Henry's debate against the Stamp Act. Programs begin at 7, 8, and 9 P.M. in July and August. Admission is $4 for adults and $2 for children.

▪ **Black music.** Performers revive the music and examine the cultural experiences of eighteenth-century Afro-America. Check the calendar of events for time and place. Admission is free for general admission ticket holders.

▪ **Bruton by candlelight.** Organ recitals in the Bruton Parish Church at 8 P.M. Programs run January and February on Saturday; March through June and September through November, on Tuesday and Saturday; and July and August on Tuesday, Thursday, and Saturday. Admission is free.

▪ **Eighteenth-century theater.** Early American comedies are performed in period costumes at the Williamsburg Lodge. Programs begin at 8:30 on Saturday, year-round. Admission is $4.

▪ **Afternoon musicale.** Fifes and drums, bagpipes, harpsichords, and other instruments are featured in light musical programs in the Music Teacher's Garden. Programs begin on Sunday at 1, 2, 3, 4, and 5. Admission is free.

▪ **Wren Chapel recital.** Eighteenth-century organ music is played on Saturday at 11. Admission is free.

Programs outside Colonial Williamsburg include:

▪ **The Virginia Shakespeare Festival** (Phi Beta Kappa Hall, College of William and Mary; phone: 253–4469 or off-season 753-4000) has performances from July 5 to August 18, nightly at 8 (except Monday) and Sunday at 2. Recent productions included *Hamlet* and *Equus.* Tickets cost $6 and $8.50.

▪ **Williamsburg Players** (2 Hubbard Lane; phone: 229-1679 or 877-6468) is a new community theater group that performs everything from comedy to serious drama from January through May. Performances are Thursday to Saturday at 8.

6. ANTIQUES AND CRAFTS

- The top antique store is **Swan Tavern** (104 Main Street, Yorktown; phone: 898–3033), which specializes in fine eighteenth-century English antiques.
- **York Antique Mall** (2007½ Richmond Road, three miles west of Williamsburg; phone: 220–2752) has 14 dealers selling "a little bit of everything," from old clothing to jewelry and furniture. Closed Tuesday and Wednesday.
- **Alley Antiques** (Prince George Street, Merchant's Square; phone: 229–9299) sells eighteenth-century silver, Victorian glass, and collectibles.
- **Bruton Antiques** (Lightfoot, corner of Routes 60 and 646, next door to The Pottery; phone: 565–0841) deals exclusively in English antiques from 1800 to 1920.
- The **Craft House** (Bus Stop #6; phone: 229–1000) is a must for visitors to Williamsburg. *See #4, What to See and Do* for details.
- Goods made by Williamsburg craftspeople are for sale within the Historic Area at **Prentis Store, Tarpley's Store, Geddy Silversmith Shop,** the **Colonial Post Office, Golden Ball Jewelry Shop, Dubois' Grocer's Shop, McKenzie's Apothecary,** and the **Raleigh Tavern Bakery.**

7. TOURS

- Two-hour general walking tours, limited to 20 people, focus on various aspects of Colonial Williamsburg, such as the shops, the homes, and the public buildings. The **Garden Tour** includes discussion of eighteenth-century garden design, plant material, and the lives of colonial plantsmen. Twentieth-century gardeners who wish to cultivate eighteenth-century plants are given horticultural information. Tickets for both of these tours are sold at the Information Center. Tickets cost $3 for adults and $1.50 for children. Without a general admission ticket, tickets cost $6 for adults and $3 for children.
- *See #18, After Hours,* for candlelight tours and evening lantern tours.
- You can leave your cars in the Information Center parking lot and tour Jamestown, Yorktown, and Carter's Grove by bus or limousine. Contact **Smith Limousine Service** (Patrick Henry Air-

port, Newport News; phone: 877-0279). You can arrange in advance to be picked up at your hotel.

8. WALKS

▪ Colonial Williamsburg is made for walkers; be sure to wear comfortable shoes. For country walks, visit the 2,500-acre **York River State Park** (10 miles north of Williamsburg; phone 564-9057). You can also take the 20-minute ferry across the James River to Scotland Wharf and visit the **Chippokes State Park** (off Route 10, about 10 miles south of Williamsburg; phone: 294-3625). Chippokes contains a seventeenth-century plantation that is open to the public and is still being farmed.

9. BIKING

▪ A pamphlet called *Biking Through Virginia's Historic Triangle* is available at the Information Center and at the bike rental shops. The 20-mile route takes you past the College of William and Mary, downtown Williamsburg, Waller Mill Park, Yorktown, and Jamestown. Biking signs mark the route, which varies from a three-lane highway to a private bike lane.

▪ Children in particular will enjoy biking through the streets of colonial Williamsburg. Also recommended is a five-mile loop around **Jamestown Island.**

▪ **Williamsburg Lodge** (phone: 229-1000) rents bikes to guests and to visitors with admission tickets to Colonial Williamsburg.

▪ Visitors with or without tickets can rent bikes at **Bikes Unlimited** (759 Scotland Street; near Hospitality House, a five-minute walk from Merchant's Square; phone: 229-4620). Bikes are also rented at **Bikesmith** (101-A Penniman Road; phone: 229–9858).

10. BOATING AND FISHING

▪ **James River Experience** (Richmond, about 1¼ hours from Williamsburg; phone: 794–3493) runs white-water raft trips on the James River—all within the city limits of Richmond.

▪ **Waller Mill Park** (Route 645, off Route 60 west, about seven miles from Williamsburg) rents rowboats and canoes for paddling and fishing on the reservoir.

▪ **York River State Park** (10 miles north of Williamsburg; phone: 564-9057) has interpretive two-hour canoe trips along the

York River. Canoes and equipment are provided. Trips begin on Wednesday at 9, Saturday at 10, and Saturday at 3:30. Phone for reservations.

11. SWIMMING

▪ Williamsburg can be insufferably hot in midsummer; after walking through the colonial village for a few hours, nothing could be finer than a dip in a pool. Most larger motels have them. The ideal solution is to stay in the **Williamsburg Inn, Lodge,** or **Motor House.** The Motor House has its own pool; the Inn and Lodge share one. These colonial Williamsburg lodgings are conveniently located so that you can go for a quick swim and return to the Historic Area without losing much time.

12. SKIING

▪ **James River Experiences** (Richmond; phone: 794–3493) rents skis, but the nearest downhill areas are 3¼ hours west at **Wintergreen** (phone: 325-2200) and **Massanutten** (phone: 703/289-9441).
▪ **Blue Ridge Mountain Sports** (Norfolk; phone: 461-2767) also rents skis.

13. RIDING

▪ **Pleasant Walks Stables** (1699 Richmond Road, about one mile from the Historic Area; phone: 229–6124) offers guided trail rides.

14. TENNIS

▪ Colonial Williamsburg (phone: 229-1000, ext. 3169) has eight courts near the **Williamsburg Inn.** Weekend tennis packages are available, costing, per person, from $180 off-season at the Motor House to $341 in-season at the Inn. Rates include two breakfasts and dinners.
▪ Tennis is available at **Holiday Inn's 1776 Resort, John Yancey Motor Hotel, Minuet Manor-Superior Motel, Quality Inn—Fort Magruder, Sheraton Patriot Inn,** and the **Williamsburg Hilton.**
▪ The **College of William and Mary** (phone: 253-4000) has courts open to the public.
▪ The town of Williamsburg (phone: 220-0807) has free public courts in **Kiwanis Park** (Longhill Road) and **Quarterpath Park** (Pocahontas Street).

15. GOLF

▪ The **Williamsburg Inn** (phone: 229-1000) has two courses, the world-class 18-hole Golden Horseshoe Golf Course and the nine-hole Spotswood Course. Weekend golf packages are available, costing from $155 per person at the Motor Lodge off-season, to $365 per person at the Inn in-season. Rates include two breakfasts and two dinners.

▪ The **Williamsburg Golf Club** (phone: 229-9085 or 877-6744) is open to nonmembers.

▪ **Kingsmill Golf Club** (West of Busch Gardens; phone: 253–3906) has a championship 18-hole course that is part of the Busch Gardens complex.

▪ **Holiday Inn's 1776 Resort** (phone: 220-1776) has a par-3, 18-hole course.

16. FOR KIDS

The following three tours are designed for children. Other family tours are listed in the *Family Guide* available at the Visitor Center. Tickets, costing $4, are sold at the Information Center and at the Courthouse of 1770. All run from mid-June to late August.

▪ **Once Upon a Town** tours introduce children aged 4 to 6 to the life, music, games, and crafts of youngsters growing up 200 years ago. Children dress up in period costumes, handle household items, see how food was grown and prepared, and participate in period games and country dances. Programs run from Tuesday through Saturday at 10 and 2.

▪ **Tricorn Hat Tours** is a two-hour experience in eighteenth-century life for visitors aged 7 to 12. Children see an early flintlock fired, puzzle their way out of a holly maze, lock friends in the pillory in the Gaol, play bowls off Market Square Green and mail a broadside printed in the Colonial Printing Office. Daily at 2.

▪ **The Townsteaders** is an experience in eighteenth-century town life for visitors aged 8 to 14. Children try their hand at flax breaking, spinning, weaving, candle dipping, and cooking in a colonial kitchen. The program takes place in the Powell-Waller House daily at 10.

Other entertainments for children:

▪ Children usually enjoy the stocks and pillory in the **Court House** and the collection of eighteenth-century arms in the **Magazine.** Let them watch one of the crafts demonstrations—anything from cabinetmaking to baking *(see #4, What to See and Do)*.

- Popular attractions include the grammar school in the Wren Building of the **College of William and Mary;** the student's room in the **George Wythe House,** and the toys in the **James Geddy House.**
- The "Visitor's Companion" lists times for special family tours of the Capitol.
- Ride through town in a horse-drawn carriage or stage wagon *(see #4, What to See and Do).*
- *See #18, After Hours* below for evening music and theater programs.
- A colonial militia company, with fife and drum unit composed of high school boys from Williamsburg, parades on Market Square Green and executes eighteenth-century drill maneuvers. Performances are held on Tuesday, Thursday, and Friday at about 5:45 in July and August, and at 5:15 in the spring and fall.
- The **Virginia Shakespeare Festival** (Phi Beta Kappa Hall, College of William and Mary; phone: 253-4469) has matinees for children.
- **Busch Gardens** (Route 60, five miles east of Williamsburg. Phone: 253-3350) is a European-theme amusement park divided into seven Old World villages, each filled with rides, restaurants, shops, live performances, and other attractions. Don't miss the "Hats Off to Hollywood" Musical Revue. The Loch Ness Monster is one of the world's tallest and fastest roller-coaster rides, with double interlocking loops. Open weekends only from March 30 to May 11 and from September 4 to October 27. Open daily from May 12 to September 3. Admission is $13.95 for adults and children.
- **Jamestown Island** has a flat, scenic five-mile road that is safe for biking. Parents can make the trip by car while children bike ahead. One mile from the island is **Jamestown Festival Park,** which contains full-scale models of the ships the first settlers arrived in, and a full-scale reconstruction of the fort they built in 1607.
- **The Williamsburg Inn, Lodge, and Motor House**—all near the Information Center—have swimming pools with lifeguards where older children may be safely left. Rather than drag unwilling children through a full day of Colonial Williamsburg, you may want to take them on a morning tour of the Historic Area, and then leave them at the pool in the afternoon.

17. DINING

- The **Williamsburg Inn** (phone: 229-2141), with its bronze and crystal chandeliers and hand-painted Chinese wall panels, is the most elegant restaurant in town. The newer Regency Dining Room is the

favorite; for a table on summer weekends, make reservations at the
same time that you reserve your room. The atmosphere is formal and
sedate—not a place for young children. A pianist or harpsichordist
plays during dinner. On weekends, there is dancing after 9. Popular
appetizers include smoked fillet of trout and avocado stuffed with
crab meat. Entrées, priced from $15.75 to $23, include braised quail
with raisins, Dover sole, and rack of lamb. Ties are required. All
major credit cards are accepted. Reservations are advised.

▪ **King's Arms Tavern** (Duke of Gloucester Street; phone: 229-
2141) is part of Colonial Williamsburg. On pleasant days and evenings, meals are served in the garden under a scuppernong grape
arbor. Lunch, priced from $4.50 to $7, includes panfried rabbit in a
casserole with wine sauce and onions, Yorkshire meat pie, and fried
chicken. Popular desserts are greengage plum ice cream and raisin
rice pudding. For dinner, try the peanut soup. Entrées, priced from
$10.50 to $15.75, include such eighteenth-century favorites as oyster
pie with Virginia ham, Cornish game hen, braised venison, and colonial game pie (duck and rabbit with bacon, onions, and russet
potatoes in a pastry crust). Reservations are accepted for dinner only.
Ties are optional. All major credit cards are accepted.

▪ **Chowning's Tavern** (Market Square, in the Historic Area;
phone: 229-2141) is an eighteenth-century ale house that features
traditional colonial fare. Lunches, costing from $3.45 to $5.50, include Welsh rabbit, Brunswick stew, and sandwiches. The tavern's
garden is a lovely place to sit in the late afternoon and enjoy clams on
the half shell and chilled ale in a pewter mug. Dinner entrées, priced
from $8.50 to $15, feature barbecued spareribs and sautéed backfin
crabmeat. Dress is casual. During dinner, minstrels entertain with
eighteenth-century ballads and tunes. The wicket bar, open during
meal times, serves such drinks as punch, grog, julep, and sangaree.
Dress is casual. Reservations are advised for dinner. All major credit
cards are accepted.

▪ While Chowning's Tavern specializes in beef, the more formal
Campbell's Tavern (Waller Street in the Historic Area; phone: 229-
2141) specializes in seafood. Brunch, priced from $4.25 to $6, includes pecan waffles with sausage and a shad roe or crabmeat and
cheddar cheese omelette. Eighteenth-century vocal and instrumental
music is presented every night by costumed players. Try the spoon-
bread and sweet potato muffins. Dinner entrées, priced from $10.75
to $16.50, include crab imperial, sautéed crab cakes, and Chesapeake
Bay jambalaya (oysters, scallops, shrimps, and clams braised with a
jambalaya sauce, with baby okra, served on a bed of rice). Popular
desserts are fig ice cream, rum cream pie, and pears in port wine.

Reservations are advised for dinner. Ties are optional. All major credit cards are accepted.

▪ **Surrey House** (Surry; phone: 294-9655) is a downhome family restaurant across the James River. It has no atmosphere but is packed with locals who are serious about their corn bread, peanuts, and Smithfield ham. Visitors who cross the ferry *(see #4, What To See and Do)* can stop here for a Virginia ham roll sandwich, a chocolate peanut sundae, a bowl of peanut soup, or a do-it-yourself peanut butter sandwich. (This $2.85 delight consists of a cutting board with a jar of peanut butter, slices of bread, honey, a rasher of bacon, a jar of raisins, a cup of jelly, a ripe banana, apple wedges, and "a little cheese.") Dress is casual. Complete dinners cost as little as $6.95.

▪ The **Trellis Restaurant** (Merchant's Square; phone: 229-8610) uses old pine boards to create a smart, contemporary feeling. The bricked-in patio bordered by pink petunias is a lovely spot for lunch if you're shopping in Merchant's Square or visiting the nearby Wren building.

▪ Families on a tight budget can drive north on Route 60 to dozens of fast-food restaurants within five miles of the Historic Area.

18. AFTER HOURS

▪ *See #5, The Arts* for evening theater and concerts.

▪ Colonial Williamsburg runs evening lantern tours of selected craft shops from March to mid-June and from early September to early December. The tours run on Monday, Wednesday, and Friday from 8:30 to 10 or 10:30. Tickets are sold at the Information Center and at the Courthouse of 1770, and cost $3.50.

▪ **Capitol by Candlelight tours** are self-guided walks through the Capitol building, which remains open Saturday nights from 8 to 10. Admission is free with a general admission ticket.

▪ **Chowning's Tavern** (Duke of Gloucester Street; phone: 229-2141) takes you back to the world of an eighteenth-century tavern, with a magician, boisterous ballads, and colonial games such as Loo and Goose. The entertainment is in the taproom from 9 to 1.

▪ Visitors interested in twentieth-century nightlife should head for the bars at the **Williamsburg Inn** or **Lodge** (phone: 229-1000). Other nightspots include **The Adams** in the Ramada Inn East (phone: 229-4100), **The Board Room** in the Sheraton Patriot Inn (phone: 565-2600), **Governor's Retreat Lounge** at the Williamsburg Hospitality House (phone: 229-4020), the **J.B. Lounge** at the Magruder Quality Inn (phone: 220-2250), the **Greenery** at George

Washington Inn (phone: 220-1410), and the **Rainbows** at the Williamsburg Hilton (phone: 220-2500).

▪ **Upstairs/Downstairs,** in the basement of the **W&M Family Restaurant** (500 Jamestown Road, near the campus; phone: 220-9804) caters to the college set and is always jammed. There's music on the jukebox, but no dancing. **The Pub,** on the College campus, has live music and dancing.

19. LODGING

Visitors have a choice of staying in an accommodation owned and operated by Colonial Williamsburg, in a private guest home in the City of Williamsburg, or in a motel or resort in the greater Williamsburg area. There are some 70 places to stay, but if you arrive on a summer weekend without a reservation you may have to go as far as Newport News or Richmond to find a room. The Lodging Desk at the **Visitor Center** (phone: 229-1000) can make reservations both at the Colonial Williamsburg properties and at some guest houses. The desk is open daily in-season from 8 A.M. to 10 P.M. and off-season from 9 to 6. If they can't help you, phone the **Innkeepers of Williamsburg** (phone: out-of-state 800/446-9244; in Virginia 800/582-8977, locally 220-3330). The Innkeepers's office is open daily, mid-March through October, from 8 A.M. to 10 P.M.; off-season daily from 9 to 7.

COLONIAL WILLIAMSBURG

The **Colonial Williamsburg Foundation** maintains the Williamsburg Inn, Lodge, and Motor House, and dozens of restored eighteenth-century guest cottages within the Historic Area. The shuttle bus—free to holders of general admission tickets—stops near all these lodgings, so you can park your car on arrival and not have to see it again until you leave. The lodgings are close enough to the Historic Area that you can run back "home" for a quick dip in the pool without losing too much time, a real plus on sultry summer weekends. All reservations are made through the Reservation Manager, Colonial Williamsburg Foundation, P.O. Box B, Williamsburg 23185. Phone: out-of-state, 800/446-8956; in Virginia, 800/582-8976; locally, 229-1000. All major credit cards are accepted.

▪ The **Williamsburg Inn** is truly the epitome of elegance and good taste. The 224 guest rooms are furnished in the Regency manner, with the dignity of a Virginia country estate. The high-ceilinged rooms are decorated with muted Schumacher fabrics, original paintings and prints, and brass candlestick lamps. The Regency Dining

Room is the most elegant restaurant in town. Facilities include golf, tennis, and swimming. Doubles, with private bath, cost from $98 to $135 without meals.

• Visitors who want a total eighteenth-century experience should stay in one of the 26 colonial homes, shops, taverns, and cottages that are operated as guest facilities by the Williamsburg Inn. These restored properties—all in the Historic Area—range from a large, 16-room tavern to a tiny cottage tucked away in a garden. The **Peter Hay Kitchen Suite,** for example, is a one-family house with a kitchen and living room downstairs, and a bedroom upstairs. In the **Bracken House** you'll be sleeping in the former home of the Reverend John Bracken, who served as rector of Bruton Parish Church for 45 years and as president of the College of William and Mary from 1812 to 1814. The **Brick House Tavern** has rooms upstairs, just as it did when it was owned by Cole Digges, a member of the Governor's Council from 1720 to 1744. Living in the Historic Area, you can wander the streets at dawn and dusk, before the crowds descend, and get perhaps the truest sense of town life in pre-Revolutionary America. Rooms are decorated in eighteenth-century style, but with modern conveniences; and guests have access to all the facilities at the Inn, only a short walk away. Doubles, with private bath, cost $85 to $135. Suites or complete houses (for two to eight people) cost $175 to $385. "The Tavern Plan," for three days and two nights, including an admission ticket, a brunch, and a dinner, is reasonably priced.

• In terms of elegance and cost, the **Williamsburg Lodge** is midway between the Inn and the Motor House. The Lodge has a convention center ambience; the Motor House is a comfortable motel. The main incentive for staying at either place is first, the facilities—pool, golf, tennis—and second, their accessibility to the Historic Area by foot or free shuttle-bus. Doubles at the Lodge cost $75 to $120 in-season and $51 to $120 from December 1 to 15 and in January and February. Doubles at the Motor House cost $61 to $67 in-season and $32 to $67 from December 1 to 15 and in January and February. The Motor House has a two-night "Leisure Plan" that includes two nights at the Motor Inn, an hour's tennis daily, two breakfasts, two dinners, and an admission ticket to the Historic Area.

GUEST HOMES

In Williamsburg as elsewhere, a night in a guest home can be a risky business. If you're lucky, you'll find yourself in a quiet home, with twice the warmth of a motel at half the price. Without luck, you'll wind up in the home of an inveterate talker in a room with paper-thin walls and a downstairs bathroom full of curlers and hair-nets. Usually, the more rooms in the guest house, the more privacy you can expect. The people who run the Lodging Desk in the Infor-mation Center can help you find a house that meets your needs. Rates range from $20 to $35 per couple.

• **The Elms** (708 Richmond Road; phone: 229-1551) is a clean, attractive guest house. The owners live downstairs; the guests, up-stairs. The four guest rooms have friendly and unpretentious furnish-ings. Doubles, one with private bath, cost $18 to $22. No credit cards are accepted.

• **Mrs. Moody's Guest House** (110 Glenn Circle; phone: 229-1953) is in a cul-de-sac in a quiet, residential part of town. Mrs. Moody is a disarmingly bright, loquacious lady who is quick to make you part of her family. Doubles, with shared bath, cost under $20. No credit cards are accepted.

MOTELS

Popular motels include the **Fort Magruder Inn** (Route 60 East; phone: 220-2250 or 800/228-5151); **Patrick Henry—Best Western** (York and Page Streets; phone: 229-9540 or 800/528-1234); **Ramada Inn East Motor Hotel** (351 York Street; phone: 229-4100 or 800/228-2828); **Econo-Travel Motor Hotel** (442 Parkway Drive; phone: 229-7564 or 800/446-6900); **Hospitality House** (415 Richmond Road, Route 60, two blocks from the Historic Area; phone: 229-4020); **Holiday Inn's 1776 Resort** (Route 60 bypass; phone: 229-7600); **Williamsburg Hilton** (1600 Richmond Road, two miles west of the Historic Area; phone: 229-1134); **Howard Johnson's Motor Lodge** (1800 Richmond Road, Route 60; phone: 229-2781 or 800/654-2000); **Sheraton Motor Inn** (506 North Henry Street, within walking distance of the Historic Area; phone: 229-6605).

20. EMERGENCIES

• **Williamsburg Community Hospital** (1238 Mount Vernon Avenue; phone: 253-6000).

• **Ambulance service** (phone: 229-1313).

21. HOW TO GET THERE

BY CAR. *From New York:* New Jersey Turnpike south to I-95. At Richmond take I-64 south to Williamsburg. *From Philadelphia* and *from Washington:* I-95 south. At Richmond take I-64 south to Wil-liamsburg.

BY BUS. Take Greyhound *from New York* (212/635-0800), *from Philadelphia* (215/568-4800) and *from Washington* (202/565-2662).

BY TRAIN. Take Amtrak *from New York* (212/736-3967), *from Philadelphia* (215/824-1600), and *from Washington* (202/484-7540).

BY PLANE. *From New York* and *from Philadelphia:* take USAir to Patrick Henry International Airport, Newport News or People's Express from Newark to Norfolk International Airport ($29). Limousines are available for the 16-mile drive from the airport to Williamsburg.

22. FOR FURTHER INFORMATION

▪ For accommodations in Colonial Williamsburg and information on things to see and do, write to **Colonial Williamsburg Travel Department,** P.O. Box C, Williamsburg 23185. Phone: locally 804/229-1000, in Virginia 800/582-8976, out-of-state 800/446-8956.

▪ For accommodations in the general Williamsburg area, phone (do not write) the **Williamsburg Hotel/Motel Association,** open May through September, 8 A.M. to 10 P.M.; off-season, 9 A.M. to 6:30 P.M. PHONE: locally 804/220-3330, in Virginia 800/582-8977, out-of-state 800/446-9244.

▪ For information on things to see and do in the Williamsburg area (outside Colonial Williamsburg), write to the **Williamsburg Area Tourism and Conference Bureau,** P.O. Box GB, Williamsburg, 23187.

23. RECOMMENDED READING

▪ The more you know beforehand about Colonial Williamsburg, the more rewarding your trip will be. Nothing makes less sense than waiting on line at the crowded Information Center to purchase the Official Guidebook, and then wasting an hour of your weekend trying to decide what to see first. Call the mail-order department toll-free at 800/446-9240 and order books by phone. Credit cards are accepted. A larger selection of books is available from the **Information Center Book Store,** where credit card purchases are also accepted. You will have to make a long-distance call here to 804/229-1000, ext. 2691. Salespeople will suggest appropriate books for you and your children. A must is the *Colonial Williamsburg Official Guidebook* ($2.50, including postage). Also informative is *Colonial Williamsburg: Its Buildings and Gardens* ($6.70, including postage).

▪ Books for children include: Ronald Syme's *John Smith of Virginia* (New York: Scribner, 1959); *The Colonial Williamsburg Activities Book* (Williamsburg, $2.95); and Cornelia Meigs's *Fair Wind to Virginia* (New York: Macmillan, 1964).

▪ Visitors to Jamestown may want to read *Captain John Smith's History of Virginia,* ed. by David F. Hawke (New York: Bobbs-Merrill, 1970).

▪ Visitors to Carter's Grove and other southern plantations should look in libraries for Clifford Dowdey's *The Great Plantation* and Emmie Ferguson Farrar's *Old Virginia Houses.*

▪ The **Book Store** at the Visitor's Center sells books on the various eighteenth-century crafts still practiced here today, such as printing, silversmithing, and blacksmithing.

Tangier Island, Virginia

(Area Code, 804; Zip Code, 23440)

---

1. DISTANCES

BY CAR AND FERRY. *From Philadelphia,* 5½ hours; *from Baltimore,* 5 hours; *from Washington,* 4½ hours.

BY CAR AND AIR TAXI. *From Philadelphia,* 4¼ hours; *from Baltimore,* 4 hours; *from Washington,* 3½ hours.

2. MAJOR ATTRACTIONS

▪ A closely knit community of watermen who still speak with the same Elizabethan twang as their seventeenth-century forebears.

▪ A boardinghouse that serves the best crab cakes on earth.

▪ An ingenuous, hard-working people happy to share their way of life with you.

▪ A welcome escape from the frenetic pace of the mainland.

3. INTRODUCTION

A sense of generations. Pride in hard physical labor. Humility before the forces that shape our lives.

These are feelings we can rediscover by visiting an island like Tangier.

The island, 3½ miles long and 1½ miles wide, lies in the southern waters of the Chesapeake, 20 miles from Reedville on Virginia's Northern Neck and 14 miles from Crisfield, Maryland, on the Delmarva Peninsula.

The 700 people who live here are neither childlike nor quaint. They have cars waiting on the mainland to whisk them to the nation's capital three hours away. They have HBO and onion dip, and lead hard, unromantic lives wresting a living from the sea. But their isolation and their constant battle against the seasons give them a sense of community and purposefulness that mainlanders search for in vain.

On a warm summer Saturday, water claps against the crab shacks in Job's Cove as the 90-foot cruise boat *Captain Thomas* nudges against the dock and 150 passengers step tentatively ashore. The path, recently paved and widened to 10 feet, is bordered by chain-link fences, and visitors are pressed between them like bulls stampeding through the walled streets of Pamplona. Very standoffish, these fences seem, until one learns that they were put up, not to keep tourists at a distance, but to discourage local drivers from destroying each other's lawns.

Half the group crowd into the Chesapeake House, where long wooden tables are set with platters of clam fritters and crab cakes. The other half climb into Cushman golf carts and tour the island. It is a short trip.

Two hours later the crowds are back aboard the *Captain Thomas* and the island returns to its peaceful self. Weekend guests now have a chance to stroll quietly by the rows of houses on either side of the island, and to explore the salt marsh that separates them. The marsh, with its waving grasses and snowy egrets, is beautiful to weekend visitors who don't have to live with the insects that breed there. The Environmental Protection Agency is not a favorite among the people of Tangier, who would fill in the marsh if they could. "I'd like to tie one of those government people to a chair out there, then ask him what he thought of the marsh," an islandman told me. "Not that there would be anything left of him by the end of the day."

There are no traffic lights, road signs, or house numbers on Tangier Island. Homes are white, no-nonsense affairs with clapboard or aluminum siding. The grander ones have tracery over screened-in porches, where women in aprons sit on summer afternoons swatting flies. The policeman has a silver Honda Civic, but most islanders ride about on bikes.

Tangier is known as the soft-shell crab capital of the world. Go down to the harbor before dawn or in the late afternoon and you will see watermen scooping up crabs from wooden floats and separating the dead ones from those about to lose their shells. Crabs have outside skeletons (exoskeletons) that they must shed each time they grow. The trick is to remove the crabs from the water and pack them in ice before new skeletons harden. It's a laborious process, and watermen are at it from dawn to dusk.

The Romantic poets could afford to see nature through sentimental eyes. But on Tangier, where people get their living from the sea, nature is an awesome power that is treated with wariness and respect. After all, a single storm could wipe the island off the map.

When John Smith sailed by in 1610, Tangier was six feet higher and extended three-fourths of a mile farther into the bay. Erosion now carries away from 24 to 27 feet a year. Barnacle-encrusted bottles or clay pipes occasionally wash ashore, recalling the sad fate of former island communities such as Oyster Creek, Canaan, and Cinnamon Ridge.

The island is only about five feet above sea level at its highest point and is sinking at the rate of 20 inches a century. What was once woods and fields is now marshland. The dead are buried in concrete boxes so that water does not seep in at high tide. By the year 2100 the entire island may be under water.

The dead are buried today in the Methodist churchyard, but not many years ago they were buried in family plots, located in back yards across the island. At dusk couples sit on their porches staring out at broken gravestones across the street—a lesson in mortality as deep and narrow as any Methodist sermon.

Death belongs to life here, and religion is no Sunday affair. When church bells ring at 7:15 at night, men and women, black Bibles clutched to their chests, leave their homes and walk the narrow lanes to church. Tuesday is women's prayer meeting. Wednesday is general prayer meeting. Friday is choir rehearsal. On Sunday, the Lord's day, all work is frowned on, and services are held all day long. After church there are fund-raising parties for people who have fallen on bad times, or visits to the sick.

"There is a way that seems right to man," says a sign in an islander's window. "But in the end it leads to death."

Crockett, Parks and Pruitt are the names on most tombstones, and the names of 80 percent of the people living on Tangier today.

Though the island was named by John Smith on one of his forays from Jamestown in search of salt, silver, and a route to the "south sea," he never settled there. Nor did a man named West, who purchased the island from the Indians for two overcoats and upon threat of extinction.

The first permanent settler was John A. Crockett, who arrived in 1686 from Cornwall. Crockett and his wife, Tangier's answer to Adam and Eve, had four sons and daughters, who brought husbands and wives back with them from the mainland. In 1800 the population of Tangier was 79—33 of them Crocketts, 20 Evanses, and 13 Parkses. Almost all islanders today are descendants of these first settlers and speak with the same Cornish accent, spiced with double negatives and island slang.

The British landed on Tangier during the American Revolution and later used the island as a staging ground for their attack on Baltimore's Fort McHenry. Ask any islandman and he'll be happy to tell you how the fiery Reverend Joshua Thomas, invited to give a parting sermon to 12,000 British troops, told them to expect defeat and exhorted them to prepare for death. The British were routed and returned only long enough to bury their dead. It was during this attack that "The Star-Spangled Banner" was written.

Tangier is Methodist today, but when church bells ring many of the younger generations choose to remain home or to zoom about town on motorbikes, making visitors scurry to the curb for safety.

There are other signs of change, too. White picket fences have been replaced by wire. Hugh Haynie's market has two outdoor pay phones. The town policeman rides around with a radar gun, giving tickets to teenagers who exceed the 15-mph limit. Now that cable TV has arrived, screened-in porches are empty after dark; you can see the ghostly colors flickering through closed windows as you walk by. Behind the town is a paved airstrip where up to 80 private planes land on summer weekends so that wealthy Washingtonians can enjoy some of Hilda Crockett's famous crab cakes at the Chesapeake House. Hilda Crockett is no longer alive.

Despite these concessions to life on the mainland—which are bound to increase with time—life on Tangier Island remains basically unchanged. Watermen still rise at dawn, check their buster floats, and sail out into the bay.

I was talking to one of these men—he is married and in his mid-20s—when the subject turned to nude bathing on Assateague Island, only a few hours away. He guffawed, then paused and said, "A nude beach ain't really half as nice as one woman by yourself. You can't do nothin' with a whole bunch of women."

The subject turned to his life as a waterman. Could he explain to readers how he spent a day?

"You can only learn so much on paper," he said. "You've got to tell your readers to come with me and learn how it really is."

So I'm telling you to go to Tangier Island and learn how it really is.

4. WHAT TO SEE AND DO

A woman returning to the mainland was overheard to say, "Is that all there is? I might just as well have stayed in the trailer."

The woman should have been warned that Tangier is not for those who seek turnstile attractions or breathtaking views, but for those curious souls who are willing to ask questions and discover a way of life different from their own.

- Some 500 visitors march through **Chesapeake House** for lunch on a warm summer Saturday or Sunday. Overnight guests should eat lunch on the mainland or bring a picnic, and save the **Chesapeake House** for dinner, when they will have the dining room to themselves.

- Stop in and say hello to **Vernon Bradshaw** at his arts and crafts store a few minutes' walk from the harbor. He'll be happy to answer questions about the island, or sell you the "Visitors Guide," which has a road map and self-guided tour.

- If you're staying overnight and able to walk or ride a bike, avoid the Cushman golf carts that tour visitors around the island. You can make the same trip on foot in less than two hours. Walk through Canton, with its narrow lanes that capture the mood of Tangier 30 years ago.

- Study the plant and bird life in the marshes.

- Buy a box of dressed and frozen jumbo soft-shelled crabs to take home with you.

- Arrange to spend a day with a waterman, free of charge. They usually go out before dawn and return home between noon and 2 P.M. **Juke Marshall** (phone: 891-2481) will take you, so will **Michael Parks.**

- In the afternoon and early evening go down to the harbor and watch the watermen at work. The idea of exploiting tourists—or of tourists exploiting them—does not seem to have reached the island yet. Proud of living in the soft-shell crab capital of the world, and flattered by your interest, they will be happy to show you how they make a living and to answer your questions. To reach **Michael**

Parks's soft-shell crab farm, turn right at the Methodist Church (facing the harbor) and continue over the rails of the boat launch. Follow a short trail through the marshes, then continue along the water's edge to a rough plywood ramp on pilings over the water. In summer, Michael returns to his crab shed after dinner, around six. Watch him scoop up the blue-claw crabs from long trays and check to see which are about to lose their shells. In the hour or two before a new shell hardens, Michael packs the still-wriggling crabs in ice and ships them in cardboard boxes to the mainland.

▪ In the early evening, go down to **County Dock** and dangle your feet over the side. Watch the sun set while birds cry and the skiffs and scows clap against the pilings.

6. ANTIQUES AND CRAFTS

A few modest craft shops line the main street, all less than a five-minutes' walk from the harbor.

▪ **Chesapeake Island Arts & Crafts** is run by Vernon Bradshaw, who will answer questions about Tangier. He sells maps, local crafts, and stationery printed with his own line drawings of the island.

▪ **Sandy's Place** is a museum of memorabilia that sells such local goods as bonnets, model fishing boats, and Christmas stockings.

▪ **Jim's Gift Shop** sells Mrs. Annie Parks's bonnets and hand-carved wooden sailors.

8. WALKS

▪ The island has about three miles of roads and paths—a good two hours' walk, if you take your time. The "Visitor's Guide," available at most shops or at the **Captain's Galley Restaurant** back in Crisfield, includes a map of Tangier with a self-guided tour.

▪ Visitors who object to motorbikes should go for morning walks, when all the young men are out fishing. Don't miss an area called **Canton,** with its narrow lanes; it typifies Tangier as it was earlier in the century. In the salt marshes, stand still and watch the great blue herons and the snowy egrets stalking their meals.

9. BIKING

▪ **Euna Dise** (phone: 891-2425) rents bikes for $12 to $15 a day. There is a sign outside her home, a short walk from **Chesapeake House.**

10. BOATING AND FISHING

- **Grace Brown** (phone: 891-2535) has a sunfish for use by overnight guests.

11. SWIMMING

- The sea nettle situation changes from year to year. In 1982 it was so bad that no one went swimming from early July to mid-October. During the summer of 1984, the nettles were no problem, and the beach was used in July and August.

16. FOR KIDS

- Rent bikes and cycle around the island *(see #9, Biking)*.
- Watch and talk to the watermen in the early morning (around 5:30) or while they're working in their crab sheds in the early afternoon and evening. Spend a day with them on the boats *(see #4, What to See and Do)*.
- A somewhat sober exercise, but an interesting history lesson, would be to list names on tombstones in family plots across the island. "Crockett" should win. See who comes in next: Evans, Parks, Pruitt, or Dies (Dize).

17. DINING

- Lunch and dinner at the **Chesapeake House** (phone: 891-2331) is an unforgettable experience. Meals are served family-style at long tables covered with platters of cold smoked Virginia ham, clam fritters, crab cakes (only two per person, alas), hot yeast rolls, thick sweet corn pudding, homemade coleslaw, pickled beets, peas, potato salad, and apple sauce. The crab cakes are so delicious, you may never want to eat them anywhere else. Dessert is a lemon-flavored pound cake. Liquor is not sold or served on the island, but you may bring your own.

The same meal is served for lunch or dinner and never varies. On summer weekends, from 300 to 600 visitors troop in and out of the Chesapeake House on day excursions from Reedville and Crisfield. Overnight guests may prefer to miss the crowds and wait for dinner at 5. The meal by itself costs $8. Breakfast and dinner are included in the cost for overnight guests. Dress is casual. No credit cards are accepted. The Chesapeake House is closed from November 1 to April 1.

▪ Weekend visitors can lunch at the **Captain's Galley Restaurant** in Crisfield while waiting for the 12:30 boat for Tangier. But save room for dinner at 5!

19. LODGING

▪ Most overnight visitors head directly for the **Chesapeake House** (Tangier 23440; phone: 891-2331), a few minutes' walk from the harbor. It was founded in 1940 by Hilda Crockett, a descendant of John Crockett, the island's first settler. Neighbors complain that the house has lost its family quality since Hilda died and the business was taken over by two of her daughters. Indeed, rooms are unnecessarily run-down for a prosperous establishment that feeds more than 1,000 visitors on a summer weekend. But who could believe the food was ever any better?

Overnight guests are usually housed in five rooms across the street. Because you are on an island, you could, if you insisted, call the furnishings "funky," but "boardinghouse chic" would be going too far. (When I removed the wooden stick holding up a window the entire window fell into the room. "Sorry," said the sign on the bathroom door, "bathroom is out of order. Please use one of two downstairs.") The two downstairs rooms are cooler on summer nights. One has four beds, reserved for families. The other has the house's only air-conditioner, which the sisters like to save for elderly guests. (Ask whether it's taken.) The four rooms in the main building are said to be in worse repair.

If the Chesapeake House were on the mainland, a night here might prove disastrous, but on Tangier it is simply part of the total experience. If you care about creature comforts, stay with the Browns across the island (see below). But wherever you stay, be sure to join guests of the Chesapeake House on their screened-in porch. At dinner you will have developed "May-I-trouble-you-for-the-ham-please-pass-the-applesauce" relationships, and by the time the sun goes down you will feel that you are among friends. Rooms with shared bath are $26 per person, including a big eggs-and-bacon breakfast and crab-cake dinner. No credit cards are accepted. Closed November 1 to April 1.

▪ At the Chesapeake House you are left alone in a very basic boardinghouse; at **Jim and Grace Browns'** (Tangier 23440; phone: 891-2535) you are made to feel part of a family in a modern, mainland-style home. Few visitors know that the Browns' home exists, for it is a 15-minute walk from the Chesapeake House, and there are no signs announcing it. Grace Brown was born on the island, but moved as a young child to Wilmington. She and her husband returned for a visit a few years ago and fell so completely in love with Tangier that they decided to stay. The two carpeted rooms are large and comfortable—one even has an exercise bike in it—and central air-conditioning should be installed by summer. The worst you can say about the rooms is that they are mainland modern, a little bit of Wilmington on Tangier. The house has a wraparound upper deck with dramatic views of the town and the bay.

Grace is a warm, intelligent woman—a potter who gives ceramic lessons to the ladies on the Island. She is also the first woman ever to be elected to the Town Council, quite a feat on an island where women are expected to stay at home and take care of children. She will pick you up at the harbor; let you use her Sunfish; arrange for a day on a crab boat or a motorboat trip to neighboring Smith Island for dinner. No credit cards are accepted. Open all year.

▪ **Euna Dies** (Box 24, Tangier; phone: 891-2425) accepts guests in her home. No credit cards are accepted. Rooms are $8 per person, without meals. She is open all year, but the guest room is not heated. There are plenty of blankets, however.

▪ **Vernon Bradshaw** (Box 84, Tangier) will be happy to arrange overnight accommodations with families.

▪ **Somer's Cove Motel** (R. R. Norris Drive, P.O. Box 387, Crisfield, Maryland; phone: 301/968-1900) is a friendly motel a short drive from the dock from where the Tangier ferry leaves.

20. EMERGENCIES

▪ A nurse visits the island on weekends and can be found at the **Health Center,** near the Methodist Church. Ask any islander for directions. She can arrange for immediate boat or plane transportation back to the mainland.

21. HOW TO GET THERE

From Philadelphia and Baltimore it is usually faster to drive to Crisfield, Maryland. From southwestern Washington and the Alexandria area it is usually faster to drive to Reedville, Virginia. Crisfield, however, has year-round ferry service, and the ferry trip is 30 minutes shorter.

BY CAR TO CRISFIELD. *From Philadelphia:* I-95 or the New Jersey Turnpike south to Route 13 south, then Route 413 to Crisfield. *From Baltimore and Washington:* Route 50 south to Salisbury, then Route 13 south and Route 413 to Crisfield.

BY CAR TO REEDVILLE. *From Baltimore:* Route 3 south to Route 301 south. Route 17 south to Tappahannock, then Route 360 east to Reedville. *From Washington:* I-95 south to Fredericksburg. Route 17 south to Tappahannock. Route 360 east to Reedville.

FERRY FROM REEDVILLE. From May through September, the 150-passenger cruise boat *Captain Thomas* leaves Reedville at 10 A.M. and returns from Tangier at 4:15. Contact Captain Stanley Bowis, Tangier & Chesapeake Cruises, Warsaw, Virginia 22572. Phone: 804/333-4656. The trip takes 1¾ hours. Off-season, a supply boat usually leaves Reedville on Thursdays around noon.

FERRY FROM CRISFIELD. From Memorial Day through October, several boats leave daily from Crisfield at 12:30 P.M. and return at 5:15. The largest and most comfortable is the 90-foot cruise boat *Steven Thomas,* which leaves from the City Dock at the foot of Main Street. The trip takes 1¼ hours. Reservations are advised on weekends; contact Captain Rudy Thomas, Tangier Island, Virginia. Phone: 891-2240. Roundtrip tickets cost $12. Passengers can also take a small mail boat that leaves Tangier at 8 A.M. throughout the year, and returns from Crisfield at 12:30. If you miss the scheduled boats, you might be able to get a lift with a crabbing boat. For information, ask around the harbor, or at the Captain's Galley Restaurant (phone: 301/968-0300) in Crisfield.

PLANE FROM NORTHERN NECK, VIRGINIA. You can charter a plane carrying up to three passengers for $70 one way from St. Mary's County Airport, 6½ miles north of Lexington Park on Route 235. Phone: 301/373–2101.

PLANE FROM CRISFIELD (DELMARVA PENINSULA). An air taxi runs between Crisfield and Tangier. Contact Saiters Air Craft Service; phone: 301/968-1572. To reach the airport, take a right turn on Route 413 just before the town of Crisfield. Follow signs to the airport.

22. FOR FURTHER INFORMATION

▪ **Virginia State Travel Service,** 11 Rockefeller Plaza, New York, NY 10020. Phone: 212/245-3080 OR 906 17th St., NW, Washington, DC 20006. Phone: 202/293-5350.

▪ **Vernon Bradshaw,** Box 84, Tangier, has taken upon himself the role of local historian and good will ambassador. He will be happy to answer questions and help arrange for weekend stays with local families.

23. RECOMMENDED READING

- James Michener. *Chesapeake.*
- William Warner. *Beautiful Swimmers: Watermen, Crabs and the Chesapeake Bay* (1977 Pulitzer Prize-winner).
- "Visitors Guide to Tangier Island," "History of Tangier Island," and "Something Fishy from Tangier" are small booklets for sale on the island.
- Tangier Island was featured in *National Geographic* in November, 1973.

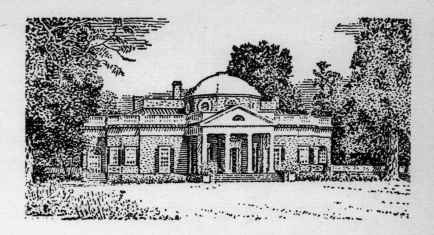

Charlottesville/Monticello, Virginia

(Area Code, 804)

1. DISTANCES

BY CAR. *From Washington,* 2½ hours; *from Baltimore,* 3¼ hours; *from Philadelphia,* 5 hours.

BY BUS. *From Washington,* 3½ hours; *from Baltimore,* 5 hours; *from Philadelphia,* 6½ hours.

BY TRAIN. *From Washington,* 2¼ hours; *from Baltimore,* 3¼ hours.

2. MAJOR ATTRACTIONS

- Jefferson's Monticello and the University of Virginia—two of the glories of American architecture.
- An opportunity to experience Southern hospitality by staying in a private home—anything from a geodesic dome to an antebellum mansion.

3. INTRODUCTION

Here, in the foothills of the Blue Ridge, the author of the Declaration of Independence and the nation's third President founded the University of Virginia and built his stately home at Monticello. Presidents Madison and Monroe lived here too, as did Thomas Walker, discoverer of the Cumberland Gap, and the explorers Lewis and Clark. But Thomas Jefferson is Charlottesville's first son, and a visit here is a pilgrimage to honor the man and his contributions to American culture.

When Jefferson's father died he left his 14-year-old son the property on top of one of the highest hills in the area. Jefferson named it "Monticello," which means "little mountain" in Italian. The house, based on Greco-Roman designs revived by the Italian Renaissance architect Andrea Palladio, looks out across a wide, tree-edged lawn with sweeping views of Charlottesville and the distant Blue Ridge Mountains.

No other American home so completely reflects the personality of its owner. For some 40 years, between 1769 and 1809, Jefferson was constantly involved with its construction and enlargement. In later years he wrote that on his mountaintop "all my wishes end where I hope my days will end, at Monticello."

The house was more than a place to retire to; it was a man's effort to give physical expression to his most profound values and sensibilities. It was also an escape from the circle of intrigue that surrounded him as President. "Hunger to return to 'the family,' as symbolized in later life by Monticello, became chronic with Jefferson," writes Fawn Brodie in her best-selling biography. "As a boy the area meant vacation from school, reunion with his kin, fishing, daydreaming. When he was a man, Monticello came to mean the Elysian fields, a haven from the brutality of politics."

It's impossible to tour Monticello today without asking oneself first, why Jefferson's dream house took the form of a monument to antiquity; and second, how America's foremost spokesman for democracy could have built himself such a baronial estate.

Until Jefferson built Monticello, American homes were built on Georgian models, imported from England. Jefferson turned to Greece and Rome for his inspiration because, like other patriots of his day, he wanted to free his country from cultural dependence on England.

Jefferson's father, denied a formal education, directed his son to have a formal classical training, which influenced Jefferson throughout his life. A creature of the American Enlightenment, he believed beauty could be defined within the mathematical forms of the classical world. His model was the Roman Republic—Rome before the time of the emperors. The Republic had a ruling aristocracy and slaves—as Jefferson himself was a slave-owning Virginia gentleman—but every free man was a citizen. In the architecture of this ancient world Jefferson found a lightness and a sense of order that flattered his own sensibilities, and that had no antecedents in the American experience.

On first glance, Monticello seems no more than a tribute to the past; in reality it is a blending of the values of the old world and the new. Double sliding glass walls that keep the heat in, dumbwaiters, a combination chaise-desk that let him write while reclining—these and other gadgets are born of the American frontier spirit.

Jefferson loved the logic and symmetry of antiquity; but he also had a practical, resourceful, "Ben Franklin" side that allowed him to bend tradition to accomodate his personal needs. As Lewis Mumford notes, Jefferson was a combination of the Renaissance man who sought to transcend provinciality through the universal forms of the ancients, and an American pioneer whose bent was mechanical and utilitarian.

Monticello is open to the public as a monument to Jeffersonian ideals. Visitors must be struck, however, by the contradiction between Jefferson the democrat and Jefferson the benevolent monarch, living in his ivory tower.

Which is the real Jefferson? It's impossible to say, for the contradictions are in the man himself and reflect his dual heritage as a product of both the Enlightenment and the American frontier. (Until his eighteenth year Jefferson had never even seen a hamlet with more than twenty houses!)

On one hand, Jefferson the aristocrat feared the growing power of the proletariat. He built a rotating kitchen door with shelves so that he would not have to look at his servants while he ate. He believed in universal education, but only up to a certain age, when the masses would be weeded out. "Never," he wrote in 1811, "have I ever been able to conceive how any rational being could propose happiness to himself from the exercise of power over others." Did he not see the contradiction in the fact that he held absolute power over slaves on his own plantation?

"In ruling at Monticello he held on to the past," writes Fawn Brodie, "preserving the world of his childhood . . . the ancient world of his parents in which he now lived as master and adult. In acquiescing in the postponement of the end of slavery . . . he postponed also his own aging, and in a sense his own death, and indeed the death of Monticello."

To point out the contradictions in Jefferson's nature is not to belittle him or to challenge his position as America's greatest spokesman for the ideals of the Revolution. There was no self-interest in his devotion to democracy. Leading the comfortable life of a baron, he stood to gain nothing from the Revolution but an early death. While other leaders, such as Patrick Henry and John Adams, turned conservative, Jefferson remained the most consistent revolutionary of all the founding fathers.

Is there no way, then, to reconcile Jefferson's egalitarianism, his love of the people, his "democratic simplicity," with Monticello? Perhaps there is.

In his excellent study, *The Jefferson Image in the American Mind,* Merrill Peterson finds a clue in a provocative essay by John Dos Passos. "Dos Passos saw nothing strange in the fact that Monticello and the Declaration of Independence were the cardinal achievements of the same man," writes Peterson; "indeed, the first was father to the second. Jefferson, like 'a free nobleman with the sky over his head . . . takes it for granted other men must be as good as he.' Planned full scale to the human figure . . . Monticello was 'a house where a free man could live in a society of equals.' As for the gleaming portico seemingly so incongruous with the surrounding wilderness, it acted as a spiritual frame for the American task otherwise formless and materialistic. It served Jefferson, and he meant it to serve America, as an ideal of beauty, conduct, and workmanship in the great republic of which he was one of the founders. Monticello, Dos Passos affirmed, 'would make manifest in brick and stucco his own adaptation to the Virginia frontier of an antique Roman sense of the dignity of free men.'"

. . .

Like Monticello, the University of Virginia is an expression of the philosophy and the sensibilities of a single man, Thomas Jefferson. Those who consider old age a time of decline should bear in mind that, at the age of 75, Jefferson surveyed the site, drew up blueprints for most of the buildings, planned the curriculum, and hired most of the faculty. The cornerstone of the first building was laid in the presence of Madison and Monroe in 1817, but the conception had formed in Jefferson's mind at least seven years earlier, when he advised against the common practice of erecting a large central building that housed students in huge, ugly dormitories. "It is infinitely better," he said, "to erect a small and separate building for each separate professorship, with only a hall below for his class, and two chambers above for himself; joining the lodges with barracks for a certain portion of students. . . . The whole of these arranged around an open square of grass and trees would make it . . . an academical village, instead of a large and common den of noise, of filth, and of fetid air."

The university is structured as a rectangle, open on one side. As Kenneth Clark points out in *Civilization*, "Jefferson's romanticism is shown by the way in which he left the fourth side of the courtyard open, so that young scholars could look across to the mountains still inhabited by the Indians who had been his father's friends."

There are 10 two-story pavilions—one for each professor—and between them are single-story dormitories for students. The whole is united and connected in front by a covered colonnade of graceful white arches and pillars. No two pavilions are alike, but all are derived from the work of Palladio and from such actual antique models as the Theater of Marcellus and the Temple of Trajan. Jefferson wanted the pavilions to inspire students with the ideals of antiquity. His love of privacy is seen in the small gardens outside the court-yards, enclosed by serpentine walls. The dominant central building is the rotunda, a scale model of the Roman Pantheon adapted to the services of a library and a planetarium.

Nothing like the University of Virginia had ever been built before; no prototypes existed anywhere on earth. As at Monticello, Jefferson the Renaissance man and Jefferson the frontiersman fused the past and present in a single design that gave expression to his own ideal self. At the center was the rotunda, the repository of all knowledge, with a view of the stars. Surrounding it were the pavilions—each one unique, but all united by a single vision. Between the pavilions lived the students, who were to be led by classical models toward wisdom and truth.

Jefferson dedicated his last years to his university because he believed that the principles of democracy could not be safeguarded except by an educated electorate. "I have sworn upon the altar of God eternal hostility against every tyranny over the mind of man," he wrote. "Enlighten the people generally, and tyranny and oppressions of body and mind will vanish like spirits at the dawn of day."

Jefferson died on July 4, 1826, exactly 50 years after the signing of the Declaration of Independence. John Adams died on the same day. On his deathbed, Adams said, "Jefferson still lives."

No one who visits Monticello or the University of Virginia today could disagree.

4. WHAT TO SEE AND DO

▪ Make your first stop at the **Thomas Jefferson Visitor's Center** (at the intersection of Routes I-64 and 20 south) for maps, brochures, and a free reservation service. Biking maps, available on request, are useful for planning back-road drives. The Historic Driving Tour map describes the homes and sights between Charlottesville and Castle Hill. Request the city map published by Charlotte Ramsey Realtors.

▪ To reach Monticello (phone: 295-8181 or 295-2657) from the Visitor's Center, go south on Route 20, then left on Route 53. The five-minute drive takes you past Michie Tavern, but visit Monticello first, as early in the day as possible, and avoid 30-minute waits on summer afternoons. Since the upper floors are closed to the public, the guided tour lasts only 15 minutes, after which you are free to wander about the grounds. Service quarters—storerooms, wine cellars, and so on—are covered with terraces and open in only one direction, in accord with Palladio's notion that a house, like a man's body, should be partly hidden. Recently restored and opened to the public is **Jefferson's Grove,** an 18-acre park on the northwest side of the mountain. Jefferson trimmed the trees there to form a canopy under which he could stroll and admire the wide variety of plant life. Monticello is open daily March through October from 8 to 5; off-season, 9 to 4:30. Admission is $4 for adults, $1 for children 6 to 11.

▪ **Michie Tavern** (phone: 977-1234), one-half mile below Monticello on Route 53 east, has a fine collection of pre-Revolutionary furniture. Built in 1735, it served as Patrick Henry's boyhood home until it was sold to John Michie, who enlarged it and established a tavern. The taproom is the only existing colonial bar in Virginia. According to tradition, the "round dance" or waltz was introduced to America in the upstairs ballroom, possibly by Jefferson's daughter, who had learned the dance in France. Jefferson, Monroe, and Madison entertained here; General Lafayette was among their guests. The house/museum was disassembled and brought to its present site in 1927. A $5- to-$8 lunch is served in a converted log cabin. The house is open daily from 9 to 5. Admission is $3.

▪ **Ash Lawn** (phone: 293-9539), the 550-acre estate of James Monroe, is only a few minute's drive from Michie Tavern. Return past the entrance to Monticello on Route 53 and turn right on Route 795. The Monroes moved here because of their friendship with Jefferson, who wanted to create "a society to our taste" near Monticello. While Monroe was serving as ambassador to France, Jefferson personally selected the house site, oversaw the construction, and sent his gardeners to start the orchards. Monroe moved into what he called his "cabin-castle" in 1799. He hoped to retire here after his Presidency (1817–1825), but financial difficulties forced him to sell the property in 1826. It was eventually bequeathed to the College of William & Mary, his alma mater, and reopened to the public in 1975. Many of the furnishings, such as the Hepplewhite table, the Duncan Phyfe chairs, and the hand-carved mahogany bed, were Monroe's own. The house is filled with French decorative arts, which many post-Revolutionary Americans preferred to English furnishings. There are picnic facilities on the grounds, and weaving demonstrations daily from April through October. Open daily from March through October from 9 to 6, and from November through February from 10 to 5. Admission is $3. Children under 6 are admitted free.

▪ **Castle Hill** (Cobham; phone: 293-7297) is a fine example of a Piedmont tobacco plantation manor house. From Ash Lawn, return to Route 53 north. Turn right on Route 732, then left, across the Rivanna River, on Route 729. From Shadwell, Jefferson's birthplace, continue northeast on Route 22E to Cismont. Bear left on Route 231 for two miles. The manor house offers visitors an opportunity to compare architectural styles, since it includes both the original clapboard house built in 1765, and a Federal section added in 1824. The 1100-acre estate is noted for its beautiful terraced gardens and its ancient boxwoods. Castle Hill was the home of Thomas Walker, who was a legal guardian for young Thomas Jefferson and the "Father of Kentucky." He was also the discoverer of the Cumberland Gap in 1750. Open daily, March through November, from 10 to 5.

▪ It's expensive—$65 per passenger—but the 30- to 45-minute balloon ride up to 5,000 feet over Monticello and the neighboring countryside is an unforgettable experience. Flights range from one to 20 miles from the **Boar's Head Inn,** depending on wind conditions. Contact the inn (phone: 296-2181) for details.

▪ The spectacular Skyline Drive along the summit of the mountains in Shenandoah National park begins less than 45 minutes from Charlottesville. *See The Skyline Drive* chapter for details.

▪ For a lovely drive through the **Piedmont region** of Virginia, take Route 20 south to Scottsville (about 30 minutes from Charlottesville), and stop at a vineyard and at the home of Earl Hamner (author of "The Waltons") along the way. Scottsville, the original county seat, has the third largest number of Federal-style buildings in the state. The museum and consignment shop, open weekends from 10 to 5, April 15 to November 15, is perfect for gifts and mementos. A canoe-rental shop here *(see #10, Boating and Fishing)* can arrange for three-hour canoe trips on the James River.

▪ From Scottsville, turn right on Route 6, drive about five miles, and follow the signs to the last pole-drawn ferry in the state. The free trip on the **Hatton Ferry** takes 10 to 20 minutes, depending on the water level. Open Wednesday through Sunday from 9 to 5.

▪ Fans of the TV show "The Waltons" will want to make a side trip to **Schuyler,** the tiny town where Earl Hamner, Jr., author of the show, grew up, and the area about which he writes. You can see the Hamner home from the outside (it's closed to the public), and have an ice cream cone at the little general store, just as John Boy and his brothers and sisters did. TO GET THERE from Scottsville: Drive west on Route 6 for about 12 miles, then turn left on Route 800 for two miles to Schuyler. Driving south from Charlottesville, follow Route 20 south to Keene. Turn right on Route 715. At Esmont, turn right on Route 6. After about six miles, turn left on Route 800 for two miles to Schuyler.

▪ Between Charlottesville and Scottsville (9.6 miles south of I-64 on Route 20) is the seven-acre **Montdomaine Vineyard** (Carter's Bridge; phone: 977-6120). Open by appointment only.

▪ Tour local wineries (by appointment only), about 13½ miles south of Charlottesville, by contacting **Montdomaine Cellars** (Route 6, Box 168A, Charlottesville 22901; phone 971-8947 or 977-6120).

▪ Jefferson considered his role in founding the **University of Virginia** of greater importance than his service as President of the United States. The Rotunda, restored to its original shape and design in 1976, is open to visitors daily from 9 to 4:45. Volunteer students lead hour-long tours of the campus during the school year at 10, 11, 2, 3, and 4; and during the summer at 11 and 2. Phone ahead to confirm the schedule (phone: 924-7969). Visitors who want to explore the campus on their own, including the room occupied by Edgar Allan Poe, can get information and a printed brochure in the administrative office in the Rotunda.

5. THE ARTS

▪ The **Virginia Players** (Drama Building, Culbreth Road, Charlottesville; phone: 924-3376) is a university group that performs during the academic year. Recent productions range from *As You Like It* to *Charlie's Aunt.* The **Heritage Repertory Theater** uses the same facilities.

▪ **Ash Lawn** (phone: 293-9539) has a summer program of concerts and opera from early July through mid-August. Visitors may picnic on the lawn before performances in the boxwood garden.

Tickets, costing $6 for adults, $3 for children under 12, may be reserved by phone. For children's theater, *see #16, For Kids.*

6. ANTIQUES AND CRAFTS

▪ The **Visitor's Center** (at the intersection of Routes 64 and 20 south) has, on request, a mimeographed list of craft and antique shops in the county.

▪ **Paula Lewis** (4th and Jefferson Street; phone: 295-6244) has one of the most varied collections of quality quilts, modern and antique, in the country. Most are from Pennsylvania and Ohio, but some come from as far away as Montana. Also on sale are pillows, calico fabrics, hooked rugs, and folk art.

▪ **Lewis Glaser Quill Pens** (107 West Main Street; phone: 293-8531) sells the same feather pens and pewter inkwells that he sends to Supreme Court justices.

▪ Charlottesville has a group of quality antique stores on Main Street between 10th and 14th Streets, a short walk from the University of Virginia and the restaurants on Elliewood Ave.

▪ **Ann Wood's** (1211 West Main Street; phone: 295-6108) has a national reputation for her American and English furniture, porcelain, and silver. Closed Sundays.

▪ **Bernard Caperton** (133 West Main Street; phone: 293-2383) has eighteenth- and nineteenth-century furniture and accessories, including Tiffany lamps. Closed Sundays.

▪ **McGuffey Art Center** (201 2nd Street; phone: 295-7973) displays and sells contemporary jewelry, batik, stained glass, and other crafts by local artisans, many of whose studios are on the premises. Closed Monday.

▪ **Signet Gallery** (212 5th Street NE) features the work of some 70 contemporary American artists and craftsmen. Work includes garnet and lapis jewelry, hand-painted silk clothing, stoneware, cutlery, and leather bags. Closed Sunday and Monday.

▪ **1740 House** (Route 250 west, 1½ miles past the Boar's Head Inn; phone: 977-1740) features eighteenth- and early nineteenth-century formal, country, and primitive furniture and accessories. Open daily.

▪ The **Crafter's Gallery** (Route 250 west, 9 miles west of Charlottesville; phone: 295-7006) features the work of dozens of contemporary American craftspeople, including painters and potters. Open daily.

▪ Visitors who drive to Hatton's Ferry or to the home of Earl

Hamner, author of the Waltons, will enjoy the **Scottsville Museum and Consignment Shop,** open on weekends.

7. TOURS

▪ **Balloon trips** over Albermarle County can be arranged through the Boar's Head Inn (phone: 296-2181). *See #4, What to See and Do.*

▪ The **Visitor's Center** (at the intersection of Routes 64 and 20 south) has a self-guided walking tour map of downtown Charlottesville. The historic area is bordered roughly by East High Street, East Jefferson Street, and 2nd and 7th streets.

▪ Those who plan to visit **Castle Hill,** some 13 miles east of Charlottesville, should pick up a free Historical Driving Tour guide at the Visitor's Center, which describes many of the sights and plantation houses along the route.

8. WALKS

▪ The **Visitor's Center** (at the intersection of Routes 64 and 20 south) has a self-guided walking tour map of historic Charlottesville. Walk along East Jefferson and East High, between 2nd and 7th streets, to see some fine examples of early nineteenth-century architecture and a famous equestrian statue of Stonewall Jackson.

▪ The 250-acre **Pen Park** (two miles northeast of downtown Charlottesville by way of Park Street and Rio Road) has two miles of nature trails along the Rivanna River, with picnic tables at either end.

▪ **Mint Springs Valley Lake** (Route 684, west of Crozet) has 445 acres with nature trails along Bucks Elbow Mountain.

▪ **Sugar Hollow Reservoir** (Whitehall, Route 614) is the start of a 4½-mile hiking trail that leads to the top of the Blue Ridge Mountains. Take Barracks Road (Route 654) to Route 614. Continue past Whitehall to the reservoir.

▪ There are many hiking trails in the Blue Ridge, less than an hour's drive from Charlottesville. *See The Skyline Drive* chapter for details. For topographical maps, rental equipment, and free advice, stop at **Blue Ridge Mountain Sports** (1417 Emmet, Charlottesville; phone: 977-4400).

9. BIKING

▪ There are no bike rental stores in Charlottesville. Both **Skyline Schwinn** (923A Preston Plaza; phone: 295-3009) and **Blue Wheel**

(Elliewood Avenue; phone: 977-1870) have regional bike maps. Routes include some lovely 10- to 15-mile back-road loops through farm country and eighteenth- and nineteenth-century estates in Albemarle County. Roads are hilly, so 10-gear bikes are recommended.

10. BOATING AND FISHING

▪ The four county lakes—**Chris Greene** beyond the Charlottesville Airport; **Mint Springs** and **Beaver Creek** near Crozet; and **Totier Creek** near Scottsville—all have fishing from 8 A.M. to dusk. Maps with locations are available at the Visitor's Center (at the intersection of Routes 64 and 20 south). Chris Greene Lake has rowboats and canoes to rent. Fishing permits are sold in the clerk's office at the Albemarle County Courthouse (Courthouse Square, East Jefferson Street; phone: 296-5869), K-Mart, Best's, and Carter's Gun Works.

▪ Call the county game warden (phone: 296-5830) for advice on the best rivers and lakes for fishing.

▪ **James River Runners** (Scottsville, about 30 minutes south of Charlottesville; phone: 286-2338) rents canoes and tubes for trips down the James River. (The 340-mile river is the longest in the U.S. contained in one state.) Rates per person range from $7.50 for a three-mile trip to $21 for a 32-mile overnight trip. There are some class I and II rapids that are fun for beginners and islands for picnics or camping along the way.

▪ **Blue Ridge Mountain Sports** (147 Emmet, Charlottesville; phone: 977-4400) rents canoes and kayaks for trips down the Rivanna and James Rivers. No pick-ups, but roof racks are available.

▪ Visitors with their own tubes will enjoy a 2½-mile trip down the **Rivanna River** from the old Woolen Mill to Shadwell Bridge. The mill is at the eastern end of East Market Street.

11. SWIMMING

▪ There are swimming pools at the **Boar's Head Inn, Prospect Hill** and many of the local motels.

▪ **Washington Pool** (Washington Park, corner of 10th Street and Preston Avenue) and **Onesty Pool** (Meade Park, intersection of Meade Avenue and Chesapeake Street) are open from June 10 through Labor Day, daily from 12 to 7, Sunday from 1 to 7.

▪ **Chris Greene Lake** (about 12 miles northwest of Charlottesville, near the airport) has a bath house, a sandy beach, and lifeguards.

▪ **Mint Springs Lake** (1½ miles from Crozet, about 12 miles from Charlottesville) has a bath house, a sandy beach, and lifeguards.

12. SKIING

▪ **Wintergreen** (Wintergreen, 48 miles southwest of Charlottesville; phone: 325-2200) claims it has the most extensive snow-making equipment in the East. Three lifts—two triple and one double—serve seven slopes. There is skiing nightly, except Monday, from 7 to 11. Weekday lift tickets cost $16; weekends, $24. TO GET THERE: I-64 west to Route 250 west. Turn left on Route 6 for seven miles to Route 151. Turn right on Route 664 for four miles to the entrance.

▪ **Massanutten Ski Area** (McGaheysville, 40 miles northwest of Charlottesville; phone: 703/289-9441) has five lifts—four double-chair and one J-bar—for nine slopes. There is skiing nightly from 6:30 to 10. Weekday lift tickets cost $17; weekends, $22.

13. RIDING

▪ **Foxfield Stables** (seven miles from Charlottesville on Free Union Road; phone: 973-4886) has Western or English trail riding. Take Barracks Road (Route 654), then turn right on Route 601 toward Free Union.

▪ **Montfair Stables** (20 miles west of Charlottesville; phone: 823-5202) has English or Western trail riding, and guided trail rides to the top of the Blue Ridge. Overnight rides with camping are also available. Take Barracks Road (Route 654) to Whitehall, then go right on Route 810.

14. TENNIS

▪ **Pen Park** (two miles northeast of downtown Charlottesville by way of Park Street and Rio Road) has eight unlighted courts. Free.

▪ **McIntire Park** (one mile north of downtown Charlottesville by way of McIntire Road) has 11 lighted courts that cost 25¢ an hour.

▪ Tennis and squash are available at the **Boar's Head Sports Club.**

▪ **Ivy House Tennis Club** (2350 Old Ivy Road; phone: 977-0066) has courts open from 8 A.M. to dark at $10 an hour.

15. GOLF

▪ **Pen Park** (two miles northeast of downtown Charlottesville by way of Park Street and Rio Road) has a public nine-hole course.

▪ **McIntire Park** (one mile north of downtown Charlottesville by way of McIntire Road) has a public nine-hole course.

16. FOR KIDS

• The guided tour of Monticello takes less than 15 minutes—not long enough for anyone to get bored. Children should be fascinated by some of Jefferson's gadgets, such as the seven-day calendar clock, the dumbwaiters, and the revolving serving door in the dining room. The more children know beforehand about Jefferson, the more rewarding will be their visit. Discuss Jefferson's life and philosophy with them, or send them to the library for some children's books.

• The **hot air balloon ride** is an unforgettable experience *(see #4, What to See and Do)*.

• **Ash Lawn** (phone: 293-9539), the home of James Monroe, has a Sunday afternoon series of puppet shows and musicals that interpret life in the late eighteenth century for children aged 3 to 12. Admission $2.

17. DINING

Since there are no consistently first-class restaurants in the Charlottesville area, pick an atmosphere you like, refuse to be upset if a meal isn't perfect, and allow yourself to be pleasantly surprised if it is.

• For a romantic evening, dine at **Prospect Hill** (Trevilians, 14 miles east of Charlottesville; phone: 703/967-0844), a 200-year-old manor house with two colonial-blue dining rooms. Guests are invited to arrive early and stroll about the grounds, sipping Chablis. A brass bell announces dinner, which begins with a grace. There is no menu—guests usually do not know what will be served until they sit down—but the cuisine is French. The complete dinner costs $20. (It may include French barley soup, salad, beef medallions sautéed in wine sauce, and a dessert of ladyfingers soaked in rum and covered with a layer of chocolate mousse.) Ties are optional, but who would visit an elegant manor house inelegantly dressed? Visa and Mastercard are accepted. Reservations are required. Dinners are served Wednesday through Saturday at 7:30. (For more information on Prospect Hill, *see #19 Lodging*.)

• **C & O Restaurant** (515 Water Street; phone: 971-7044) is the other top eating spot, with the advantage of being near the center of town. Prospect Hill, with its soft old-world atmosphere, is for couples who enjoy candlelight and the solace of the past. The C & O is for a tougher, more urbane, perhaps more adventuresome crew, who want to be stunned by something daringly new. The entrance to the C & O is next to an exterminating company, across from the

Chesapeake & Ohio railroad tracks. Downstairs, in what used to be a diner, is the bar and lounge. Upstairs is the dining room, seating only 30. Walls, floors, shutters—everything is painted white, and there are no pictures to distract you from the main show, the meal itself. The chef, Spencer Graham, was a religious studies major who went on to *nouvelle cuisine.* Try the melon soup, made with cranshaw and cantaloupe, sometimes mango and papaya. Entrées, priced from $17 to $26, include veal chops with chanterelle mushrooms (flown in from Oregon), and scallops in a light grapefruit, mustard, and cream sauce. Who can pass up fresh blackberries for dessert? Ties and jackets are requested. All major credit cards are accepted. Reservations are required.

▪ **Le Snail** (320 West Main Street; phone: 295-4456) has a Viennese chef who specializes in boned, baked trout in pastry, beef Wellington, and rabbit tenderloin in currant wine sauce. Entrées, priced from $10.25 to $12.95, tend to be more traditional French than *nouvelle cuisine.* The style is Old World, with lots of velveteen. Jackets are required. All major credit cards are accepted. Reservations are recommended.

▪ While visiting the University of Virginia, stop for an inexpensive lunch at restaurants on Elliewood Avenue. Popular among students are **Martha's Café** (phone: 295-3418) and the slightly more formal and expensive **Lena's Dance** (phone: 293-6900).

18. AFTER HOURS

▪ **C & O Restaurant** (515 Water Street; phone: 296-8280) has live music Thursday through Saturday from 8:30 to 2. The crowd is mixed, with a large college contingent.

▪ An under-30 crowd is attracted to the bars around the university, between Elliewood and 14th streets, north of University Avenue. Most popular are **The Virginian, El Greco's, T.J.'s,** and the **Mine Shaft.**

▪ The over-40 crowd heads for the **Boar's Head Inn** (Route 250 west; phone: 296-2181).

▪ **McIntire Park,** one mile north of downtown Charlottesville by way of McIntire Road, has 11 lighted tennis courts that cost 25¢ an hour.

▪ The **Farmington Hunt Club** (Barracks Road, Route 654, about 10 minutes west of Charlottesville; phone: 296-4796) has polo matches on Friday nights in summer. Call to confirm schedule.

19. LODGING

▪ For a taste of Southern hospitality, enjoy bed and breakfast in any of 140 homes within the Charlottesville area that have opened their doors to overnight guests. **Guesthouses Bed & Breakfast, Inc.** (phone: 979-7264 or 979-8327 from 1 to 6 P.M.) can arrange for accommodations in anything from a single room with a fourposter bed, to a geodesic dome powered by a windmill, to a historic manor house with its own tennis court. Rooms run from $40 to $80 a night, including breakfast.

▪ **Prospect Hill** (Route 1, Box 55, Trevilians 23170, 14 miles east of Charlottesville; phone: (703) 967-0844) is one of the most charming, romantic inns in the East. Rows of 140-year-old boxwoods lead to the manor house on a former 1,576-acre plantation. The original English settlers moved here because the rolling farmland reminded them of the Cotswolds. The former plantation owners returned from the War Between the States to find their property overgrown and their slaves gone. Like other families in similar straits, they added bedrooms to the manor house, enlarged the slave quarters, and began taking in guests from the city. The present owner, Bill Sheehan, a retired marketing executive for a plastics company, has been here since 1977 with his French wife, working hard to restore the property to its former glory. There are only seven guest rooms, each with a fireplace and private bath. The Overton Room in the main building has a couch where you can cuddle up in front of a fire, and a private breakfast porch overlooking the pool. In the former slave quarters, imaginative use is made of small space. Dormer rooms of white plaster and unfinished heart pine are decorated with braided rugs and four-poster beds with white cotton spreads. Doubles, some with shared bath, cost $40 to $50 per person, including breakfast; $60 to $70 per person, including breakfast and dinner. Visa and Mastercard are accepted. (For additional information, *see #17, Dining.*)

▪ **Boar's Head Inn** (Route 250 west, Charlottesville 22905; phone: 296-2181) is a mock colonial-style complex—a theme Holiday Inn—built in 1966. A stuffed boar's head hangs to one side of the registration desk, above the plain carpet. Talbots designed the boar's head ties worn by the desk clerks. The inn is perfect for those who want a relaxed, comfortable, motellike environment and a wealth of sports facilities, including tennis, swimming, paddle tennis, and squash. Doubles cost $63 to $73.

▪ **Best Western's Cavalier Inn** (corner of Routes 29 north and 250 Business; phone: 296-8111) is on the campus of the University of

Virginia. Facilities include a swimming pool. Doubles cost $40 to $50.

▪ **Quality Inn** (I-64 and Route 250 east; phone: 977-3300) has miniature golf, tennis, and swimming. Doubles cost $40 to $50.

20. EMERGENCIES

- ▪ **University Hospital** (phone: 924-0211).
- ▪ **Martha Jefferson Hospital** (phone: 293-0111).

21. HOW TO GET THERE

BY CAR. *From Washington:* South on Route 29.

BY BUS. Trailways *from Washington* (phone: 202/537-5800) or *from Baltimore* (phone: 301/752-2115).

BY TRAIN. Amtrak *from Washington* (phone: 202/484-7540) or *from Baltimore* (phone: 301/539-2112).

BY PLANE. Piedmont Airlines (800/251-5720) flies into the airport eight miles north of Charlottesville *from New York* and *from Washington.*

22. FOR FURTHER INFORMATION

▪ **Thomas Jefferson Visitor's Center** (at the intersection of Routes 64 and 20 south; phone: 293-6789 or 944-1783). Mailing address: P.O. Box 161, Charlottesville 22902.

▪ **Charlottesville and Albemarle Chamber of Commerce** (corner of Market and 5th Street N. E.; phone: 295-3141). Mailing address: P.O. Box 1564, Charlottesville 22902.

23. RECOMMENDED READING

▪ Fawn M. Brodie. *Thomas Jefferson: An Intimate History* (New York: Bantam Books, 1975).

▪ Adrienne Koch and William Peden, editors. *The Life and Selected Writings of Thomas Jefferson* (New York: Random House Modern Library, 1944).

▪ "Thomas Jefferson: Agrarian Democrat," in Vernon L. Parrington, *The Colonial Mind, 1620–1800* (New York: Harcourt, Brace, 1972), pp. 347–362.

Rehoboth Beach, Delaware

Area Code, 302; Zip Code, 19971

1. DISTANCES

BY CAR. *From Washington*, 2¾ hours; *from Philadelphia*, 3 hours; *from Baltimore*, 2¾ hours; *from New York*, 4½ hours.

BY BUS. *From Washington*, 3 hours; *from Philadelphia*, 4 hours; *from Baltimore*, 2½ hours.

2. MAJOR ATTRACTIONS

- Beautiful ocean beaches for families and singles.
- A sophisticated nightlife for both the young and the not-so-young.
- Enough top restaurants to fill a month of weekends.
- A choice of modern motels or charming country inns; of muscle shirts or Polo shirts; of cherry dip-top flavor cones or broiled quail and gelati.

3. INTRODUCTION

Thank the Methodists and the U.S. Highway Department. The Methodists, who founded Rehoboth Beach just over a hundred years ago, gave the town a low-keyed family atmosphere it still enjoys today. The Highway Department built Route 1 to the west of town so that instead of a "strip"—the plague of other shore communities—Rehoboth has parks, rambling old boarding houses, and quiet, residential neighborhoods with $400,000 homes. Dewey Beach, a Frisbee's throw to the south, allows drinking on the beach (unlike Rehoboth) and siphons off the loud, shiny singles crowd. "You won't find mom, pop, and the kids in Dewey Beach," a coed told me. "They're all in Rehoboth Beach."

One reason there's so much expensive good taste in Rehoboth is the type of people summering here—mostly diplomats and professionals from Washington and Baltimore who can afford to keep the Polo Shops and the elegant French restaurants in business, and who have a stake in keeping the community low-keyed.

Not that Rehoboth is without its honky element, far from it. The Chamber of Commerce holds each summer a Best Body on the Beach Contest, where "gorgeous specimens of flesh compete for prizes." Rehoboth has its share of T-Shirt Riot Stores, Video Parlors, and Fudge Kitchens. But the world of cherry dip cones and fries is confined essentially to the boardwalk and the ocean end of Rehoboth Avenue, and weekend guests can, up to a point, choose to ignore it.

Most won't. Most, remembering what it was like to be a child, will eagerly submit to the pleasures of an oceanside boardwalk, knowing that when they've had enough they can retreat to a more sophisticated world of country inns and elegant dining.

That's what makes Rehoboth so unique—this mix of Ralph Lauren and muscle shirts; of orange slush and frogs' legs Provençale. The two worlds seem to coexist here without threatening each other, and on a weekend escape you can enjoy the best of both.

4. WHAT TO SEE AND DO

▪ The main attraction is of course the beach. You can walk south and submit to the gorgeous singles scene at Dewey Beach, or head north to the relative quiet of Cape Henlopen State Park, which begins about a mile north of the boardwalk. After 3, join the crowds heading for the jam session at The Bottle and Cork in Dewey Beach.

▪ Within a six-block area, on either side of Rehoboth Avenue, are dozens of clothing and specialty shops; it would take more than a weekend to see them all. Among the best are **The Ralph Lauren Polo Shop** (86 Rehoboth Avenue); **Crabtree & Evelyn** (33 Baltimore Avenue); **Mostly Irish** (33 Baltimore Avenue); **The Sea Shell Shop** (37 Rehoboth Avenue); and **Penny Lane Mall** (phone: 227-6666). Almost every store has a postseason clearance sale in September, with summerwear priced up to 50 percent off.

▪ **Cape Henlopen State Park** (ten minutes north of Rehoboth; phone: 645-6852) has free summer talks on Wednesday and Saturday at 7:30 P.M. on subjects ranging from acid rain to shore birds.

▪ The area around Rehoboth Beach is flat as a pancake. Rent a bike and head north to Cape Henlopen State Park or through the tree-lined residential streets of Henlopen Acres. The boardwalk is open to bikers until 10 A.M. only.

▪ When you've had enough sun, or when there isn't any, head north about ten minutes to the historic town of **Lewes** (pronounced Lewis), founded in 1631. There are ten antique stores here *(see #6, Antiques and Crafts)*, and a number of interesting historic buildings to explore. You can go on a guided walking tour, which will get you inside some of the buildings, or on a self-guided tour, using a walking map from the Historical Society. *See #7, Tours,* for details.

▪ There's plenty of crabbing and clamming around Rehoboth Bay and Love Creek, and in the Lewes–Rehoboth Canal area. Check with bait and tackle stores such as **Mac's** (Route 1, Dewey Beach; phone: 227-7213) for details.

▪ Don't miss the nightly auctions at **Stuart Kingston Gallery** at the northern end of the boardwalk (phone: 227-2524). Goods—mostly new jewelry and rugs, but also antique furniture—are placed in auction by someone like yourself who stopped by during the day and agreed to make the first bid. If you like a maple Duncan Phyfe bureau, dated 1820, for example, you can buy it for the appraised value of $2,500 or agree to place an opening bid of $1,000. There needs to be at least one countering bid—the auctioneer will probably ask for $1,500—and then the bureau is yours for a bid of, say, $1,600, if no one bids again. The auctioneer is wonderfully manipulative and condescending, and even if you have no intention of buying, it's fascinating in a frightening sort of way to watch how he gets people who wander in off the boardwalk to shell out $3,000 for, say, a yellow diamond ring.

▪ For sailing and fishing, you have your choice of two bays, Rehoboth and Delaware, and two lakes, Silver and Gerar. For fishing, there are two inlets, Indian and Roosevelt, and of course the Atlantic Ocean. *See #10, Boating and Fishing,* for details.

▪ See the Rehoboth of yesterday in the **Anna Hazzard Museum** (Martin's Lane), a Methodist camp meeting–era building now serving as the resort's first museum. Open Memorial Day through Labor Day on Saturday and Sunday from 1 to 4, or by appointment.

▪ Evening cruises along the Lewes shoreline, usually beginning at 7 P.M., are available at **Angler's Fishing Center** (Angler's Road, Lewes; phone: 645-6080/8212). The head boat *Judy V* (five miles south of Rehoboth on Route 1; phone: 227-4440 or 422-8940) has evening cruises on Indian River Inlet.

▪ On your way home, stop for fresh fruits and vegetables along Route 1. The closest market to the ferry for visitors heading north is **Homestead Market** on King's Highway, open daily in season from 10 to 6 and on Sunday from 10 to 5. Visitors heading west and south can stop at Isaac's Family Farm (phone: 856-7245) or O'Day's Market (337-7575).

5. THE ARTS

▪ The **Rehoboth Art League** (Dodds Lane, Henlopen Acres; phone: 227-8408) sponsors Friday evening chamber music concerts in the Chambers Studio from July through early September. You can join or listen to amateurs and professionals play chamber music on Saturday mornings. The Art League also sponsors art exhibits from mid-March through September.

6. ANTIQUES AND CRAFTS

▪ Antiques are surprisingly scarce for such an affluent area. Best bet are the ten antique stores in Lewes (a ten-minute drive north of Rehoboth), almost all within three blocks of each other on Front, 2nd, and 3rd streets between Market Street and Savannah Road. The **Golden Goose** (phone: 645-6343) sells new and antique quilts and folk art. **The Antique Corner** (401 King's Highway; phone: 645-2400) specializes in antique jewelry, silver boxes, and old toys. Ask at any of the stores for a map of antique dealers in Lewes.

▪ For antique furniture, combine your drive to Lewes with a trip to **The Brick Barn** and **York's Antiques** (both on Route 9 toward Georgetown, about five miles from Rehoboth).

▪ There are nightly auctions, mostly of new jewelry and rugs, at the Stuart Kingston Galleries on the boardwalk. *See #4, What to See and Do.*

▪ Best bet in Rehoboth is **Antiques and Old Things** (81 Rehoboth Avenue; phone: 227-1344), with its small but tasteful collection of crystal and eighteenth- and nineteenth-century furnishings.

▪ **Tideline Gallery** (41 Rehoboth Avenue; phone: 227-4444) sells smart contemporary American crafts, from hand-blown glass to platinum-plated vases, dolls, wooden toys, and batiks.

▪ There's an occasional find at **The Treasure House** (Route 1, off Ann B. Street, Dewey Beach; phone: 227-2401). Also on Route 1 in Dewey Beach is **The Studio Gift and Antique Shop,** selling the largest selection of antique duck decoys in the area.

7. TOURS

▪ The choice is yours: a surrey ride or a Jolly Trolley ride, both departing from Rehoboth Avenue at the boardwalk. The **Jolly Trolley** (phone: 227-2280) takes you on a ten-mile narrated tour of Rehoboth and Dewey Beach. **Horsedrawn Tours of Rehoboth** (phone: 227-2210) takes you on a 30-minute clip-clop around town. Up to four of you can sign up for a private tour in a horse-drawn hansom cab.

▪ The **Lewes Historic Society** (phone: 645-8346) runs worthwhile 90-minute walking tours of historic Lewes that include the **Zwaanendael Museum,** with its collection of Americana; the **Colonel David Hall House,** which was built in 1790 and still retains its original woodwork and paneling; the 300-year-old **Ryves Holt House;** and a beautifully restored eighteenth-century farmhouse, the **Rabbit's Ferry House.** Tours begin on Tuesday, Thursday, Friday, and Saturday at 10:30. Adults, $2, children free. Tickets are sold in the Society's Country Store, one of a complex of restored buildings.

8. WALKS

▪ From Rehoboth you can maneuver north along the beach through the muscular singles scene on Dewey Beach, or head north to the relative solitude of Cape Henlopen State Park. If so inclined, you can walk some seven miles along the shore to Delaware Bay. Solitude will be yours here, as well as the unforgettable smell of king crabs (members of the spider family) spawning in summer. To avoid the parking problems and crowds in Rehoboth, bike or drive north along a street called Duneway to the two parking lots in the Gordon Pond Wildlife Area. From here, at the southern end of the Cape Henlopen State Park, walk north along the beach.

▪ **Cape Henlopen State Park** (ten minutes north of Rehoboth; phone: 645-8983) has over 2,500 acres of open shoreline, bayshore, pinelands, and cranberry bogs. Head south along the beach from the north parking area and pass beneath 80-foot dunes, the highest between Cape Hatteras and Cape Cod. The Seaside Nature Center at the entrance has a salt-water aquarium. The self-guiding Seaside Nature Trail (.6 miles) takes you through low sand dunes, dense thickets, and the bayshore, which can be a revelation at low tide. The **Pinelands Nature Trail** is a two-mile loop that takes you across "walking" dunes and a pitch-pine forest. Bring lots of bug repellent in summer!

• For a lovely walk through suburban Rehoboth, with its $400,000 homes, walk around Lake Gerar, down Park Avenue, and north through Henlopen Acres.

9. BIKING

• Biking is permitted in Rehoboth on the boardwalk and in the commercial district only between 5 A.M. and 10 A.M. Most stores rent children's bikes and bikes with baby seats or training wheels. The area is so flat, it could have been smoothed with a trowel. Bike north through Henlopen Acres or along the new wooded bike path in Henlopen State Park. Most rentals cost $6 a day; **Boardwalk Bikes** (at Virginia Avenue) charges $5. You'll find the greatest variety of bikes at **Bob's Rentals** (North 1st Street and Maryland Avenue; phone: 227-7966). Other rental stores include **Resort Rental Service** (8 North 2nd Street, across from the Post Office; phone: 227-9470) and **Wheels** (8 South 1st Street; phone: 227-6807).

10. BOATING AND FISHING

BOATING

• **Waples Mill Pond Canoeing** (Routes 1 and 5, Milton, about 20 minutes north of Rehoboth; phone: 684-8084) rents canoes for trips on the pond and along the Primehook Creek through the most remote regions of the National Wildlife Refuge. You can paddle 7½ miles one way, or 15 miles round trip. Fall is an ideal time, when birds are migrating and trees are showing off their fall plumage.

• For sailboat rentals on Rehoboth Bay and surfboard rentals and instruction, contact in Dewey Beach the **Waterfront Restaurant** (McKinley Street; phone: 227-9292); **Dewey Beach Surf and Sport** (Route 1; phone: 227-8288); and **Dewey Beach Sailing and Water Sports Center** (Dagsworthy Street; phone: 227-1777. **The Rehoboth Bay Sailing Association** (phone: 227-9008) offers sailing lessons.

• For early evening cruises, *see #4, What to See and Do.*

FISHING

- For the latest story on fishing, phone the **Fisherman's Hotline** at 645-4241.
- You can buy a ticket and rub rods with other fishermen, or charter your own boat. The main action is in Indian River Inlet, where trout and blues are caught, as well as flounder and tautog. Deep-sea trips to Baltimore Canyon for marlin, tuna, and dolphin can also be arranged. Serious anglers begin fishing in April for mackerel, which stay around till the blues chase them north in May. The bluefish season lasts all summer. Trout arrive with warmer water.
- **Fisherman's Wharf** (7 Vermont Avenue, Lewes, about ten minutes north of Rehoboth; phone: 645-8862/8541) has half-day fishing trips departing at 8 A.M. and 1:30 P.M., and eight-hour trips departing at 7 A.M. Private charters can also be arranged.
- **Angler's Fishing Center** (Angler's Road, Lewes; phone: 645-6080/8212) has four- and six-hour family fishing trips departing at 8 and 9 A.M.
- Land-based anglers find that surf-fishing peaks in the spring and fall, both in Cape Henlopen State Park and on the open sections of the beach south of Dewey Beach.

11. SWIMMING

- There's supervised swimming both in front of the boardwalk in Rehoboth and in Cape Henlopen National Park, a ten-minute drive to the north. Singles in search of adventure should walk south to Dewey Beach. Most of the larger motels have private pools.
- The best bay swimming is at Lewes Beach and in Delaware Seashore Park, south of Dewey Beach, off Tower Road.
- For scuba diving lessons, contact the **Rehoboth Dive Center** (Route 1, Midway; phone: 645-6800) or the **Old Inlet Dive Shop** (Route 1, Dewey Beach; phone: 227-0999).

14. TENNIS

- Rehoboth has public courts (phone: 227-3598) at the end of Lake Avenue on Deaville Beach and at the Junior High School on State Road.
- Dewey Beach, just south of Rehoboth, has five courts at **The Runaround** (phone: 227-6053) on McKinley Street on the Bay.
- In the Lewes area, just north of Rehoboth, there are public courts at Cape Henlopen High School and in Cape Henlopen State Park (phone: 645-8983).

15. GOLF

▪ **Old Landing** (phone: 227-3131) is a regulation 18-hole course.
▪ **Midway Par 3** (Route 1, four miles north of Rehoboth; phone: 645-7955) is an 18-hole course with 50- to 150-yard greenways. The cost is $4, including clubs.

16. FOR KIDS

▪ Rehoboth Beach, unlike Dewey Beach to the south, is a family resort, where children are welcome. The beach and boardwalk should provide a weekend's worth of fun for any child.
▪ Bike rental shops *(see #9, Biking)* have a large assortment of children's bikes, some with training wheels. Kids can pedal along the boardwalk until 10 A.M.
▪ **Rehoboth Summer Children's Theatre** (Olive Avenue, near the beach; phone: 227-6766) performs 45-minute plays from late June through August. The curtain rises Tuesday and Thursday at 7:30 P.M.
▪ **See #15, Golf,** for golf at Midway Par 3.
▪ The city of Rehoboth sponsors volleyball, touch football, softball, and other competitive sports nightly in summer from 7 to 11 on a lighted portion of the beach between Rehoboth and Olive Avenues.

17. DINING

▪ When I asked dozens of summer residents where they would take weekend guests to dine, the same restaurants were mentioned again and again. Garden Gourmet and Chez la Mer were the top two, or among the top three, on every list. Fran O'Brien's was the place to go for prime ribs. Most everyone raved about the food at the Blue Moon, but while some loved the smart, modern decor, others found it forbidding. Most had heard positive things about Astral Plane, but because it had opened only recently they had not dined there themselves. The Corner Cupboard has a solid reputation; so has a Middle Eastern restaurant called The Camel's Hump. The Back Porch Café was rated good to excellent, depending on how people reacted to its distinctive decor.
▪ Since Rehoboth's restaurants, unlike those in other shore communities, are civilized enough to accept dinner reservations, it makes sense to search around in the morning, find one with the right mood, and make reservations for the evening. If you're arriving Friday night on a summer weekend, call ahead, or you may end up eating french fries and orange slush on the boardwalk. Most restaurants have an

indoor dining area and an outdoor patio; specify your choice when making reservations.

▪ French Provençale cooking is the specialty at **Chez La Mer** (2nd Street and Wilmington Avenue; phone: 227-6494), with an emphasis on veal and fresh fish. Two popular dishes are veal with red wine and mushrooms, and shrimps and bay scallops cooked with tomatoes and basil. For dessert, try the chocolate mousse laced with citrus flavor. Entrées are priced from $9 to $15. All major credit cards are accepted.

▪ It's hard to believe that a restaurant as elegant as the **Garden Gourmet** (4121 Route 1 at Phillips Street, just south of the Route 1A or Rehoboth Avenue turnoff; phone: 227-4747) is on Route 1. The mood is early American in this lovingly restored 85-year-old farmhouse, with its crystal chandeliers, soft lighting, and muted Williamsburg blue wainscoting. The alcove, with only three tables, is a particularly intimate place to dine. Appetizers include smoked fish, usually marlin or tuna, with either a cucumber or a mustard horseradish sauce. Entrées, priced from $14 to $20, include flounder à l'orange flamed in Grand Marnier; grilled tournedos; and scallops of veal sautéed with prosciutto and mushrooms and finished with cream and Emmenthaler cheese. All major credit cards are accepted.

▪ **Fran O'Brien's** (59 Lake Street; phone: 227-6121) is the place to go for prime ribs ($14). Entrées, including several fresh fish dishes, range from $10 to $17. If loud music disturbs your digestion, finish your last sip of coffee by 10, when the music starts.

▪ The multi-leveled **Back Porch Café** (21 Rehoboth Avenue; phone: 227-3674) looks like a stage set for *Porgy and Bess.* Tables are set in an open courtyard under a catalpa tree; in a long, narrow art gallery with pull-down movie-theater seats; under a skylight of French doors; and on a trellised balcony with two soft globe lights that look like moons. "Creative international cuisine" aptly describes the menu, which includes roast duck glazed with soy molasses; calves' liver sauteed with leeks, prosciutto, and white wine; and veal sautéed with oysters, shallots, artichoke hearts, and fresh sage cream, served over fettucine. The imaginative brunch includes a Thai seafood séviche of shrimps, scallops, and oysters with peppers, shallots, peanuts, ginger, and a minted lime vinaigrette. Entrées are priced from $12 to $16. Visa and Mastercard are accepted.

▪ **The Blue Moon** (35 Baltimore Avenue; phone: 227-6515) is a high-profile, style-conscious restaurant. Most outrageous is the bar, with magenta lights reflected in its stainless steel ceiling. Walls in the main dining room are an almost Mediterranean blue. The outdoor dining area is much softer, thanks to the stars. Appetizers include oyster bisque and baked goat cheese on fresh greens with rosemary baguettes. Entrées, priced from $11.50 to $14.50, include Pasta Puttanesca (various seafoods in a red sauce over tagliatelle noodles) and grilled lamb chops with minted chutney butter. For dessert, try the frozen sabayon with raspberry sauce or a Key lime tart.

▪ The atmosphere at the **Corner Cupboard Inn** (50 Park Avenue, between 1st and 2nd streets; phone: 227-8553) is more relaxed than smart and trendy—the very opposite of The Blue Moon. It is the sort of familiar place that long-time summer residents call their own and return to year after year. Entrées, priced from $9 to $14.50, include broiled fish, lobster, duckling, and scallops. The breakfast menu includes kidney stew; Sunday brunch (which is lovely on the open porch) includes broiled kippers. BYOB. All major credit cards are accepted.

▪ The reputation of **Astral Plane** (Rehoboth Avenue; phone: 227-1191) has been soaring since it opened last year. As with its sister restaurant in Philadelphia, you will either love or hate its wild, playful eclecticism, which its owners aptly call "organized madness." The art deco room has a Chinese corner and a ceiling made from a parachute. There are large rattan fan-back chairs, Victorian ceiling fans, purple walls, Oriental carpets, and flowery chintz tablecloths. The food is as original as the decor: a classic French dish made with tofu instead of veal; Thai-style chicken; breaded shrimp in a spicy Creole sauce with scallions in a nest of pasta. Entrées range from $8 to $14. A special bargain is the $10 three-course meal, which might include gazpacho, scallops scampi, and German chocolate cake.

▪ The **Camel's Hump** (21 Baltimore Street; phone: 227-0947) is popular even among those with no particular passion for Middle Eastern food. The ambiance is 1960ish, which could be a plus or minus, depending on your sensibilities. Entrées, priced from $10 to $13.50, include broiled eggplant stuffed with beef, almonds, raisins and mushrooms and baked with sherry and spices.

▪ For Italian food, particularly eggplant Parmesan, the first choice among summer residents is **Adriatico Ristorante** (North 1st Street and Baltimore Avenue; phone: 227-9255). Check out the atmosphere before you go. Another restaurant with decent reviews is **The Summerhouse** (78 Rehoboth Avenue; phone: 227-3895), which features an award-winning white gazpacho and a dish of crabmeat baked with green and red peppers, mozzarella, and onions.

▪ If you want to eat cheap, pig out on a $1.50 bucket of fries at **Thrasher's** (Rehoboth Avenue, near the boardwalk). Locals under 25 head for **The Frog Pond** for 50-cent drafts. Some say **Lou's Pizza**, off the boardwalk, is the best. Locals all swear by the spaghetti at

Mrs. Florio's Restaurant, made fresh and served in her home behind the post office in Lewes (about ten minutes north of Rehoboth). Now there's a place none of your friends have been to!

18. AFTER HOURS

▪ Stroll along the boardwalk and submit to miniature golf, cherry dip cones, and all those other tacky pleasures you think you've outgrown. There are nightly auctions at the Stuart Kingston Gallery *(see #4, What to See and Do)* at the northern end of the boardwalk. When you've had enough, leave the lights and the board-walk behind and continue north along the beach.

▪ There's a pride of nightclubs both in Rehoboth Beach and nearby Dewey Beach; you won't have time to try them all in a weekend, but most attract the same handsome, well-heeled crowd. What makes the Rehoboth night scene so special is the fact that 45-year-old Washingtonians with diplomatic pouches go to the same bars as Georgetown coeds. The not-so-young will feel right at home in Rehoboth.

▪ The fish in the tank behind the bar at **Fran O'Brien's** (55 Lake Avenue; phone: 227-6121) are less confined than the hundreds of guests packed into this popular night spot—which is why people keep trying to get in. The crowd is smart, tan, and visibly self-assured. Of all the local watering holes, the over-30 crowd will be most comfortable here.

▪ The preppy college and postcollege crowd heads to the **Sum-merhouse** (78 Rehoboth Avenue; phone: 227-3895), and sometimes to **Obie's By the Sea** (Olive Avenue on the Boardwalk; phone: 227-6261) and **Kelly's** (112 Rehoboth Avenue; phone: 227-7655).

▪ The bar scene in Rehoboth is pretty tame compared to what nearby Dewey Beach has to offer. There are three night spots within staggering distance of each other, so if one doesn't please you, finish up your drink and move on. The **Bottle and Cork** (Route l; phone: 227-8545) gets the youngest crowd. The **Rusty Rudder** (Dickinson Street on the Bay; phone: 227-3888) is the largest, holding more than 700 bodies at one time. The **Waterfront** (McKinley Street on the Bay; phone: 227-9292), like the **Rusty Rudder,** attracts a crowd ranging from 20 to 50, with an emphasis on 25 to 35.

▪ Couples who have tried everything else, or perhaps nothing else, should slip into a private hot tub at **Naturally Hot** (Route 1 and Read Street, Dewey Beach; phone: 227-2390). The cost is $7.50 a person per hour. There's a $20 minimum after 10.

▪ For an intimate spot no one knows about, walk to the end of

Rehoboth Avenue and, facing the boardwalk, turn left and look up at the **Café des Arts.** On one side of the small roof is an air-conditioner exhaust that, unless it has been covered, still competes with the sounds of the surf. On the other side of the open roof is a space just big enough for one table, and the two of you.

19. LODGING

▪ There is no central reservation number, but the **Chamber of Commerce** (302/227-2233) will send you a list of lodgings and give you the names of places to call. Rates drop as much as 60 percent in the off-season; one typical hotel charges $55 in summer, $36 in the spring and fall, and $27 in winter. Most hotels and boardinghouses require a two- or three-night weekend reservation, but of course there are always last-minute cancellations. If you arrive on a summer weekend without a reservation, plan to sleep in your car. If you're calling at the last minute, ask the Chamber of Commerce for motels in nearby Lewes; I had luck finding a room the day before my arrival at the **Cape Henlopen Motel** (phone: 645-2828). All lodgings listed below are within a block or two of the ocean.

▪ If you're staying at an inn or boardinghouse, remember that rooms vary tremendously in decor and amenities; discuss alternatives with the innkeeper before making reservations. A room that includes breakfast is a real plus. So is private parking; you don't want to spend your weekend slipping quarters into 12-hour meters. Air conditioning can be nice for an afternoon snooze. Is the early Methodist influence responsible for so many twin-bedded rooms?

▪ Some of you would rather stay in a tired old boardinghouse with Salvation Army furniture than submit to the anonymity of a motel. If that's the case, you're in luck in Rehoboth, for within a few blocks of the ocean are several old boardinghouses, somewhat the worse for wear, which were built to house the Methodists, who came here to pray. The alternative does not have to be a motel, though, for at least three, perhaps five of these old buildings have been lovingly restored.

▪ Particularly charming are the Corner Cupboard Inn and the Lord & Hamilton Seaside Inn. The Corner Cupboard Inn is considerably more expensive and includes dinners in its price—which means you can't experience the various restaurants Rehoboth has to offer. The Lord & Hamilton is only a few minutes' walk from most shops and restaurants; the Corner Cupboard is perhaps a 15-minute walk away. On the other hand, the Corner Cupboard is in a beautiful, quiet residential section of Rehoboth, light-years away from the hubbub on Rehoboth Avenue. The Corner Cupboard gives you the sense of being in an old, established country inn; the Lord & Hamilton is more like a private home, where you get to know your hosts on a first-name basis.

- The original **Corner Cupboard Inn** (50 Park Street, between 1st and 2nd avenues; phone: 227-8553) was built as a private home for the present owner's aunt in 1927; today the 16 rooms are spread among three buildings. Popular rooms are the Blue Room, with a four-poster bed, and the Porch Room, with a somewhat masculine, hunting lodge ambiance. My least favorite was the Panelled Room, which is just what it says. Doubles, almost all with private bath, cost $95 to $140 for two, including breakfast and dinner. All major credit cards are accepted.

- **Lord & Hamilton Seaside Inn** (20 Brooklyn Avenue; phone: 227-6960) is a three-story Victorian house with a wide, wrap-around porch. Room 1 has a cherry canopy bed and a powder room. Some upstairs rooms show a Laura Ashley influence, with designer sheets and towels, soft purple walls, and an antique child's bed and commode. Dick Hamilton is Director of Drug Abuse Prevention for Maryland; his wife Marge is a former antique dealer and guide for the Winterthur Museum in Wilmington. Doubles cost $40 to $50 from mid-June to mid-September, and $30 off-season, including a delicious continental breakfast of fresh fruits and freshly baked breads. No credit cards are accepted.

- The **Pleasant Inn Lodge** (1st Street & Olive Avenue; phone: 227-7311) may not be quite as well kept up as the Lord & Hamilton, but it still has a great deal of character and charm. The Lodge is a Victorian four-square house with a widow's walk. Rooms are mostly furnished with period antiques and fresh flowers. Doubles, all with private bath, cost $55 to $75 in season. Off-season rates run as low as $25. Visa and Mastercard are accepted.

- What distinguishes the 70-year-old **Abbey Guest House** (31 Maryland Avenue; phone: 227-7023) from your run-of-the-mill boardinghouse is the narrow tongue-and-groove wainscoting that runs right up to the ceiling, and across it as well. The owner summed up the appeal of the Abbey when she said, "It's just an old-fashioned tourist home. It's the way they used to do it before motels." Doubles, most with shared bath, cost from $20 to $40 in season. No credit cards are accepted.

- Furnishings in the **Lord Baltimore** (16 Baltimore Avenue; phone: 227-2855) are basic, but clean and friendly. This is the sort of place you'd appreciate if you started coming here every summer as a child. Room 1 has a stamped tin ceiling. Room 8 may be your best bet, despite the orange carpet. Doubles, some with private bath, cost from $25 to $45. Visa and Mastercard are accepted.

▪ A motel with some of the charm of an inn is the **Dinner Bell Inn** (2 Christian Street; phone: 227-2561). All the following motels are clean and modern; all have pools and are near or on the beach: **Atlantic Sands** (Baltimore Avenue at the Boardwalk; phone: 227-2511); **Admiral Motel** (Baltimore Avenue at the Boardwalk; phone: 227-2103); **Oceanus** (62nd Street; phone: 227-9436); **Beach View** (6 Wilmington Avenue; phone: 227-2999); **Commodore Motel** (50 Rehoboth Avenue; phone: 227-9446 or 800/245-2112); **The Breakers** (2nd Street and Maryland Avenue; phone: 227-6888/4721 or 800/441-8009).

20. EMERGENCIES

▪ **Beebe Hospital** (424 Savannah Road, Lewes; phone: 645-3000).
▪ **Beebe Clinic** (Route 1 and Washington Street, Rehoboth Beach; phone: 227-2191).

21. HOW TO GET THERE

BY CAR. *From Washington:* the Beltway to John Hanson Highway (Route 50/301) to Route 50. Left on Route 404, left on Route 16, right on Route 1, south to Rehoboth Beach. *From Baltimore:* Route 3, Route 100, Route 2, Route 50, Route 404, Route 16, Route 1 south to Rehoboth. *From New York:* New York Thruway south to Garden State Parkway to Cape May/Lewes Ferry (609/886-2718 or 302/645-6313), then south five miles to Rehoboth. The ferry makes four 70-minute trips daily from November through mid-April and about 15 trips daily from late June to early September. Before Memorial Day and after Labor Day the ferries are seldom filled, except for holiday weekends. In summer, be sure to arrive 45 minutes before departure. No reservations are taken.

BY BUS. Trailways (95 Rehoboth Avenue; 227-7223) has direct service *from Washington, Philadelphia,* and *Baltimore.*

BY PLANE. Chesapeake Air (Arlington, Virginia; phone: 703/276-0222) flies regularly from Washington's National Airport to Rehoboth. One-way tickets on five-passenger planes cost about $50. Taxis from the airport are available from Rehoboth Limo & Taxi Service (phone: 645-8100 or 227-7900).

22. FOR FURTHER INFORMATION

- **Rehoboth Beach Chamber of Commerce** (73 Rehoboth Avenue, Rehoboth Beach 19971; phone: 302/227-2233).
- **Rehoboth City Manager,** Municipal Building, Rehoboth Beach 19971; phone: 302/227-6181.
- Delaware Beaches Information Number: 302/645-5213 or 800/441-1329.

23. RECOMMENDED READING

- Check bookstores on Rehoboth Avenue for *Room for One More Summer* by Dan Terrill, a delightful, informal history of Rehoboth Beach. Guides to Rehoboth are sold at **Brouseabout Books** (41 Rehoboth Avenue; phone: 227-0905); at **Gingerbread Square Mall** (55 Rehoboth Avenue; phone: 227-3573/7400), and at **The Bookateria** (110 Rehoboth Avenue; phone: 227-1241).

Skyline Drive, Virginia

(Area Code, 703)

1. DISTANCES

(Times are calculated from the northern end of the Skyline Drive at Front Royal. Add another two hours from the southern end at Waynesboro. The 105.4 mile trip along the drive takes 3½ to 4 hours by car, without stops.)

BY CAR. *From New York,* 6½ hours; *from Philadelphia,* 4½ hours; *from Baltimore,* 2¼ hours; *from Washington,* 1½ hours.

2. MAJOR ATTRACTIONS

▪ More than 100 miles of scenic highway along the crest of the Blue Ridge Mountains, with spectacular views of the Virginia Piedmont and the Shenandoah Valley.

▪ Hundreds of miles of scenic trails, ranging from quarter-mile leg stretchers to overnight hikes past waterfalls, trout-filled streams, spectacular overlooks, and mountain people's homesteads.

- The Luray Caverns—the largest in Virginia.
- Horseback riding; golf; picnicking; craft and antique shops; fresh fruit and vegetable stands.
- Blanket-cool evenings, even in mid-summer when Washington and New York are sweltering in summer heat.

3. INTRODUCTION

The Skyline Drive twists and turns for 105.4 miles along the crest of the Blue Ridge Mountains of Virginia. The Swiss love it here because their mountains are craggy and remote, and the Blue Ridge are green to the summit and tamed with flowers like trilliums and touch-me-nots. In summer a blue-green haze hangs over the valleys, softening the edge of things, like a landscape in a dream.

This is "ooh-and-aah" country. Visitors park their cars in dozens of spacious overlooks and enjoy breathtaking views of the Shenandoah Valley to the west and the rolling Piedmont country to the east. The more energetic set off on hundreds of miles of well-groomed trails, ranging from easy, hour-long nature walks to strenuous daylong hikes to waterfalls, trout streams, and stands of 300-year-old hemlocks.

The Drive runs through the Shenandoah National Park, which offers a full range of outdoor activities, from horseback riding to campfires and conducted walks. The restaurants are several notches above most park-run facilities, and the overnight cabins and lodges are the next best thing to summer camp.

Luray, only nine miles west of the Drive, has the most spectacular caverns in Virginia. To the east of the Park are sleepy country towns like Sperryville and Criglersville, where farmer's markets sell sweet white corn and craft shops offer hand-split white oak baskets and corn husk wreaths made of cinnamon sticks, statice, and golden yarrow.

Shenandoah, the rangers point out, can be called a recycled park. It was not saved, but re-created. It was once a magnificent forest with an abundance of wild game, and fish in every stream; but when the Park was created in 1936 the land was cleared, the soil eroded, and the wildlife gone. When the region was incorporated into the National Park System it became a protected area, and has returned to its natural state.

The rich lowlands were first settled by pioneers moving westward through Virginia and southward from Pennsylvania. They bought large tracts of land along the slopes for grazing, and allowed poorer settlers to build homes and gardens there, in return for pro-

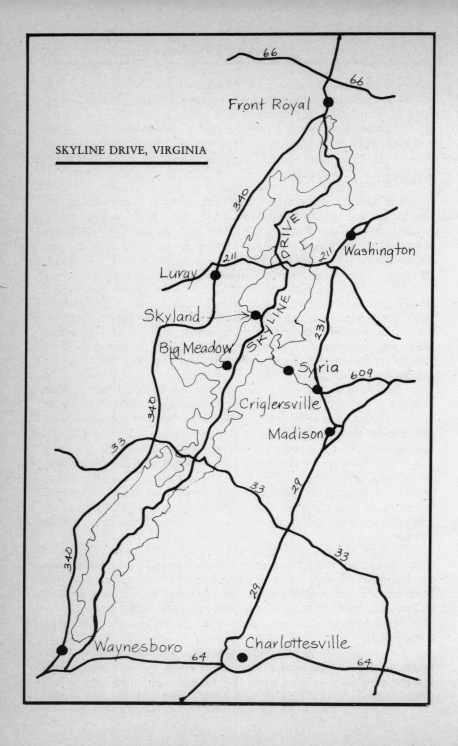

SKYLINE DRIVE, VIRGINIA

tecting the owners' flocks. Some mountain people were employees, and others were squatters. From the mid-1800s to the Civil War, they lived in the hollows and atop the broad ridges, growing vegetables and apples; raising chickens, pigs, and cows; and producing tanbark, honey, furs, and moonshine. They were a self-sufficient people with their own culture—their own way of smoking meats, their own music, their own crafts.

After the Civil War the impoverished landowners in the valley sent in logging crews, who stripped the forests. The mountain people had nothing left to hunt but squirrel or rabbit. The soil either washed away or was misused, and the mountain people moved to higher lands, where in desperation they burned trees to get sunshine for their crops.

The notion of developing a park in southern Appalachia had been tossed around for several decades when the Secretary of the Interior set up a committee in 1924 to recommend locations. The idea of a park near the nation's capital appealed to legislators, but the federal government, accustomed to acquiring park land without cost, refused to pay. Some 24,000 private individuals, including children tapping their piggy banks, contributed a million dollars. The Virginia legislature added another million and authorized condemnation of thousands of acres of land. In 1930, 2,000 mountain people were living in the park area, some of whom refused to move. Litigation went on for years. Resettlement communities were finally established near the Park, where displaced persons could buy homes with no down payments and with low-interest, 30-year mortgages.

Today most of the mountain people have been assimilated into the "outside" world. Battered tubs and buckets, unmarked gravestones, stone walls overgrown with brambles, a few wizened old apple trees—these are the visible reminders of their culture. The home crafts are lost or forgotten, except to a few of the elderly, and to a few young idealists who come with their tape recorders to preserve the past.

Meanwhile, in the Park, the scarred earth continues to heal. Black locusts grow in what were once open fields, and in their shadow have come oaks and hickory and pine. Birds have returned, and small mammals, and deer and bear.

The decline of an independent breed of mountain men is a sad story, but a story with a happy ending. For the damage to nature has been reversed, and the gift of wilderness has been given back to the people as part of their priceless natural heritage.

4. WHAT TO SEE AND DO

▪ Visitors whose idea of happiness is a drive through beautiful country will want to follow the Skyline Drive for its entire length—105.4 miles—between **Front Royal** (Mile 0.0), at the northern entrance, and **Waynesboro** (Mile 105.4), at the southern entrance. The speed limit is 35 mph, but traffic usually makes it impossible to complete the trip in under four hours.

▪ The Drive lies within the **Shenandoah National Park.** Admission is $2 per car. As you enter, be sure to request a free copy of the *Overlook*, the Park newspaper, which lists all current activities. The paper is also available at concessions along the Drive.

▪ Visitors who stay in the Park only long enough to take an hour's walk will probably develop a deeper and longer-lasting appreciation of the region than visitors who try to "do" the entire Skyline Drive in an afternoon. It's a long, tiring trip to make in a day. Many through-drivers find themselves jumping out of their cars at all the early overlooks, afraid of missing a single view. But by the fifth overlook the views begin to look the same. Visitors are therefore encouraged to enter or exit from the Park at one of three crossings: Route 211 (Mile 31.5), Route 33 (Mile 65.7), or Route 641 (Mile 105). The two lodges, **Skyland** (Mile 41.7) and **Big Meadows** (Mile 51), are along this stretch of road, from Route 211 to Route 33, a 34.2-mile trip. Nearby are **Luray Caverns** and the craft and antique shops in **Criglersville** and **Sperryville** (see below).

▪ Dozens of trails lead from the Drive, ranging from hour-long rambles to overnight treks. Trails are described in the "Park Guide" ($1) and other publications on sale at lodges and visitor centers. For longer walks, be sure to bring water and to wear sturdy hiking boots. Evenings can be chilly, even in midsummer; don't leave home without a heavy sweater or jacket.

▪ There are ranger-conducted activities at **Skyland Lodge** and **Big Meadows Lodge.** All are listed in the *Overlook* newspaper. Programs run from April through October, from 9 A.M. to 10 P.M. Trips from Skyland include a night walk to **Miller's Head;** a four-hour hike to **Whiteoak Canyon;** a two-hour hike to see the few remaining virgin hemlocks at **Limberlost,** and a two-hour walk in search of birds and wildflowers. Trips from Big Meadows include a three-hour hike to **Lewis Falls;** a four-hour hike to the top of the highest peak in Shenandoah; a one-hour wildflower hike, and a one-hour demonstration of the skills and crafts of the mountain people.

▪ **Luray Caverns** (Luray, nine miles west of the Route 211 entrance to the Skyline Drive; phone: 743-6551) are the largest in Virginia. The 1¼-mile, one-hour tour takes you through a fantastic dream world, where the only guide you need is your senses. Arthur Rackham would have delighted in the ghoullike shapes, with eyes that seem to follow you wherever you go. A booklet distributed at the caverns explains how they were made. The hollowing out began as rain and snowmelt penetrated through cracks in the rock made during the shifting of the earth's crust. As the water seeped down, it dissolved carbon dioxide in the decaying vegetation on top and turned it into dilute carbonic acid. The acid in the water began eating at the limestone, opening up rooms and passages. Underground streams grew in force as openings were widened and extended. Clay, which is insoluble, was suspended in the water. As the water began to seep into lower passages, or to evaporate, the clay settled to the floor. Other insoluble materials such as quartz were left protruding from the walls and ceilings, like cauliflower heads. When the water in the caves was reduced to a slow seepage, "decorations" began to appear. Drops of water left tiny deposits of calcite (crystallike forms of limestone) hanging from the ceiling or rising from the floor where they fell. (The iciclelike formations on the ceiling are stalactites; the ones on the floor are stalagmites. Where they meet they form columns or pillars.) Other decorations were made when water, carrying minerals, spread fanlike over the walls or floors, or built deposits on protruding ledges. Some of the pillars in the Luray Caverns are about seven million years old and more than 60 feet in height. The wet, shiny formations are still being created—about one cubic inch every 120 years. Within the Caverns today is the world's only **Stalacpipe Organ.** The stalactite formations, which hang from the ceiling, are tuned to concert pitch and tapped by rubber-tipped plungers under the organist's control.

Tours of Luray Caverns leave every 20 minutes mid-March to mid-June, from 9 to 6; mid-June to Labor Day from 9 to 7; Labor Day to mid-November from 9 to 6; and mid-November to mid-March from 9 to 4. The cost is $7 for adults and $3 for children aged 7 to 13. Included with the price of admission is a tour of an antique car museum that contains everything from an 1892 Benz to Valentino's 1925 Rolls-Royce.

▪ **Skyline Caverns** (Front Royal, one mile from the northern entrance to the Drive; phone: 635-4545), a smaller version of Luray Caverns, boasts some unique anthodite formations. Luray is more impressive; Skyline is less expensive and more convenient for visitors passing through Front Royal. Tours run June through Labor Day from 8:30 to 7; from Labor Day through October from 9 to 6, and off-season from 9 to 5. Tours cost $6 for adults and $3 for children aged 7 to 13.

▪ **Thunderbird Museum and Archaeological Park** (Route 737, about six miles south of Front Royal, off Route 340; phone: 635-7337) has displays of over 11,000 years of human history, and a working archaeological site. Excavations began here in 1971 under the sponsorship of *National Geographic* magazine and the National Science Foundation. Children in particular will want to watch an actual "dig" in progress, as summer volunteers scrape the earth for signs of human life 4,000 years ago. Admission is $2 for adults, $1.50 for children aged 8 to 12.

▪ Near the exits to the Drive are fruit and vegetable stands, and a number of orchards where you can pick your own fruit in season. **Beech Spring Fruit Stand** (Sperryville; phone: 987-8209) sells fruits and raw honey. **Harmony Hollow Orchard** (Front Royal; phone: 636-2009) features late-summer raspberries. TO GET THERE: From the intersection of Routes 55 and 522 at Front Royal, go two miles south on Route 522, turn right on Route 604 for two miles. **Hartland Orchard** (Markham; phone: 364-2316) lets you pick your own cherries. TO GET THERE: Take I-66 east from Front Royal to Markham. Follow signs on the service road (Route F284) for one mile to the orchard. **Jordan River Farm** (Huntly; phone: 636-9388) has strawberries and vegetables. TO GET THERE: Drive south from Front Royal for 10 miles on Route 522, then turn east for two miles on Route 637.

▪ On your way to or from the Skyline Drive, stop in the town of **Washington** (Route 211, 13 miles east of the Skyline Drive). The streets—Wheeler, Jett, Porter, and Calvert—have not changed their names since George Washington laid them out 225 years ago. The town has several gift and antique stores, a first-rate artist's cooperative *(see #6, Antiques and Crafts)*, and a famous restaurant, the **Inn at Little Washington** *(see #17, Dining)*. One and a quarter miles west of Washington is **Mountain Green Farm** (Blue Ridge Avenue; phone: 675-3219) where you can pick your own apples.

▪ A group of unique American homes exist in **Page County**. Built when the area was on the American frontier, and Indian attacks were a constant threat, they contain forts within their walls. They were usually conical, constructed of thick stone, and located in basements. They were kept supplied with food and usually contained both a fireplace and a tunnel that entered the wall above the water level. Sometimes they were built over flowing springs. These forts are within the walls of private homes, and no effort is made to attract visitors. But if you have a flaming interest in seeing one, the **Luray Chamber of Commerce** *(see #22, For Further Information)* may be able to arrange a visit.

5. THE ARTS

■ **Wayside Theater** (Middletown, 13 miles west of Front Royal, off exit 77 of I-81; phone: 869-1776 or off-season 869-1782) is a first-rate summer stock theater. The 1985 season runs from June 5 to August 31 and includes *Barefoot in the Park, Crimes of the Heart,* and *The Gin Game.* Performances are Wednesday through Saturday at 8, Sunday at 6:30, and Wednesday and Saturday at 2:30. Tickets are $9.50 and $10 for evening performances, $8 for matinees. The theater is conveniently located for visitors who arrive in Front Royal on a Friday night and do not want to set off into the mountains until morning. Theatergoers can dine at the **Wayside Inn** (phone: 869-1797), a block away.

■ The **Rappahannock Players** (phone: 675-3412) have a summer theater program in the town of Washington (Route 211). The **Rappahannock Country Dancers** (phone: 675-3412) have monthly square- and contra-dancing.

■ **Luray Caverns** (nine miles west of the Route 211 entrance to the Skyline Drive; phone: 743-6551) has a "Singing Tower" where free 45-minute carillon recitals are given from March through May at 2, June through September 15 at 8 P.M., and September 16 through October at 2. This old-world instrument has 47 bells ranging in size from 12½ pounds to 7,640 pounds.

6. ANTIQUES AND CRAFTS

■ Visitors who enter or leave the Drive on Route 211 will pass through the town of **Sperryville,** which has a half-dozen antique and craft stores, usually open weekends only.

■ **Faith Mountain Herbs and Antiques** (Box 199, Sperryville 22740; phone: 987-8824) is a real find. Cheri Woodard harvests her own herbs in the backyard and dries them in the attic of her 1790 house, which was once called the Dew Drop Inn. Shelves are lined with naturally scented soaps, gaily printed sachet bags, and mason jars full of juniper berries, yarrow, and seedless rose hips. Upstairs is a small but first-rate collection of antiques, furniture, and quilts. In 1984, an arrowback chair sold for $195, and a double-size Victorian walnut bed went for $895.

■ Also in Sperryville is **Chipmunk Hollow,** which specializes in homemade Christmas decorations, and **The Sperryville Emporium** (phone: 987-8235), which specializes in pottery.

■ If you are visiting **Graves Mountain Lodge** *(see #17, Dining* and *#19, Lodging),* or heading back to Washington, D.C., on Route

29, make a short side trip to **Criglersville** (Route 670, off Route 231). The **Handcraft House** (phone: 923-4640) is your best bet in the area for locally made crafts. Gifts include old quilts, hearth brooms, wooden toys, hand-painted china, crocheted pillows, rag rugs, hand-woven shawls, and silver jewelry. The shop is open on weekends from April to November.

▪ **Swinging Bridge Pottery** (S.R. 2, Box 351A, Criglersville, one-quarter mile north of town on Route 670; phone: 923-4244) is Bob van Kluyve's home and studio, where he makes oil lamps with pottery bases and porcelain stoneware, which he will inscribe for you. Bob is an active member of the newly formed **Blue Ridge Arts Council,** and will be happy to send you a map with the names and addresses of some 25 craftspeople in the area, including printmakers, quilters, musical instrument makers, cabinetmakers, and leather-smiths.

▪ **Doll House Emporium** (Brightwood, Route 29, 10 miles south of Culpepper; phone: 547-2200) sells homemade dollhouses and furnishings, and dollhouse tapestries. Open daily year-round.

▪ **The Little Shop** (Madison, off Route 29, about 15 miles south of Culpepper; phone: 948-4147) sells locally made quilts and quilt fabrics.

▪ Anyone interested in beautiful white oak baskets should head for the home of **W.C. and Lucy Cook** (1318 East Main Street, Luray, nine miles west of the Route 211 exit of the Skyline Drive; phone: 743-3832). "Our store doesn't have a name," says Mrs. Cook. "We just make baskets. We've been making them for 52 years in the shop in back of the house. This basket goes back as far as 1500." The Cooks are written up in various crafts books sold in Williamsburg, where they helped make the first craft film on—what else?—basket making. Open daily year-round.

▪ Visitors to Front Royal will want to stop at **Constant Spring Gallery of Fine Crafts** (South Royal Avenue; phone: 635-7010). The shop is run by the owners of the nearby **Constant Spring Inn,** a short distance from the entrance to the Skyline Drive. Local crafts, all handmade, include low-sudsing soaps, quilts, table mats, aprons, pottery, and cornhusk dolls.

▪ Visitors passing through the town of Washington (Route 211) en route to or from the Skyline Drive should make a point of visiting **Rush River Company** (phone: 675-3410), a cooperative of first-rate craftsmen, including the nationally known cabinetmaker Peter Kramer. There are several other craft, antique, and quality gift stores in town *(see #4, What to See and Do).*

8. WALKS

The **Shenandoah National Park** has some 400 miles of hiking trails, ranging from leisurely 30-minute strolls to a 95-mile section of the Appalachian trail. The more popular routes are described in the "Park Guide," on sale for $1 at Park concessions. Serious hikers should buy topographical maps and Henry Heatwole's *Guide to Skyline Drive* ($3.50), which was revised in 1981. Overnight campers need backcountry permits, which are free at ranger stations (*see #20, Emergencies* for locations), Skyland Lodge (Mile 41-43), and Big Meadows (Mile 51.2). Remember, most trails begin at the crest of the Blue Ridge and head downhill. The return trip can take twice as long.

Here is a list of waterfalls:*

TRAILHEAD LOCATION	WATERFALL (STREAM)	ROUNDTRIP HIKE FROM SKYLINE DRIVE	HEIGHT (IN FEET)
Mile 22.2	Big Falls (Overall Run)	4.0 miles	93
Mile 22.2	Twin Falls (Overall Run)	4.0 miles	29
Mile 42.6	Whiteoak No. 1 (Whiteoak Run)	4.6 miles	86
Mile 42.6	Whiteoak No. 2 (Whiteoak Run)		62
Mile 42.6	Whiteoak No. 6 (Whiteoak Run)	7.2 miles	60
Mile 42.6	Whiteoak No. 5 (Whiteoak Run)		49
Mile 42.6	Whiteoak No. 4 (Whiteoak Run)		41
Mile 42.6	Whiteoak No. 3 (Whiteoak Run)		35
Mile 45.6	Cedar Run Falls (Cedar Run)	3.4 miles	34
Mile 49.4	Rose River Falls (Rose River)	2.0 miles	67
Mile 50.7	Dark Hollow Falls (Hogcamp Branch)	1.5 miles	70
Mile 51.2	Lewis Falls (Hawksbill Creek)	2.0 miles	81
Mile 62.8	South River Falls (South River)	2.6 miles	83
Mile 81.1	Doyle River Falls (Doyle River)	2.8 miles	63
Mile 84.1	Jones Run Falls (Jones Run)	3.4 miles	42

Below are some of the most beautiful hikes, recommended by park rangers and by Henry Heatwole, author of the *Guide to Skyline Drive.*

▪ **Limberlost Trail** (Mile 43.0) is a 1.2-mile circuitous route, which climbs about 130 feet and takes about an hour round trip. About 0.6 miles from the start, the trail makes a sharp left turn in

*Reprinted from the "Park Guide" with permission.

front of a hemlock more than three feet in diameter. This is an area of big hemlocks from 350 to 400 years old, called the **Limberlost.** In the summer, Limberlost is one of the best places in the park to find mushrooms, Indian pipes, mosses, pine drops, and other plants that thrive on deep shade. The trail crosses a small stream, the source of **Whiteoak Run,** which, growing considerably, forms the six beautiful waterfalls of Whiteoak Canyon.

▪ **Whiteoak Canyon** is described by Heatwole as "the scenic gem of Shenandoah; a place of wild beauty; a shady place of great boulders under tall hemlocks, of cascades and pools and sheer rock walls and a steep gorge with six waterfalls. The trail from the Drive to the first waterfall is in good condition and the walking is easy. But further down it gets steeper, and parts of it are rough and rocky." There are numerous trails to the canyon, which tend to be overrun with visitors on summer weekends. The shortest begins at the north end of the parking lot at the south end of *Skyland.* The walk, 4.6 miles round trip, to the first waterfall, takes about 4½ hours. The waterfall can also be reached from the **Limberlost Trail** described above.

▪ **Hawksbill Mountain** has an elevation of 4,050 feet, which makes it the highest point in the Park. The easiest route is from the **Upper Hawksbill Parking Area** at Mile 46.7. From here, it's a 2.1-mile, two-hour walk to the summit and back.

▪ **Rose River Falls** can be reached from **Fishers Gap** at Mile 49.4. The 2.7-mile, 2½-hour round-trip walk is not too difficult and takes you to a rather small but pretty waterfall. The longer **Rose River Falls** walk, returning via **Hogcamp Branch,** is a four-hour, four-mile walk, but in addition to the falls you will see dozens of pools and cascades.

▪ **Hightop Summit** is a three-mile, three-hour round-trip walk from Mile 66.7. Views are spectacular.

▪ The "Park Guide" lists five 1½-hour nature trails: the **Fox Hollow Nature Trail** (Mile 4.6), **Traces Nature Trail** (Mile 22.2), **Stony Man Nature Trail** (Mile 41.7), **Store of the Forest Nature Trail** (Mile 51) and **Deadening Nature Trail** (Mile 79.5).

▪ The **Potomac Appalachian Trail Club** (1718 North Street, NW Washington, D.C. 20036) has six trail cabins located within the park, where visitors can stay overnight. Write months in advance for reservations.

10. BOATING AND FISHING

BOATING

- The **Shenandoah River** flows north along the western edge of the Shenandoah National Park, and is a favorite among canoeists.
- **340 Outfitters** (Route 340, three miles south of Front Royal; phone: 635-5440) rents canoes for trips lasting from 2½ hours to five days. Canoeists are usually transported upstream to Luray, and then paddle back downstream. Novices can portage around one short stretch of Class III rapids.
- **Downriver Canoe Campany** (Route 340, ten miles south of Front Royal, to Bentonville, then one-half mile west on Route 613 to the river; phone: 635-5526) rents canoes and provides a shuttle service.
- **Shenandoah River Outfitters** (Luray, about 14 miles west of the Route 211 exit of the Skyline Drive; phone: 743-4159) rents canoes and provides a shuttle service.

FISHING

- The **Shenandoah** has perch in the early spring, and bass throughout the summer.
- There are some 50 trout streams in the **Shenandoah National Park,** which can be reached by trails leading from the Skyline Drive. Visitors can purchase a five-day Virginia fishing license at any concession facility along the Drive. The season runs from early April through mid-October.

11. SWIMMING

- Swimming is not permitted in the Shenandoah National Park, but all major streams have small pools where you can get thoroughly wet and *very* cool.

12. SKIING

- **Massanutten Village Ski Resort** (McGaheysville, off Route 33, about 15 miles west of the Route 33 exit of the Skyline Drive; phone: 289-9441) has five lifts leading to nine trails. Lifts cost $17 on weekdays, $22 on weekends, and $12 at night.

13. RIDING

- Beginning and advanced riders can join guided trail rides through the Shenandoah National Park from **Skyland Lodge** (phone:

999-2211). Visitors may sign up one day in advance at the front desk. Rides cost $7 an hour. Wagon rides are available at **Big Meadows Lodge** (phone: 999-2211).

▪ **Graves Mountain Lodge** (Syria; phone: 923-4231) has guided trail rides in the foothills of the Blue Ridge Mountains for both guests and nonguests.

▪ **Old Mill Stables** (Woodville, Route 522, about 1½ miles from Sperryville; phone: 987-8215) has 1½- to two-hour rides on open and wooded trails.

14. TENNIS

▪ **Caverns Country Club Resort** (Luray, nine miles west of the Route 211 exit of the Skyline Drive; phone: 743-6551) has four tennis courts. Weekend tennis packages include lodging in two nearby motels.

▪ **Graves Mountain Lodge** (Syria, about 23 miles south of the Route 211 exit of the Skyline Drive; phone: 923-4231) has courts that may be used by nonguests. Phone for reservations.

15. GOLF

▪ **Caverns Country Club Resort** (Luray, nine miles west of the Route 211 exit of the Skyline Drive; phone: 743-6551) has a par-72, 18-hole course. Weekend golf packages include lodging at nearby motels.

▪ **Greene Hills Golf Club** (Stanardsville, eight miles east of the Route 33 exit of the Skyline Drive; phone: 804/985-7328) has an 18-hole course open to the public.

16. FOR KIDS

▪ **Luray Caverns** are a must *(see #4, What to See and Do)*.

▪ For an introduction to archaeology, visit a "dig" in the **Thunderbird Archaeological Park** *(see #4, What to See and Do)*.

▪ See entries under *#9, Biking; #10, Boating and Fishing; #12, Skiing; #13, Riding;* and *#14, Tennis.*

▪ Nothing could be deadlier for a young child than a four-hour trip down the Skyline Drive in a single afternoon, with the Shenandoah Valley framed through the car window. If you need to drive the entire length, plan to stop in one place for at least two or three hours. Short nature trails *(see #8, Walks)* are ideal for youngsters. Many trails lead from picnic grounds; parents can wait here with their chicken wings while children go on hikes.

▪ **Big Meadows** has a free, one-hour "Kids Corner" walk for children aged 8 to 12 that parents do not have to join. Check the *Overlook* newspaper for details on this and other ranger-conducted activities suitable for children.

17. DINING

▪ If you can afford the steep prices, the best dining on your way to or from the Skyline Drive is the **Inn at Little Washington** (Washington, Route 211, about 13 miles east of the Skyline Drive; phone: 675-3800). The other Washingtonians, in the nation's capital, think nothing of driving here just for dinner. The salmon-colored building—a former country store—sits at the crossroads of a charming village that George Washington laid out in 1749. The town is rapidly becoming a center for the arts, and visitors will want to browse through the galleries and craft shops before dinner *(see #4, What to See and Do)*. What makes the inn special is the attention to detail in cooking and decor. Dining room tables are built from local cherry wood. An English painter was hired to hand-grain the wood trim in the 24-foot center hall. Even the bathroom has imported French wallpaper and fresh flowers. "We're called a French restaurant because we use French terms on the menu," explains chef and part-owner Patrick O'Connell, "but what we emphasize is regional cuisine—doing something new and original with local produce." Appetizers include timbale of fresh lump crab meat and spinach mousse under glass, and baked fresh oysters in champagne sauce. Entrées, priced from $20.50 to $24.95, include fresh local trout cooked in parchment; sweetbreads sautéed with three mustards; and veal Shenandoah made with apples, cider, and Calvados. A popular dessert is white chocolate ice cream with a hot dark chocolate sauce. Ties are optional. Reservations are advised. Mastercard and Visa are accepted.

▪ On the Skyline Drive itself, full-service restaurants are located at **Skyland Lodge** Mile (41-43), open April through November; **Big Meadows Lodge** (Mile 51.2), open May through October; and **Panorama Restaurant** (Mile 31.6). Panorama Restaurant has lovely views, but an abbreviated menu, and more of the atmosphere of a cafeteria. Menus and prices at Skyland and Big Meadows are identical. The dining rooms have more warmth than one might expect from concession-run operations in a national park. The Big Meadows dining room, with its wormy chestnut ceilings, has a bit more character.

Food is straightforward. Dinner entrées, priced from $7.25 to $11.50, include Virginia baked ham and roast beef. Dress is casual. All major credit cards are accepted.

▪ When we were going to press, the 214-year-old **Conyers House** (phone: 987-8025; *see #19, Lodging*) was about to open a gourmet restaurant with a chef formerly of the famous Inn at Little Washington. Weekend seatings will be limited to about 15, so reservations are a must.

▪ Snack bars and grocery stores along the Drive are located at **Elkwallow Wayside** (Mile 24.1), open May through October; **Big Meadows Wayside** (Mile 51.2), open April through October; **Lewis Mountain** (Mile 57.6), open late May through October; and **Loft Mountain Wayside** (Mile 79.5), open April through October.

▪ The following picnic areas have tables, fireplaces, drinking fountains, and toilets: Mile 4.7, **Dickey Ridge;** Mile 24.1, **Elkwallow;** Mile 36.7, **Pinnacles;** Mile 51.2, **Big Meadows;** Mile 57.5, **Lewis Mountain;** Mile 62.8, **South River;** Mile 79.5, **Loft Mountain.** The Big Meadows area tends to get crowded; some visitors will prefer the smaller areas at Pinnacles or Lewis Mountain.

▪ **Graves Mountain Lodge** (Syria, about 27 miles south of the Route 211 entrance to the Skyline Drive; phone: 923-4231) is famous for its country-fresh home-style meals and unlimited helpings. Guests sit on straight-back chairs at long wooden tables, where pass-the-mashed-potatoes-relationships develop quickly. The Graves family's own 6,000-acre farm supplies most of the meat, fruit, and vegetables. Lunch is served from 12:30 to 1:30, and dinner from 6:30 to 7:30. Nightly specials include roast beef on Thursday, rainbow trout on Friday, sirloin steak on Saturday, and country ham on Sunday. Complete dinners range from $8.50 to $15. Dress is casual. Reservations for nonguests are required. Visa and Mastercard are accepted.

▪ Visitors who enter or leave the Drive at Waynesboro—the southern end—have a choice of restaurants in **Charlottesville** (*see #17, Dining* in the chapter on Charlottesville).

▪ Visitors who enter or leave the Drive at Front Royal—the northern end—can dine at the **Constant Spring Inn** (413 South Royal Avenue; phone: 635-7010). The decor here is as home-style as the cooking. Dinners, priced from $5.25 to $8, include baked Virginia ham, pan-broiled fillet of perch with baked rice, homemade biscuits, and hot apple cobbler. Dress is casual. Reservations are accepted. Visa and Mastercard are accepted.

▪ If you're visiting the Luray Caverns, or staying in the Luray area, try dining at the nearby **Mimslyn Inn** (Luray; phone: 743-

5105). The Mimslyn is a 50-year-old antebellum-type hotel with High Corinthian columns, 58 functioning rooms, and a dining room that comfortably seats 250. The Mimslyn is a holdover from an earlier age, when proper Washingtonians came here for a month to escape the heat. Meals are a notch or two above those on the Drive. The 12 acres of gardens, with beeches, clipped hedges, and songbirds, are lovely for an after-dinner stroll. Entrées, ranging from $4.95 to $15, include Virginia ham, fried chicken cooked in an iron skillet, and shish kebab. Ties are optional. Reservations are accepted. All major credit cards are accepted.

18. AFTER HOURS

- Both the **Skyland Lodge** (Mile 41-43; phone: 999-2211) and **Big Meadows Lodge** (Mile 51.2; phone: 999-2221) have lounges with nightly entertainment.
- **Skyland** and **Big Meadows Lodge** have ranger-conducted activities from 7:30 to 9:45 or 10 at night. From Skyland you can walk to **Millers Head** and watch the sunset and the lights appear in the valley below. Big Meadows has campfire programs. For a schedule of night activities, check the *Overlook* newspaper, available at lodges and visitor centers.

19. LODGING

- On the Drive itself, motel-type units and rustic cabins are available at both **Skyland** (Mile 41.7), open April through November, and **Big Meadows** (Mile 51.2), open May through October. The restaurant at Big Meadows Lodge is closed in winter, but some 40 rooms are kept open through December, and meals are served at the Big Meadows Wayside. Big Meadows is the larger of the two areas and has more facilities, including bike rentals and twice as many ranger-conducted tours. Some will prefer the slightly more rustic and age-worn charm of Big Meadows. Rooms at both resorts are small but clean, with pine walls and calico bedspreads. Nothing quaint or elegant, but a convenient and comfortable place to sleep after a day in the great outdoors. The play areas are alive with the sounds of children, who have plenty of opportunities to make new friends. There are many different types of accommodations, some with partial views, some with full views. Whatever you choose, make reservations months in advance. Doubles with private bath cost from $22 to $43. Suites are available for $65. Visa and Mastercard are accepted. For reservations, contact **ARA Virginia Sky-line Co., Inc.**, P.O. Box

727, Luray 22835. Phone: 743-5108 off-season, 999-2221 in season for Big Meadows, 999-2211 for Skyland.

▪ Front Royal has a string of motels on Route 340 (South Royal Avenue, only a short distance from the northern entrance to the Drive). Among the closest are **Quality Inn** (phone: 635-3161), **Scottish Inn** (800/251-1962), and **Pioneer Motel** (635-4784).

▪ If you leave or enter the Drive at Front Royal and insist on avoiding motels, stay at the family-run **Constant Spring Inn** (413 South Royal Avenue, Route 340; phone: 635-7010). This large white stucco building, with pillars and wide front porch, was built in antebellum style in the 1920s. Room #3 is a good bet; if occupied, try #10. Doubles with private bath cost $27 to $35 per person, including breakfast and dinner. No credit cards are accepted.

▪ **Graves Mountain Lodge** (Syria, about 26 miles south of the Route 211 entrance to the Skyline Drive; phone: 923-4231) sits among apple and peach orchards in the Rose River Valley, which nudges the east shoulder of the Blue Ridge Mountains. This is not a place for couples in search of a wine-and-candlelight ambience (a Pepsi machine greets you in the entrance), but for people—families in particular—who want comfortable, modern rooms, hearty, family-style meals, exquisite views, and a wide range of healthy outdoor activities. Facilities include swimming, horseback riding, tennis, basketball, golf privileges at a nearby 18-hole course, and fishing in a trout-stocked stream. Kids can say hello to the animals on the 6,000-acre farm, where most of the fruits and vegetables are grown, or climb trails that lead right up to the Skyline Drive. The motel is on a slope above the main lodge. Sitting on their balconies, guests have a spectacular view of the entire valley, with its fruit trees and barns. A more tranquil setting would be hard to find. The motel units are as homey as motel units can be, with reproduction antique furniture, homemade calico curtains, and the smell of pine. Visitors who want a more rustic and private setting (though a less spectacular view) have a choice of various cabins and cottages, including a modernized eighteenth-century farmhouse. Summer reservations, particularly on weekends, should be made in spring, since many families book a year in advance. Doubles, with private bath, cost $49 per person, including three meals. Cabins run from $36 to $52.50 per person, including meals. Breakfast, as wholesome as the farm itself, includes eggs, sausage, scalloped apples, hot biscuits, apple butter, juice, milk, and coffee. *(See #17, Dining.)* Visa and Mastercard are accepted. TO GET THERE: From the Route 211 exit of the Skyline Drive, head east to Route 231. Turn left (south) to Route 670 at Banco. Turn right and drive 3½ miles, past the Syria General Store, to the Lodge. The entrance is on the left. If you're driving north from Madison (Route 29), turn left on Route 231 and at Banco turn left again on Route 670 and drive for 3½ miles. From Culpepper, take Route 29 south, turn right on Route 609 to Route 670. Continue straight on Route 670 for 3½ miles.

▪ The 214-year-old **Conyers House** (eight miles south of Sperryville, off Route 231 on Slate Mills Road; phone: 987-8025) is the charming home of Norman and Sandra Cartwright-Brown in the foothills of the Blue Ridge. Only one of the five guest rooms in the main house has central heating; visitors in winter sleep under electric blankets. "L. L. Bean is more appropriate here than Gucci and Anne Klein," says Mrs. Cartwright-Brown. "In winter sockless preppies will catch pneumonia, and guests will understand why their forefathers wore flannel nighties to bed." (Rumor has it that Roger Mudd stayed here one night and left his flannel nighties behind.) "Grampie's Room" has a four-poster bed with a crocheted bedspread, a nineteenth-century rocking chair, a winding clock dating back to 1793, and a working fireplace. "Helen's Room" has a three-quarter-length 1820 rope braid bed, which is great for sleeping in a fetal position. Thirty paces in back of the house is the most elegant chicken coop in Rappahannock County. One of the guest rooms in this restored structure has exposed beams, and soft chintz curtains from a pattern in the Victoria and Albert Museum. Doubles at Conyers House cost $75 to $100, including breakfast and afternoon tea.

▪ Visitors to Luray Caverns (nine miles west of the Route 211 entrance to the Skyline Drive) can make Luray their base for daily forays into the Blue Ridge Mountains. The **Luray Caverns Motel East** (phone: 743-4531) and **West** (743-4536) have doubles for $38, with tennis, golf, and swimming at the nearby **Caverns Country Club. The Mimslyn Inn** *(see #17, Dining)* is operating as a bed-and-breakfast inn, with doubles from $40 to $44; facilities include a pool. **Guesthouses** (P.O. Box 5737, Charlottesville 22905; phone: 979-7264 or 979-8327) has four bed-and-breakfast properties in the Luray area, including a farmhouse with a Swedish sauna and a cedar-log home on five shady acres. **The Inn at Little Washington** (phone: 675-3800) is expected to have several rooms this summer. *See #17, Dining.*

20. EMERGENCIES

▪ Contact a ranger or call the emergency number (phone: 999-2227) at **Park Headquarters.** Personnel at park concessions can contact rangers for you. The four **Ranger Stations** within the park, open during normal working hours, are: Mile 22.1, **Piney River**, directly across from Matthews Arm Campground Entrance; Mile 51.2, **Big Meadows,** located at Campground Entrance or follow the signs; Mile 41-43, **Skyland, Boulder Cabin;** Mile 73.2, **Simmons Gap,** take road on the east side of Skyline Drive.

▪ If you have a medical problem that needs immediate attention and can't locate a phone or ranger, drive to the nearest hospital:

From the north entrance to the Drive (Mile 0.0), go north on Route 340 to **Front Royal;** from Panorama (Thornton Gap, Mile 31.5) go west on Route 211, nine miles to **Luray;** from Swift Run Gap (Mile 65.5), go west on Route 33, 25 miles to **Harrisonburg;** from the south end of the Drive (Rockfish Gap, Mile 105.4), go west on Route 250, four miles to **Waynesboro.**

21. HOW TO GET THERE

BY CAR. *From Washington:* I-66 west to Front Royal. (Visitors who want to explore only the more dramatic sections of the Drive can join it further south by taking I-66 west, Route 29 west to Warrenton, and Route 211 west to the Skyline Drive.) *From Baltimore* and *from Philadelphia:* I-95 south, I-495 south, and I-66 west. *From New York:* New Jersey Turnpike south to I-95 south, I-495 south, and I-66 west.

BY BUS. (There is no public transportation along the Drive.)

BY AIR. The nearest major airport is Dulles, 65 miles to the east, where cars can be rented. Allegheny Commuter Airlines (phone: 800/428-4253) flies from Washington to Shenandoah Valley Airport at Weyer's Cave, where Hertz and Avis cars can be rented.

22. FOR FURTHER INFORMATION

▪ For general information on park activities along the Drive: **Shenandoah National Park,** Route 4, Box 292, Luray 22835. Phone: 703/999-2243.

▪ For trail books, maps, and other detailed information on the wildlife, plants, and geology of the region: **Shenandoah Natural History Association,** Route 4, Box 292, Luray 22835. Phone: 703/999-2243, ext. 57.

▪ For overnight reservations along the Drive: **ARA Virginia Sky-Line Company, Inc.,** P.O. Box 727, Luray 22835. Phone: 703/743-5108 (weekdays from 8 to 5).

- For information on sights and accommodations in Front Royal and vicinity (the northern end of the Drive): **Front Royal Chamber of Commerce,** P.O. Box 568, Front Royal 22630. Phone: 703/635-3185.
- For information on sights and accommodations in the Shenandoah Valley (the region to the west of the Drive): **Shenandoah Valley Travel Association,** P.O. Box 488E, New Market 22844. Phone: 703/740-3132.
- For lodgings and attractions in the Luray area: **Luray Chamber of Commerce,** 6 East Main Street, Luray 22835. Phone: 703/743-3915.
- For overnight reservations at Skyland Lodge and Big Meadows Lodge: Phone: 703/999-2211 or 703/743-5108.
- For a 24-hour recorded message on the weather and park closings (in winter): phone 703/999-2266.

23. RECOMMENDED READING

- Visitors who pass through Front Royal can pick up books on the Blue Ridge at **Royal Oak Bookshop** (207 South Royal Avenue, Route 340, a short distance from the Drive entrance; phone: 635-7070).
- *Shenandoah Valley Magazine* is both a useful visitor's guide that lists upcoming events and an introduction to the people and folklore of the region. The July "Vacation & Leisure" issue is particularly valuable to summer visitors. Copies are sold at newsstands in major cities, and at gift shops along the Drive. For subscriptions or individual copies ($2), contact Shenandoah Valley Magazine, Box 17, Mint Spring 24463. Phone: 885-0388.
- For trail books, maps, and other detailed materials on the plants, wildlife, and geology of the region, contact the **Shenandoah Natural History Association,** Route 4, Box 292, Luray 22835. Phone: 703/999-2243, ext. 57. Particularly valuable are the "Park Guide" and the more detailed *Guide to Skyline Drive* by Henry Heatwole. Heatwole's book describes all the trails in the Shenandoah National Park.
- On entering the Drive, be sure to request a copy of the National Park newspaper, *Shenandoah Overlook,* which lists all ranger-conducted activities. The paper is also available at all concessions along the Drive.
- Other useful books for hikers are *Circuit Hikes in Shenandoah National Park* (a P.A.T.C. publication) and *Guide to the Appalachian Trail* (a P.A.T.C. publication). These and other books are for sale at the Visitor Centers and at gift shops in the Park.

Cape May, New Jersey

(Area Code, 609; Zip Code, 08204)

---

1. DISTANCES

BY CAR. *From New York,* 3½ hours; *from Philadelphia,* 2 hours; *from Washington,* 3½ hours.

BY BUS. *From New York,* 5 hours; *from Philadelphia,* 3½ hours.

2. MAJOR ATTRACTIONS

• A National Historic Landmark town with dozens of restored late nineteenth-century guest houses only minutes from the ocean.

• Some 600 wooden buildings surviving from the Gingerbread Age.

- Some of the best birdwatching on the Eastern seaboard.
- Hiking and biking trails, tennis, golf, fishing, swimming.
- First-rate restaurants for every taste and budget.

3. INTRODUCTION

The past is the future in the New Jersey seashore resort of Cape May. Motels and Skeeball parlors stretch along the beachfront like a giant piece of saltwater taffy; but behind them is the greatest concentration of late nineteenth-century houses in the country. So rich is this Victorian confection that Cape May has been designated a National Historic Landmark, the highest honor that can be bestowed on an American cultural property.

What was considered hopelessly old-fashioned 15 years ago is now the city's greatest asset. Visitors are booking months in advance for weekends in restored guest houses with high French windows and sweeping verandas brushed by buttonwood leaves and cooling breezes from the sea. The young, eager couples who run these homes are as interested in you as in the past, and a weekend stay with them is the next best thing to a visit with friends.

Sun lovers and surfers flock here in July and August, staying in 30 or more efficiency motels and dozens of turn-of-the-century guest houses and hotels. Old-timers know, however, that Cape May shows its true colors on mild weekends in September and October, when sun umbrellas have been stored away, the last piece of fudge has been sold, and the only commotion is the flapping of gulls' wings over Delaware Bay.

Those who seek a sweaty singles scene can join the disco crowd at Wildwood, 20 minutes north along the coast. Cape May is for those octogenarians, families, and young lovers who are happy feeding on gingerbread in a glowing world of sun and sand.

Some visitors will be content to loll about their oceanfront motels with heated pools and miniature golf courses, literally turning their backs on history. (Motels such as the *Golden Eagle* have children's programs that allow parents to turn their backs on their offspring as well.) The more energetic will wander among the Victorian buildings, or take advantage of an exhaustive schedule of activities, including a Victorian fair, antique car parade, concerts, dances, vintage movies, treasure hunts, arts and crafts shows—even a baby parade and a four-day clamshell-pitching contest.

In the early days, Cape May (named in 1621 after Cornelius Mey, a representative of the Dutch West India Company) belonged to the fishermen—first, Indian oystermen, then New England whalers.

In the early 1800s Southern gamblers and plantation owners helped convert this whaling and farming community into a famous resort. They flocked north by railroad and steamboat, bringing their luggage and slaves. During the town's heyday, from 1850 to 1900, its only rivals were Newport, Saratoga Springs, and Long Branch.

Each summer day some 3,000 visitors arrived by steamer, including many wealthy Philadelphia Main Liners and five Presidents: Pierce, Buchanan, Grant, Arthur, and Harrison. President Harrison made Congress Hall (still standing) his summer White House. He lived in a secluded Cape May Point cottage and commuted by electric train to his offices in the huge hotel.

"Our local government is rigid and definite in its ideas of right and wrong," says an 1865 ordinance, "and is to a great extent responsible for the city's high moral tone. The cultured and refined people who patronize our hotels diffuse about the place a high bulwark, which patrons of disreputable habits cannot penetrate."

From the ashes of a disastrous fire in 1878 rose the unparalleled collection of late Victorian buildings that make Cape May so distinctive today. As Willard Randall points out in *Smithsonian* magazine (September 1978), the town's master carpenters and Philadelphia's best architects joined forces to satisfy the whims of status-hungry millionaires. The frame structures, writes Randall, show "virtually every imaginable variation of lattice, scroll and fretwork, bargeboard, and brackets, with architectural designs spanning eight major styles generally considered to be under Victorian influence. Beneath exuberantly competitive ornamentation, Cape May's houses were designed with summers always in mind: long porches and balconies for rocking chairs, shaded high windows opening to sea breezes. Evidently the most popular among newly rich merchants and bankers was American Bracketed, a graft of Renaissance Revival onto Italian villa style."

Cape May was never mauled by twentieth-century progress because bans on liquor and gambling sent tourists scurrying to newer watering holes such as Atlantic City. In the early 1960s Cape May was beginning to develop its own brand of saltwater-tacky architecture when pro-Victorian forces fought and won their battle to preserve their city's priceless heritage.

4. WHAT TO SEE AND DO

Visitors have an opportunity to view some 600 authentic Victorian buildings, the largest collection in the country. The information booths on Washington Street Mall and at 405 Lafayette Street, across from the bandstand, have free self-guided walking tour maps. High-lights include:

• The **Pink House** (33 Perry Street) is the most elaborately deco-rated house in town—a photographer's dream and a house painter's nightmare.

• **Congress Hall** (Beach and Congress) was President Harrison's summer White House.

• The **Mainstay Inn** (635 Columbia; phone: 884-8690) is an elegant villa built in 1872 as a gambling house and a gentleman's club. Tours and afternoon tea begin at 4 from April through October, on Tuesdays, Thursdays, and weekends. Tea and tour are $3.50.

• The 16-room **Emlen Physick House** (1048 Washington Street; phone: 884-5404) was built in 1881 by the renowned nineteenth-century architect Frank Furness. Of particular interest are the hooded dormer windows, the massive chimneys, the textured wall coverings, the marble bathroom, and the original Furness bedroom suite. The museum contains furniture, toys, and costumes of the Victorian pe-riod. Admission is $4 for adults, $1 for children ages 12 to 17. Open June and September on Wednesdays and weekends from 12 to 4; May and October on Sundays from 12 to 4; July and August, daily, except Monday, from 10 to 4.

• **Wilbraham Mansion** (133 Myrtle Avenue; phone: 884-4717) is a private home open to the public, with period furnishings and decorations as impressive as those in the Emlen Physick House. Open April through November at 11. Tours cost $3. Closed Tuesday and Wednesday.

• The **Mid-Atlantic Center for the Arts** (phone: 884-5404) of-fers both walking and trolley tours of historic Cape May. The 90-minute walking tour begins at the Washington Street Mall informa-tion booth. Tours run in May and October on Sundays at 10; June and September on Wednesdays and Sundays at 10; July and August on Wednesdays and weekends at 10, and on Mondays and Thursdays at 7 P.M. Tours cost $4 for adults, $3 for children.

• The 45-minute **trolley rides** begin at Beach and Gurney. They run in June and September from 10 to 3; and in July and August daily from 6:30 to 9:30. Trips cost $3.

• The **Cape May Art League** (1050 Washington Street; phone: 884-8628) runs two open-house tours in Cape May County on the second Saturday and Sunday in July. Tours cost $10.

• **Historic Cold Spring Village** (Seashore Road, 10 minutes north of downtown Cape May; phone: 884-1811) is a collection of 15 restored buildings that bring to life the history of southern New Jersey. Children in particular will enjoy watching the craftspeople at work, and exploring the Nathaniel Douglass House—now an ice cream parlor.

▪ Whether you bike or drive, take the two-mile trip to **Cape May Point.** The state park here has self-guided nature trails *(see #8, Walks).* The beach at the Point is the least crowded and you can search for Cape May diamonds—semiprecious stones of pure quartz. In Victorian times it was fashionable to make pins from the stones; the clear ones were most prized. There is also a 120-year-old lighthouse, a half-sunken ship offshore, and—on clear nights— spectacular sunsets.

▪ The **Cape May Bird Observatory** (phone: 884-2736) conducts hawk watches in the Cape May Point State Park from September through November. The largest hawk migration in North America— more than 88,000 birds last year—passes through each fall. The observatory also sponsors a fall lecture series on Saturday evenings.

▪ The **Stone Harbor Bird Sanctuary,** ten miles north of Cape May, has a pull-off area with pay binoculars, where you can watch egrets and herons from March through September.

▪ **Yearick Hedge Gardens** (Fishing Creek; phone: 886-5148) is a collection of some 75 California privet hedges trimmed in fanciful shapes, such as a clipper ship, a statue of liberty, and a baseball game. What began as a hobby 54 years ago now attracts thousands of visitors each year. Open daily from 9 to dusk. Donations of 50¢ are requested. TO GET THERE: Follow signs to the county airport. At the entrance blinker turn south on Breakwater Road.

▪ Write or stop at one of the information booths for an updated calendar of events.

5. THE ARTS

There is a surprising absence of serious music or theater in the Cape May area. Best bets are:

▪ The **Jersey Cape Performing Arts** (Phone: 884-0054 or 884-1987) produces light drama, musicals, and children's plays throughout the year.

▪ The **Mid-Atlantic Center for the Arts** (1048 Washington Street, at the Emlen Physick Estate; phone: 884-5404) is completing an outdoor stage for musical and theatrical events in summer.

▪ **Convention Hall** (phone: 884-3323 or 884-8411) offers free evening concerts every Sunday, July through September.

▪ The **Cape May Art League** (1050 Washington Street; phone: 884-8628) sponsors group shows and exhibits of local and nationally

known artists in the 1876 Carriage House, the oldest building on the
Emlen Physick Estate. Shows run from March through November.

6. ANTIQUES AND CRAFTS

No stores in Cape May have consistently top-quality antiques.
Collections both in the city and along Route 9 are extremely personal
and eclectic, which makes for great browsing and the possibility of an
occasional "find." Cape May shops include:

- **Nostalgia Shop** (408 Washington Mall; phone: 884-7071).
- **Travis Cove** (621 Lafayette Street; phone: 884-5959).
- **Antiques Et Al** (Hughes and Ocean Streets; phone: 884-
2206).
- Victorian **Pink House** (33 Perry Street; phone: 884-2525).
- **Convention Hall** (phone: 884-8411) has antique sales June
through September, every Monday from 10 A.M. to 10 P.M.
- **Route 9** north from Cape May to Egg Harbor, about a 50-
minute drive, has dozens of antique shops you may want to explore
on your way home.

7. TOURS

- The information booths on the Washington Street Mall and
across from the bandstand on Lafayette Street have free self-guided
walking tour maps of historic Cape May.
- The **Mid-Atlantic Center for the Arts** (phone: 884-5404) runs
walking and trolley tours of the historic district *(see #4, What to See
and Do)*.
- **Cottages by Twilight** is a two-hour tour of four private cottages run from July to mid-September, Tuesday at 8. The cost is $8.
Mansions by Gaslight is a 2½ hour tour of four of Cape May's finest
homes. Tours run from mid-June to mid-September, Wednesday at
7:30. The cost is $10.

8. WALKS

- **Cape May Point State Park** (two miles from Cape May;
phone: 884-2159) is world-famous among bird watchers. The half-
mile nature trail follows a boardwalk through marshland where in
autumn thousands of birds regroup before striking out across the
bay. Crouching in a blind at the edge of a pond, you can see blue
herons alighting among the rustling reeds and wild swans gliding by

and disappearing into the gathering mist. The park has two other nature trails, both under two miles long. The three trails are only a short walk from the Cape's least developed ocean beach, where you can jog or search for Cape May diamonds. For information on recent and unusual birds sighted in the area, call the 24-hour birding hotline at 884-2626. The **Cape May Bird Observatory** (phone: 884-2736) has additional information.

▪ **Stone Harbor Bird Sanctuary** (Stone Harbor, about 10 miles north of Cape May) has 21 acres designated as breeding habitats for egrets and herons. Breeding season is at its peak in May and June. Morning and evenings are best, when birds are just leaving their roosts and coming home. The park is maintained by the town.

▪ **Higbee Beach Track** (just north of Cape May Point) is a dune habitat with the last vestiges of natural holly forest in New Jersey. There is an unpatrolled beach (not advisable for swimming—the bay is murky) maintained by the New Jersey Division of Fish and Game. TO GET THERE: Turn right on Bay Shore Road and left on New England Road, which terminates at the parking lot.

9. BIKING

▪ Bicycles were so much the rage in the Gay Nineties that the city council established an eight mph speed limit. The sport itself is in full gear again, and bikes can be rented from numerous hotels and bike rental shops, such as **Village Bike Rentals** (Ocean and Washington streets; phone: 884-8500).

▪ Pick up a self-guided bicycle touring map at either information booth and set off early in the morning before the light breeze has a chance to pick up. Best bet is an easy two-mile pedal along Sunset Boulevard to Cape May Point (see #4, What to See and Do).

10. FISHING AND BOATING

▪ The budget-minded who don't mind rubbing reels with strangers can sign up for four- or eight-hour deep-sea fishing trips during the day or night. Serious fishermen will want to charter their own boats and head for big game fish in the Canyon. The Chamber of Commerce (see #22, For Further Information) will send you a packet of fishing brochures on request.

▪ **South Jersey Marina** (off Route 9, one mile from the Garden State Parkway; phone: 884-2400) has the largest fleet of party boats in south Jersey. The trips of four, six, and eight hours cost from $14 to $22 per person. The night trip—chumming for bluefish from 7

P.M. to 3 A.M.—costs $25. Charter boats are also available for $350 and up. Marlin, tuna, shark, and swordfish are caught at the Canyon, 70 miles offshore.

▪ **Miss Chris Fishing Center** (Third Avenue and Wilson Drive; phone: 886-8164) also has half- and full-day party boats in search of mackerel, weakfish, flounder, sea bass, and bluefish. Prices range from $12 to $22. Charter boats to the Canyon are also available. Surf fishermen can buy bait here and get information on the best fishing spots.

▪ **Pharo's Marina** (Lafayette Street, one block past the bridge; phone: 884-4309) has boat charters.

▪ There is excellent surf fishing at **Cape May Point**, either from the beach or along the jetties. Angle for striped bass in early June, for weakfish from July through October, and for flounder and bluefish throughout the summer.

11. SWIMMING

▪ Supervised beaches along the boardwalk get crowded on summer weekends. Two miles away at Cape May Point is an undeveloped beach where there are no pinball flippers competing with the sound of the surf. The bay meets the Atlantic here and waters can be turbulent, so children should never swim unsupervised.

▪ Most beachfront motels have their own swimming pools.

13. RIDING

▪ **Hidden Valley Ranch** (Bay Shore Road, Cold Spring, about 3 miles northwest of Cape May; phone: 884-8205) has English and Western riding. Guided trips include a 45-minute trail ride around the farm for $8.50, and a 90-minute ranch and beach ride down to Delaware Bay for $16. Closed Sundays. Open all year, but reservations are necessary off-season.

14. TENNIS

▪ The **elementary school** on Lafayette Street has public courts. No charge.

▪ The **Cape May Tennis Club** (Washington Street, adjoining the Emlen Physick Estate; phone: 884-8986) has nine clay and four hard-surface courts, all outdoors.

▪ The **Jersey Cape Racquet Club**, 11 miles up the Garden State (phone: 465-4312), has both indoor and outdoor courts at $5 to $16 an hour.

■ The **Stone Harbor Golf and Tennis Club,** 13 miles up the Garden State (phone: 465-9270), has courts at $6 an hour per person. While some family members play tennis, others can play golf.

15. GOLF

■ The **Avalon Golf Club** (Cape May Court House, one mile south of exit 13 on the Garden State Parkway; phone: 465-4389) has a par-72, 18-hole course.
■ **Stone Harbor Golf Club** (Cape May Court House, two miles south of exit 13 on the Garden State Parkway; phone: 465-9270) has a par-72, 18-hole course. Tennis courts are also available.

16. FOR KIDS

■ Even the most unresourceful child will have trouble getting bored in Cape May. The town fathers have planned an exhaustive schedule of activities from vintage movies to treasure hunts and baby parades. Concerts, dances, and films are held in Convention Hall. A calendar of events is available from the information booths at the mall and boardwalk, and at the Welcome Center on Lafayette Street, across from the bandstand. For further information, phone Terry Brown (884-8411) at **Cape May City Hall.**
■ Trolley tours of historic Cape May *(see #4, What to See and Do).*
■ Deep-sea fishing, particularly at night; miniature golf; following the self-guided nature trail at **Cape May Point State Park;** searching for Cape May diamonds at Cape May Point; swimming; biking; riding; playing tennis.
■ The **Jersey Cape Performing Arts** (phone: 884-0054 or 884-1987) produces plays and puppet shows for children.
■ **Yearick Hedge Gardens** has some 75 hedges sculptured in the forms of animals, ships, buildings, etc. *(see #4, What to See and Do).*
■ **Historic Cold Spring Village** *(see #4, What to See and Do)* has weekend square dances.

17. DINING

■ **Alexander's** (653 Washington Street; phone: 884-2555) is the most elegant and expensive restaurant in town. The 1880 house seats 45 in five intimate, candlelit dining rooms. Each room, from the parlor to the glass-enclosed porch, has its own atmosphere, so tell the hostess what you're looking for when calling for a reservation. Some visitors will love, others will resent, the somewhat self-conscious effort by the owners to create the ambience of a formal Victorian world. Popular appetizers are cream of crab soup and sausage nut strudel. Entrées, ranging in price from $14 to $20, include sweetbreads with mushrooms; calves' liver sauced with orange and Dubonnet; and baked sea trout with sour cream, dill, and bacon sauce. Save room for the chocolate fondue, homemade black licorice ice cream, or brandy Alexander pie. Bring your own wine. Reservations are necessary. All major credit cards are accepted. Dress is optional, but most guests like to dress up.

▪ The **Mad Batter** (19 Jackson Street; phone: 884-5970) is a favorite among local people who want a more relaxed atmosphere, but who still demand a first-class meal. Dining is more casual, either indoors or on the front porch under a striped yellow awning, where you can watch the activity on the street. The cooking is "original"— standard ingredients combined in new and imaginative ways. Omelets, crepes, and smoked fish highlight the breakfast menu. Lunches include an Indonesian rice salad ($6); smoked fish salad with chopped egg ($5.50); and an Oriental salad with shrimps, scallops, and Chinese vegetables, seasoned with a light ginger and tamari sauce. Dinner entrées, priced from $8 to $20, include back fin crab cooked in a thin pastry crust with spinach, ricotta cheese, and onions; and scallops sautéed in white wine, garlic and butter, with peppers, onions, and tomatoes, all served on a bed of rice. A favorite dessert is Black Velvet, a sponge cake with a chocolate mousse center and heavy dark chocolate icing. Dress is casual. Reservations are advisable. Bring your own wine. Mastercard and Visa are accepted.

▪ **Louisa's Café** (104 Jackson Street; phone: 884-5882) is a very small, friendly restaurant for the young at heart, offering quality food at extremely reasonable prices. Pen and ink drawings of old Cape May line the white walls. Votive candles squat beside fresh flowers on red, yellow, and blue calico tablecloths. The owners, Louisa Hull, 27, and Doug Dietsch, 28, are as fresh and green as the salads they grow from seed in the backyard. A favorite appetizer is paté of sturgeon, which Louisa smokes over hickory chips. Entrées, listed on a chalkboard, range in price from $7 to $12 and include sea trout sautéed with slices of fresh ginger, sesame oil, and sherry; and fettucine (made fresh each morning) with pesto sauce. An infamous dessert is chocolate orange black bottom pie made with a graham cracker crust and dark chocolate custard, flavored with Grand Marnier and orange rind. Dress ranges from blue jeans to black tie. No reservations are accepted; on summer weekends, come early, add your name to the list, and return in an hour. No credit cards are accepted.

▪ The **Merion Inn** (phone: 884-7252) has advertised old whiskies and fresh seafood since 1885. Today it is the busiest restaurant in town. The three rooms seat 98. The menu is traditional, with an emphasis on fish and beef. Entrées on the "Early Bird Special," served from 4:30 to 6 P.M., cost $7. After 6, entrees range from $10 to $18, and include lamb chops, broiled lobster tail stuffed with crab meat, and flounder stuffed with crab Imperial. Dress is optional, but the atmosphere is strictly tie-and-jacket. No credit cards are accepted. No reservations are taken: just sign up, then go home and change. Open weekends in April and October, and daily from May through September.

▪ The **Lobster House** (Fisherman's Wharf, two miles north of the mall; phone: 884-8296) is perfect for visitors who appreciate the lobster-and-steak ambience of a harborside seafood restaurant. Entrées, ranging in price from $8 to $20, include lobster, crab Imperial, and a popular Schooner Dinner of boiled crabs, shrimp, clams, and scallops served in a steaming kettle. All major credit cards are accepted. Dress is casual. No reservations are accepted, and two-hour waits are not unusual on summer weekends. Time passes quickly sipping cocktails aboard the schooner *American* or watching boats reeling about the harbor. Those with an aversion to crowds and long waits should consider lunch served aboard the schooner rather than dinner.

18. AFTER HOURS

▪ Though the serious disco crowd will head to Wildwood, about 20 minutes north along the coast, Cape May does have its share of nightlife for couples and singles. The under-30 set will head to any of the following four places (moods change depending on the season and the group that's playing, so poke your head in and see if the atmosphere is right):

Old Shire Tavern (on the mall; phone: 884-4700) is relatively subdued, particularly if a swing jazz band is playing. Nearby is **Harvey's Restaurant** (phone: 884-5648), a restaurant by day, a saloon with dancing by night. **Gloria's** (Beach and Decatur; phone: 884-3774) has very live rock music, dancing, and an active singles crowd. **The Ugly Mug** (phone: 884-3459) has rhythm and blues groups and a singles crowd.

▪ Couples young and old who appreciate the art of talking will head for the **King Edward Room** at the **Chalfonte Hotel** (phone:

884-8934). The bar at the **Merion Inn** (phone: 884-7252) attracts an older crowd. The waiters sing for you at the bar at the old **Colonial Hotel** (phone: 884-3483).

▪ Visitors determined to soak up some local color should stop in at **Mayer's Bar** (Route 9, near the Lobster House; phone: 884-8980), where local fishermen drop their lines.

▪ For those who want to gamble away their weekend, **Atlantic City** is only 45 minutes away.

19. LODGING

Each guesthouse reflects the very personal tastes of its owners, and each room has its own special flavor. Except for the **Mainstay,** which is authentically High Victorian, and to a lesser degree the **Abbey,** furnishings tend to be eclectic, ranging from grandmother's Victorian armoire to early Sears to Beachfront Modern. Discuss rooms with owners before making reservations. On summer weekends most guest houses require a two-night and sometimes a three-night reservation. The budget-minded will want to stay where full breakfasts are served. Motels usually accept one-night reservations and rent efficiencies, a real plus for budget-minded families. Prices at all lodgings are lower during the off-season.

▪ The **Mainstay** (635 Columbia Avenue; phone: 884-8690) is the most lavishly and faithfully restored guest house, run by two arch-preservationists, Tom and Sue Carroll. Breakfasts of homemade bread and coffee cake are served on a sweeping veranda; or in a formal dining room with a 14-foot ceiling and French windows with lace curtains and red satin swags with tassels.

A pair of wealthy gamblers built this elegant villa in 1872. A few cozy rooms in the new wing were added in 1890 to house six Irish maids, but most are decorated in happily pretentious Victorian manner, with Oriental carpets, matching vanities, bouquets of peacock feathers, and chamber pots. The bathrooms have wood-framed copper bathtubs surrounded by potted ferns and Maxwell Parrish-like paintings of young girls and their lovers. Doubles in the Mainstay or in the newly restored 1870 "cottage" next door, some with private bath, cost $44 to $77, including breakfast and afternoon tea. Make summer reservations before March. No credit cards are accepted.

▪ The **Abbey** (Columbia Avenue and Gurney Street; phone: 884-4506), like the Mainstay, is so splendid a house that nonguests pay a fee to go on guided tours. The 1869 building is one of the finest examples of Gothic Revival architecture in town. The seven large guest rooms are furnished with gas lighting fixtures, marble-topped dressers, beds with high walnut headboards, and other period antiques. Who would mind sharing a bath in a tower, complete with stained glass windows, oriental rug, and brass chandelier? Doubles, some with private bath, cost $50 to $80, including breakfast. No credit cards are accepted.

▪ **Windward House** (24 Jackson Street; phone: 884-3368) has a wonderful confusion of Victorian antiques, and an innkeeper who works hard at making you feel welcome in her home. Doubles, some with private bath, cost $40 to $70, with breakfast included in the off-season. No credit cards are accepted.

▪ The **Brass Bed** (719 Columbia Avenue, phone: 884-8075) is an 1872 Gothic Revival house that was completely restored two years ago. The eight rooms are furnished with period antiques: marble-topped night tables, armoires and, of course, brass beds. Breakfast is served in a formal dining room with an ornate gasolier and three sets of French doors. Doubles, some with private bath, cost $40 to $65, including breakfast. No credit cards are accepted.

▪ **Poor Richard's** (17 Jackson Street; phone: 884-3536) is a textbook version of a gingerbread house, built in Second Empire style in 1882. Rooms are furnished with nineteenth- and early twentieth-century pieces. Doubles, some with bath, cost $34 to $57 without meals. No credit cards are accepted.

▪ **Seventh Sister Guesthouse** (10 Jackson Street; phone: 884-2280) was built in 1888 as a private home. Furnishings are cheerful, with plants, wicker, and lots of bright beach colors. Doubles, all with shared bath, cost $35 to $50. No credit cards are accepted.

▪ The **Chalfonte Hotel** (phone: 884-8934) is the last of the great Cape May hotels, with 104 rooms, some with private porches. So venerated is the hotel that groups of students from all over the northeast volunteer their services several times each year to help restore and maintain the building. Some architectural students even get credit for their help. The hotel has a certain boardinghouse chic that Main Liners return to year after year; but others will be put off by the very basic furnishings. Doubles, 11 of them with private bath, cost $49 to $98, including breakfast and dinner. Visa and Mastercard are accepted.

▪ Motel rooms, without meals, run from $55 to $105 for two. Most larger motels have pools. Motels with the broadest range of services include **Stockholm** (phone: 884-5332); **Best Western's Marquis de Lafayette** (phone: 884-3431 or 800/528-1234); **Golden Eagle Inn** (phone: 884-5611 or 800/257-8550); and **Atlas** (phone: 884-7000). The **Colonial Motor Lodge** (phone: 884-3483) has both a motel and a 100-room hotel, where doubles, including two meals, are more reasonably priced.

20. EMERGENCIES

- **Burdette-Tomlin Hospital** (Cape May Court House; phone: 465-2000).

21. HOW TO GET THERE

BY CAR. *From New York:* follow the Garden State Parkway south to the end. *From Philadelphia:* cross the Delaware Memorial Bridge, follow Route 40 south to the Garden State Parkway, and continue south to the end. *From Washington and Baltimore:* take Routes 301, 404, and 18 east to Lewes, Delaware, and cross to Cape May on the Cape May—Lewes Ferry (for schedules, phone: 609/886-2718 or 302/645-6313). Ferries run from 7:30 A.M. to 8:30 P.M., with additional crossings on summer weekends. No reservations are accepted for the 70-minute trip, so be sure to reach the ferry dock at least 45 minutes before departure.

BY BUS. Transport of New Jersey has service from New York (phone: 212/594-7181) and Philadelphia (phone: 800/526-4514).

BY PLANE. Allegheny Airlines (phone: 800/428-4253) has a commuter service from Philadelphia, with connecting flights to New York and Washington. The taxi ride from Cape May County Airport to Cape May takes 10 minutes.

22. FOR FURTHER INFORMATION

- Write to Publicity Department, Box CA, City Hall, Historic Cape May, 08204. Phone: 884-8411, ext. 20, 27, or 28.
- **The Welcome Center** (405 Lafayette Street, across from the bandstand; phone: 884-3323 or 884-8411, ext. 28) has a complete list of current activities, restaurants, accommodations, etc. Use the hot line here free of charge to make room reservations. Open May through October.
- There is a small version of the Welcome Center at the booth at Washington Street Mall.
- For information about the county, contact the **Cape May Chamber of Commerce** (Cape May Court House 08201; phone: 465-7181). Special booklets on birding and fishing are available on request.

- The Chamber of Commerce runs a visitor's center off Milepost 18 of the Garden State Parkway (Seaville Service Area), open from mid-May to mid-September. There's another visitor's center open year-round at Milepost 11 of the Garden State Parkway (Crest Haven Road).

23. RECOMMENDED READING

Books on Cape May are for sale at **Keltie's News Store** on the mall. Best bets are:

- *Cape May: Queen of the Seaside Resorts* (The Art Alliance Press, Philadelphia).
- Robert Alexander. *Steamboat for Cape May* (Cape May Geographic Society) and *Ho! for Cape Island* (Edward Stern & Co., Inc.)

Bay Head, New Jersey

(Area Code, 201; Zip Code, 08742)

1. DISTANCES

BY CAR. *From New York,* 1½ hours; *from Philadelphia,* 1½ hours; *from Baltimore,* 3¼ hours.

BY BUS. *From New York,* 2¼ hours; *from Philadelphia,* 2½ hours.

BY TRAIN. *From New York,* 2 hours.

2. MAJOR ATTRACTIONS

▪ An exclusive residential community along the Jersey shore with attractively restored boardinghouses for weekend guests.

▪ A wide, immaculately clean ocean beach without noise or crowds.

▪ A 1⅓-mile stretch of oceanfront with virtually no commercial development. Yet restaurants, golf, tennis, and other services are only minutes away.

3. INTRODUCTION

Weekend visitors to the Jersey shore do not have to submit to motel communities with fast-food chains rattling at their doors. The posh residential community of Bay Head has more than a mile of virtually private beachfront and several lovely boardinghouses and inns for weekend guests.

Accommodations in the past few years have been dramatically upgraded. Inns which I described in the first edition of *The Great Weekend Escape Book* as "spartan" and "monastic" are now comfortable and quaint. As soon as renovations are complete, The Bluffs will probably join my list of most highly recommended inns in the northeast. Three other inns, all under new ownership, have been completely redecorated. And Conover's Bay Head Inn is as charming as ever.

Bay Head has lost its battle to keep its beachfront private. But since eating and drinking are prohibited on the beach, and badges for daytrippers cost $8 per person, the crowds have stayed away. I walked along the ocean one warm Sunday night in early September and met no one. The only litter along a mile-long stretch of beachfront was two Styrofoam cups.

At midday, when the heat gets oppressive, visitors can walk a block inland for some lemonade at Dorca's Sidewalk Café, or stroll among a dozen fancy shops selling everything from designer pillow cases to Tiffany flatware. Those who seek a more active weekend can enjoy golf, tennis, sailing, crabbing, or deep-sea fishing. In the early evening, residents and visitors brush themselves off and head for the bar at The Bluffs. The Bluffs is a local secret, and a drink here is the next best thing to membership in a private club.

The town of Bay Head has the atmosphere of a private club, too. Drive south along the coast and at Bay Head the four-lane highway abruptly narrows to two. The blinking neon sights of the Jersey shore are suddenly replaced by tree-shaded lawns in a turn-of-the-century residential community, without a billboard or parking meter in sight. The main artery, Route 35, is clogged with traffic on summer weekends, but the surrounding streets are lined with large old wooden cottages with weathered shingle siding and white trim. These are the summer homes of people who do not have to announce their wealth.

The summer traffic crawls for three miles through Bay Head and through the even more insular community of Mantoloking. Then the road widens again and cars accelerate back into the twentieth century. The state highway department would love to open this bottleneck, but cannot, because the citizens of Bay Head and Mantoloking are

opposed to change. Barricaded behind a wall of old money, they have
the luxury of cultivating the past while availing themselves of all the
modern-day services in nearby Point Pleasant.

Not that there haven't been changes. To the dismay of some
residents, Bay Head theater has been converted into a small shopping
center. Several summer homes are available for group rentals, and
many of the older families have scurried off to Mantoloking, which is
residential only. Other families that used to settle in for the summer
with their servants now drive down for long weekends. Like other
Jersey shore towns, Bay Head has lost much of its homogeneity; to
call it pure WASP, as many like to do, is to cultivate the myth that
history is no more than the story of kings and queens.

Despite these minor changes, the people who come to Bay Head
still believe in words like family, privacy, and tradition. College girls
guard the entrances to the beach and make sure that everyone has a
badge. Eating is forbidden on the beach, which further discourages
outsiders; and there are no loud radios drowning out the sound of the
surf.

Other communities have their fudge; Bay Head has boutiques
and fancy gift shops run by men like Dick Waterhouse, a member of
the Bay Head Yacht Club, who goes to work in a pink button-down
shirt, lime-green bermudas, and tassled loafers. His shop has a refrigerator full of frozen chicken-in-wine dinners. Ducks, those sym-
bols of leisure and wealth, are printed on everything from pillows to
party napkins.

Half of Bay Head seems to work for the other, but everyone you
ask says he was delighted with a recent article in *Town and Country*
called "New Jersey's Gold Coast," which included the following
description:

"Every summer is distinguished by a bash or two. Last summer
Lee Bristol III of Bay Head and his friend Greg Matthews, both 21,
threw a formal debutante ball for themselves, because, said the Bris-
tol-Myers heir, 'We were tired of girls being the only ones introduced
to society.' Jimmy and Betty Kellogg's son Peter, a New York
financier, tossed a toga party in Bay Head that featured invitations in
Latin, a whole roasted pig, and 'chariot races' in which male guests
pulled female-piloted boat trailers through a street conveniently
closed by local police."

It seems appropriate that the Bay Head Yacht Club is the focal
point of the community, since Bay Head has been a boating center
since its founding in 1877. Unlike several other Ocean County
towns, it was created for neither religious nor industrial purposes,
but simply for investment and the pursuit of leisure.

The resort was founded by three men associated with the Princeton Bank and Trust Company. One of them, William Harris, also had strong connections with Princeton University. Forming the Bayhead Land Company, they purchased the land, laid out a grid of streets, and leveled the dunes. Lack of easy transportation was a major deterrent to settlement, but the coming of the railroad in 1882 brought with it a wave of summer visitors from Pittsburgh, New York, and Philadelphia. Horse-drawn carriages met the train at Bay Head Junction and carried summer visitors to their hotels, rooming houses, and private cottages. The great hotels—the Bellevue, the Bluffs, the Grenville, Grenville Arms, and Ocean View—were built in the town's heyday, between 1886 and 1899. The Grenville, Ocean View, and the Bluffs still stand today, though somewhat the worse for wear.

"My grandfather and grandmother, the Mercer Biddles, arrived as early as April," wrote Adele Schoettle of Philadelphia in the *Chestnut Hill Local.* "They were followed by vans full of furniture and Victorian bric-a-brac. In June, my mother, father, sister, aunt and uncle and two first cousins would arrive. The rest of the entourage included a practical nurse for my grandfather, a babysitter for my sister and me and a German governess for my cousin. . . . We had four maids, two German and two Irish, and a chauffeur."

Visitors to Bay Head today live on a smaller scale, but they are just as determined to preserve the unhurried, uncommercial quality of their lives. "The threat of intrusive development in Bay Head today is minimal," says a Historical Site Inventory published in 1981, "and it is hoped that the future loss of buildings will result only from natural causes. Scale, materials and plantings are all harmonious. A sense of permanence rather than seasonal transience prevails. . . . Even nonresidents tend to be of long standing, and the rooming houses and hotels are largely booked by returning clientele."

If the author of this report had his way, Bay Head would be no more than a dot on the map south of Point Pleasant. But newcomers are discovering the charms of Bay Head, and making it their secret, too.

4. WHAT TO SEE AND DO

The shops in Bay Head are stocked with goods that satisfy the needs of a well-heeled summer crowd. The Sandpiper, the Sea Horse, Lilly Pulitzer, the Monogram Shop, and the Hunny Pot are all run by members of the Bay Head Yacht Club and carry merchandise that reflects their own conservative and expensive tastes.

- The **Sandpiper** (536 Lake Avenue; phone: 892-9090) is a gift and party shop that carries everything from frozen baked ziti to decorative wooden ducks.

▪ The **Sea Horse** (41 Mount Street; phone: 899-0910) is a quality clothing store.

▪ **Magpie for Lilly Pulitzer** (412 Lake Avenue; phone: 892-9093) specializes in colorful resortware for the green pants and madras jacket set.

▪ The **Hunny Pot** (55 Mount Street; phone: 899-9099) is one of the best-known needlepoint shops in the northeast. Also for sale here are espadrilles, lamps, and gifts.

Other nearby shops include:

▪ The **Bay Head Cheese Shop** (81 Bridge Avenue; phone: 892-7585) is a good bet for picnic supplies. (Picnicking is forbidden on the ocean beach; ask your guest house about lunch arrangements.)

▪ **Mark Fore and Strike** (68 Bridge Avenue; phone: 892-6721) is a quality clothing store for men and women with branches in the Hamptons and Palm Beach.

▪ **The Maker's Mark** (519 Main Avenue; phone: 899-4424) has handsome homemade silver and gold jewelry.

▪ The **Jolly Tar** (56 Bridge Avenue; phone: 892-0223) is a glorified gift shop with Tiffany sterling flatware, Waterford crystal, and Wedgwood china.

▪ **Shopper's Wharf** (70-72 Bridge Avenue) is a collection of shops in what was once a movie theater. Stores include the **Memory Shop** *(see #6, Antiques)* and **Morning Star Quilts and Calicos** (phone: 892-2236).

▪ **Allaire State Park** (about 14 miles northwest of Bay Head; phone: 938-2371 or 938-2253) contains the remains of an iron foundry and the village that grew up around it. The blacksmith shop, general store, carpentry shop, bakery, and other buildings are in operation from May through Labor Day under the auspices of the New York State Historical Society. Admission is $2 per car. TO GET THERE: Take Route 35 north to Brielle circle, then Route 34 west. Follow signs to the park.

▪ Visitors returning to New York should try to save an hour of daylight for a short side trip to Ocean Grove. If you've never been here before, you're in for a delightful shock. For who could imagine the existence of a nineteenth-century religious community less than 65 miles from Times Square? Adventurous young couples are beginning to move into the area and change its complexion, but it still retains the flavor of another age.

"God's Square Mile," as it was called, began as a Methodist meeting ground in 1869. Until a few years ago no cars, driven or parked, were allowed on the streets on Sunday. Ordinances forbade such Sunday activities as lawn mowing, window washing, and newspaper deliveries. Visitors today still enter through brick pillars engraved with the words, "Enter into these gates with Thanksgiving, and unto His courts with praise." Look around—is anyone under 60? Summer guests rock peacefully on the wide, three-tiered porches of huge old Victorian boardinghouses with names like **The Quaker** and **The Sampler Inn:** The guests, like the hotels they've been returning to for 40 to 50 years, seem brittle with age. Stroll north along the boardwalk, pass through an enclosed area, and suddenly you're in Asbury Park. Walk another 100 yards, then retrace your steps back to Ocean Grove. The contrast is overwhelming. One moment you're in a fudge-and-taffy world; the next, in a Victorian world of ladies crocheting on creaking porches under the eye of God. If you have children, let them pass through this portal between the past and present: the contrast will burn a place in their memories that will last a lifetime. TO GET THERE: Drive north on Routes 35, 34, and 71.

5. THE ARTS

▪ The **Garden State Philharmonic Symphony Orchestra** (Toms River, phone: 349-6277) gives several concerts each year, usually in November, January, and April.

▪ **Red Oak Music Theater** (472 Somerset Avenue, Lakewood, about 12 miles west of Bay Head; phone: 367-1515) is a community and professional theater that offers well-known musicals in the fall and spring. Recent productions include *Grease* and *Godspell.*

▪ The **Fine Arts Center at Ocean County College** (Route 549, Dover Township, about 12 minutes from Bay Head; phone: 255-4000) has a community theater in the spring and summer. Recent productions included *The Elephant Man, West Side Story,* and *Tintypes.* The same facility runs a year-round program of dance, opera, mime, and classical music.

▪ **Ludlow Thurnston Art Gallery** (Lake Avenue; phone: 295-2300) features quality paintings, prints, and etchings. The **Anchor and Palette Gallery** (45 Mount Street; phone: 892-7776) sells old Bay Head prints and original work by local artists.

6. ANTIQUES

▪ The best bet for antiques is the **Point Pleasant Antique Emporium** (Bay and Trenton Avenue, Point Pleasant; phone: 892-2222). The quality is uneven, but you're bound to find something from the booths of more than 100 dealers.

▪ **Bay Head Carousel** (410 Main Avenue, on Route 35; phone: 899-3633) sells ice cream cones, but it also has the most tasteful collection of serious antiques in the area, including nineteenth-century pine chests and early American tables, dressers, and chairs.

▪ **Jeannette's Consignment** (517 Main Avenue; phone: 899-4488), billed as "a storeful of non-essentials," has lots of wicker, some antique furniture and jewelry, and a few beautiful antique quilts.

▪ **Mary Pellerito** (184 Bridge Avenue, Bay Head; phone: 892-1830) sells new and old decoys, antiques, and primitives.

▪ Local antique stores are listed in "Ocean City Attractions," a pamphlet available from the **Ocean County Office of Public Information** (see #22, For Further Information).

▪ Auctions are held on Friday nights at 7:30 at **Willinger Enterprises, Inc.** (626 Ocean Road, Point Pleasant; phone: 892-2217.)

▪ Saturday night auctions are held at 7 at **Carl's Auction** (1125 Arnold Avenue, Point Pleasant; phone: 892-6040).

8. WALKS

▪ **Island Beach State Park** (15 miles south of Bay Head on Route 35; phone: 793-0506) is a 3,000-acre peninsula bordering Barnegat Bay, with a wildlife sanctuary and nature trails. Admission is $3 on weekdays, $4 on weekends. The park opens at 8; you may be turned away after 9 on summer weekends.

▪ **Allaire State Park** (Route 537, about 14 miles northwest of Bay Head; phone: 938-2371) has miles of hiking and nature trails (see #4, What to See and Do).

9. BIKING

Traffic on Route 35 between Mantoloking and Point Pleasant can be vicious on summer weekends; bikes are a great way to get around.

▪ **Point Pleasant Bicycle** (2701 Bridge Avenue; phone: 899-9755) rents bikes in season, and has information on bike paths in state

and county parks. Bikers are allowed on boardwalks from 6 to 10
A.M.

10. BOATING AND FISHING

CANOEING

Within 30 minutes of Bay Head are two of the loveliest rivers in
the Jersey Pine Barrens, the **Manasquan** to the north and the **Toms** to
the south. Both are discussed in two helpful guide books, James and
Margaret Cawley's *Exploring the Little Rivers of New Jersey* and
Robert Parnes' *Canoeing the Jersey Pine Barrens.*

▪ **The Toms,** according to Parnes, is the second longest canoe-
able stream in the Pines and the most popular river outside the Whar-
ton State Forest. The actual distance from Bowman's Mill Bridge at
Route 528 to Barnegat Bay is over 30 miles. The closer to the headwaters you get, the more beautiful the route; but low water levels
may make the upper sections impassable. Downstream from Whitesville the stream is negotiable year-round. The swampy shores found
on the upper river become firm and sandy below Whitesville, with a
heavy growth of oak and scrub pine. In places, the stream is only
about 15 feet wide, and each bend brings a new view. The sandy
banks are ideal for picnicking and swimming. For information and
canoe rentals, contact **Pineland Canoes** (Brick Town; phone: 892-
8811), **Albocondo Camp Grounds** (Toms River; phone: 349-4079),
or **Surf and Stream Canoe Rentals** (Route 571, Toms River; phone:
349-8919).

▪ Debris on the upper **Manasquan** makes canoeing difficult, but
you should have no difficulty below Route 547 through **Allaire State
Park.** "The river does have its attractive features," writes Parnes, "the
most outstanding of which are the precipitous banks of limonite that
are stained with rusty hues and support mountain laurel and beech
trees. Another is the section within Allaire State Park, where fine
stands of sycamores and holly trees grow." For details and canoe
rentals, contact **Mohawk Canoe Livery** (phone: 938-7755).

SAILING

▪ **Teal Sailing School** (668 Main Avenue, Bay Head; phone:
295-8225) offers private sailing lessons on both the bay and ocean
from mid-May through mid-October on a fiberglass Rhodes-19.
Sloops not used in classes may be rented.

▪ **Windsurfing Bay Head** (76 Rear Bridge Avenue at Twilight
Lake; phone: 899-9394) is run by Ted Smith.

FISHING

- At **Ken's Landing** in Point Pleasant, Captain Ken (phone: 477-6441 or 892-9787) and Captain Jack (phone: 892-5358) offer half-day fishing trips, from 8 to 12:30 and from 2 to 6:30. They also go night fishing for blues at 7:30. Half-day trips cost $13 for adults, $9 for children. Night fishing, which may last until 4 A.M., costs $28.
- **Bogan's Brielle Boat Basin** (Higgins Avenue, Brielle; phone: 528-8377 or 528-5014 has party boats for half-day ($13), full-day ($22), and night ($28) fishing.
- The Manasquan is famous for its fluke grounds and crabbing. Rowboats and fishing gear are available at **Chapman's Boat Sales and Service** (1500 Riverside Drive, Brick Town; phone: 840-9100).
- For fishing and crabbing on Barnegat Bay, rent boats and equipment from **Starck's Landing** (728 Princeton Avenue, Brick Township; phone: 892-7558).
- **C & C Sail** (Bay Avenue, Point Pleasant; phone: 295-3450 or off-season 800/638-0426) offers bareboat charters with or without captain, on both Barnegat Bay and the ocean. Boats sleep from four to six people.

11. SWIMMING

- Guests at hotels and boardinghouses are given badges permitting them on the ocean beach.
- Some visitors prefer swimming in the bay, particularly those with young children. A favorite place is **Cattus Island County Park** (Fischer Boulevard, Toms River).

13. RIDING

- **Bill French's Riding Stable** (Route 2, Farmingdale; phone: 938-4480) offers one-, two-, and three-hour rides along wooded trails in the nearby Allaire State Park.
- **Circle A** (Route 547, two miles from Allaire State Park) offers rides through the nearby Allaire State Park.
- **Lazy K Riding Stables** (Old Freehold Road, Toms River, about 10 miles south of Bay Head) has riding for novice and experienced riders on 100 acres of wooded trails. No reservations are required.

15. GOLF

- **Spring Meadow Golf Club** (about 14 miles northwest of Bay

Head; phone: 449-0806) is an 18-hole course within the Allaire State Park.

 • **Jumping Brook Golf Club** (Neptune, about 14 miles north of Bay Head; phone: 922-8200) has a championship 18-hole, par-72 course.

 • **Bel-Aire Golf Club** (Wall Township, about 14 miles north of Bay Head; phone: 449-6024) has an 18-hole, par-60 course.

14. TENNIS

 • Bay Head's two municipal courts are for residents only. If you plan to play several times it might be worth buying a season pass. Some hotels and guest houses may be able to provide you with keys for the courts, particularly off-season.

 • **Allaire Racquet Club** (Wall Township, about 14 miles northwest of Bay Head; phone: 681-3366) has two outdoor and six indoor courts.

 • **Atlantic Club** (Wall Township, about 14 miles northwest of Bay Head; phone: 223-2100) has outdoor tennis courts and indoor racquetball courts.

16. FOR KIDS

 • Sign up for sailing classes at the **Teal Sailing Academy** (phone: 295-8225, *see #4, What to See and Do*).

 • Bike to Point Pleasant and succumb to miniature golf, swim, ride, play tennis, join a party boat for four hours of fishing in the Atlantic, or go crabbing in the bay.

 • If you're returning to New York, save an hour before dark to visit **Ocean Grove** *(see #4, What to See and Do)*.

17. DINING

Someone would do very well with a small, elegant French restaurant in the Bay Head area. No such place now exists. Summer residents head for the Bay Head Yacht Club, which is limited to members and guests.

 • Most local innkeepers send discriminating guests to **Churchill's** (Route 71, Brielle, about four miles north of Bay Head; phone: 528-7833), which is more formal than most local seafood restaurants, and has a larger selection of meat dishes. Entrées range in price from $10 to $15. The menu is straightforward: charcoaled lamb chops, charcoal-grilled swordfish, shrimp stuffed with crabmeat, and broiled flounder. A favorite dessert is Key lime pie. There's no dress code, but ties are usually worn. No reservations are accepted. Most major credit cards are accepted.

▪ The restaurant at **The Bluffs** (892-1114) now serves three meals a day and is in walking distance of The Bentley Inn and Conover's Bay Head Inn. The atmosphere is more that of a comfortable coffee shop than of a formal restaurant. Best bet are the $9.95 lobster dinners on Wednesday and Saturday.

▪ Those who want elegance should drive about 14 miles northwest to the **Spring Meadow Inn** (Allaire Road, Wall Township; phone: 449-4511). This French restaurant was awarded four stars by both the *Asbury Press* and the *Trenton Times.* The turn-of-the-century building seats 111 in three dining rooms, one on a porch overlooking the golf course. A popular appetizer is coquille Niçoise (shrimps sautéed with white wine and herbs). Entrées, priced between $9.75 and $18, include breast of chicken with crab meat, sealed in pastry with mushroom sauce; and medallion of veal in white wine topped with tips of white asparagus and king crab meat. For dessert, try the German apple wrapped in puff pastry. Jackets are required. Reservations are advised. All major credit cards are accepted.

▪ For a varied menu, including the best seafood dishes in the area, dine in the garden room at the **Old Mill Inn** (Old Mill Road, Spring Lake Heights; phone: 449-5371). In summer, come early for drinks on the patio beside the lake. Entrées range from $10 to $19. No reservations are accepted, so expect an hour's wait on summer weekends. Dress is informal. All major credit cards are accepted.

▪ **The Shrimp Box** (Inlet Drive, Point Pleasant Beach; phone: 899-1637) is favored by most locals for the freshness of its seafood and the size of its portions.

▪ Another local favorite is **The Crab's Claw Inn** (601 Grand Central Avenue, Route 35, Lavallette, about four miles south of Bay Head; phone: 793-4447). Entrées, ranging in price from $8 to $19, include a platter of broiled or fried shrimps, scallops, and crab meat; and King Neptune's delight, a combination of lobster tails and crabs' legs. The Inn serves over 100 kinds of beer and has a wine-dispensing system that lets you taste over 100 wines by the glass. Dress is casual. No reservations are accepted. All major credit cards are accepted.

▪ **Jack Baker's Lobster Shanty** (Channel Drive, Point Pleasant, one mile north of Bay Head; phone: 899-6700) and **Jack Baker's Wharfside** (Channel Drive, Point Pleasant, one mile north of Bay Head; phone: 892-9100) are popular among visitors all along the coast. Menus at both restaurants are exactly the same, but prices at the **Lobster Shanty** are about $2 higher. The fish of the day—

bluefish, hake, etc.—costs $6. Other entrées, ranging in price from
$7.95 to $14.95, include zuppa di pesce—lobster tails, shrimp, scallops, mussels, and clams steamed in a red sauce with wine and garlic,
served with linguine and white clam sauce. The Shanty has a rock
band in the pub after 10. Dress is casual. No reservations are accepted. All major credit cards are accepted.

• **Evelyn's** (507 F Street, Belmar; phone: 681-0236), noted in
The New York Times as a popular seafood restaurant, is about 10
miles north of Bay Head on Route 71. It seems unnecessary to travel
so far for a seafood dinner, but visitors might want to stop here en
route to Ocean Grove *(see #4, What to See and Do)*. Complete
dinners range in price from $9 to $13, and include tempura fried
lobster and stuffed shrimp with crabmeat. Dress is informal. No
reservations are accepted. All major credit cards are accepted.

• **Dorcas Sidewalk Café** (58 Bridge Avenue, Bay Head; phone:
899-9365) is your best bet for breakfast and lunch. The shaded outdoor veranda is perfect for afternoon milk shakes and an hour's
respite from the sun. Everything on the luncheon menu is priced
under $6. Best bet is the shrimp salad.

18. AFTER HOURS

• **The Bluffs** (phone: 892-1114 or off-season 899-3067) attracts a
sophisticated postcollege crowd. As one local put it, "singles come
here who have accomplished something in life." No place in Ocean
County has quite the same panache *(see #19, Lodging* for details).

• A less homogeneous 25-to-40 singles crowd heads for **The Red
Ranch** (2655 River Road, off Route 70, Wall Township, about six
miles north of Bay Head; phone: 528-7555). The cocktail lounge has
live music, but no dancing.

• **Park Place** (Central and Ocean aves. on the Boardwalk, Point
Pleasant; phone: 295-8577) attracts a younger singles crowd. The
dance floor is upstairs, above the jukebox and video games.

• **The Ship Wheel** (503 Higgins Avenue, Brielle; phone: 528-
5554) attracts an under-25 crowd. Music ranges from disco to Top 40
to country and western.

• **Ken's Landing** in Point Pleasant *(see #10, Boating and Fishing)* has moonlight sails along the Jersey shore from 8 to 9:30 in 70-
foot and 95-foot boats. Both **Ken's Landing** and **Bogan's Basin** have
all-night fishing trips for blues.

• For Friday and Saturday night auctions in nearby Point Pleasant, *see #6, Antiques and Crafts.*

19. LODGING

▪ **The Bluffs** (575 East Avenue; phone: in-season 892-1114, out of season 899-3067) was originally the bachelor quarters of the largest and most prominent of Bay Head's hotels. It replaced the much larger, original 1890 hotel, which was demolished by a 1953 hurricane. In the first edition of this book I wrote: "The spartan simplicity of the rooms has been described as 'WASP chic.' Those who demand elegance or Old World Charm may describe them otherwise."

What a transformation the Bluffs has undergone since then! Even the summer regulars—the folks from Chestnut Hill and the Main Line—are delighted with the change. Rooms have been completely redecorated in soft, matching pastel colors. Beds—some of them king-size with wicker headboards—are covered with soft, fluffy pillows and comforters. Oceanfront rooms now have decks with comfortable beach furniture. Not all rooms have been refurbished yet; be sure to request one, if possible with an ocean view.

The Bluffs is the town's one hotel that is off Route 35—a plus for light sleepers. It's also the only hotel directly on the beach. The season runs from late June through September. Doubles, almost all with private bath, cost from $55 to $75. Singles in the very basic "bachelor's annex," with shared bath, cost $18 to $20. The hotel has no sign in front; the owners cultivate anonymity, and people who stay here are supposed to know where it is.

All other hotels and guest houses are located on Route 35, where summer weekend traffic resembles the Long Island Expressway at rush hour. Since cars are moving slowly, noise is not too serious a problem, particularly if your room has air conditioning. But visitors who cherish quiet should request back or side rooms. Conover's Bay Head Inn and The Bentley Inn have the advantage of being a few minute's walk from most of the shops and the restaurants at The Bluffs and Dorca's. The Gables and the Sands are a 10-to-15-minute walk to the north. None of the inns is more than two blocks from the ocean. Ask about their so-called continental breakfasts; most are in fact full breakfasts, with fresh fruits and homemade breads.

▪ Everything is tidy and beautifully kept up at **Conover's Bay Head Inn** (646 Main Avenue; phone: 892-4664), one of the most charming and comfortable guest houses in town. The 12 rooms contain a miscellany of oak and maple Victorian furnishings and reproduction wicker. The owner, Beverly Conover, has hand-quilted the bedspreads and color-coordinated the towels and sheets. Hallways are carpeted with thick Berber carpeting. Doubles, some with private bath, cost from $43 to $85, including a luscious breakfast. All major credit cards are accepted.

   ▪ Former guests at **The Bentley Inn,** formerly the Ark Royal (694 Main Avenue, on Route 35; phone: 892-9589 or 899-8668) will not recognize it today. For the past year the new owners, Terry and Jim Alberts (he a former New York corporate executive), have been hard at work transforming a rambling, run-down boardinghouse into a charming 20-room inn. There's still more to do, but everything is bright, clean, sophisticated, and tasteful, and the Alberts are warm, enthusiastic hosts. The Inn is open year-round. Doubles cost $50 to $60, including a continental breakfast with fresh fruit, croissant, and freshly baked breads. All major credit cards are accepted.

   ▪ **Bay Head Sands** (2 Twilight Road, on Route 35; phone: 899-7016) has a friendly, bed-and-breakfast ambience, thanks to the hard work of its young new owners. The Coke machine and refrigerator, once in the main hallway, are now safely hidden in closets, and the walls, though still paneled, are painted and stenciled. There are nine rooms, five with private bath. Doubles cost $46 to $65, including a continental breakfast. All major credit cards are accepted.

   ▪ Forty gallons of paint went into the refurbishing of **Bay Head Gables** (200 Main Ave, on Route 35; phone: 892-9844) last year, when it was taken over by Don Haurie and Ed Laubusch, a school teacher and an engineer from northern New Jersey. If you like art deco, you'll love the Gables. Every room is a personal statement on art deco themes, with Jeff Kahn and early Vogue posters, charcoal gray carpets matched with white chenille spreads, expensively uphol-stered couches and chairs, even a maroon velvet fainting couch. Best bets are the two back rooms with private sunning porches and rooms #8 and #9, facing the ocean—all four of which have twin beds (which could be pushed together). Doubles, two with private bath, cost $40 to $70, including a large continental breakfast. All major credit cards are accepted.

   ▪ **The Rooming House** (672 Main Avenue; on Route 35; phone: 899-2585) is just what its name suggests: a clean, comfortable, unpre-tentious place to lay your head at night. Six rooms share two baths. A breakfast basket is provided on request. Room #5 has recently been redone. Doubles cost $40 in-season, $20 off-season. No credit cards are accepted.

20. EMERGENCIES

   ▪ **Point Pleasant Hospital** (phone: 892-1100).
   ▪ Ambulance (phone: 892-1100).

21. HOW TO GET THERE

BY CAR. *From New York:* the Garden State Parkway south to exit 98. Route 34 south to the second traffic circle. Follow Route 35 south to Bay Head. *From Philadelphia:* Route 70 east or the new 195 east and Route 35 south.

BY BUS. *From New York:* Asbury Park-New York Transit (phone: 212/267-6035 or 201/892-0465). The New York-Long Branch Bus Company (phone: 212/962-1122 or 201/291-1300) runs a mid-week commuter service to Battery Place in lower Manhattan. *From Philadelphia:* Transit of New Jersey (phone: 800/526-4514). Buses from New York and Philadelphia go to Point Pleasant, a few minute's taxi ride from Bay Head.

BY TRAIN. *From New York:* the North Jersey Coastline Train (phone: 212/736-6000 or 800/242-0212).

BY PLANE. *From Washington:* Colgan Airways (phone: 800/336-5016) flies to Monmouth County Airport (*phone:* 201/681-3701), which is a 15-minute taxi ride from Bay Head. You can rent a car from Thrifty (phone: 938-2776) at the Monmouth County Airport. North American Land and Sea Airlines (phone: 609/597-4152) flies *from New York* (phone: 212/772-0259), and *from Philadelphia* (phone: 215/334-7704).

22. FOR FURTHER INFORMATION

▪ For information on programs in the arts and historic places to visit, contact the **Ocean County Cultural and Heritage Commission,** 38 Hadley Avenue, Toms River 08753. Phone: 244-2121, ext. 2200.

▪ For information on accommodations, marinas, restaurants, etc., contact the **Ocean County "hot line"** at 201/929-2163.

▪ The nearest **Chamber of Commerce** is in Point Pleasant (phone: 899-2424).

▪ For brochures and additional information, contact Don O'Rourke at the **Ocean County Office of Public Information,** Administration Building, C.N. 2191, Toms River, NJ 08753. Phone: 201/244-2138.

23. RECOMMENDED READING

▪ Robert Jahn. *Down Barnaget Bay: A Nor'easter Midnight*

Reader. Available at the **Bay Head Bookhouse** (89 Bridge Avenue; phone: 899-6995).

▪ "Ocean County Attractions" is a complete list of local services. It is available from the **Ocean County Office of Public Information.**

Gettysburg
Pennsylvania

(Area Code, 717; Zip Code, 17325)

---

1. DISTANCES

BY CAR. *From New York,* 4½ hours; *from Philadelphia,* 2½ hours; *from Washington,* 2 hours.

BY BUS. *From New York,* 7 hours; *from Philadelphia,* 4½ hours; *from Washington,* 2¼ hours.

2. MAJOR ATTRACTIONS

▪ The site of one of the bloodiest battles in world history—the battle that turned the tide against the Confederacy during the American Civil War.

▪ Orientation programs, tours, films, museums, and activities to help you understand and relive the conflict.

▪ An original draft of the Gettysburg Address and the site where Lincoln delivered it.

3. INTRODUCTION

The outcome of the Battle of Gettysburg hung on possession of a three-mile strip of high ground, just south of town. For three days—July 1, 2, and 3, 1863—Union troops held the heights, despite Confederate efforts to dislodge them. On the third day, General Robert E. Lee ordered a suicidal frontal attack known as Pickett's Charge that left more than 7,000 Confederate soldiers dead. This was the turning point of the war. Though the conflict dragged on for two more years, the road for Lee lay southward to Appomattox and defeat.

Some three million visitors travel to Gettysburg each year to tour the 3,000-acre battlefield and to stand near the spot where Lincoln delivered his immortal Gettysburg address. The only signs of war today are the hundreds of statues and cenotaphs that dot the fields and woodlands where the battle raged. In such a pastoral setting, it is difficult to believe that 51,000 soldiers, almost one of every three in both armies, were wounded or slain.

Numerous tours of the battlefield are available by bus, car, foot, horse, and bike. But whichever you choose, the more you know beforehand about Gettysburg, the more enjoyable and rewarding your trip will be. Orientation programs are a must, but the information comes too fast to be completely absorbed. To get the most out of your trip here, first read one of the books listed in *#23, Recommended Reading*. Parents should try to visit when their children are studying the Civil War in school. A book that describes the Battle of Gettysburg within the context of the war as a whole should be required reading for all young visitors.

At the very least, one should have a general sense of what transpired during those three fateful days in July.

The two armies had never planned to meet in Gettysburg. In June of 1863 General Robert E. Lee had organized the Army of Northern Virginia into three infantry corps and begun marching westward from Fredericksburg, Virginia, through gaps in the Blue Ridge Mountains, into Pennsylvania. This was the second time in a year that Lee had carried the war to northern soil. His first invasion had been turned back at Antietam, in Maryland. His hope now was to take Harrisburg, then Philadelphia; to demoralize Union troops, and to encourage the British and French to aid the Confederacy.

While most of Lee's army, almost 75,000 strong, moved north up the Shenandoah Valley, three brigades of Confederate cavalry under General J. E. B. Stuart rode ahead to scout the Union army. The report that Stuart was supposed to make was delayed until July 2, leaving Lee in the dark about the size and movement of Union troops.

President Lincoln, meanwhile, learning that Lee was heading north, ordered the Army of the Potomac to follow. General George G. Meade assembled his army near Frederick, Maryland, and sent his first corps and a division of cavalry north to Gettysburg to scout the Confederate forces. On June 28, Lee was in Chambersburg (northwest of Gettysburg), with his army stretched eastward in a 50-mile crescent to Carlisle and York. A brigade that Lee sent to Gettysburg to find supplies and to "see what General Meade is up to," came across the forward column of Meade's cavalry.

On July 1, Confederate troops attacked Union troops on McPherson's Ridge. The outnumbered Union troops were driven back through town. Thousands were captured before they rallied on Cemetery Ridge south of Gettysburg. Meanwhile Lee's army arrived and took positions on Seminary Ridge.*

July 2 began with the two armies on two parallel ridges about one mile apart. The men in blue on Cemetery Ridge faced the men in gray on Seminary Ridge. Lee's strategy was to attack Union forces on both flanks. The attack on the left, at the Peach Orchard and Little Round Top, left the Union forces in shambles. On the right flank, at Cemetery Hill and Culp's Hill, the entrenched Union forces stood fast.

On July 3, Lee's artillery began a fierce bombardment of Union lines in order to soften up the center, and to continue the offensive he had begun the day before. He then ordered some 12,000 troops under George E. Pickett to charge across the open field and attack the center of the Union line. Union troops responded with a barrage of musketry and cannon fire. In 50 minutes the battle was over. Some 7,000 Confederate soldiers were killed, captured, or wounded.

*Some of this information is drawn from the booklet "Gettysburg," published by the National Park Service and distributed at the Visitor's Center.

Others ran or staggered back to Seminary Ridge where Lee watched. "This was all my fault," he murmured.

On both sides, 172,000 men had been committed to the battle— 97,000 of them Union, 75,000 of them Confederate. There were 51,000 casualties in what became the bloodiest battle in American history.

The bloodshed continued for another two years, but the Confederacy never recovered from its losses at Gettysburg. Henceforth, the Confederacy was on the defensive, fighting on its own soil until Lee surrendered to Grant at Appomattox Court House on April 9, 1865.

Even before the dead were buried, sightseers came to search for lost relatives and to view the carnage. The governor of Pennsylvania joined with the governors of 18 northern states whose troops had fought at Gettysburg to provide a proper burial place for the Union dead. Together they purchased seventeen acres of the battlefield to establish the Gettysburg National Cemetery.

At the ceremony to consecrate the grounds, Edward Everett, the greatest orator of the day, was asked to be the principal speaker. President Lincoln and other national figures were invited, too. Lincoln was asked to make "a few appropriate remarks."

Lincoln arrived by train and spent the night at the home of David Wills, whose house still stands on Lincoln Square. Funeral music was played and thousands of visitors and mourners lined the one-mile route as the procession of notables marched solemnly to the cemetery. A prayer was offered. Then Everett arose and delivered a classical oration of nearly two hours' duration. President Lincoln followed with a 272-word, 10-sentence speech that took less than three minutes to deliver. When he returned to his seat he turned to his friend Lamon and remarked, "Lamon, that speech won't scour. It is a flat failure."

Contrary to popular belief, Lincoln did not write the Gettysburg Address on the back of an envelope on the train trip to Gettysburg. He took great pains with its formulation. He wrote the first draft in Washington and revised it at the home of David Wills the night before the dedication. He may have completed a second draft back in Washington. Altogether he made five copies—all extant. During the summer, one of them is on display at the Cyclorama. It is impossible to see this simple, handwritten document and not be moved by its lofty sentiments and by the tragedy that inspired them.

4. WHAT TO SEE AND DO

▪ First stop should be the **National Park Visitor's Center** (off Business Route 15 at the south end of town; phone: 334-1124). Here you can arrange for a private guide licensed by the Park Service, purchase books on the Civil War, pick up battlefield maps, obtain tour tickets to the Eisenhower estate, and explore one of the largest collections of Civil War artifacts in the country. Here, too, you can watch an informative 30-minute Electric Map orientation program. Sitting in an amphitheater, visitors look down on a 750-square-foot topographical model of the battlefield with lights indicating landmarks and movement of troops. Admission is $1.50 for adults, free for children under 16. The Visitor's Center is open daily from Memorial to Labor Day from 8 to 6; off-season, from 8 to 5. Electric Map shows run from 8:15 to 5:15 in summer; off-season, from 8:15 to 4:15.

▪ First see the **Electric Map,** which gives an overview of the entire battle, and then walk across the street to the **Gettysburg Cyclorama,** which focuses on the third day of the battle, at the moment when Pickett's Virginians pierced through Union lines at Cemetery Ridge—the so-called High Water Mark of the Confederacy. The story is dramatically told on a canvas 356 feet in circumference and 26 feet high. This famous 1884 cyclorama is interesting in itself as an example of a popular late nineteenth-century art form. Before the advent of film, no other pictorial representation gave the illusion of reality quite as convincingly as a cyclorama. The narrated show runs daily from Memorial to Labor Day, from 9 to 4:30. Admission is $1 for adults, free for children under 16.

▪ An original draft of the **Gettysburg Address** is on display in the Cyclorama building daily from Memorial to Labor Day from 8:30 to 5.

▪ Now that you have some perspective on the events at Gettysburg, it's important to get an overview of the battleground itself. Most tours, particularly those by bus, will confuse you unless you have first had the opportunity to stand above the fields and ridges and take in the entire battlefield with a single sweep. The ideal and most extravagant solution is to take a short helicopter ride over the battlefield *(see #7, Tours).* A more economical solution is to ride the elevator to the top of the 307-foot **National Tower** (phone: 334-6754). Opponents of the tower call it an eyesore and a desecration of hallowed ground; nevertheless, it does offer you a sweeping 360-degree view of the battlefield. Children can climb the 1,016 steps to the top. The tower's 12-minute taped program here is difficult to follow; but you can stay on the observation deck as long as you want and, with the aid of maps, identify most of the major landmarks in the fields and ridges below. Admission is $2.50 for adults, $1.55 for children ages 6 to 14.

▪ A less spectacular but equally useful sense of perspective is gained by climbing any of the three observation towers provided by the park. Admission is free. The one near **Culp's Hill** offers the best overview of the battlefield. The southern tower overlooks the **Wheatfield** and **Little Round Top,** scenes of the second day's battle. It also looks down on the Eisenhower estate.

▪ You're now ready to tour the battlefield at ground level. Various tours are listed in *#7, Tours,* below. If you decide against a guide and have limited time, you might want to focus entirely on Pickett's Charge, the third day of battle. At **Cemetery Ridge,** at what is known as **The Angle,** near the copse of trees, you have a clear field of vision across to **Seminary Ridge,** and you can imagine the smoke clearing and the sight of 12,000 men lined shoulder to shoulder, advancing toward you. Or you can stand at the **Virginia Memorial on** Seminary Ridge and watch the battle from where Lee stood. Families with children (big or small) will want to come down from Seminary Ridge and follow the mile-long Confederate march through open fields to Cemetery Ridge. Imagine Union gun batteries opening fire on you, double cannisters tearing holes in your lines as you advance. (Remember, only one of the three of you will come back alive.)

▪ If you plan to trace the three-day battle, follow the movement of Confederate troops, since Lee's army was on the offensive.

▪ After touring the battlefield, it's fitting to visit the **National Cemetery.** Enter directly across from the Visitor's Center and follow in Lincoln's footsteps. Bear right along upper Cemetery Road; a union army cannon is on the crest. You will see hundreds of small granite blocks inscribed with numbers marking the graves of 979 unknown soldiers. (They didn't have dog tags in those days.) The various state plots describe a huge semicircle around the **Soldiers National Monument**—the large white monument to the left. On this spot stood the wooden platform where Lincoln spoke to some 10,000 dignitaries, soldiers, and civilians, many of them relatives of the dead. This is an ideal place for children to recite the Gettysburg Address.

▪ Having survived the front lines, you're ready for R & R. There are dozens of activities to choose from, some more commercial than others.

▪ The **Gettysburg Headquarters of Robert E. Lee** (eight blocks west of Lincoln Square on Route 30; phone: 334-3141) is now a war museum with sabers, uniforms, and surgical instruments. Photo buffs will want to see a display of Brady's original battlefield photographs. On July 1, 1863, Lee established his personal headquarters in this old stone house, in the rear center of his advancing troops. Admission is free. The museum is open mid-April through November from 9 to 9 and off-season from 9 to 5.

▪ If you liked Ike, you'll want to visit his 495-acre retirement estate on the **Eisenhower National Historic Site,** just over Seminary Ridge. Ike and Mamie lived in 17 places during their lifetime, but this 15-room modified Georgian house, which they purchased in 1951, was the only one they called home. Khrushchev, Nehru, Churchill, and de Gaulle were among the overnight guests. Gettysburg had a special meaning for the 34th President, for in 1918 the 28-year-old captain was ordered here to train a 5,600-man American tank corps, his first military assignment. He went with his bride of two years, Mamie Doud Eisenhower from Denver. Tickets to the estate can be purchased at the Eisenhower Tour Information Center within the Park Visitor's Center. The farm is open daily from April through Thanksgiving and Wednesday through Sunday off-season. Closed in January. The estate is accessible only by tour bus, which runs every 15 minutes from 9 to 4:30. The bus costs 85¢ for adults, 60¢ for children under 16. The tour lasts about 90 minutes. Tickets are distributed for the next available bus, so if you happen to arrive behind 200 Boy Scouts, you may be out of luck. Best bet is to pick up tickets early in the morning.

▪ The **Gettysburg Railroad** is the real thing, and should not be confused with the Lincoln Train Museum, which offers a simulated train ride. The railroad (one block west and north of Lincoln Square, off Constitution Avenue; phone: 334-6932) takes you on a 16-mile, 90-minute round trip to Biglerville. A 1920 steam engine pulls coaches built as early as 1890. Trips run on weekends from June through October. The cost is $3.50 for adults, $2 for children under 12. Several times each season, the train makes a scenic 50-mile round trip to Mt. Holly Springs. Call for details. The cost is $8.50 for adults, $5.25 for children under 12.

▪ Honest Abe lives again at **A. Lincoln's Place Theater** (777 Baltimore Street; phone: 334-6049)—a live 40-minute portrayal by actor James A. Getty. Lincoln tells his homespun stories, recalling his personal and political life from the days in New Salem to the night at Ford Theater. Shows run from mid-June to Labor Day, daily at 1:30, 4, 7, and 9; and in spring and fall daily at 2 and 8.

▪ **The Conflict** (213 Steinwehr Avenue; phone: 334-8003) is an honest effort to deal cinematically with the entire scope of the Civil War. The four-part multimedia program uses six projectors. The four segments—antebellum America through New Orleans, through the Emancipation Proclamation, through the Gettysburg Address, and through Appomattox—are shown at various times throughout the day. Also recommended is a single 45-minute presentation, *Three Days at Gettysburg*, shown at 12, 2, 3, 6, and 9. Admission is $3.25 for adults, $2.50 for students.

▪ Visitors who plan to see several of the attractions described previously will save money with a package plan on sale at the **Gettysburg Tour Center** (778 Baltimore Street; phone: 334-6296).

▪ Among the more commercial activities are the **Lincoln Train Museum,** which houses over 1,000 model trains; the **Hall of Presidents and First Ladies,** a display of life-size wax figures with authentic reproductions of First Ladies' gowns; and the **National Civil War Wax Museum** *(see #16, For Kids)*.

▪ The town of **Fairfield,** eight miles west of Gettysburg on Route 116, is neglected by visitors and commercial interests alike—which helps explain its charm. The main street is lined with beautiful early American homes. The drive here takes you past cornfields, "fresh eggs" signs, and splendid old barns. The **Fairfield Inn** (phone: 642-5410) is a good bet for lunch or dinner. A few miles past Fairfield is **Ski Liberty** (phone: 642-8282), which has grass skiing and a four-minute, 3,400-foot Alpine slide.

▪ The **Gettysburg Travel Council** on Carlisle Street has a 36-mile scenic valley tour map. The ride takes you down narrow, winding secondary roads, past the 128-year-old **Sachs Mill Bridge,** one of the country's finest examples of a latticed covered bridge, to **An Apple a Day Farm Market,** near Biglerville. Make a side trip to Fairfield, and return to the proposed route at Orrtanna. Visitors who love unusual architecture should not miss **Round Barn Orchards** (phone: 334-4486), a farm market open from April through November daily from 9 to 6. The round barn was built in 1914 from plans drawn in Illinois. TO GET THERE: From Gettysburg, follow Route 30 for eight miles to a crossroads, where a left turn takes you to Cashtown, and a right turn to Arendtsville. Take the right turn and drive two-thirds of a mile.

▪ There are two wineries in the area. **York Springs** (15 miles north on Route 15 to York Springs, then about three miles northwest on Route 94; phone: 528-8490) has free tours and tastings. Open daily from 10 to 6. **Adams Country Winery** (Route 30, about 10 miles west of Gettysburg; phone: 334-4631) is open daily from 12:30 to 6. Closed Tuesday and Wednesday.

5. THE ARTS

▪ **Totem Pole Playhouse** (Fayetteville, 30 minutes west of Gettysburg; phone: 352-2164) is a professional summer theater. Recent productions include *Annie* and *Best Little Whorehouse in Texas.* The season runs from April through November. Tickets are $8.75 to $10. Performances are given Tuesday through Saturday at 8:30, Wednesday and Saturday at 2, and Sunday at 3.

▪ **Allenberry Playhouse** (P.O. Box 7, Boiling Springs 17007; phone: 258-6120), about 30 miles northwest of Gettysburg, has musicals and comedies from April through November. Tickets cost $7.25 to $10.75.

6. ANTIQUES AND CRAFTS

▪ **The Maples Antiques** (207 East Middle Street, Gettysburg; phone: 334-1729), specializes in oriental rugs and eighteenth- and early nineteenth-century period and country furniture.

▪ **American Pie Antiques** (15 Seminary Ridge, Gettysburg; phone: 334-5919) sells anything from flint and cut glass to primitives.

▪ **Gettysburg Unlimited** (4th and Water Streets; phone: 334-6400) is a collection of 100 dealers with headquarters two blocks from Lincoln Square. Most merchandise is in the flea-market class, which is fun for browsing and occasional finds. Open Sunday from 10 to 5.

▪ **New Oxford** (about 10 miles east of Gettysburg on Route 30) has a half-dozen shops.

▪ The **Gettysburg Travel Council** on Carlisle Street has a map with locations of 21 antique stores in the general area.

▪ The gavel falls at **Jim's Country Auctions** (four miles north of Gettysburg on Route 15; phone: 334-6354) on Friday nights at 6:30. **Dave Redding** (phone: 334-6941 or 334-6598) holds his auctions on Wednesday nights at 5:30, and occasionally on Saturday. TO GET THERE: Drive one mile north of Gettysburg on Route 34 and bear right at the car wash on Table Rock Road for 2½ miles.

▪ **American Print Gallery** (219 Steinwehr Avenue; phone: 334-6188) has over 10,000 original prints of military scenes, sporting events, advertisements, etc.

▪ **American Image Gallery** (215 Steinwehr Avenue; phone: 334-0751) has original Civil War photographs on display and for sale.

- **Gallery 30** (30 York St, one-half block east of Lincoln Square; phone: 334-0335) is a bookstore with a gallery of original paintings, photographs, and sculpture.

7. TOURS

You can tour the battlefield in a helicopter, on a bus, on a ranger-conducted walk, or in your own car with a licensed battlefield guide.

- The helicopter tour is short and expensive, but gives you a dramatic overview of the battlefield. **Agrotor's, Inc.** (three miles south of Gettysburg on Route 15; phone: 334-6777) has four-minute flights that take you up Cemetery Ridge, across Pickett's Charge, down Seminary Ridge. The cost is $8 for adults, $7 for children. Longer flights can be arranged.
- At the **Park Visitor's Center** (phone: 334-1124) you can arrange for a guide licensed by the National Park Service to join you in your car. The cost is $12 for the 1½- to 2-hour trip. Some guides have a tendency to stop at every monument and cannon, providing more information than you can ever absorb. Before the tour begins, therefore, spell out how long you want the tour to take and what you hope to see and learn.
- **Battlefield Bus Tours** (Gettysburg Tour Center; phone: 334-6296) offers scenic open-air bus trips through the countryside; but it's not always easy to follow the narrative through earphones as you speed along. "This land about us was not made for war," says the narrator, as the sounds of artillery boom in your ear. "I'm not spittin' in the wind when I tell you. . ."
- Ninety-minute Auto-Tape tours can be rented from the **National Civil War Wax Museum** (phone: 334-6245).
- Walking-tour maps of the downtown Gettysburg historic district are available without charge from the **Gettysburg Travel Council** on Carlisle Street.
- The **National Park Service** organizes ranger-conducted walks and lectures through the summer season. Call or stop in at the Visitor's Center (phone: 334-1124) for details. Most popular programs, all free, are: **1.** Daily 20-minute walks through the National Cemetery. Once or twice an hour, from the Lincoln Speech Memorial, across from the Visitor's Center. **2.** Daily 30-minute walks to the High Water Mark on the third day of fighting. Once or twice an hour, from in back of the Cyclorama Center. **3.** Pickett's Charge, a two-hour afternoon walk from the Virginia Memorial (stop #8 on the official map). **4.** Little Round Top—20-minute talks on the sec-

ond day's fighting. Once or twice an hour, from the ranger station at Little Round Top. **5.** Valley of Death walk—a two-hour afternoon walk through Little Round Top, Devil's Den, and the Valley of Death, beginning at the bicycle tour parking area.

8. WALKS

▪ The free Gettysburg battlefield map published by the **National Park Service** recommends several walks, including a one-mile Big Round Top loop trail, and a one-hour trip from the Cyclorama Center to the High Water Mark of the Confederacy.

▪ The **Gettysburg Travel Council** on Carlisle Street has a free 1½-mile walking-tour map of the town of Gettysburg. Points of interest include the house where Lincoln slept the night before he delivered his address, and the many artillery-pocked houses that survived the battle.

▪ **Caledonia State Park** (15 miles west of Gettysburg on Route 15; phone: 352-7271) has miles of hiking and nature trails. The Appalachian Trail runs through this area.

▪ For guided walks, *see #7, Tours.*

9. BIKING

▪ **Lawvers** (280 Barlow Street; phone: 334-3295) rents bikes. A free map, available at the Park Visitor's Center, shows two bike trails through the battlefield, one four miles and one seven miles long.

10. BOATING AND FISHING

▪ The **Scenic Valley Tour** *(see #4, What to See and Do)* takes you past The Narrows, a deep cut in a ridge of the South Mountain Range—probably the coolest spot in summer. The Conewago River flows through, stocked with trout. TO GET THERE: Take Route 34 north to Biglerville, and Route 234 west about 10 miles. The creek runs near the side of the road.

▪ **Caledonia State Park** (15 miles west of Gettysburg, off Route 30; phone: 352-2161) has stocked streams.

▪ Fishing licenses are sold at all sporting goods stores.

11. SWIMMING

▪ Many motels have swimming pools, a real plus in the hot summer months.

- **Ski Liberty** (eight miles west of Gettysburg on Route 116; phone: 642-8282) has a pool.
- **Caledonia State Park** (15 miles west of Gettysburg, off Route 30; phone: 352-2161) has a swimming pool.
- There is a pool open to the public at the **Battlefield Campgrounds** on Route 134 south.

12. SKIING

- **Ski Liberty** (about eight miles west of Gettysburg on Route 116; phone: 642-8282) has five lifts leading to 14 trails.
- Call the **Bureau of Forestry** (phone: 352-2211) for information on cross-country ski trails surrounding the Caledonia State Park. The Appalachian Trail goes through this area.

13. RIDING

- **National Riding Stables** (at the Artillery Range Campground, Route 134, one mile south of the Visitor's Center; phone: 334-2469 or 334-1288) has historic rides through the battlefield for both beginners and advanced riders. Trips run from April through October.
- **Liberty Valley Stables** (Fairfield; phone: 642-5569) has 90 miles of mountain and wooded trails. Private lessons are available. Take Route 116 west to Fairfield. When the road turns into Gingle Street, turn right at the first stop sign and drive 100 yards.

14. TENNIS

- The **Gettysburg Area High School** (two blocks south of Lincoln Square) has free public courts.
- The **Community Recreation Park** (Breckenridge Street, four blocks southwest of Lincoln Square) has free public courts.
- **Ski Liberty** (eight miles west of Gettysburg on Route 116) has courts. Call for fees and reservations.

15. GOLF

- **Carroll Valley Golf Club** (Route 116, about 10 miles west of Gettysburg at Ski Liberty; phone 642-8211) has an 18-hole public course.
- **Caledonia Golf Club** (in Caledonia State Park, 15 miles west of Gettysburg on Route 30; phone: 352-7271) has an 18-hole, par-68 course.

16. FOR KIDS

▪ Act out Pickett's Charge, walking from Seminary Ridge to Cemetery Ridge *(see #4, What to See and Do).*

▪ Buy **William Frassanito's book of Brady photos** *(see #23, Recommended Reading)* and try to locate the very spot where each of them was taken.

▪ **National Civil War Museum** (Business Route 15, south of Lincoln Square; phone: 334-6245) has 200 life-size figures in 30 scenes depicting important moments in the war. The tour ends with a re-creation of Pickett's Charge, with Lincoln rising waxily from the carnage to recite the Gettysburg Address.

▪ Children will easily tire of one- or two-hour car trips through the battlefield. They will, however, enjoy biking seven miles along a battlefield route listed in the free visitor's map available at the **Park Visitor's Center.**

▪ **The audiovisual presentation,** *Three Days at Gettysburg,* and the 40-minute live portrayal of Lincoln at **A. Lincoln's Place** *(see #4, What to See and Do)* provide useful background information for children.

▪ Walk to the top of the **National Tower** *(See #4, What to See and Do).*

▪ The **Park Service** has several programs for children and evening campfires on the grounds where the Confederates camped. Schedules vary. Phone the Visitor's Center at 334-1124 for a schedule.

▪ Memorize the Gettysburg Address and recite it on the very spot where Lincoln delivered it *(see #4, What to See and Do).*

17. DINING

▪ Residents have reservations about all local restaurants, but **The Dobbin House** (89 Steinwehr Avenue; phone: 334-2100) is generally considered the best Gettysburg has to offer. It was built fourscore and seven years before the Gettysburg Address and served as both a private dwelling and a school of classical learning. In case you don't recognize the building's antiquity, the management has printed its menus on fake parchment with burned edges. Waitresses in period costumes serve customers at canopied bedsteads in the upstairs rooms. All very hokey and overdone—but charming nonetheless. A popular appetizer is baked onion soup. Entrées, ranging in price from $11 to $23, include lamb chops and prime ribs of beef. Dress is casual. Reservations are recommended. All major credit cards are accepted.

- **Farnsworth House** (401 Baltimore Street; phone: 334-8838) is an 1810 structure complete with bullet holes from the Battle of Gettysburg. Like the owners of the Dobbin House, the managers here feel a need to assault you with a sense of the building's antiquity. Fortunately, both places have enough natural charm to survive. The outdoor shaded garden at the Farnsworth House is particularly lovely, if the weather's not offensively hot. Entrées range from $6 to $16. The house specialty is Colonial Game Pie—pheasant, duck, and turkey blended with mushrooms, bacon, and red currant jelly, served with an egg crust on long grain and wild rice. While waiting for dinner, see how many grammatical mistakes you can find in the menu! Save room for the homemade black walnut ice cream or the walnut apple cake with hot nutmeg sauce. Dress is casual. Reservations are recommended. Visa and Mastercard are accepted.

- **Fairfield Inn** (Main Street, Fairfield, eight miles west of Gettysburg on Route 116; phone: 642-5410) was a stagecoach stop on the "Great Road" from York to Hagerstown. Be sure to reserve a table in the older section, which dates from 1757. The management prides itself on having no professional cooks—what the "local ladies" cook at home is what they prepare for guests. The menu shows a Pennsylvania Dutch influence—creamed chicken with a biscuit dough, corn soup, pumpkin fritters, hot bacon salad dressing. Vegetables tend to be very overdone, and the pies made with canned fruits, which is a real sin, with so many fresh fruit and vegetable markets in the area. The inn can be recommended for visitors, particularly families, who want a reasonably priced meal and an opportunity to visit the beautiful old town of Fairfield. Full course dinners range in price from $9.95 to $13.95. Dress is casual. Reservations are needed on summer weekends. Visa and Mastercard are accepted.

18. AFTER HOURS

- **The Springhouse Tavern,** in the basement of the 1776 Dobbin House (89 Steinwehr Avenue; phone: 334-2100), is a lovely, subdued, late-night spot for drinks, sandwiches, and classical music.

- The **Old Cellar Tavern** in the 1810 Farnsworth House (401 Baltimore St; phone: 334-8838) has a jukebox, which makes for a somewhat livelier, more singles-oriented scene than at The Springhouse Tavern.

- The college crowd heads for **The Pub** (no music) or **The Retreat** (DJs or live bands, with dancing; phone: 334-3388). A less polished crowd gathers at the **Tract Inn** (Tract Road, nine miles south of Gettysburg, off Route 15; phone: 642-8395) for country and western music.

▪ In winter, there's night skiing at **Ski Liberty** (phone: 642-8282). *See #12, skiing.*

▪ Evening activities include battlefield campfire talks (details at the Visitor's Center), performances at **A. Lincoln's Place Theater** (phone: 334-6049), and showings of *Three Days at Gettysburg* (phone: 334-8003). **Lee's Gettysburg Headquarters** is open until 9 *(see #4, What to See and Do).*

19. LODGING

▪ **Twin Elms** (228 Buford Avenue; phone: 334-4520) is a comfortable brick home surrounded by the historic Gettysburg Battlefield. It is within walking distance of museums, the National Cemetery, swimming, golfing; the Eisenhower farm is close by, as well as diverse eating places. Your hostess is a former teacher and history buff who enjoys having guests. Rooms with shared bath cost $15 per person.

▪ **Fairfield Inn** (Main Street, Fairfield, eight miles west of Gettysburg on Route 116; phone: 642-5410) is for visitors who are seriously committed to old inns. It was built as the plantation home of Squire William Miller, who settled in Fairfield in 1775. It has been an inn since 1823, when it served as a stagecoach stop and drover's tavern on the road between York and Hagerstown. Rooms today are sparsely but beautifully decorated with serious antiques. The owners have a genuine interest in the past, and have made every effort to decorate rooms with period furnishings. There are two rooms above the restaurant in the 1757 inn, and another four rooms in an 1800 house across the street. Fairfield itself is a charming town, barely touched by time. Some visitors will resent having to drive eight miles for a place to sleep; others will delight at the opportunity to slow down after the pace of Gettysburg. The absence of air-conditioning may be a problem on hot summer nights. All rooms, with shared baths, cost $40 to $50. Visa and Mastercard are accepted.

▪ Motels include the **Howard Johnson's Motor Lodge** (301 Steinwehr Avenue, eight blocks south of Lincoln Square on Business Route 15; phone: 334-1188); **Quality Inn Gettysburg Motor Lodge** (380 Steinwehr Avenue, eight blocks south of Lincoln Square on Business Route 15; phone: 334-1103); **Sheraton Inn,** (five miles south of Gettysburg on Business Route 15; phone: 334-8121); **College Motel—Friendship Inns** (Carlisle Street, three blocks north of

Lincoln Square on Business Route 15; phone: 334-6731); **Gettysburg Travelodge** (10 East Lincoln Avenue, on Business Route 15, north of Lincoln Square; phone: 800/255-3050); **Penn Eagle Motel—Superior Motels** (1½ miles east of Lincoln Square on Route 30; phone: 334-1804); **Stonehenge Lodge—Best Western** (at site of the National Tower on Route 97; phone: 334-6715).

20. EMERGENCIES

▪ **Gettysburg Hospital,** South Washington Street, Gettysburg. Phone: 334-2121.

21. HOW TO GET THERE

BY CAR. *From New York:* I-78 west to Harrisburg, then go south on Route 15; *from Philadelphia:* Pennsylvania Turnpike west to Route 15 south; *from Washington:* Route 270 north to Frederick and Route 15 north; *from Baltimore:* Routes 140, 97 and 15 north.

BY BUS. *From New York* (212/635-0800) and *from Philadelphia* (215/568-4800) take Greyhound. *From Washington* (202/737-5800) take Capitol Trailways.

BY PLANE. The nearest airport is at Harrisburg, 28 miles from Gettysburg.

22. FOR FURTHER INFORMATION

▪ **Gettysburg Travel Council, Inc.** (Carlisle Street, Gettysburg 17325; phone: 334-6274) carries information on all activities and points of interest not covered by the National Park Service. Headquarters are one block north of Lincoln Square, off Business Route 15, in the train station where Lincoln arrived on November 18, 1863, to make his "few appropriate remarks."

▪ Gettysburg **Chamber of Commerce,** 33 York Street. Phone: 334-8151.

▪ For information on the battlefield, phone **Visitor's Center** at 334-1124.

23. RECOMMENDED READING

▪ The Gift Shop in the Park Visitor's Center has many books on the Civil War.

- Michael Shaara's *Killer Angels: A Novel about the Four Days at Gettysburg* was a Pulitzer Prize winner in 1975.
- MacKinley Kantor's *Andersonville* is a gripping novel about prison conditions during the war.
- Bruce Catton's Civil War books are a must. Particularly valuable are *Glory Road: The Bloody Route from Fredericksburg to Gettysburg* and *Gettysburg: The Final Fury.*
- Civil war buffs will want to look at the extensive catalogue of obscure and reprinted works on the Civil War available from Morningside House, 260 Oak Street, Dayton, Ohio 45410 (phone: 513/461-6736).
- War buffs, photographers, and children of all ages will enjoy William A. Frassanito's *Gettysburg: A Journey in Time.* What could be more fun than to stand on the very spots where Brady took his famous Civil War photographs and to take your own pictures there today? (Children will undoubtedly enjoy posing as casualties on either side.)

Lancaster County, Pennsylvania

(Area Code, 717)

1. DISTANCES

BY CAR. *From New York*, 4 hours; *from Washington*, 2½ hours; *from Philadelphia*, 2 hours.

BY BUS. *From New York*, 4½ hours; *from Washington*, 3¼ hours; *from Philadelphia*, 2¼ hours.

2. MAJOR ATTRACTIONS

▪ The Old Order Amish—a twentieth-century people committed to eighteenth-century ways.

▪ Beautiful, rolling farmland with working Mennonite farms where visitors can stay overnight.

▪ Pig roasts, quilt sales, visits to pretzel factories, amusement parks, museums, and model farms—a list of activities four seasons long and as tempting as shoofly pie.

3. INTRODUCTION

There are windmills in Paradise, and horses and buggies, and rich, rolling fields furrowed by mule-drawn plows.

Paradise, of course, is a village slightly east of Eden, in the heart of Pennsylvania Dutch County, 70 miles west of Philadelphia. The Old Order Amish live here with their Old World ways. Some five million people come to gape at them each year, more than twice the number of visitors to Yosemite National Park or the Grand Canyon, and the contrast between old and new, between plain and fancy, is shocking, funny, wonderful, and obscene.

Most of the shops and amusement parks are stretched along Routes 30 and 340. The contradictions are most painfully evident here: in the distant windmill framed by the golden arches of McDonalds; in the buggy tethered outside the Wonderland Cinema where George Burns stars in *Oh God, Book II.* Go and observe these contradictions, for they will help you answer your most profound questions about happiness and progress. Children in particular should go while they are still establishing priorities. Ask them the right questions and they will return home with an educational experience that they will remember for a lifetime.

After the shopping and the rides, leave the trappings of the modern world behind and discover another Lancaster along the back roads, where the Amish live. The quiet beauty of the county is captured in their prosperous farms standing in the hollows of gently rolling fields. It is a green daytime world that assaults you with its wholesomeness. Dogs bark, bees hum, cows swish their tails. Laundry lines flap their shadows on lengths of lawn. Nature speaks in whispers here, and night is meant for sleep.

No wires lead to these farms because the Old Order Amish shun electricity and have no TVs or phones. They follow a rigid code of dress that both honors conformity and forces them to seek for beauty that lies within.

Leave Route 30, with its blinking neon sights, and you will see Amish men wearing broad-brimmed black hats and homemade "barn-door" trousers that fasten with hooks and eyes instead of buttons. The women wear ankle-length dresses fastened with pins, and their hair is tucked severely back into bonnets.

No one can see these people without being overwhelmed by the wholesome simplicity of their lives. Coming upon them in their fields or in their horse-drawn carriages is as startling and wonderful as stepping back into an earlier America, when people lived close to the soil and moved to the slow, steady rhythm of the seasons.

Who are the Amish? Historically, they can be traced back to the followers of Menno Simons, a sixteenth-century Dutch priest who believed that Martin Luther and other religious reformers did not go far enough in returning the church to its spiritual foundations. They also rejected infant baptism (hence the name Anabaptist), insisting that believers should be baptized voluntarily as adults and commit themselves freely to a Christian life.

Dissension arose among these Mennists, or Mennonites, over interpretation of Paul's advice to the Corinthians (Cor. 1: 5–11) that believers should not associate with sinners. The fiery young Swiss bishop Jakob Ammann argued that sinners should be shunned, not just excluded from the communion table; and he and his followers became known as Amish Mennonites.

At William Penn's invitation, a group of Mennonites from Germany settled near Philadelphia in 1683. The Amish followed in 1727. Collectively they are known as Pennsylvania Dutch, a corruption of the word "Deutsch," meaning German.

There are numerous Mennonite and Amish sects, but it is the most conservative, Old Order Amish who delight us with their old-fashioned ways. They have no cars, not because they consider them inherently evil, but because cars take us away from home and therefore weaken family and community ties. Their farms have no electricity, not because they abhor modernity, but because TVs and telephones are links to a world of nonbelievers. The family that plows together stays together, they believe, and hard labor keeps one close to God.

Our shifting attitudes toward the Amish are telling commentaries on ourselves. A decade or two ago we dismissed them as quaint curiosities, laughable and ignorant. For how could anyone familiar with the conveniences of modern life deliberately turn his back on them? Today, however, we view the Amish with respect and a certain romantic awe. They are a living tribute to a way of life which, in our headlong rush toward the future, we have left behind.

One of the most telling differences between cultures is how the elderly are treated. As the Amish grow older they gain in prestige and respect. Retirement is gradual and voluntary, with no dependence on federal aid. No nursing homes or park benches for the elderly—they live in houses built for them on land adjoining their children's property, and busy themselves in useful, dignified activities such as carpentry, caring for livestock, gardening, and quilting. There is a continuity between generations and divorce is virtually unknown.

Is it any wonder that the number of Amish—and the number of people who come to see them—is increasing?

4. WHAT TO SEE AND DO

What a waste of valuable time, leafing through hundreds of brochures at the **Visitor's Bureau,** deciding what to do. If time allows, write ahead and plot your weekend in advance. (For addresses, *see #22, For Further Information.*) Be sure to specify your interests; the Visitor's Center has enough brochures to fill a hay wagon.

The Pennsylvania Dutch Country encompasses such a large area that it makes sense to begin with a guided tour *(see #7, Tours)* and then return on your own to places that interest you. Save more commercial activities for Sunday, when Mennonite-run markets, shops, and museums are closed. Credit cards are seldom honored, so be sure to bring traveler's checks or cash. Summer weekends are busy; fall weekends are crowded. Try to visit before Memorial Day, during the week, or after Columbus Day.

It is easy, especially with children, to get caught up in a world of shops and rides and completely miss what is unique about Lancaster County. Set at least a few hours aside to walk or bike down country lanes parallel to Routes 30 and 340 *(see #9, Biking).* On Sundays you will pass Amish children playing on farms or families riding their buggies home from church.

Remember, the Amish consider a photograph a graven image. (The Exodus 20:4 commandment states, "Thou shalt not make to thyself a graven thing, nor the likeness of anything that is in the heaven above or in the earth beneath nor of those things that are in the waters under the earth.") If you must take pictures, shoot only from a distance when you can't be seen. Under these conditions, a 200mm zoom or telephoto lens is extremely useful.

▪ **Kitchen Kettle** (Route 772 west, in Intercourse, a block from Route 340; phone: 768-8261) is a group of popular shops featuring baked goods, relishes, Pennsylvania Dutch T-shirts, and hay-scented candles. Check out the homemade fudge and funnel cakes, made of batter squeezed through a funnel into hot lard, cooked to a crispy brown and sprinkled with sugar.

While tourists stream through the Kitchen Kettle, many miss the neighboring **People's Place** (Main Street, Intercourse; phone: 768-7171). Yet here is a fine place to begin your trip. The 30-minute three-screen slide presentation *Who Are the Amish?* is worth the $2 admission charge ($1 for children). There's a Mennonite bookstore and an Amish Story Museum featuring the three-dimensional paintings of Aaron Zook, which even small children will find fascinating. The museum costs $2 for adults, $1 for children. Both museum and film cost $3.50 ($1.50 for children). Closed Sundays.

▪ Don't leave Lancaster without a visit to at least one farmer's market. The most authentic and the least visited by tourists are in downtown Lancaster. Baked goods, Lebanon bologna, scrapple, *Schmierkase* (a tangy local cheese), homemade ice cream, pickles, relish—just about anything made on a farm is sold at these markets. The 250-year-old **Central market** in downtown Lancaster is open Tuesdays and Fridays. The **Southern Market**, 106 South Queen Street, also in downtown Lancaster, is open Saturdays from 6 to 2.

▪ If time is limited, go to **Bird-in-Hand Farmer's Market** (Route 340, Bird-in-Hand) and check out the mushroom butter and Mrs. Zimmerman's sweet peppers filled with cabbage. Tour buses are usually lined up outside, so there's nothing quaint about the market but its name. But it's impossible to leave without a jar of pickled something. Open Friday from 8:30 to 5:30 and Saturday from 8:30 to 5:30.

▪ If you go to the downtown Lancaster farmer's markets, consider combining the trip with a walking tour of historic **Lancaster** *(see #7, Tours)* and a visit to **Wheatland** (1120 Marietta Avenue; phone: 392-8721), the Victorian home of America's only bachelor President, James Buchanan. Wheatland is 1¼ miles from downtown Lancaster on Route 23. It is open daily, April 1 to November 30, from 10 to 4:30. Admission is $3.

▪ Train buffs should head directly to Strasburg and jump aboard the oldest operating standard-gauge train line in the world, the **Strasburg Railroad** (Route 741, Strasburg; phone: 687-7522). You can take the 45-minute roundtrip to Paradise in the same nineteenth-century open coach featured in *Hello, Dolly.* There's a stop for those who want to picnic along the way; pick up some goodies at a farmer's market, or stop at the country store in Strasburg. Trains leave hourly, on weekdays (every 30 minutes on summer weekends) from 12 to 3, Saturday from 11 to 4, and Sunday from 12 to 4. The noon train on Sunday is crowded. On weekends, arrive at least 20 minutes before departure. Tickets are $3.75 for adults, $1.75 for children under 12.

▪ **The Railroad Museum of Pennsylvania** (east of Strasburg on Route 741; phone 687-8628) has an outstanding collection of railroad equipment and memorabilia. Open daily 10 to 5; Sunday, 11 to 5. Admission is $1.50; free to children under 12 and senior citizens.

▪ Visitors will get some sense of Amish life by visiting **The Amish Farm and House** (Route 30, six miles west of Paradise; phone: 394-6185); **The Amish Village** (Route 896, two miles north of Strasburg; phone: 687-8511); or **The Amish Homestead** (Route 30 at the bypass; phone: 392-0832). The Homestead, an actual working farm, is the most authentic; however, it is important to remember that no Old Order Amish would ever participate in one of these commercial undertakings. All are open daily.

▪ The **Hans Herr House** (1849 Hans Herr Drive, Willow Street, Lancaster; phone: 464-4438) is the oldest Mennonite meeting house in America, restored to its medieval-style Germanic charm. Don't miss the antique varieties of fruit trees in the orchard. Open April through October, 9 to 4, and November through March, 10 to 3. Closed Sundays.

▪ **Julius Sturgis Pretzel House** (Route 772, Lititz; phone 626-4354) offers tours in its 200-year-old factory building. You can watch both hard and soft pretzels being made, and kids will love the chance to make their own. Open Monday to Saturday from 9 to 5; the last tour is at 4:30. Admission is 75¢ for adults, 50¢ for children.

▪ Children will probably not let parents escape without a trip to **Dutch Wonderland** (Route 30, 4½ miles east of Lancaster), a 44-acre amusement park featuring a monorail, dolphin and sea lion show, and waterflume ride. Admission is $6 with selected rides, $9 with unlimited rides. Open daily.

▪ On your way back home, take Route 272 to exit 21 of the Pennsylvania Turnpike and stop at the **Pennsylvania Farm Museum of Landis Valley** (Landis Valley, three miles north of Lancaster; phone: 569-0401), a complex of original and faithfully restored eighteenth- and nineteenth-century buildings. Special exhibits focus on the Conestoga Wagon and the Pennsylvania Rifle. Open daily except Monday, from 9 to 5; Sunday 12 to 5, April through October. Off-season, open daily from 10 to 4:30, Sunday from 12 to 4:30. Admission is $2. Children under 12 are admitted free.

▪ From the Farm Museum continue on Route 272 to **Ephrata Cloister** (at the junction of Routes 272 and 322 east, Ephrata; phone: 733-6600). Founded by the Seventh Day Baptists in 1732, it was one of the few Protestant monasteries in the New World. Tours run daily from 9:30 to 4; Sunday from 12 to 4. Admission is $2.50 for adults, $1 for children 6 to 18. Children under 12 are admitted free. Craft demonstrations from 7 to 9 P.M. precede a musical drama on summer Saturdays and Sundays *(see #5, The Arts)*.

▪ Continuing north on Route 272 from Ephrata, you will pass **LeRoy Pfautz' Farm Market** (Stevens; phone: 733-6694), open June through November from 9 to 9. Crossing the turnpike entrance, continue on Route 272 to three large antique emporia, **Renninger's, Shupp's Grove,** and **Black Angus** *(see #6, Antiques and Crafts).*

5. THE ARTS

▪ **Fulton Opera House** (downtown Lancaster; phone 397-7425), the oldest opera house in the country still in operation, was named for Robert Fulton, who lived in Lancaster. John and Ethyl Barrymore and Sarah Bernhardt performed here. *Man of La Mancha* and Agatha Christie's *Ten Little Indians* were among recent summer productions. Opera, concerts, and plays are performed on selected weekends throughout the year.

▪ **Green Room Theater** at Franklin and Marshall College (College Avenue, Lancaster; phone: 291-4015) offers three plays during the academic year, ranging from serious drama to comedy.

▪ **Ephrata Cloister** (junction of Routes 272 and 322 east, Ephrata; phone: 733-6600 or 733-4811) offers performances of the *Vorspiel,* a musical drama depicting 18th-century cloister life. Summer performances on Saturdays and selected Sundays at 9 P.M.

6. ANTIQUES AND CRAFTS

▪ **Pandora's Box** (just east of Route 30, on Route 340; phone: 299-5305) is your best bet for old quilts. Those under 100 years old sell for $100 to $1,000. Antique Amish quilts start at $1,500. It's an expensive but sound investment. For example, a 50-year-old round-the-world quilt that sold in 1967 for $130 is worth $500 today.

▪ Local newspapers list dozens of auctions each weekend where you can bid on anything from hooked rugs to grandfather clocks. The antique business is pretty sophisticated in Lancaster, so unless you're lucky don't expect any great bargains.

▪ Antique hunters should stalk the many shops along Route 340 from the Route 30 intersection east to Intercourse.

▪ **Renninger's** and **Black Angus** (Route 272, Adamstown, 2 miles east of Exit 21 of the Pennsylvania Turnpike) together comprise one of the largest antique emporiums in the country. Dozens of dealers sell everything from old books and prints to Victorian blouses, corner cupboards, pewter, and local stoneware. Black Angus has higher quality goods, but fewer "finds." At Renninger's you can occasionally get a good deal, but make sure you know what you're buying. Both are open year-round, Sunday only, from 8 to 5. Two miles away is **Shupp's Grove**, another collection of antique shops, open Saturday and Sunday from 8 to 5.

▪ **Ebersol Chair Shop** (101 Centerville Road, Gordonville; phone: 768-8820) specializes in hand-painted children's furniture made of poplar. Open weekdays from 8 to 5, Saturday from 9 to 4:30.

▪ **Mrs. Raymond Kauffman's Quilt Shop** (Minerva's Hand-mades, 31 South Weavertown Road, Ronks, just west of Intercourse; phone: 768-3966) has a large collection of new quilts, and will also make them to order for $150 to $350. Also for sale are calico fabrics and locally made rag rugs and stuffed toys. Open Monday through Saturday from 8 to 5.

▪ **Folk Craft Museum** (off Route 340, Witmer; phone: 397-3609) has a shop selling locally made tinware, copperware, pottery, hand-blocked stationery, and placemats—a happy alternative to the mass-produced gifts and mementos for sale elsewhere. Open daily, April through November, from 9:30 to 5.

▪ The work of 60 craftsmen is for sale at the **Market House Craft Center** (lower level of the Southern Market Building, Queen and Vine Streets, Lancaster; phone: 392-7797 or 295-1500) from October through December.

7. TOURS

▪ **Dutchland Bus Tours** (phone: 392-8622 or 687-8671) and **Conestoga Tours** (phone: 299-6666) offer four-hour rides through the Amish countryside, with stops at farmer's markets and craft shops. Visitors are picked up at various motels and restaurants. Tours begin daily at 8:30 and 1:30. Cost is $9 for adults, $7 for children under 15.

▪ **Abe's Buggy Rides** (Route 340, just west of Bird-in-Hand; phone: 392-1794) offers two-mile, 15-minute tours in an Amish family carriage. Cost is $6 for adults, $3 for children. Open all year. Closed Sundays.

▪ **Forest Ridge Stables** (Vintage Road, about three miles from Paradise; phone: 442-4259) offers four-mile, one-hour buggy rides through the Amish countryside.

▪ One of the great bargains of the area are the $5-an-hour (for a minimum of two hours) private Mennonite guides who will get in your car and lead you down country roads to one-room schoolhouses, grist mills, and farmer's markets. Guides should also be able to lead you to small roadside stands for a unique opportunity to talk with Amish farmers. Discuss beforehand the places to be visited. Be aware that guides—some more than others—are anxious to tell you about their faith. ("The Lord has presented us with a unique challenge," says a booklet distributed to all guides. "We need to nudge the person one step further in his pilgrimage.") It may make sense to sign up for the minimal two-hour tour and then extend the time if all is going well. Reservations are made through the **Mennonite Information Center** (phone: 299-0954).

- **Aerial Tours** from Smoketown Airport (Route 340, between Bird-in-Hand and Lancaster; phone 394-6476) cost $12.50 for adults, $6.25 for children.
- **Autotapes** may be rented from the **Visitor's Center, Dutch Wonderland** (Route 30), and **Howard Johnson's Motor Lodge Gift Shop** (Route 30).
- For walking tours of downtown Lancaster, *see #8, Walks.*

8. WALKS

- History and architecture buffs will want to take a walking tour along the red brick streets and crooked alleys of **Lancaster,** the oldest inland city in the nation. Laid out in 1730, it served as the state capital from 1799 to 1812. For one day, September 27, 1777, it was the U.S. capital, when the Congress met here during its retreat from Philadelphia.
- Self-guided walking tour maps are for sale at the **Walking Tour Office** (15 West King Street, off the main square in downtown Lancaster; phone 392-1776), open daily from 9:30 to 3:30; Sunday 12:30 to 3. Closed Sunday, November through March. Open Tuesday and Friday in January and February. Guided tours, including a slide presentation, begin daily at 10 and 1:30, and Sunday at 1:30. Cost is $2.50.
- Hess Road, Eby Road, Groffdale Road, Centerville Road, Scenic Road, and Musser's School Road are all lovely for country walks. They are located just north of Route 772, about two miles northwest of Intercourse. For details, see the **Pennsylvania Dutch Tour and Guide Map,** free at the Visitor's Bureau.

9. BIKING

- A book of suggested biking routes is available through Sutter Hudson, Director, **Lancaster Bicycle Club** (2714 Royal Road, Lancaster; phone: 394-8220).
- Many motels and farms have bikes that guests may rent or use.
- For a bike trip through the Amish countryside, start at Hess Road, off Route 772, about two miles northwest of the intersection of Route 772 and 340 in Intercourse. Turn right on Eby Road, right on Groffdale Road, and right on Scenic Road. For details, see the **Pennsylvania Dutch Tour and Guide Map** at the Visitor's Bureau.
- **Pennsylvania Bicycle Touring** (P.O. Box 87, Bird-in-Hand; phone: 392-1676) offers weekend bike tours on Amish country back-

roads with lodging in country inns and farm homes. Weekend trips, including breakfasts and dinners, cost $115.

11. SWIMMING

▪ **Lancaster County Swimming Pool** (phone: 299-8215), in the County Park, is allegedly the largest in the eastern United States. TO GET THERE: Take Route 30 west to Route 462 to downtown Lancaster. Turn right on Broad Street and continue one mile to the park entrance.

▪ Most motels and some guest farms have pools or ponds for swimming.

12. SKIING

▪ **Host Farm and Corral** (phone: out-of-state, 800/233-0121; in-state, 800/732-0454; local, 299-5400 or 299-5500) has its own modest ski slope with snow-making facilities.

13. RIDING

▪ **Circle M Ranch** (2111 Millersville Road, 5 miles southwest of downtown Lancaster; phone: 872-4651), has guided 45-minute rides around the property.

▪ **Forest Ridge Stables** (Vintage Road, three miles from Paradise; phone: 442-4259) offers guided 45-minute rides through woods on the owner's property.

14. TENNIS

▪ **Lancaster County Central Park** (phone: 299-8215) has four lighted courts *(see #18, After Hours)* for night tennis. Take Route 30 west into Route 462 to downtown Lancaster. Turn right on Broad Street and continue one mile to the park entrance.

▪ **Buchanan Park,** behind Franklin and Marshall College in downtown Lancaster, has six courts.

▪ There are tennis courts on the **Franklin and Marshall** and the **Steven's Trade School** campuses in Lancaster and at community parks in Ephrata, Lititz, New Holland, Safe Harbor, and Manheim.

15. GOLF

▪ **Host Farm and Corral** (Route 30, Lancaster; phone: out-of-state, 800/233-0121; in-state, 800/732-0454; local, 299-5400 or 299-5500) has 18- and nine-hole courses.

▪ **Overlook Public Course** (Route 501, three miles north of Lancaster; phone: 569-9551) has 18 holes.

16. FOR KIDS

▪ Children staying on a Mennonite farm can fish, feed calves, ride ponies, even help with the milking. Ask for farms with children the same age as yours *(see #19, Lodging)*.

▪ **People's Place** *(see #4, What to See and Do)* has a prize-winning 30-minute slide presentation on Amish life and the three-dimensional paintings of Aaron Zook. There is also a full-length feature film, *Hazel's People*, starring Pat Hingle and Geraldine Page, which provides a fine introduction to Mennonite life. The film is shown April through October at 6 and 8 P.M., daily except Sunday.

▪ Ride bikes down country roads *(see #9, Biking)* to get a firsthand view of Amish life.

▪ Ride the **Strasburg Railroad** *(see #4, What to See and Do)*.

▪ Visit the **Dutch Wonderland Amusement Park** *(see #4, What to See and Do)*.

▪ Go for a buggy ride with **Abe** or with **Forest Ridge Stables** *(see #7, Tours)*.

17. DINING

There are more than 40 restaurants in the area, many specializing in such local foods as chicken corn soup, platters of chicken, beef, and ham, chow chow (a mix of pickled vegetables), apple butter, pepper cabbage, and shoofly pie (made of molasses or brown sugar sprinkled with a crumbly mixture of flour, sugar, and butter).

▪ In a class by itself is **Groff's Farm Restaurant** (Mount Joy; phone, 653-1520). James Beard calls it "one of the steadfast outposts of Americana." Many of Betty Groff's recipes appear in *The American Heritage Cook Book* and in *Country Goodness*, her own collection of recipes. Dinner is served in a 1750 farmhouse. The feast begins with dessert (chocolate cake), moves on to spiced cantaloupe, winds its way through chicken Stoltzfus (stewed chicken over a biscuit dough), roast beef, sugar peas with brown butter, dandelion salad with hot bacon dressing, and comes to a heavenly rest with blackberry crumb pie or creme de menthe parfaits. There is one sitting for lunch, between 11:30 and 1, and two for dinner, at 5 and

7:30. Meals are by reservation only. Call three weeks ahead for Friday night, six for Saturday night. The set price is $12.50 to $14.50. Open Tuesday through Saturday year-round except for a few weeks in January. Visa and Mastercard are accepted. TO GET THERE: Take Route 30 west to Route 283 west. Take the first Mount Joy exit (Route 230) into town. Continue one-half block past the traffic light to a Y. Bear left onto Marietta Ave. After four blocks, turn left onto Pinkerton Road. The farm is the fourth on the left—about 1¼ miles from Mount Joy.

• **Cameron Inn Estate** (Mount Joy; phone: 653-1773) is the 14-room former home of Lincoln's first Secretary of War. Because it's owned by Abe and Betty Groff (see their Farm Restaurant listed above), you can expect a first-rate meal. Entrées, priced from $9 to $14.50, include brook trout and veal steak with white wine, mushrooms, and shallots. Favorite desserts are Black Forest cake and spiced sickle pears. Visa and Mastercard are accepted. Reservations are requested.

• A favorite spot for sampling local specialties is **Plain 'n' Fancy** (Route 340, near Bird-in-Hand; phone: 768-8281). Food is healthy and honest, and there is plenty of it. Platters of meats, noodles, and relishes are served on long tables in a barn that seats 800. Pass-the-chow-chow-relationships develop rapidly. The set price is $9.50, or $3.95 for kids. Visa and Mastercard are accepted. Reservations are necessary.

• **Stoltzfus' Farm Restaurant** (Route 772, east of Intercourse; phone: 768-8156 or 768-8811) is smaller than Plain 'n' Fancy, serving only 200. Homemade sausage and roasted chicken highlight a menu that includes peppered cabbage, sweet potatoes, and shoofly pie. Meals are served on platters. Unlike Plain 'n' Fancy, families usually get their own table. The set price is $8.25. No credit cards or reservations are accepted. Expect a 30- to 60-minute wait on summer weekends.

• **The Lemon Tree** (1766 Columbia Avenue, Route 462, a 10-minute drive west of downtown Lancaster; phone: 394-0441) offers gourmet dining in a converted 1856 farmhouse. A favorite appetizer is oysters Galasayres (oysters wrapped in prosciutto, with garlic butter and sauce béarnaise). Entrées, ranging in price from $8.50 to $15, include sweetbreads sprinkled with curry powder and sautéed in olive oil; and roasted, boneless duck glazed with citrus-fruit sauce. Jackets are recommended. Reservations are advised. All major credit cards are accepted.

• **Old Greenfield Inn** (1858 Hempstead Road, one-half mile east of the **Visitor's Bureau**; phone: 393-0668) features a continental cuisine. Entrées, priced from $10 to $18, include veal with mushrooms in a creamy white sauce, and baked flounder stuffed with crab meat. Dress is optional. Reservations are recommended. Visa and Mastercard are accepted.

18. AFTER HOURS

▪ Cabaret at the **Host Farm and Corral** (Route 30; phone: out-of-state, 800/233-0121; in-state, 800/732-0454; local, 299-5400 or 299-5500) features performers such as Ben Vereen, Bobby Vinton, and Shirley Jones. Both the farm and the corral have cocktail lounges.

▪ **Treadway Resort Inn** (Route 30; phone: 569-6444) has a cocktail lounge.

▪ **Lancaster Dispensing Company** (3335 North Market Square, one block from the Fulton Opera House; phone: 299-4602) has live music Wednesday through Saturday and a crowd in the 21-40 range.

▪ **The People's Place** shows a full-length feature film with insights on Mennonite life, daily except Sunday at 6 and 8 P.M. A good bet for families (see #4, What to See and Do).

▪ **Lancaster County Central Park** has four lighted tennis courts. The $1 tokens that turn the lights on are sold at the park entrance from 8:30 to 4:30. After hours you can buy tokens from the ranger, if you're lucky enough to find him driving through the 560-acre park. You can also order tokens by mail from the Park Office, Lancaster County Parks Department, Rockford Road, Lancaster 17602; phone: 299-8215. TO GET THERE: Drive toward downtown Lancaster on Routes 30 and 462, turn left on Broad Street, and continue one mile to the park entrance.

▪ On moonlit nights, take a stroll down a country road, past some Amish farms. You will have no trouble imagining yourself back in the nineteenth century.

19. LODGING

Accommodations range from plain to fancy, from farm homes to lavish resorts. For under $22 a night per room you can have the unforgettable experience of staying on a Mennonite farm. The Mennonites, unlike the more conservative Amish, have no objections to air-conditioning, TV, and other amenities of modern life, so you needn't worry about a lack of creature comforts. Rooms tend to be decorated simply, with a disarming lack of pretension. Some farms serve breakfast, a real plus for budget-minded visitors, and almost all forbid smoking and alcohol. If you have children, try to find farmers with children the same age as yours. Credit cards are usually not accepted. Reservations can be made through the **Mennonite Information Center** *(see #22, For Further Information).*

▪ One lovely tourist farm is run by **Ellen and Roy Neff** (R.D. #1, Paradise 17562; phone: 687-7837.) Their three guest rooms, one with private bath, are in the second story of a restored 200-year-old farmhouse. The 115-acre dairy farm has cows, chickens, pigs, ducks, cats, and a dog named Husky. Children who are visiting can help feed the calves, fish in a trout-stocked stream, even help with milking.

▪ The family of Ray and Reba Ranck (Black Horse Road, R.D. #1, Paradise 17562; phone: 687-6729) has operated the 100-acre **Rayba Acres Farm** since 1863. Here too, visitors can go for picnics and get a firsthand view of life on a working farm. Some evenings the three Ranck children like to organize guests for a softball game. But dusk is a time for strolls down country roads where the only sound is the creaking of waterwheels, and the only movement, the shifting colors of an evening sky.

▪ Other popular farms, somewhat farther away, are the **Nolt Farm** (Mount Joy 17552; phone: 653-4192) and **Rocky Acre Farm** (R.D. #3, Mount Joy 17552; phone: 653-4449).

▪ Those who like old inns should consider the **Cameron Inn Estate** (Mount Joy 17552; phone: 653-1773.). This 14-room former home of Lincoln's first Secretary of War is set on 15 acres with its own stocked trout stream. Rooms are tastefully decorated with oriental carpets and expensive reproductions of four-postered, canopied beds covered with locally made quilts. Doubles, some with private bath, cost from $45 to $80, including a continental breakfast. Consider dining one evening here, and another at Groff's Farm Restaurant, only three miles away. Visa and Mastercard are accepted.

▪ **Witmer's Tavern,** at the sign of Pandora's Antiques (2014 Old Philadelphia Pike, Route 340, Lancaster 17602; phone: 299-5305) is a lovingly restored inn that once catered to pioneers waiting for their Conestoga wagons and Pennsylvania rifles to be made before heading west. Rooms have antiques and fireplaces. Those upstairs are more private. Doubles with shared bath cost $50 to $70, including a continental breakfast. No credit cards are accepted.

▪ A dozen years ago a man named Donald Denlinger put a low bid on 19 cabooses auctioned for scrap and found himself with 475 tons of rolling stock. He renovated them, fitted them with TVs and showers, and turned them into the **Red Caboose Motel** (Strasburg; phone: 687-6646). Rooms are snug but when was the last time you slept on a train? Meals are served in two Victorian-style dining cars complete with globe lamps and plush red drapes. Doubles cost $35. Visa and Mastercard are accepted.

▪ **Host Farm and Corral** (Route 30, Lancaster 17602; Phone: out-of-state, 800/233-0121; in-state, 800/732-0454; local, 299-5400 for the coral, 299-5500 for the farm) is a full-service resort with two golf courses, indoor and outdoor pools, and tennis courts, miniature golf, indoor ice-skating, even a ski slope and lift. The supervised children's program continues until the cabaret closes at midnight. Doubles, including breakfast and dinner, cost from $100 to $130, depending on the season. All major credit cards are accepted.

▪ **Treadway Resort Inn** (Route 30, Lancaster 17601; phone: out-of-state, 800/631-0182; local, 569-6444) has an indoor pool and sauna and a movie house next door. Doubles cost $52 to $71. All major credit cards are accepted.

20. EMERGENCIES

For an ambulance, dial 911. There are emergency rooms in three Lancaster hospitals:

- **Lancaster Osteopathic Hospital** (Phone: 397-3711).
- **Lancaster General Hospital** (Phone: 299-5511).
- **Saint Joseph Hospital** (Phone: 291-8211).

21. HOW TO GET THERE

BY CAR. *From New York or Philadelphia:* take the Pennsylvania Turnpike west from Philadelphia. At exit 22 take Route 23 west (the scenic route) or at exit 21 take Route 222 south (the fast route).

BY BUS. *From New York:* Greyhound (phone: 212/635-0800). *From Philadelphia:* Greyhound (phone: 215/568-4800). *From Washington:* Greyhound (phone: 202/565-2662) or Trailways (phone: 202/737-5800).

22. FOR FURTHER INFORMATION

▪ **Pennsylvania Dutch Visitors Bureau,** 1799 Hempstead Road, Lancaster, 17601. Phone: 717/299-8901. Located east of Lancaster on Route 30 bypass and Hempstead Road Interchange.

▪ **Mennonite Information Center,** 2209 Mill Stream Road, Lancaster 17602. Phone: 717/299-0954.

23. RECOMMENDED READING

• John Hostetler. *Amish Society* (Johns Hopkins, $6.95). The definitive work on Amish life.

• Carolyn Meyer. *Amish People* (Atheneum, $7.95). A must for all children *before* visiting Lancaster. Why not read it aloud on the drive down?

Hershey, Pennsylvania

(Area Code, 717; Zip Code, 17133)

---

1. DISTANCES

BY CAR. *From New York*, 4 hours; *from Philadelphia*, 2 hours; *from Washington*, 2½ hours.

BY BUS. *From New York*, 5 hours; *from Philadelphia*, 2 hours; *from Washington*, 3 hours.

BY TRAIN. *From New York*, 3½ hours; *from Philadelphia*, 1¾ hours; *from Washington*, 3½ hours.

2. MAJOR ATTRACTIONS

- A quality hotel/resort only minutes from five golf courses.
- A simulated chocolate factory tour—the next best thing to Charlie's Chocolate Factory.
- A child's fantasy land, with amusement rides, Hershey Kiss lampposts, and streets with names like Cocoa Avenue and Chocolate Avenue.

3. INTRODUCTION

As the posters say, there's a little bit of Hershey in all of us.

Who can visit the town without feeling a tinge of excitement as he drives beneath chocolate kiss lampposts along East Chocolate Avenue? Chocolate-brown buses pass by with visitors on their way to Hersheypark and Chocolate World. To the left is the Cocoa Motel. And over there is the $80 million Hershey Medical Center. Was it built for chocolate lovers who didn't know when to stop? Hanging over the town is the thick, reassuring smell of chocolate—an explosion of sweetness from the great Hershey bar in the sky.

A trip to Hershey is even sweeter for those who know the extraordinary story of the man who founded the factory town in the fertile farmland of Lebanon Valley.*

Milton Snavely Hershey was born in 1857 only miles from the site of present-day Hershey, the son of a freethinking farmer and a strict, penny-pinching Mennonite. Success did not come easily to him, not at first. All thumbs, he lost his first job as a printer's devil from dropping too much type and letting an old straw hat fall into the rollers. Apprenticed to a Lancaster confectioner, he forgot to turn the blower off one night and by morning the street outside was covered with peanut shells.

When Hershey failed as a caramel maker in New York City, he tried again in Lancaster. Things were looking pretty bleak until an English candy importer bought some caramels from his pushcart and liked them enough to place an order. By 1894 Hershey was doing a million dollars of business a year and owned the largest caramel factory in the world.

"Frank, I'm going to make chocolate!" he told his cousin in 1893 after inspecting a European-made chocolate-molding machine at an

---

*This introduction is based on material in Roy Bongartz's article on Milton Hershey in *American Heritage* (June 1973), and is adapted with permission of American Heritage Publishing Co.

exposition in Chicago. And when another caramel company offered to buy him out for one million dollars, Hershey just melted in their hands.

A chocolate factory, of course, wasn't enough for a man with Hershey's dreams and ambition—he wanted to build a whole new town: "an industrial utopia . . . that has no poverty, no nuisances, and no evil." Employees would not live in mean row houses as they did in the mining and mill towns of Pennsylvania, but in homes of their own, with lawns and gardens. "Hershey had left school in the fourth grade," writes Roy Bongartz, "but this was 1901, the quintessential moment of the self-made man, and Hershey was serenely confident that he could build a utopia as much as anyone else."

Making more money than he knew what to do with, he founded the world's largest orphan school, the Milton Hershey School, where today some 1,500 orphaned or underprivileged children are given a completely free education, including room, board, and clothing. In Hershey's day the boys helped with the milking operation and learned useful trades. "We do not plan to turn out a race of professors," said Hershey.

In addition to the school and the world's largest chocolate factory, Hershey built a hotel, an airport, a sports arena for a professional hockey team, four golf courses, a zoo, an amusement park, a garden with 35,000 roses in it, a theater, and so on and on—all in Hershey. The drug store, cafeteria, department store, bank, even the ice cream parlor were owned by Hershey. As suspicious as his penny-pinching mother, he would patrol the town, telling employees to sweep their streets or mow their lawns. He was not above firing street workers for leaning on their shovels. When he ordered a man to stop fishing in the town park, the culprit—the town barber—argued back, and Hershey simply had his equipment, which of course Hershey owned, hauled away.

At the same time, however, Hershey would spare nothing to save a clubfooted boy who had gained his sympathy. When he built a sugar mill town called Central Hershey 28 miles outside of Havana, he bought his employees an ocean beach, hired doctors and dentists for them, and founded another orphanage for children who had lost their parents in a train wreck. When he couldn't convince the five local churches to let him build them a single church which they could use in turn, he gave each church $20,000 to fix up its old building. During the Depression he gave away his home at High Point to be used as a country club for his employees and kept only a couple of rooms upstairs for himself.

Employees had free entertainment and low taxes but there were no utopian labor practices in Hershey such as paid vacations or guaranteed wages. Talk to old-timers in Hershey today and they will tell you they were grateful to Milton Hershey for seeing them through the Depression, but resentful of his almost feudal paternalism—what a *Fortune* reporter called "the sweet and oppressive odor of charity."

Any hope for a utopia disappeared in 1937 when workers went on strike for higher wages. Hershey himself reportedly acted "like a kid who's had his face slapped," but workers who had seen all this wealth paraded before them felt it was time to get some of it for themselves.

Today, the town of Hershey is changing, as the Hershey Foods Corporation divests itself of local holdings and more and more outsiders move in with few permanent ties to the community. But while you're playing golf or enjoying the amusement park, remember that these and other activities were built originally for the enjoyment of Hershey's employees. And as you drive down Chocolate Avenue try to see this town as a monumental tribute to the drive and fortune of a single man with a utopian vision of how sweet life could be.

4. WHAT TO SEE & DO

▪ **Chocolate World** (phone: 534-4900)—Hershey's answer to the tunnel of love—was opened in 1973, when the actual chocolate factory was no longer able to accommodate the tens of thousands of visitors each year. An open car on a conveyer belt takes you on a 10-minute trip through a simulated world of chocolate—from cocoa beans in the tropics to the wrapping of candy bars in Hershey. It's more an exercise in wowmanship than an honest effort to teach how chocolate is made—but fun, nonetheless. Admission is free. Open April 1 to June 8 and September 4 to October 31 from 9 to 4:45; November through March Monday to Saturday, from 9 to 4:45; Sunday 12 to 4:45; June 9 to Labor Day from 9 to 6:45. Expect a 30-minute wait on summer weekends.

▪ **Hersheypark** (phone: 534-3900) is a theme park that features a 1919 carousel with hand-carved wooden horses, a 1946 wooden roller coaster, a waterflume ride, and live musical entertainment. The Sooperdooper Looper, with its full 360-degree loop, was named one of the four great steel roller coasters by none less than the nationally recognized roller coaster expert, Gary Kyriazi. The Kissing Tower, with its bubbled, kiss-shaped windows, rises 330 feet above the park for splendid views of the surrounding countryside. An afternoon here is fun for amusement park fans, but it is no Disneyland. Waits can be long, particularly on summer weekends, and the dining is strictly fast food. Parents might consider leaving teenage children here while they make a trip to the Hershey Gardens or Hershey Museum. Admission, including all rides, is $13.95, for ages 9 and over; $10.95 for children 5 to 8. Open weekends in late May and in September; open daily May 24 to Labor Day. Admission after 5 P.M. is $8.95.

▪ **Hershey Gardens** is a 23-acre park with six gardens: a formal English garden with hemlock and barberry, a rock garden with Alpine plants, a colonial garden with perennials and herbs, a Japanese garden, a fountain garden, and an Italian garden with a large marble terrace. There are over 35,000 roses, thousands of daffodils, tulips, and annuals, and countless varieties of azaleas, magnolias, rhododendron, and chrysanthemums. After a dizzying day of games and amusements, come here in the later afternoon, perhaps with a book, and enjoy the quiet and solitude. Guests in the nearby Hotel Hershey will want to walk here after dinner. Admission is $2.50 for adults, $1.25 for children 12 to 18.

▪ **Hershey Museum of American Life** (phone: 534-3439) has displays on American Indian art and life in the nineteenth century, including an unusual display of games and toys, and Pennsylvania Dutch folk art and crafts. An apostolic clock built during an 11-year period by a late nineteenth-century Lancaster County artisan is controlled by weights that move beautiful sculpted figures. Open Memorial to Labor Day from 10 to 6; off-season, from 10 to 5. Admission is $2.50 for adults, $1.25 for children 5 to 18.

▪ See planets, galaxies, and star clusters through five telescopes at the **Edward L. Naylor Astronomical Center and Observatory** (Lewisberry, about 30 minutes from Hershey; phone: 938-6041 or 234-4616). Open from dusk to 11 or 12 P.M. on Sundays from June through August. Admission is free. TO GET THERE: Drive 1.4 miles west of Lewisberry on Route 382. Turn left on Brenneman, then the second left on Observation Drive (a dirt road).

▪ **Hersheypark Arena** (phone: 534-3911) is home of the Hershey Bears, members of the American Hockey League since 1938. They have frequent home matches on Wednesdays and Saturdays from October through March. Arena entertainment includes such superstars as Diana Ross and Billy Joel.

▪ **Indian Echo Caverns** (three miles west of Hershey, off Route 322; phone: 566-8131) offers a 45-minute walk through some of the most beautiful caverns north of Virginia. Open Memorial to Labor

Day, daily from 9 to 6; April to June and September and October, from 10 to 4; in March and November, open weekends only from 10 to 4.

▪ **Penn National Race Course** (Grantville, 10 miles north of Hershey, on Route 743; phone: 469-2211) has thoroughbred racing year-round.

▪ **Dan-D Village** (three miles west of Hershey off Route 39; phone: 566-2541) has a display of animated, hand-made, turn-of-the-century dolls, a gift and antique shop, and an orchard where you can pick your own apples in the fall.

▪ Visitors interested in Hershey's "utopia" will want to walk past some of the original houses that Hershey built for his employees on East Caracas Street and Aruba Avenue, both off Cocoa Avenue.

5. THE ARTS

▪ **Hershey Theater** (corner of Chocolate Avenue and Cocoa Avenue, P.O. Box 395, Hershey; phone: 534-3405) presents plays such as *Evita* and *Agnes of God.*

▪ **The Forum** (3rd Street, at the corner of Commonwealth and Walnut, Harrisburg; phone: 787-1874) is rented out to various groups, including the **Harrisburg Symphony Orchestra,** which gives frequent performances.

▪ **Harrisburg Community Theater** (513 Hurlock Street, at 6th Street, Harrisburg; phone: 238-7381) is a local group performing such plays as *Grease, Follies,* and *H.M.S. Pinafore.* Open October through June.

6. ANTIQUES

▪ Returning to Philadelphia or New York, take Pennsylvania Turnpike exit 21 north two miles on Route 272 to **Renninger's** or **Black Angus.** Together they comprise one of the largest antique emporiums in the country. Dozens of dealers sell everything from old books and prints to Victorian blouses, corner cupboards, pewter, and stoneware. Black Angus has higher quality goods, but fewer "finds." At Renninger's you can occasionally get a good deal, but make sure you know what you're buying. Both are open year-round, Sundays only, from 8 to 5.

▪ Over 50 dealers sell everything from Depression glass to Hummels at **Ziegler's Antique Mall** (corner of Routes 322 and 743, Hershey; phone: 533-4267).

7. TOURS

▪ A self-guided walking tour map of the historic district in nearby **Harrisburg** is available from the **Chamber of Commerce** (114 Walnut Street, Harrisburg; phone: 232-4121).

8. WALKS

▪ There are some lovely trails open to the public in the pine forests surrounding **Hotel Hershey.**
▪ **Shank Park** has 89 acres of wooden trails. From Route 322 turn south on Bullfrog Valley Road to the park entrance.
▪ Local residents like to take walks through the fields and wooded areas around **Owl Hill,** in back of Hershey Cemetery. Take Airport Road (Hersheypark Drive) east. At Route 743, turn left, then make the first left. Continue to the cemetery.

9. BIKING

▪ Rentals are available at the **Hershey Lodge** (533-3311) and **Hotel Hershey** (533-2171).
▪ **South Hills** is one of the loveliest, most exclusive areas of Hershey. From the Information Center, take Route 39 east to Route 322 east. Continue about three miles. At Don's Pier turn right. Take the fork to the right onto South Hills Road.

10. BOATING AND FISHING

▪ The **Seaplane Base** (Wormleysburg, across the river from Harrisburg; phone: 763-7654) rents canoes and Jon boats (with or without motors) for trips up and down the Susquehanna River—about three miles in each direction. TO GET THERE: Park at the foot of Walnut Street, Harrisburg, and walk across the bridge. Or take I-83 south to exit 21. Follow the road north along the river to Front Street.

11. SWIMMING

▪ There are pools at the **Hershey Lodge** (533-3311), **Hotel Hershey** (533-2171), and the **Best Western** (533-5665).

12. SKIING

▪ There are cross-country ski trails and equipment rentals at the **Hershey Hotel Golf Course** (533-2171).

▪ **Ski Roundtop** (Route 15 or 83 to Lewisberry, about 20 minutes from Hershey; phone: 432-9631) has five double-chair lifts and snow-making equipment for 10 downhill slopes. Lift tickets cost $17 on weekends, $16 on weekdays, and $10 for night skiing from 5 to 10.

13. RIDING

▪ **Hotel Hershey** (533-2171) has riding facilities for both guests and nonguests.

14. TENNIS

▪ Courts available at the **Hershey Lodge** (533-3311) and **Hotel Hershey** (533-2171).

▪ **Hershey Racquet Club** (University and Briarcrest Avenue, Hershey; phone: 533-5995) has indoor courts for nonmembers at $8 an hour, plus $4 per person guest fee.

15. GOLF

Hershey prides itself on having more golf per square foot—72 holes on five courses—than anywhere else in the world.

▪ The 18-hole **Hershey Parkview Golf Course** (adjacent to Chocolate World; phone: 534-3182) is rated one of the top public courses in the country.

▪ **Hershey Country Club** (phone: 533-2462) has two championship 18-hole courses.

▪ **Hotel Hershey** (533-2171) has a wooded nine-hole course.

▪ **Spring Creek Golf Course** (East Chocolate Avenue; phone: 533-2847) has a nine-hole course.

▪ Both the **Hotel Hershey** and the **Hershey Lodge** offer golf package weekends.

16. FOR KIDS

▪ There is very little in Hershey that is *not* for kids. **Chocolate World** and **Hersheypark** (*see #4, What to See and Do*) are musts. For a unique experience, take them to the **Astronomical Center and Observatory** in Lewisberry *(see #4, What to See and Do)* for a look at the stars. Tennis, riding, biking, swimming—all are available at both **Hotel Hershey** and the **Hershey Lodge.**

17. DINING

▪ The elegant dining room at **Hotel Hershey** (phone: 533-2171) has stained glass windows looking out on formal gardens, where guests can stroll before dinner. Space is limited, so if you are staying at the **Hershey Lodge,** make dinner reservations at the hotel at the same time that you book your room. The complete dinner, including appetizer and dessert, costs $19.50. Jackets are requested. All major credit cards are accepted.

▪ Complete dinners at the **Hearth Restaurant** in the **Hershey Lodge** (phone: 533-3311) run from $10 to $18. Dinners in the Tack Room at the Lodge run from $11 to $22. Ties are optional. Reservations are recommended. All major credit cards are accepted.

▪ **Alfred's Victorian Restaurant** (38 North Union Street, Middletown, about six miles from Hershey; phone: 944-5373) is on *Gourmet* magazine's list of fine restaurants and also on the National Register of Historic Places. The 20-room Victorian mansion has four dining rooms and specializes in fresh seafood and northern Italian cuisine. Included among the 30 entrées, ranging in price from $10 to $23, are 10 pasta dishes. A favorite is tortellini Alfredo—homemade pasta tossed in butter, cream, prosciutto, and parmesan cheese. Jackets and reservations are recommended. All credit cards are accepted.

▪ **Au Jour le Jour** (540 Race Street, Harrisburg; phone: 236-2048) is an intimate French restaurant, seating 40, in the historic district of downtown Harrisburg. Entrées, priced from $12 to $18, include fresh seafood and tournedos of beef with a sauce of shallots, red wine, and cream. Jackets and reservations are recommended. American Express is accepted.

18. AFTER HOURS

▪ There is nightly dancing and entertainment at Hotel Hershey's **Iberian Lounge** (phone: 533-2171) and at the **Antique Auto Pub** at the Hershey Lodge (phone: 533-3311). The hotel is more formal and elegant and worth a visit, even if you don't stay there.

▪ **Hershey Lodge** (phone: 533-3311) has lighted tennis courts and a movie theater.

▪ Watch the stars and constellations through powerful telescopes at the **Edward L. Naylor Astronomical Center and Observatory** (1¼ miles west of Lewisberry on Route 383 and Brenneman and Observatory drives; phone: 938-6041 or 234-4616). Facilities are open to the public on Sundays, June through August, from dusk. Admission is free.

- **Ski Roundtop** *(see #12, Skiing)* has night skiing in season.

19. LODGING

Hotel Hershey (800/533-3131 or 717/533-2171) and **Hershey Lodge and Convention Center** (800/533-3131 or 717/533-3311) are both under the same general management, and facilities at both resorts are available to all guests. But in mood and appearance the two resorts are light-years apart.

- The modern lodge, with 460 rooms, is for those who like the motellike efficiency and predictability of large, expensive resort chains, such as Sheraton or Holiday Inn. Kids, and parents who want to be left alone, will love it here because of all the facilities. But the lodge could really be anywhere in the world. Facilities include tennis courts, indoor and outdoor pools, pitch and putt golf, whirlpool, and movie theater. Doubles cost $58 to $90 without meals. A three-day, two-night package, including various admissions, costs $108 per person. All major credit cards are accepted.

- **Hotel Hershey** could only be in Hershey, for it is the architectural conceit of a single man, Milton Hershey. The 250 rooms unfortunately have been given the homogenized look of modern motel units; but the hotel itself is full of character and a certain outrageous charm. In his counterattack on the Depression, Milton Hershey put the townspeople to work building this Hollywoodlike castle on a hill overlooking the town. Since he was unable to duplicate the weather he had enjoyed on trips to Egypt and Spain, he instructed his architects to paint the ceiling a sky blue with scurrying clouds. He hated being stashed away behind pillars in European restaurants and insisted that no one in his dining room would suffer the same fate. The result, a considerable architectural feat at the time, is a great circular dining room with stained glass windows overlooking formal gardens, with a gazebo supported by classical columns. When the hotel was nearly finished, Hershey imported Italian laborers to lay tile and Lowell Thomas pronounced the result, "a palace that out-palaces the palaces of the maharajas of India." The gardens and the woods behind the hotel are ideal for morning or evening walks. Facilities include indoor and outdoor pools, tennis, riding, golf, and cross-country skiing. Doubles with three meals cost $88 per person;

with breakfast and dinner, $84; and without meals, $125 for two. Visitors on a European plan can figure about $5.25 per person for breakfast, $8.25 for lunch, and $19.50 for dinner. A three-day, two-night package, including breakfasts, dinners, and admission tickets, costs $191.45 per person. All major credit cards are accepted.

▪ **Best Western** (422 West Chocolate Avenue, Hershey; phone: 800/528-1234 or 717/533-5665) has 121 units. Facilities include an outdoor pool. Doubles cost $58 to $78 with a continental breakfast.

20. EMERGENCIES

▪ The $85 million **Milton S. Hershey Medical Center** has a 24-hour emergency room (phone: 534-8333).

21. HOW TO GET THERE

BY CAR. *From New York:* New Jersey Turnpike to the Pennsylvania Turnpike. Turn north on Route 72 north (exit 20), then take Route 322 west for about 19 miles. *From Philadelphia:* Pennsylvania Turnpike to exit 20. Turn north on Route 322 for about 19 miles. *From Washington:* north on I-95 to Route 695 to I-83 north. Then go east on Routes 422 and 322.

BY BUS. Trailways to Harrisburg *from New York* (phone: 212/730-7460), *from Philadelphia* (phone: 215/569-3100) and *from Washington* (phone: 202/737-5800).

BY TRAIN. Amtrak to Harrisburg *from New York* (phone: 212/736-4545), *from Philadelphia* (phone: 215/824-1600), and *from Washington* (phone: 202/484-7540).

BY AIR. USAir flies between Harrisburg and *New York* (phone: 212/736-3200) or *Washington* (phone: 202/783-4500). Hershey Lodge and Hotel Hershey offer free limousine service for guests from the Harrisburg Airport and train station, about a 15-minute drive from Hershey.

22. FOR FURTHER INFORMATION

▪ **Hershey Information Center,** Airport Road, Hershey, Pennsylvania 17033. Phone: 534-3005.
▪ **Harrisburg & Hershey Tourist Promotion Agency,** 114 Walnut Street, P.O. Box 969, Harrisburg, Pennsylvania, 17108. Phone: 232-4121.

New Hope, Pennsylvania

(Area Code, 215; Zip Code, 18938)

1. DISTANCES

BY CAR. *From New York;* 1½ hours; *from Philadelphia,* 45 minutes; *from Washington,* 4 hours.

BY BUS. *From New York,* 2¼ hours; *from Philadelphia,* 1½ hours; *from Washington,* 5 hours.

2. MAJOR ATTRACTIONS

- A tree-shaded canal with mule-drawn barge trips, and a 150-year-old towpath for cyclists and walkers.
- Dozens of quality craft, antique, and novelty shops offering everything from homemade licorice ice cream cones to $12,000 Hepplewhite sideboards.
- A first-rate summer theater for adults, and a unique educational game park for children.
- Inner-tube trips down the Delaware River.
- Romantic dining in cozy inns overlooking the Delaware Canal.

3. INTRODUCTION

William Lathrop. Edward Redfield. Dorothy Parker. S. J. Perelman. James Michener. Moss Hart. Richard Rodgers. Pearl Buck. Paul Simon. Ann Miller.

These are just a few of the artists and writers who discovered the beauty of New Hope and returned to stay. They stayed with friends or at the Logan Inn on Main Street, and then they came back and bought places of their own.

The tourists followed and turned this quiet river town into a weekend playground complete with antique stores and galleries, elegant restaurants in restored old inns, and shops selling everything from rag rugs to Victorian blouses.

Visitors today who expect a genuine cobblestone artist's colony may be disappointed by the commercialism of Main Street. (To use the toilet in the Visitor's Center you must buy a token from the Chamber of Commerce and drop it in a turnstile.) But wander down side streets or along the canal and you'll discover the same small town charm that attracted New York's literati in the 1930s.

The setting is idyllic—to the east is the wide, rippling Delaware—pastoral rather than wild; and to the west is the sleepy canal, with overhanging trees reflected in its mirrorlike surface. A stroll along the towpath is a journey back in time, to a nation that traveled by water. For more than a century mules walked this same grassy path, pulling coal barges from Easton to Bristol.

For those who want a more active weekend, the curtain rises each summer on one of the country's most popular straw-hat theaters. The list of crafts and antique stores is several days long. Antique dolls, bonsai, silver jewelry, decoys, and Edwardian dresses are just a few of the hundreds of items beckoning to you through store windows. Young and old are equally at home here. The bohemian legacy remains in the town's willingness to accept everyone, and the response to the question, "Where do you go for nightlife?" is usually, "Straight or gay?"

New Hope began in 1681 as a land grant from William Penn to Thomas Woolrich, who never left his home in England. Members of his family settled in the early eighteenth century. John Wells bought half the tract in 1717 and obtained a license to run a ferry and tavern. The original Ferry Tavern is now part of the Logan Inn. New Hope was then no more than a ferry slip on the Old York Road (Route 202) linking pre-revolutionary New York and Philadelphia. Its name changed with its ferry masters—first Wells' Ferry, then Coryell's Ferry.

In the fall of 1776, Washington's army, driven back by the British, crossed the Delaware and encamped just south of Coryell's Ferry in an area known today as the Washington Crossing State Park. While his men rested, Washington and his generals plotted their counteroffensive. They commandeered all boats along the Jersey shore and hid them on an island below the town. Then, on Christmas Eve, Washington's armada stole downstream, crossed the freezing river, and began its march on Trenton. The Hessian mercenaries, still staggering from Christmas celebrations, were defeated at dawn on December 26, and the tide of the war began to turn.

Industry began in New Hope with Benjamin Parry's grist and lumber mills in 1784. When fire destroyed the mills, Parry had them rebuilt and called them New Hope Mills, hence the town's name. Parry built himself a fieldstone house in the center of town, which is now the Parry Mansion, open to the public.

Construction of the Delaware Canal began in 1827, but it was not in full operation until 1840. Mule-drawn barges carried Bushkill whiskey and coal to Bristol and returned to Easton with manufactured and imported goods. In 1862, some 3,000 barges passed through New Hope, each about 87 feet long and 10½ feet wide, with a 100-ton capacity.

The coming of the railroad closed most of the mills and other industries along the river. The last mule-drawn barge went by in the early 1930s. Today the canal is part of the Roosevelt State Park. Visitors can walk along the grassy, tree-shaded towpath and feel themselves back in another era.

With the end of river traffic and the closing of the canal, New Hope returned to obscurity as a sleepy river town. In the 1920s and '30s it was discovered by artists and writers, and became a fashionable country retreat for the Algonquin Roundtable set: Alexander Woollcott, Dorothy Parker, and others. Today the literati are tucked away in their summer homes in the beautiful countryside of Bucks County; and Main Street is filled with weekend visitors, enjoying the comforts of the present and satisfying a nostalgic yearning for the past.

4. WHAT TO SEE AND DO

Visitors who think that Bucks County is no more than a walk down Main Street in New Hope may be disappointed. There are dozens of charming shops, but little merchandise that could not be found elsewhere. Be sure to wander along side streets, eastward to the river, westward to the canal, where you will discover many interesting shops that could not afford the high rents on Main Street. The walk, from one end of town to the other, should not take more than a morning or an afternoon.

For an experience that "belongs" to New Hope, take a walk along the Towpath *(see #8, Walks)*, and imagine yourself living here when mules pulled coal barges up and down the Delaware Canal. If the weather's warm and you don't feel a need to be alone, join the hundreds of visitors, ages 7 to 70, riding inner tubes down the Delaware River *(see #10, Boating)*. For a lovely drive, past colonial houses and antique stores, head north on Route 32, along the Delaware River and canal. Take your children to **Sesame Place**—an educational amusement park run by the same imaginative folks who brought you "Sesame Street" *(see #16, For Kids)*. For a lesson in history, take a short drive south to the **Washington Crossing State Park,** and tour the sites where Washington planned his march on Trenton. In the evening, dine at one of several elegant but cozy inns, take in a play at the **Bucks County Playhouse,** and end the day by listening to some jazz at a candlelit table overlooking the canal.

▪ The **Washington Crossing State Park** (seven miles south on Route 32; phone: 493-4076) covers the site where the general and 2,400 soldiers crossed the Delaware in a heavy snowstorm on Christmas night, 1776, took the mercenary Hessian soldiers by surprise, and captured Trenton. In the northern section of the park, four miles closer to New Hope, is the **Thompson-Neely House,** which was requisitioned for 16 days during the 1776 campaign. Meeting here with the generals was an 18-year-old lieutenant named James Monroe, who was wounded in the battle but went on to become the nation's fifth President. Also on the northern grounds is the 110-foot **Bowman's Tower,** where sentries searched for enemy movement along the opposite shore. Today the tower overlooks 100 acres of wildflowers *(see #8, Walks),* where visitors can walk along miles of nature trails. A short walk from the Thompson-Neely House are the graves of some of America's first unknown soldiers.

▪ New Hope has its own historical house—the **Parry Mansion** (Cannon Square, in the center of New Hope; phone: 794-8143 or 862-2194). Each of the ten rooms is decorated in a different period, showing the changes in life-styles from the late eighteenth to the early twentieth century. The building, run by the **Historical Society,** is open Friday through Monday from 2 to 5. Suggested contribution is $1.50 for adults, 50¢ for children under 12.

▪ A favorite among visitors is a one-hour mule-drawn barge trip along the **Delaware Canal.** Reservations should be made through the **New Hope Barge Co.** (P.O. Box 164, New Hope; phone: 862-2842).

Trips run in April on Wednesday, Saturday, and Sunday at 1, 2, 3, and 4:30; from May 1 through September 15 daily at 11:30, 1, 2, 3, 4:30, and 6; and from September 15 to November 15 on Wednesday, Saturday, and Sunday at 11:30, 1, 3, 4:30, and 6. The cost is $4.95 for adults, $2.75 for children under 12.

▪ Train buffs will want to ride the **New Hope Steam Railway** (New Hope Train Station, 32 West Bridge Street; phone: 862-5880 weekdays, 862-2707 weekends). A 1925 Baldwin steam engine pulls 1930-vintage coaches on a one-hour, nine-mile round-trip to Lahaska. Tracks are on a freight line still in operation between New Hope and Ivyland. The railway is a nonprofit corporation run by volunteers, whose idea of happiness is shoveling coal into a fiery engine. Trains run from June through October and during the first two weekends in December, Sundays only, at 1:15, 2:45, and 3:30.

▪ **Harrison Aire** (Route 179, Lambertville, New Jersey, across from the Yellow Brick Toad Restaurant; phone: 609/466-3389) has daily balloon flights.

▪ Across the river in New Jersey is the **Black River and Western Railway** (Box 83, Ringoes, NJ 08551; phone: 201/782-9600). Visitors can choose between a 70-minute round-trip ride from Ringoes (starting at Route 202, about 6½ miles from New Hope) to Flemington; and a 2½-hour round-trip ride from Lambertville (starting at the old Pennsylvania RR station on Bridge Street, just across the river from New Hope) to Flemington. The Ringoes-Flemington trip, behind a 1937 steam engine, costs $4 for adults, $2 for children. The Lambertville-Flemington trip, in one of the country's last gas and electric self-propelled cars, costs $7.50 for adults, $3.75 for children. Trains run from mid-April to the end of November. The Ringoes train runs daily in July and August; otherwise, on Saturday, Sunday, and holidays. The Lambertville train runs on Sunday only.

▪ **Wilmar Lapidary Museum** (off Route 232 and Pineville Road, Pineville, about five miles from New Hope; phone: 598-3572) has one of the country's largest collections of hand-carved semiprecious stones. Open April to December 24, Tuesday through Saturday from 11 to 5, and Sunday from 1 to 5. Admission is $1 for adults, 50¢ for children 12 and under.

▪ Psychic Thomas Jeffrey, author of *Ghosts in the Valley* and *More Ghosts in the Valley* (among other works), leads lantern ghost walks on haunted streets and trips to historic cemeteries (bring pillows and blankets!) where you will hear eerie tales guaranteed to lift your spirits. Ghost walks begin Friday and Saturday nights at seven at the Cannon on Main Street. The cost is $3.50. The graveyard trips begin every Saturday at 9 P.M. The cost is $5. For details, contact

Ghost Tours, 912 Cherry Lane, Southampton, Pennsylvania 18966; phone: 355-7046.

▪ If you are antiquing on Route 202 between New Hope and Lahaska, stop in at **Bucks County Vineyards and Winery** (phone: 794-7449), three miles west of New Hope. Tours are free during the week, $1 on weekends, and include a glass on the house, from more than a dozen varieties. A local specialty is Pennsylvania Dutch Apple Wine. At least as interesting as the winery is the **Fashion Museum.** Vineyard president Arthur Gerold is also president of Brooks-Van Horn, America's largest theatrical costumers. Dorothy's costume in *The Wiz,* Marlon Brando's in *The Godfather,* Richard Burton's in *Camelot,* Gertrude Lawrence's in *The King and I,* Frank Langella's in *Dracula*—these are only some of the original costumes on display weekdays from 11 to 5, Saturdays from 10 to 6, and Sundays from 12 to 6.

▪ No visitor to New Hope should miss a fantasy trip through **H. & R. Sandor** (Route 202 and Reeder Mill Road; phone: 862-9181)— a 1745 house full of museum-quality antiques. Who hasn't toured through restored homes, wishing the furniture on the other side of the braided velvet rope were for sale? Well, here everything *is*—from a Hepplewhite mahogany sideboard, c. 1790, for $21,000, to a Sheraton curly maple and cherry stand for $1,815. Browsers are welcome.

▪ After a walk through town, take the **Coryell's Ferry** cruise (22 South Main Street; phone: 862-2050) on the Delaware.

▪ It's difficult to imagine a more beautiful drive than north from New Hope to Riegelsville, along the Delaware River and Canal. At Phillips Mill Road is **Lenteboden** (phone: 862-2033), where Charles Mueller grows some 1,300 varieties of tulips. The gardens are open from April 1 to May 25. Bulbs are for sale year-round, daily from 10 to 6. When you get tired of driving, park your car and go for a walk or picnic along the canal, or stop for lunch at **Black Bass Hotel** (Lumberville; phone: 297-5770), **Golden Pheasant Inn** (Erwinna; phone: 294-9595) or the **Riegelsville Hotel** (Riegelsville; phone: 749-2469). Antique stores line the route. At the Black Bass Hotel, take the foot bridge to **Bull's Island,** a nesting ground for yellow-throated warblers.

▪ **Fonthill Mansion** (Doylestown; phone: 348-9461) is the architectural conceit of Dr. Henry Chapman Mercer. Mercer built his 39-room concrete castle from 1908 to 1910 from "an interweaving of my own fancies blending with memories of my travels and suggestions from several engravings." The tiles that adorn every wall and niche were fabricated in the nearby **Moravian Pottery and Tile Works** (phone: 345-6722), which Mercer founded in 1898 and which is still in operation today. The tiles are based on Pennsylvania German, Anglo-Saxon, and Aztec motifs. A lawyer turned anthropologist, Mercer assembled a vast collection of 40,000 agricultural and craft implements, which are on display in the third of his freakish forms, the **Mercer Museum** (phone: 345-0210). All three buildings are open from March 1 to December 31. The **Tile Works Gift Shop** is also open in January and February. Fonthill and Mercer Museum each cost $3 for adults and $1.50 for students. Fonthill is open Tuesday through Sunday from 10 to 3:30. Guided tour reservations are often necessary. Mercer Museum is open Monday through Saturday from 10 to 4:30 and Sunday from 1 to 4:30. The Tile Works are open Wednesday through Sunday from 10 to 5. TO GET THERE: Take Route 202 to Route 313. Turn north (right) for less than one mile to Fonthill. The Tile Works are within walking distance. The museum is one-half-mile away.

5. THE ARTS

▪ In 1939 an old eighteenth-century grist mill was converted into one of the most famous summer stock theaters in the country. The **Bucks County Playhouse** (P.O. Box 313, New Hope; phone 862-2041) runs from May through early December. Recent productions included such classic Broadway musicals as *Guys and Dolls, Pippin,* and *Annie.* Matinees are on Wednesday, Thursday, and Sunday at 2. Evening performances are Wednesday through Friday at 8:30, Saturday at 5 and 9, and Sunday at 7:30.

▪ **Miryam's Farm** (take Route 32 north and at Point Pleasant take Tohickon Hill Road; phone: 766-8037) has open house the second Sunday each month. Jazz piano, harpsichord, recorders, and dulcimers are some of the instruments you can expect to hear, either indoors in winter or on the lawn in summer. The art exhibits and craft demonstrations here were written up in *Smithsonian* magazine. Admission is free.

▪ Couples or families who want to watch movies under the stars (*The Third Man, The Lavender Hill Mob,* etc.) can attend the summer film series outside the **Mercer Museum** (Doylestown, at Pine Street and Scout Way; phone: 345-0210). Admission to the Tuesday night 8:30 showings is $1 for adults, 50¢ for children.

▪ **Washington Crossing State Park,** on the New Jersey side (Route 32 south to Washington Crossing, and over the bridge to New Jersey; phone: 609/737-1826) has an open-air theater from late June through Labor Day, featuring classical music, light opera, musical comedies, and mime. Bring chairs, blankets, and picnics. Shows cost

$4 on Wednesday and Thursday, $5 on Friday and Saturday.

▪ **Town and Country Players** (The Barn, Route 263, Buckingham; phone: 348-7566) is a summer theater-in-the-round with local
and semiprofessional actors. TO GET THERE: Follow Route 202 toward Doylestown.

▪ **Twilight Festival** (Newtown; phone: 968-8181) is a series of
musical and theatrical events from June 4 to August 15 at the **Bucks
County Community College.** Music—classical, country and western, or jazz—is performed in an outdoor amphitheater on the campus
on Friday, Saturday, and Sunday evenings. Plays are usually mysteries or light comedies. TO GET THERE: Take 232 south to Route 413.
Turn left and follow Route 413 to Newtown.

▪ The **Mercer Theatre Series** (Carriage House Courtyard,
Fonthill, East Court Street, Doylestown; phone: 348-2788 or 297-
5053) offers everything from Shakespeare to light comedies. The
community group performs during the last two weeks in June.

▪ **The Barn at the Parry Mansion,** now called the **Golden Door
Gallery** (phone: 794-8143), is operated as a commercial art gallery.

▪ The **Phillips Mill Art Exhibition** (Route 32, north of New
Hope; phone: 862-9982) features the work of some 140 contemporary artists from late September to November 1, daily from 1 to 5.

▪ For information on upcoming art shows, contact the **Bucks
County Council on the Arts,** Neshaminy Manor Center, Route 611,
Doylestown 18901. Phone: 343-2800, ext. 351.

6. ANTIQUES AND CRAFTS

Don't be content to wander up and down Main Street. High
rents have chased many of the more interesting antique dealers onto
side streets and into the surrounding countryside. At least a half-
dozen shops line Route 32 north from New Hope to Point Pleasant.
The highest concentration of antique shops is on Route 202 between
New Hope and Lahaska.

▪ **H. & R. Sandor, Inc.** (Route 202 & Reeder Mill Road; phone
862-9181) is in a class by itself. (*See #4, What to See and Do* above
for details.)

▪ **Crown & Eagle Antiques** (phone: 794-7972; out-of-state,
800/523-6054) features American Indian art—rugs, basketry, and
beadwork. Located across from the Winery.

▪ **Lippincott Antiques** (phone: 794-8328) sells eighteenth- and
nineteenth-century furniture, both formal and country.

▪ **Joseph Stanley** (phone: 862-9300) features period English furniture.

• **Duck & Dolphin** (Routes 202 and 313, Doylestown; phone: 348-2887) features fine furniture, clocks, and accessories.

• **Peddler's Village** in Lahaska attempts to be a collection of quality antique stores. It is really a pseudo-antique development of novelty and collectible shops that are fun for browsing. (**The Arts Alliance of Bucks County** [phone: 794-8405] has its offices and gallery here.) An outdoor flea market sits across the street. **The Yard,** another complex across from Peddler's Village, houses an artists' cooperative called the **Upstairs Gallery** (phone: 794-8486). Ship models, pottery, silver jewelry, and watercolors are for sale.

Auctions are listed in local papers, including *The Jersey Devil* (P.O. Box 202, Lambertville, New Jersey 08530). **Brown Brothers** (Buckingham, near the intersection of Routes 202, 263, and 413; phone: 794-7630) holds auctions every Saturday.

Best bets in New Hope are:

• **The Pink House** (Bridge Street; phone: 862-5947) specializes in eighteenth- and nineteenth-century French and English porcelain, prints, furniture, Chinese export porcelain, and American quilts.

• **Besch's Clock Shop** (86 Ferry Street; phone: 862-9319), in a small, low-ceiling room, is straight out of Dickens. The grandfather clocks alone are worth a visit.

• **Katy Kane** (38 West Ferry Street; phone: 862-5873) has a wonderful collection of Victorian and Edwardian clothing for women. Also for sale are linens and quilts.

• **James Martin Gallery** (north end of Main Street; phone: 862-2459) is a real treat for anyone interested in museum-quality woodwork. These are not the super-glossy wood carvings that say "New England." The work here has an austere, almost Oriental simplicity to it.

• **George Nakashima** is the author of *The Soul of a Tree: A Woodworker's Reflections,* published by Kodansha International. His studio is open Saturday afternoons by appointment for those familiar with and seriously interested in his work (phone: 862-2272).

• Hidden behind Main Street is **Ney Alley,** where some seven craftspeople have their studios and galleries. What a shame that so few visitors know about this narrow lane! Nearby, at 13 West Mechanic Street (phone: 968-5539 or 862-2660) is **The Decoy Shoppe,** with old decoys, original watercolors, and books.

• Lists of local antique dealers, and maps of their locations, are available from the **Chamber of Commerce** *(see #22, For Further Information)* or from **Geraldine Lipman,** Corresponding Secretary,

Bucks County Antique Dealers Association, 5 Byron Lane, Yardley 19067. Phone: 295-6142.

▪ Best bet among shops on scenic Route 32, north of New Hope, is **Ronley at Limeport** (2½ miles north of New Hope; phone: 862-2427). In addition to selling eighteenth- and early nineteenth-century American and European antiques, the Ronleys make antique lamps for period rooms.

7. TOURS

▪ **Bucks County Tours** (4 East Mechanic Street, New Hope; phone: 862-5081) runs various group trips, including walking tours through the oldest sections of town, with visits to studios of local craftsmen; Delaware Canal rides in mule-drawn barges; dinner and theater tours; and six-hour bus rides through Bucks County.

▪ Self-guided tour maps of both New Hope and Bucks County are available from the **Bucks County Tourist Commission** *(see #22, For Further Information)* and the **Information Center** on the corner of Mechanic and Main Streets.

▪ The **Bucks County Carriage Company** (phone: 343-4252 or 862-3582) offers 15- and 30-minute horse and carriage rides, starting at the Logan Inn, from 8 A.M. to midnight. Rates are from $5 to $8.50.

8. WALKS

▪ Few walks are lovelier than along the towpath that follows the **Delaware Canal.** For more than a hundred years, from 1828 to 1931, the level, grassy path was a workday route for mule teams towing coal barges along the 60-mile canal. From Point Pleasant to Lumberville you can walk on an aqueduct and across the spectacular Tohickon River Gorge before it empties into the Delaware. Below Point Pleasant the narrow path straddles an embankment, with the canal, smooth as glass, on one side, and the wide, spirited Delaware River on the other. The path moves from lock to lock, under tiny wooden bridges and shade trees, with colonial houses visible in the distance. At the **Black Bass Inn** in Lumberville, cross the foot bridge to **Bull's Island.** This New Jersey state park provides nesting grounds for the cerulean and yellow-throated warblers. It's a lovely spot for picnics. You can join other visitors along the canal in New Hope, but if you want to be alone begin your walk a few miles north of town along Route 32.

▪ **Bowman's Hill Wildflower Preserve** (three miles south of New Hope, off Route 32; phone: 862-2924) is part of the Washington Crossing State Park. Trails run through 100 acres of trillium, Dutchman's-breeches, mountain laurel, the rare fuchsia-colored jeweled shooting star, and dozens of other flowers in bloom through the spring and summer. There's also a bog with bog flowers and unusual orchids. Admission is free.

▪ The walking tour book of New Hope, with locations of some of the 181 buildings built before 1876, is out of print; your hotel may have a copy for you to look at. *A Wayfarer's Guide to the Delaware*, a walking guide to the towpath, is on sale at **Farley Bookstore** (44 South Main Street; phone: 862-2452).

9. BIKING

▪ **Kiddle Cyclery** (Buckingham, Route 202 at the intersection with Route 413, about nine miles from New Hope; phone: 794-8958) has three-gear bikes to rent.

▪ The towpath along the **Delaware Canal** is ideal for biking. The unpaved path is best with bikes that have wide-tread tires.

▪ The 4560-acre **Nockamixon State Park** (40 minutes north of New Hope; phone: 538-2151) has bikes to rent.

10. BOATING AND FISHING

BOATING

A canoe or inner-tube trip down the **Delaware River** is an exhilarating experience, but don't expect much privacy on summer weekends. The largest outfitter, in Point Pleasant, handles more than 3,000 visitors a day! When the current slows, inner tubing can be excruciatingly slow; but when you're in no rush to get anywhere, nothing could be more therapeutic than submitting to the moods of the river and stopping at an island for lunch (which you can carry with you in waterproof bags). For a particularly smooth, safe trip—ideal for families with grandparents or small children—rent a 4 × 11-foot raft with an inflated floor. The outfitters will, for a fee, transport you upstream so that you can float or paddle back to the starting point. Stretches of white water are gentle enough for novices to negotiate. Canoeists may want to paddle one way in the virtually currentless canal and then return downstream along the river.

▪ Trips of almost any length and difficulty can be arranged through **Point Pleasant Canoe Rental,** which has bases in Point

Pleasant (Route 32, about eight miles north of New Hope; phone: 297-8400) and Riegelsville (Route 32, about 26 miles north of New Hope; phone: 749-2093). Make advance reservations. At **Ralph Stover State Park,** you'll pass beneath 200-foot cliffs and the meandering swell becomes a whitewater sensation. For the final 14 miles, the creek drops an average of 60 feet per mile, with constant rapids, rock ledges, and shelves. Children must be at least 10 years old and 42 inches tall.

▪ **Jim Abbott's Marina** (Route 29, New Jersey; phone: 609/737-3446) rents canoes, inner tubes, and pedal boats.

▪ **George's Canoe Rentals** (Route 532, Washington Crossing, six miles south of New Hope; phone: 493-2366) rents canoes and pedal boats for use on the canal. This location is convenient for visitors to the **Washington Crossing State Park.**

▪ **Nockamixon State Park** (about 40 minutes north of New Hope; phone: 538-2151) has a 1,040-acre lake with rowboats, canoes, sailboats, and pedal boats to rent. TO GET THERE: Take Route 202 to Route 313 to Route 563 north; or take the slower but more scenic route north on Route 32 to Route 611, south on Route 412 and north on Route 563.

FISHING

▪ The **Tohickon Creek** (Ralph Stover State Park, north on Route 32 to Point Pleasant; then left on Tohickon Hill Road; phone: 297-5090) is usually stocked with trout. Licenses, available at all sporting goods stores, are required for anyone over 16.

▪ **Nockamixon State Park** (Phone: 538-2151) has a lake with boats to rent for fishing (mostly muskies, walleyes, large-mouth bass, and pickerel).

11. SWIMMING

▪ Several motels and inns, including the **Hotel du Village** (phone: 862-5164) and the **1740 House** (phone: 297-5661) have swimming pools.

▪ **Tohickon Valley County Park** (Route 32 north to Point Pleasant, then left on Tohickon Hill Road, about 15 minutes from New Hope; phone: 757-0571) has a public swimming pool.

▪ **Nockamixon State Park** (40 minutes north of New Hope; phone: 538-2151) has a pool. The lake here is for boating and fishing only.

12. SKIING

▪ **Belle Mountain Public Ski Area** (cross to New Jersey, take Route 29 south five miles; phone: 609/397-0043) has a rope tow and a double-chair lift. Snow-making equipment is available if weather conditions allow their use.

13. RIDING

▪ **Haycock Stables** (about 40 minutes north of New Hope; phone: 257-6271) has horses for riding in the nearby **Nockamixon State Park.**

14. TENNIS

▪ **The Fountainhead** (near the intersection of Routes 202 and 179; phone: 862-2078) has courts and also a swimming pool.
▪ **Hotel du Village** (North River Road and Phillips Mill Road; phone: 862-5164) has courts for guests.
▪ The **New Hope-Solebury Public School** (off Route 202, New Hope) has courts.

15. GOLF

▪ **Bucks County Country Club** (Route 263, Jamison, about seven miles from New Hope; phone: 343-0350) has an 18-hole, par-71 course.
▪ **Warrington Country Club** (Route 611, Almshouse Road, Warrington, about six miles from New Hope; phone: 343-1630) has an 18-hole, par-70 course.

16. FOR KIDS

▪ Less than 30 minutes south of New Hope is **Sesame Place** (I-95 south to exit 25E; phone: 752-7070). This educational play park is geared for children ages 3 to 13, but anyone raised on "Sesame Street" will love the exhibits and games. In the computer game gallery, programmed by the Children's Television Workshop, the Muppets teach spelling, counting, and other basic skills. In a replica of the "Sesame Street" studio, children can watch themselves on closed circuit TV. Science exhibits teach about lightning and gravity. Grown-ups will be green with envy as their children swim through a pond with 60,000 green plastic balls. One activity may get children wet, so bring a change of clothing! Meals in the Food Factory are nutritional, and include all-beef hot dogs and pizza made with whole wheat dough. Admission is $8.80 for children, $6 for adults. Tokens—three for $1— may be purchased for the 60 computer games. The season runs from early April through October.

- **Bowman's Hill Wildflower Preserve** (three miles south of New Hope, off Route 32; phone: 862-2924) has special children's nature programs and family nature walks on Saturday mornings in the spring and summer. Parents can leave children during the program (*see #8, Walks* for details).

- The **New Hope Steam Railway** (phone: 862-5880) runs three one-hour round-trips on Sunday from New Hope to Lahaska (*see #4, What to See and Do* for details).

- Bike along the **tow path** (*see #9, Biking*).

- Take a canoe or inner-tube ride down the **Delaware River** (*see #10, Boating*).

17. DINING

- The **Inn at Phillips Mill** (Route 32, 1½ miles north of New Hope; phone: 862-9919 or 862-2984) serves excellent French food in an intimate, candle-lit setting. The only thing worse than not eating here is dining here alone! One of the dining rooms is in a glass-enclosed terra-cotta porch that reeks in summer of lilac. Another is on a brick terrace surrounded by gardens. A popular appetizer is seafood crepes—shrimps and scallops in a light wine cream sauce. Entrées range from $9.50 for the vegetarian platter to $15.50 for Dover sole amandine. Another favorite is steak au poivre—filet mignon served with brandy and peppercorns in a cream and mushroom sauce. Try the strawberries and whipped cream pastry for dessert. Dress is optional. Reservations are recommended. No credit cards are accepted. Bring your own wine.

- **La Bonne Auberge** (Village #2, New Hope; phone: 862-2462) is not as intimate as the Inn at Phillips Mill, but enjoys a reputation as the finest, and also most expensive, restaurant in town. The farmland that once surrounded the 1780 building has been paved over and turned into a townhouse complex, which is disconcerting until you're safely inside. Dining is in two rooms—in the original building, complete with fireplace; and in the newer garden room built with cedar, with plenty of plants and open space. Popular appetizers are watercress soup and brioche of lobster. Entrées, ranging in price from $15 to $22, include roast rack of lamb with Provençale herbs, garlic, and bread crumbs; and Dover sole filled with salmon mousse and served with a lobster sauce. The Concord Cake—it goes as fast as the plane—consists of a layer of meringue filled with chocolate mousse and topped with shavings of Swiss chocolate. Ties are requested but not required. Reservations are advised. American Express is accepted. TO GET THERE: Follow Mechanic Street. Turn left into Village #2A, a townhouse complex.

▪ **Mothers** (34 North Main Street; phone: 862-9354) is ideal for breakfast, lunch, or for a light dinner. The **Playhouse** is only a short walk away. This is also a perfect spot for picnic supplies. Dinner is first-rate, but some may find it a shame to eat on the main street of town when there are so many old inns nearby. The serious breakfast menu includes poached eggs on a fried fillet of fish with lemon and caper sauce, and creamed mushrooms sherried with bacon on pumpernickel. The young owners here are very up on latest trends in food and enjoy combining ingredients in imaginative ways. Dinner entrées, ranging in price from $9.50 to $15.50, include duck with duck paté and black raspberry sauce; chicken and pistachios in a plum sauce; and veal sauteed with artichokes, pimentos, olives, and spinach. What Mothers is most famous for are its sinful desserts. The German chocolate torte (four layers of chocolate mocha sponge cake filled with coconut, and covered with pecan frosting and chocolate glaze) is one of the more modest ones. Expect to wait 15 to 30 minutes for breakfast or lunch. Reservations are accepted only for dinner, and are recommended before theater. Dress is casual. All major credit cards are accepted.

▪ Locals give the **Black Bass Hotel** (Route 32, Lumberville, seven miles north of New Hope; phone: 297-5770) mixed reviews from adequate to excellent. But everyone agrees that the setting—on the outdoor terrace overlooking the canal—is one of the most idyllic in the country. The hotel, a treasure house of English and American antiques, is worth a visit in itself. Lunch here is a good bet for visitors enjoying the beautiful drive north along the canal from New Hope to Riegelsville. Lunches cost from $5 to $9. Dinners range from $11 to $17. Favorites are Charleston Meeting Street crabmeat—lumps of back fin crabmeat in a white wine sauce, topped with Gruyère and Parmesan cheese; and New England Lobster Pie, a casserole dish with chunks of lobster in a sherried cream sauce, topped with Gruyère and Parmesan. For dessert, try the hot, deep-dish apple pie. Jackets are optional. Reservations are advised. All major credit cards are accepted.

▪ **Hotel du Village** (Phillips Mill Road, a left turn off Route 32, one mile north of New Hope; phone: 862-9911 or 862-5164) is run

by Omar Arbani, who made his reputation as the former chef at the
Inn at Phillips Mill. The turn-of-the-century country estate was once
a private girl's school, and then part of the lower campus of the
Solebury School, until Arbani purchased the property in 1976. The
large main dining room has beamed ceilings and huge fireplaces at
either end. A popular appetizer is fried mushrooms with remoulade
sauce. Entrées on the French menu range from $10 to $14 and include
tournedos of beef wrapped in bacon and topped with paté, civet
villageois (rabbit in a pastry crust), and sweetbreads with a madeira
and cream sauce. The tray of homemade French pastries includes
Napoleons and a Black Forest cake made with kirsch.

   ▪ Visitors who plan an early evening drive north along the canal
can stop for dinner at the **Golden Pheasant Inn** (Erwinna, 17 miles
north of New Hope; phone: 294-9595). Dining is in a plant-filled
greenhouse or in the dark, intimate taproom, with velvet loveseats
and Tiffany-style lamps. Entrées on the continental menu range in
price from $12.50 to $21. A regular favorite is bouillabaisse. Specialties, which change weekly, include charcoal-broiled venison steak,
pheasant, curried chicken, and sautéed sea trout. Dress is casual.
Reservations are advised. All major credit cards are accepted.

   ▪ Two other restaurants worth trying are the **Towpath House**
(18–20 Mechanic Street; phone: 862-5216), with tables overlooking
the canal; and the historic **Logan Inn** (Main Street; phone 862-5134).

18. AFTER HOURS

   ▪ After their performances, the actors at the **Bucks County
Playhouse** usually gather at the **Logan Inn** (Main Street; phone: 862-
5134). This 1727 inn, the oldest building in town, has a greenhouse/
dining room where it is always summer, and where jazz is often
played and sung after dark.

   ▪ **Chez Odette** (South River Road, New Hope; phone: 862-
2432 or 862-2773) features a jazz trio on summer weekends.

   ▪ Couples will want to listen to some serious jazz at the **Canal
House** (30 West Mechanic Street; phone: 862-2069). A more romantic setting—a candlelit table overlooking the canal—would be hard to
find.

   ▪ A younger crowd gathers at **John and Peter's Place** (96 South
Main Street; phone: 862-5981), which features first-rate rhythm and
blues groups, new wave, rock, and jazz. Down the street is the
Havana Bar and Restaurant (105 South Main Street; phone: 862-
9897). For dancing, try **Zadar's** (50 South Main Street; phone: 862-
5237) or **The Yellow Brick Toad** (Route 179 north, Lambertville,
New Jersey; phone: 397-3100).

19. LODGING

▪ Rumor has it that Richard Rodgers had the **Inn at Phillips Mill** (Route 32, 1½ miles north of New Hope; phone: 862-2984) in mind when he wrote "A Small Hotel." True or not, the eighteenth-century inn is a place for lovers—one of the most romantic spots in the country. The five small rooms are decorated with Pierre Deux and tattersall fabrics, and quilt-covered four-poster or brass beds. In the room under the eaves—the one with tiny print wallpaper—you can imagine some sixteen-year-old Jane Austen sprawled across the bed on a gloomy afternoon, writing in her diary. Guests are provided with bedside candles and Godiva chocolates. Place your breakfast request outside your door and awaken to the smell of coffee in stoneware cups and warm rolls wrapped in country French blue linen. Doubles are $55, with private bath. No credit cards are accepted.

▪ **Tattersall** (Cafferty Road, Point Pleasant, 9 miles north of New Hope on Route 32; phone: 862-2984) is a beautiful old plastered fieldstone country house with an upstairs veranda for reading on a lazy summer afternoon. The owners also run the Inn at Phillips Mill. Doubles are $60, including continental breakfast. No credit cards are accepted.

▪ **Black Bass Hotel** (Route 32, Lumberville, seven miles north of New Hope; phone: 297-5770) is beautifully situated along the canal. Rooms are filled with serious eighteenth- and nineteenth-century American and English antiques. Visiting here is a bit like sleeping in a museum—as if your guide had unhooked the rope in front of a room and invited you to spend the night. The hotel began as a haven for river travelers in the 1740s. Bargemen made lively use of the tavern in the late nineteenth and early twentieth centuries. The innkeepers were loyal to the Crown during the Revolution. Today's owner is infatuated with English memorabilia, including life-size portraits of George II, William III, and Queen Victoria. The main lounge has a pewter bar reputedly from Maxim's in Paris. The seven rooms share two baths. Doubles are $60, suites $110 including continental breakfast. All major credit cards are accepted.

▪ The **Logan Inn** (Main Street, New Hope; phone: 862-5134) is perfect for visitors who want to stay in town, within walking distance of the Playhouse and most of the shops, or for those who love the extravagances of Victoriana. Owner and village mayor Carl Lutz is unabashedly in love with anything antique, from tankards and armoires to old clocks, marble-topped dressers, and pewter bottles. Hanging in the wainscoted taproom is a portrait of Prince Albert, painted before Victoria fell in love with him. The crimson-flocked Victorian room is direct from the pages of a French memoir. Established in 1727, the Logan Inn is the oldest building in town. It is called the Logan Inn because Chief Wingohocking of the Lenni-Lenape Indians developed a rapport with James Logan, a secretary to William Penn, and traded names with the white man. Washington and his generals met here while planning their Trenton campaign. In the 1930s it became the off-Broadway headquarters for the Algonquin Roundtable crowd—Richard Rodgers, Dorothy Parker, Helen Hayes, Moss Hart, and others. Doubles are $50 with shared bath, $60 with private bath. Visa and Mastercard are accepted.

- **Riegelsville Hotel** (Riegelsville, 29 miles north of New Hope; phone: 749-2469) will be too far north of New Hope for most visitors. Rooms also lack the elegance and comfort of other inns. What it does offer, however, are reasonable prices and an ambiance that honestly captures the feeling of nineteenth-century boarding-houses along the canal. This is the real thing—not a city man's idea of what an inn should be. Doubles, some with private baths, range from $40 to $65. All major credit cards are accepted. TO GET THERE from New Hope: Take Route 32 north to Route 611. Follow Route 611 for four miles, then turn right at the traffic light in Riegelsville.

- **The 1740 House** (Route 32, Lumberville, 6½ miles north of New Hope; phone: 297-5661) is beautifully situated at the edge of the canal. Rooms are clean and comfortable, but the name "1740 House" is misleading; most rooms have been added on by the present owner, Harry Nessler. When I met him he was smarting from a review that described his place as "motel-modern." The reviewer was unfair—the rooms have more character and charm than that—but an old inn it is not. Facilities include a swimming pool and canoes. Doubles range from $55 to $61, including a buffet breakfast. No credit cards are accepted.

- **The Hotel du Village** (corner of North River Road and Phillips Mill Road, New Hope; phone: 862-9911/5164) has 19 rooms, two tennis courts and a pool. Doubles, all with bath, cost $50 to $65, including continental breakfast.

20. EMERGENCIES

- The closest ambulance rescue squad is in Lambertville, New Jersey, directly across the river from New Hope (phone: 609/397-3131). You can also call the **Bucks County Fire and Ambulance Radio Emergency** (phone: 547-5222). The nearest hospital is **St. Mary Hospital** (Langhorne; phone: 750-2000).

21. HOW TO GET THERE

BY CAR. *From New York:* south on the New Jersey Turnpike to exit 10. Then north on U.S. 287 for about 15 miles to another exit 10. Go west on Route 22 for 3½ miles and then turn right at the sign marked Flemington-Princeton, Route 202 south. Follow Route 202 south for about 25 miles and cross the Delaware River. Take Route 32 south to New Hope. *From Philadelphia:* take I-95 north to New Hope Yardley exit. Turn north on Route 32 to New Hope.

BY BUS. *From New York:* West Hunterdon Transit (phone: 201/782-6313) has service from Port Authority to the Holiday Inn in New Hope. The trip takes about 2 hours and 10 minutes. Greyhound (212/635-0800) has a 3½-hour bus trip to Doylestown, with a stopover in Philadelphia. Doylestown is a 10-mile taxi ride from New Hope. *From Philadelphia:* Septa Bus Lines (215/574-7800), Bus #55, takes one hour to Doylestown, which is a 10-mile taxi ride from New Hope. Greyhound (215/568-4800) has a 1½-hour trip to Doylestown. *From Washington:* Greyhound (202/565-2662) has a 4½-hour trip to Doylestown, with a stopover in Philadelphia.

22. FOR FURTHER INFORMATION

▪ For general information contact the **Bucks County Tourist Commission,** 152 Swamp Road, Doylestown 18901; phone: 215/345-4552. Brochures available on request include a calendar of events, driving tours, covered bridges, campgrounds, museums, parks, shopping, and dining.

▪ **New Hope Chamber of Commerce,** New Hope 18938. Phone: 862-5880. The Chamber runs an **Information Center** on the corner of Mechanic and Main Streets near the center of New Hope.

23. RECOMMENDED READING

▪ The *Area Guide Book* ($1.50) is available in local bookstores and at the **Information Center** at the corner of Mechanic and Main Streets.

▪ Ann Hawkes Hutton's *George Washington Crossed Here* should be required reading for visitors to the state park. It's for sale in the gift shop in the Memorial Building on the southern grounds.

▪ **Farley Bookstore** (44 South Main Street; phone: 862-2452) has some historical books on the county, and a walking guide to the towpath.

The Poconos, Pennsylvania

(Area Code, 717; Zip Code, 18360 [Stroudsburg], 18325 [Canadensis])

1. DISTANCES

BY CAR. *From New York*, 2 hours; *from Philadelphia*, 2½ hours; *from Baltimore*, 4½ hours.

BY BUS. *From New York*, 2 to 3 hours by Greyhound or 1 hour 40 minutes by Martz Trailways; *from Philadelphia*, 3 hours.

2. MAJOR ATTRACTIONS

- Resorts and country inns set among wooded uplands, lakes, waterfalls, and streams.
- A wealth of outdoor activities, including downhill and cross-country skiing, riding, tennis, fishing, hiking, swimming, and golf.
- Cool, dry air, even in midsummer.

3. INTRODUCTION

Drive west from New York on I-80 and all signs will point to the Delaware Water Gap, as if friends had marked the route for you. The Gap—where the river breaks through the mountains—has been the gateway to the Poconos since the arrival of the first Indian settlers. The word *Pocono* in fact cames from the Indian word *Pocohanne*, meaning "a stream between mountains."

Across the Gap, you can enter a never-never land of heartshaped bathtubs and mirrored bedroom ceilings that promoters package as the Honeymoon Capital of the World. Or you can head for the quiet beauty of the Central Poconos, in and around the town of Canadensis. Inns and resorts here cater to people who love the outdoors and are happy slowing down to the pace of the seasons. It is a clean, wholesome, daytime world, where you will see nothing more lascivious than a rhododendron leaf uncurling in the morning sun, or a robin nudging up against some mountain laurel.

So that you will not spend your weekend licking wounded expectations, bear in mind that the Poconos are rounded hills rather than mountains, with none of the stark grandeur or majesty of the Catskills or the White Mountains. Because the area was mercilessly timbered in the nineteenth century, the landscape today often has a scrawny, scrub-pine feel about it, as though you were driving through overgrown meadows.

There are some remaining stands of virgin timber, however, if you care to look for them. There are waterfalls, streams rushing through gorges, and more lakes than anywhere else in Pennsylvania. Because much of the Poconos are on a 1,500- to 2,000-foot plateau, the air is dry and cool, and you can sleep under blankets in late July when New Yorkers two hours away are sweltering in 90-degree heat.

The area, bordered roughly by the Delaware river on the east and the Lehigh River on the west, was originally covered with magnificent forests of hardwoods and evergreens—oaks, maples, chestnuts, hemlocks, and spruce up to five feet thick and a hundred feet high. Lumbering began in the 1820s when oak was cut for barrels and floated down the Delaware. After the Civil War forests began to disappear as land was cleared for farms. The town of Canadensis was named for the hemlock tree, *Tsuga canadensis*, which furnished bark for the tanning of shoe leather, the economic lifeblood of the region.

By 1900 the virgin forests were gone, and so were the lumbering and tanning industries on which the economy of the area depended. Where soil was deep and fertile, farming continued, but on stony hillsides time and nature won their battle against the farmers, and

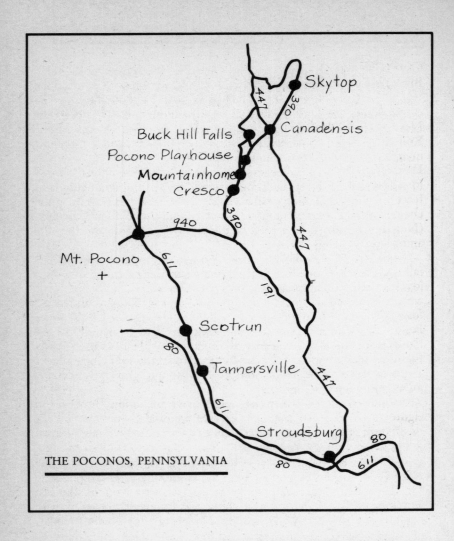

THE POCONOS, PENNSYLVANIA

land reverted to its natural state. Because of the comfortable climate, the economy survived on tourism, particularly for sportsmen; and it is the lure of the outdoors that attracts visitors to the central Poconos today.

4. WHAT TO SEE AND DO

▪ Both Skytop Lodge and Buck Hill Inn have so many activities (all listed in sections 5 to 17 below), that it seems a shame to leave the grounds except for evening trips to the Pocono Playhouse. The

Overlook Inn and other resorts in the Canadensis area have access to Buck Hill Inn facilities.

Other excursions and diversions include:

▪ A triangular drive from Canadensis northwest on Route 447 to Newfoundland; south on Route 191 to Mountainhome, and east on Route 390 back to Canadensis. Scenically, the trip is not particularly memorable, but the route includes a dozen antique stores; **Geo'Lou Farmer's Market** (Route 507, outside of Newfoundland); **Pocono Playhouse; Callie's Candy Kitchen** (Route 390, Mountainhome), featuring chocolate-covered everything, from strawberries to cream cheese, potato chips, and jelly beans; and **Earhardt General Store** (Newfoundland), where kids should be set loose with quarters among the penny candies.

▪ A drive through the farmland of **Cherry Valley**, particularly in fall, past some attractive eighteenth-century stone farmhouses and a lovely white church at the western end of the valley. From the Delaware Water Gap, drive southwest to Bossardsville, make a right at the fork at 1.2 miles to Hamilton Square and continue to Snydersville. Follow Route 209 back to Stroudsburg. The trip can include a stop at Collector's Cove *(see #6, Antiques and Crafts)* and the Quiet Valley Farm Museum.

▪ **The Quiet Valley Farm Museum** (off Bus. Route 209, 3½ miles south of Stroudsburg; phone: 992-6161) is on the National Register of Historic Places. It includes an authentic collection of eighteenth- and nineteenth-century Pennsylvania German buildings, where you can watch families pursuing such early American activities as meat-smoking and soap- and broom-making. Open June 20 to Labor Day. **Harvest Festival** takes place the second weekend in October.

▪ **Birchwood Pocono Air-Park** (East Stroudsburg; phone: 629-0222) offers 15-minute glider flights, with instruction. A small plane tows your glider up to 1,500 feet and releases you and your pilot on currents of air.

▪ The 2,131-foot **Camelback Mountain** (Big Pocono State Park; phone: 629-1661) has a road and chair lift to the summit, for impressive views of the surrounding countryside. The chair lift doesn't take passengers down, however. In winter, you must ski. Other times, either drive, walk, ski on grass, or ride the 3,200-foot Alpine slide. A book of five tickets costs $14 for adults, $12 for children under 12.

5. THE ARTS

▪ **Pocono Playhouse** (Route 390, Mountainhome; phone: 595-

7456) is summer theater at its best, with such recent productions as *Guys and Dolls* with Joey Travolta. Open late May to mid-October, and mid-December to mid-January. Tickets cost $12 to $16.

6. ANTIQUES AND CRAFTS

All of the following, except Collector's Cove, lie along the triangular Canadensis-Newfoundland-Mountainhome route listed above *(see #4, What to See and Do)*. My own favorite was Challenge Acres Antiques.

▪ **Collector's Cove** (Route 33, Scotia, eight miles south of Stroudsburg; phone: weekdays 421-7439, Sundays 992-9161) has more than 100 dealers. Auctions are held the fourth Sunday of every month. Open Sunday only from 9 to 5.

▪ **Peddlers Cove** (South Sterling, corner of Routes 507 and 191; phone: 676-3186) has nine dealers. Open May to October on weekends only from 10 to 6.

▪ **Carl Rose Auctions** (Route 507, Greentown, near Newfoundland; phone: 676-3356) has auctions once or twice monthly, usually on Saturday nights from May to October.

▪ **The Chimes** (Route 447, Newfoundland; phone: 676-3476) sells early tools, coins, antique clothing, and handmade Moravian quilts.

▪ **Challenge Acres Antiques** (Route 390 near the Route 191 intersection, Mountainhome; phone: 595-7755) sells nineteenth-century furnishings.

▪ **Marli's Arts & Antiques** (Route 447, next to the Methodist Church, Canadensis; phone: 595-2621) sells early country furniture, prints, clocks, glass, silver, and jewelry.

8. WALKS

▪ For picnics with panache, pick up some imported cheeses and gourmet snacks at **Curds & Whey** (Route 390, Mountainhome; phone: 595-3721).

▪ At **Buck Hill Falls** (Buck Hill Falls, Route 390; phone: 595-7441) the waters of the Buck Hill Creek fall through a primitive ravine with giant hemlocks, tulip trees, and stands of rhododendron. This is the best bet for people who want to "do" a spectacular falls with a minimum of legwork. Crowds are thinner than at Bushkill Falls. The more ambitious will want to walk to the top of the upper falls, or follow one of several lovely wooded trails, including a self-guided nature walk through the remnant of a primeval forest in Jenkins Wood. The property belongs to Buck Hill Inn. Parking for nonguests costs $1.

▪ **Bushkill Falls** (Route 209, Bushkill; phone: 588-6682) is the highest falls in the Poconos and also the most crowded and expensive, with access through private property. Open April through mid-November. Admission is $3 for adults, $1 for children under 12.

▪ **George W. Childs State Park** (two miles west of Dingmans Ferry) is ideal for those who are willing to walk for their waterfalls, and who object to paying for a beautiful view. This 154-acre rocky glen has three waterfalls that change Dingmans Creek to white foam. The two-mile trail takes you down one side of the gorge, past virgin white pine and hemlock, and up the other.

▪ For a spectacular view of the **Delaware Water Gap,** take the side road from the town of Delaware Water Gap (Route 611) to Lake Lenape. Park and follow the relatively easy 30- to 45-minute path to the Appalachian Trail on top of the ridge.

▪ The **Cranberry Bog in Tannersville** is a rare boreal heath bog—the southernmost on the east coast. Tours are arranged through the **Meesing Nature Center** (phone: 992-7334).

▪ **Tarkill Forest Demonstration Area** (Route 402; phone: 424-3001) has two self-guided nature trails where you can try to name the 41 trees marked by numerals. Answers are in a pamphlet available at the registration box. Take Route 209 from Stroudsburg to Marshall's Creek, then drive 18 miles north on Route 402.

▪ **Bruce Lake Natural Area** (off Route 309, adjoining Promised Land State Park; phone: 676-3428) is a 2,300-acre park. There are no roads or public facilities, but a three-mile walk, past Venus's-flytraps and pitcher plants, will bring you to a sparkling blue 48-acre glacial lake where you can fish for pickerel and bass. The Bear Wallow and Klein Trails lead to some of the few great remaining virgin trees in the area.

9. BIKING

▪ Almost all inns and hotels in the Canadensis area have bikes for guests to borrow or rent. The **Buck Hill Inn** (phone: 595-7441) may rent bikes to visitors after guests are taken care of. Phone first.

10. BOATING AND FISHING

FISHING. Fishing is a serious sport in the Poconos; someone at your hotel will know the best streams or lakes in the area. Both **Skytop Lodge** and **Buck Hill Inn** have their own stocked streams. **Promised**

Land State Park (phone: 676-3426) and **Tobyhanna State Park** (phone: 894-8671) rent boats to fishermen. **Peck's Pond Store** (Route 402) rents boats on Peck's Pond—the largest state forest lake in Pennsylvania. For fishing licenses, fly rod rentals, and hints on the best fishing holes, contact Tim Revell at Daniel's Resort (Canadensis; phone, 595-7531).

BOATING. The Poconos are bordered on the west by the Lehigh River and on the east by the Delaware River. The Lehigh River Gorge offers one of the most exciting and dramatic white-water raft trips in the east. The Delaware from Dingmans Ferry to the Delaware Water Gap offers a series of tame but lovely canoe trips for families or for those who have never gotten their paddles wet. Both Lehigh and Delaware River trips can fit into a single day of a two-day weekend in the central Poconos.

Trips on the Lehigh River run from about July 1 to mid-September, and are organized by:

- **Whitewater Rafting Adventure, Inc.** (Albrightsville; phone: 722-0285).
- **Whitewater Challengers** (White Haven, 443-9532).
- **Pocono Whitewater Rafting Adventure Center** (Jim Thorpe; phone: 325-4097 or 201/774-6975).

The Delaware is a scenic and majestic river, but avoid it on summer weekends if you cherish solitude. If you must go then, set out early in the morning, no later than 8 A.M., and return home by noon. Rental costs vary, particularly for transporting canoes, so compare prices.

For general information on Delaware canoe trips, contact the **Kittatinny Point Information Service** (Recreation Information Center, off I-80, the last exit in New Jersey; phone: 201/496-4458). The park service here runs free guided trips, including swimming, lunch stops, and canoeing instruction, daily from July 1 to Labor Day. Reservations are required. The most popular canoe trips and rental outfits are:

- From Dingmans Falls to Bushkill is a 4½-hour, 10-mile trip. Canoes are available from **Kittatinny Canoes** (at toll bridge, Route 209, Dingmans Ferry; phone: 828-2700 or 828-2338) and **Tri-State Canoe & Boat Rentals** (Route 209, Dingmans Ferry; phone: 828-2510).
- From Bushkill to Smithfield Beach, 9½ miles, about 4½ hours. This is the most challenging paddle, but no problem for anyone who has been in a canoe before. Canoes available from **Point Pleasant**

Canoe Outfitters (Route 209, Bushkill; phone: 588-6776) and
Chamberlain's Canoes (River Road, Smithfield Beach; phone: 421-
0180).

▪ From Smithfield Beach to Delaware Water Gap is a 3-hour,
6½-mile paddle. This is the easiest and shortest trip. Canoes are
available from **Chamberlain's Canoes** (River Road, Smithfield
Beach; phone: 421-0180), **Pack Shack** (Delaware Water Gap; phone:
424-8533), and **Water Gap Canoes** (Delaware Water Gap; phone:
424-5566).

11. SWIMMING

▪ All resorts and inns *(see #19, Lodging)* have their own swimming pools and/or lakes. The swimming pool is sometimes open to
nonguests at **Buck Hill Inn** (phone: 595-7441).

12. SKIING

▪ For cross-country ski rentals and information on trails in the
Canadensis area, contact the **Pocono Sport Shop** (Route 390, Mountainhome; phone: 595-7429).

There are 15 ski areas in the Poconos, all described in the "Ski
the Poconos" guide available from the **Pocono Mountains Vacation
Bureau** (1004 Main St., Stroudsburg; phone: 421-5791). The smaller
ski areas, ideal for children or beginners, are:

▪ **Buck Hill Inn** (Buck Hill Falls; phone: 595-7441) has two
poma lifts and two trails.

▪ **Tanglewood** (Lake Wallenpaupack; phone: 226-9500) has one
double-chair and two T-bar lifts leading to seven trails.

Larger areas, all within about 30 minutes of Canadensis, include:

▪ **Camelback** (Tannersville; phone: 629-1661) has eight chair
lifts and two T-bars leading to 22 slopes.

▪ **Jack Frost Mountain** (White Haven; phone: 443-8425) has six
chair lifts leading to 13 trails.

▪ **Big Boulder** (Lake Harmony; phone: 722-0101) has six
double-chair lifts leading to 11 trails.

13. RIDING

▪ **Buck Hill Inn** (phone: 595-7441) has 20 miles of riding trails
open to nonguests.

- **Carson's Riding Academy** (one mile south of Mt. Pocono on route 611; phone: 839-9841) has 50 acres of trails for beginning and advanced riders.
- **Double 'W' Farm Resort & Riding Stable** (Honesdale, four miles from Hawley Post Office, north of Lake Wallenpaupack; phone: 226-3118) has guided tours.
- **EL-J Riding Stable** (Cresco; phone: 839-8725).

14. TENNIS

- **Buck Hill Inn** (phone: 595-7441) has 14 courts open to nonguests.

15. GOLF

There are 11 golf courses in the Poconos. Those closest to Canadensis are:

- **Skytop Club** (Skytop; phone: 595-7401) lets nonguests play if they call ahead and space is available.
- **Buck Hill Inn** (Buck Hill Falls; phone: 595-7441) has 27 holes of golf.
- **Mount Airy Golf Course** (Mt. Pocono; phone: 839-8811).
- **Evergreen Park Golf Course** (Analmink; phone: 421-7721).
- **Pocono Manor Inn & Golf Course** (Pocono Manor; phone: 839-7111).
- **Pine Hollow Golf Course** (Routes 390 and 447, Canadensis; phone: 595-2198).

16. FOR KIDS

- **The Overlook Inn** *(see #19, Lodging)* does not accept children under 12. They—and therefore their parents—would probably be happier at Skytop Lodge or Buck Hill Inn, both of which offer complete children's programs.
- See entries under *#4, What to See and Do* for glider flights, Camelback Mountain Alpine Slide, Earhardt General Store, and Quiet Valley Farm Museum.
- See entries under *#8, Walks; #9, Biking; #10, Boating and Fishing; #11, Swimming; #12, Skiing; # 13, Riding;* and *#14, Tennis.*

17. DINING

- **Skytop Lodge** (Skytop, phone: 595-7401) is perfect for non-guests who want an excuse to wander through one of the most exclusive, grand old hotels still functioning in the northeast. Call at least a day ahead to find out if the maitre d' is accepting outside reservations. Dinner, with a choice of four or five entrées, comes at a fixed price of $16.50. Ties and jackets are required. Visa and Mastercard are accepted.

- **Overlook Inn** (Canadensis, *see #19, Lodging* for directions; phone: 595-7519) has excellent food. Entrées range from $10.50 to $16.50. The medallions of steak will convince you that beef can be as subtle as veal or lamb, if properly prepared. Another good choice is butterfly shrimp served with chow mein noodles layered with Alaska king crab meat and topped with a light lemon sauce. Dessert? Try the homemade black cherry tarts with fresh whipped cream or the white chocolate mousse. Jackets and reservations are requested. All major credit cards are accepted.

- The 1844 **Pump House Inn** (Canadensis, see *#19, Lodging* for directions; phone: 595-7501) is considered one of the oldest and one of the finest restaurants in the Pocono region. The three small dining rooms—the largest has 8 tables—have pewter plates, captain's chairs, botanical prints, and a shellacked dark wood ambience. Some will find the rock waterfall hokey—others, quaint. For a starter try Swiss potato soup with Gruyère, or shrimps in beer batter. Specialties include rack of lamb roasted with Dijon mustard and sautéed bay scallops with wine and mushrooms. Entrées range from $12 to $22. Jackets and reservations are requested. All major credit cards are accepted.

18. AFTER HOURS

- Most nightlife around Canadensis belongs to the cicadas and crickets. There is live music and dancing on weekends at the **Four Crown Lounge** at Buck Hill Inn (Phone 595-7441). No rock groups or disco music, however, so crowds tend to be over 30.

19. LODGING

Decide first whether you prefer the intimacy of a small inn such as the Overlook, or the services and activities of a large, impersonal resort such as Skytop or Buck Hill. Resorts may be preferable for children, yet anyone staying in the Canadensis area can, for a fee, make use of Buck Hill's facilities.

Any of the places listed below is suitable for a night's stay. Top choices are Skytop Lodge and Overlook Inn.

▪ **Overlook Inn** (Dutch Hill Road, Canadensis; phone: 595-7519) is a turn-of-the-century inn that once overlooked the Delaware Water Gap, but is now closed in by stands of hemlock and white pine. The 1,800-foot elevation makes for blanket-cool nights, even in late July. Rooms are modestly but warmly decorated with gingham curtains, chenille spreads, and old books. The lounge, with its half-finished puzzles, Scrabble boards, and worn oriental rugs, is a place to make new friends, including owners Bob and Lolly Tupper, who are quick to establish first-name relationships with their guests. The food is superb, served in an intimate, candle-lit dining room. Could there be a better sendoff than a breakfast of apple pancakes graced with a sprig of parsley, pear slices, and grapes? TO GET THERE: Take Exit 52 of I-80 to Route 447 north. Drive 18 miles to Canadensis. One-quarter mile past the traffic light, after a small steel bridge, turn right for 1½ miles to the inn's driveway. Rooms with private bath are $56 per person, including breakfast and dinner. All credit cards are accepted.

▪ The 5,500-acre **Skytop Lodge** (Skytop; phone 595-7401) was a private club until a decade ago. One senses that it opened its doors to outsiders only under financial duress, for it still prides itself on maintaining a sense of privacy and class. How could the world of Kozy Kabins and heart-shaped beds be only miles away? Some may find the atmosphere too formal; but others will succumb to its campy charm and allow themselves to be pampered.

On summer afternoons violinists play in a 110-foot pine-paneled hall, under the unblinking gaze of George Washington and an assortment of mounted deer heads and fish. Matriarchal ladies shuffle by in thick tweed suits. Men in checkered pants drive by in golf carts, under the shadow of the American flag. "Loafing," says the club information booklet, "is an important part of your vacation. In a Skytop chair, with a book or your knitting, you may soon be fast asleep under the kindly rays of the mountain sun."

For those who prefer a more active weekend, the alternatives are staggering. The 6,400-yard golf course has gradations of no more than 84 feet over 18 holes. There's pickerel and bass fishing in the upper lake, and swimming along a white sandy beach at the lower lake. Facilities include a children's camp, archery, tennis courts, an indoor/outdoor pool, an ice-skating rink, ski lifts, and miles of cross-country trails. One scheduled activity is deer spotting at dusk;

another, nighttime sledding—"old-fashioned belly-whopping" on Boathouse Hill.

Says a sign in the main lobby: "Until 6:30, throughout the lodge and about the grounds, tennis clothes, Bermuda shorts, tailored slacks and buttoned sport shirts with shirt tails tucked in plus other modest sports attire may be worn. For gentlemen in the evening, coats and ties are required. Short shorts, abbreviated costumes or extreme faddish attire is considered objectionable. Dinner is over at 8." TO GET THERE: Take Exit 52 off I-80 to Route 447 north. Drive 18 miles to Canadensis and continue north on Route 390 to Skytop. Doubles are $154 and $185, including three meals. Visa and Mastercard are accepted.

▪ **Buck Hill Inn** (Buck Hill; phone: 595-7441, Philadelphia area, 215/563-7664, New York area, 800/233-8113) and the Skytop Lodge dominate hilltops across the valley of the Brodhead, like two wealthy dowagers. Skytop sits on 5,500 acres, Buck Hill on 5,700. The latter was built at the turn of the century as a Quaker retreat. The 240-room stone fortress was falling into serious disrepair when Astrid and Jack Keuler took over on April Fool's Day in 1981, determined to turn the place around. "We're going into a new image," I was told. "Before we were called 'the romantic destination.' Now we're catering to an older crowd—the corporate family."

At last look, Buck Hill Inn was an Everyman's Skytop. Facility-wise, it probably leads the pack, with ski lifts, indoor and outdoor pools, a 27-hole championship golf course, stables, 20 miles of riding trails, a children's camp, and the finest lawn bowling courts in the east. A social staff of ten organize such activities as kite flying, darts, and professionally guided fish tours on private streams. TO GET THERE: Take Exit 52 of I-80 to Route 447 north. Drive 18 miles to Canadensis, then turn left (south) on Route 191. Rooms are $74 to $109 per person, including two meals. All major credit cards are accepted.

▪ **Sterling Inn** (South Sterling; phone: 676-3311) is more a small resort than a cozy country inn, for the 67 rooms are fresh and homey rather than venerable with age and character. Families will appreciate the range of activities, including tennis, shuffleboard, lake swimming, and hiking. Doubles, some with private bath, cost $106 to $120 on weekends, including three meals. No credit cards are accepted. TO GET THERE: Take Exit 52 of I-80 and follow Route 447 north. At Canadensis turn left on Route 191 north to South Sterling.

▪ **Pine Knob Inn** (Canadensis; phone: 595-2532), like the Sterling Inn, has the atmosphere of a small resort, with swimming, archery, tennis, shuffleboard, and other family activities. The main building was built in 1850; the cottages were added in 1930. The chef, who graduated from assistant chef at the Overlook Inn, enjoys enthusiastic reviews from critics. Meals, such as roast duckling for $8.75, are reasonably priced. Try the creamy broccoli and cheddar quiche and the praline pecan cheesecake. Doubles are $40 to $47 per person, including breakfast and dinner. Some have private baths. TO GET THERE: Take Exit 52 of I-80 to Route 447 north. The inn is one-half mile south of Canadensis.

▪ **Pump House Inn** (Canadensis; phone: 595-7501) is more a restaurant with rooms than the other way around. The five rooms are clean and comfortable, though some might question the decor. One has wallpaper with green wicker designs. Another has several aging pages of *Gourmet* magazine tacked to cork squares above the bed. Doubles are $50 to $100, all with private bath. TO GET THERE: Take Exit 52 of I-80 to Route 447 north. At the Canadensis traffic light, turn right for 1½ miles. The inn is on the left.

20. EMERGENCIES

▪ **Pocono Hospital** (East Stroudsburg; phone: 421-4000).

21. HOW TO GET THERE

BY CAR. *From New York:* I-80 west to Exit 52 (1½ miles past the Delaware Water Gap toll). Turn north on Route 447 and drive 20 miles to Canadensis. *From Philadelphia:* Northeastern extension of the Pennsylvania Turnpike to Lehigh Valley Interchange (Exit 33). Follow Route 22 east to Route 33 north and continue to Bartonsville. Take I-80 west to Scotrun exit and go north on Route 611 to Mt. Pocono. Take Route 940 east approximately 3.1 miles to Route 390. Continue north to Cresco and Canadensis. *From Washington and Baltimore:* Baltimore-Washington Expressway to Baltimore Beltway Bypass. Follow signs to I-83. Take I-83 to I-81, to I-80, to I-380 west. Go one mile on I-380 to the first exit, then east on Route 940 to Mt. Pocono. Continue on Route 940 approximately 3.1 miles to Route 390 north to Cresco and Canadensis.

BY BUS. *From New York:* Greyhound (212/635-0800) or Martz Trailways (212/730-7460) to Stroudsburg or Mt. Pocono (an additional 20 minutes). The Martz trip is up to one hour shorter. *From Philadelphia:* Greyhound (215/468-4800) to Stroudsburg or Mt. Pocono. Most inns and resorts will meet you at the bus depot for a nominal charge.

BY PLANE. USAir has direct flights from New York and Philadelphia to the Wilkes-Barre-Scranton Airport (about 30 miles from Canadensis). Most inns and resorts will meet you at the airport for a nominal charge.

22. FOR FURTHER INFORMATION

 ▪ **Pocono Mountains Vacations Bureau,** 1004 Main Street, Stroudsburg, PA 18360. Phone: 421-5791.

 ▪ There is a tourist information center at the Delaware Water Gap exit of I-80.

Cold Spring, New York

Zip Code, 10516 (Cold Spring), 10524 (Garrison); Area Code, 914

---

1. DISTANCES

BY CAR. *From New York*, 1½ hours.

BY TRAIN. *From New York*, 80 minutes.

2. MAJOR ATTRACTIONS

- A peaceful nineteenth-century Hudson River village with breathtaking views of the Hudson Highlands, only 90 minutes north of Times Square.
- Historic buildings, dozens of craft and antique shops, and at least three first-class restaurants and inns.
- Lakes, hiking trails, and nature preserves.

3. INTRODUCTION

Fifty miles north of Manhattan, the Hudson River cuts through the Appalachian Mountains, creating the Hudson Highlands, a spectacular rocky gorge that has resisted development and change. The region today has more than 340 historic landmarks, many of which you'll see as you wander through the delightful, unspoiled river village of Cold Spring.

Until 1818 Cold Spring was nothing but a tiny hamlet on the banks of the Hudson. But then James Madison chose the village as the site of one of four foundries to supply the government with weapons and ammunition. It was a natural choice, for Cold Spring was only a few miles upriver from the military academy at West Point.

By the mid-nineteenth century the foundry had become the largest in the nation. It continued to grow, building steamboat and locomotive engines, and during the Civil War manufactured munitions for the Union Army. After the war, the foundry produced iron parts for bridges, tunnels, and buildings, but the technology had changed, and in 1911 the foundry closed down for good.

Until perhaps fifteen years ago Cold Spring was a sleepy nineteenth-century town, with a blue-collar population half Irish, half Italian. But as real estate values in Westchester soared, artists and commuters headed north in search of affordable homes. Historic buildings were lovingly restored and converted into inns and restaurants. Weekend visitors flocked to the beautifully renovated Hudson House at the water's edge. An abandoned post office was transformed into a Saturday night jazz club. The Plumbush Restaurant drew three stars from *The New York Times.* Main Street property that went for $20,000 five years ago is now selling for $150,000. A new bakery will be selling croissants and imported coffees this summer. A ferry between Garrison, Cold Spring, and West Point is on its way. There's no gourmet deli yet, but no one doubts that there will be one soon.

The younger residents, the ones who drive their motorcycles and pickup trucks up and down Main Street on Saturday nights, are not so sure they like what's happening to Cold Spring. It's not the town they grew up in. But their parents, remembering when the town was boarded up and dying, are beginning to join in the facelift. After all, who can complain when home values have tripled in the past five years, and there's work now, when a few years ago there was none?

What oldtimers and newcomers agree on is that the pace of change should be controlled, and that nothing should be allowed to compromise the village's integrity and charm. So far, so good. The town still has a life of its own that survives when weekend visitors pack up and go home. Antique stores still outnumber the fudge and T-shirt shops, and dealers still close their doors when the spirit moves them, even on busy weekends. What makes Cold Spring so special today (other than its proximity to Manhattan, only 80 minutes away) is the fact that it hasn't yet turned into a Nyack or a New Hope. It's still a sleepy river village where weekend visitors can capture the spirit of an earlier America, and enjoy sights that have remained unchanged since Henry Hudson sailed by more than 350 years ago.

4. WHAT TO SEE AND DO

▪ Walk the length of Main Street from Route 9D down to the river, admiring the nineteenth-century buildings and stopping in at more than a dozen antique and craft shops. From the bandstand there's a breathtaking view of the Hudson Highlands. For the same view free from weekend traffic, turn south along Market Street and walk to the **Chapel of Our Lady Restoration** (phone: 265-2781), an outstanding example of Greek Revival architecture. The original chapel, dedicated in 1834, was the first Catholic Church in the Hudson River Valley. This is a contemplative spot for picnics.

▪ **The Foundry School Museum** (63 Chestnut Street, Cold Spring), housed in a one-room schoolhouse used by foundry workers, has exhibitions on local history focusing on the old West Point foundry. Open Wednesday from 9:30 to 4 and Sunday from 2 to 5.

▪ When you've seen enough of Cold Spring, drive south toward Garrison on Route 9D. For one of the most restful and dramatic views of the Hudson Highlands, and to tour a masterpiece of early nineteenth-century Federal Domestic architecture, stop at **Boscobel Restoration** (Route 9D, one mile south of Cold Spring; phone: 265-3638). Paintings include works from the Hudson River School of artists, including Benjamin West. In spring thousands of tulips encircle the rose garden fountain. Open April through October, daily except Tuesday, from 9:30 to 5 (last tour at 4:30); also open November, December, and March from 9:30 to 4. Admission is $4 for adults, $2 for children 6 to 14. Admission to the grounds alone is $2 for adults.

▪ **Garrison** (also called Garrison-on-Hudson and Garrison's Landing) is only a ten-minute drive south of Cold Spring. If you're not staying at Garrison's only inn, The Golden Eagle, you'll want to visit this nineteenth-century town, spruced up for the filming of *Hello, Dolly* in 1968. The town itself is full of wealthy estates, whose owners keep a low profile. What you'll see of it, besides the inn, is a cluster of homes around a railroad station, a general store that houses a funky bar, a potter's studio, a print gallery run by the wife of a former Ambassador to Peru, and a small park with a gazebo at the water's edge. The park has benches and plenty of grass and shade trees—a much more peaceful place to picnic or to appreciate the Hudson than the busy waterfront in Cold Spring. If you arrive mid-day, the inn is an ideal spot for lunch.

   ▪ Across the river (a 30-minute drive from Cold Spring) is the military academy at **West Point.** Among its graduates since 1802 are Robert E. Lee, Ulysses Grant, George Patton, and Dwight D. Eisenhower. The West Point Museum, housing the largest general military collection in the Western Hemisphere, is open daily, year-round, from 10:30 to 4:15. Autumn is an ideal time for football, foliage, and cadets on parade. For cadet-viewing times, phone 914/938-2638/3507. For football tickets, phone 914/446-4996.

   ▪ The Hudson Highlands is both the oldest and the youngest winegrowing region in the country. More than ten of these wineries are within 30 miles of Cold Spring. **Brotherhood Winery** (35 North Street, Washingtonville; phone: 496-3661) is the closest to Cold Spring, and also the oldest in America. A complete list of Hudson River wineries is available from the Chamber of Commerce *(see #22, For Further Information).*

   ▪ If you want to return home with fresh fruits and vegetables, stop at the **Maple Lawn Farm Market** (Route 9, just north of the Bird & Bottle Inn; open till 8 P.M.).

   ▪ **Franklin D. Roosevelt's home and library** (Route 9, Hyde Park; about 40 minutes north of Cold Spring; phone: 229-9115) are open to the public daily from 9 to 5. Also in Hyde Park is the **Vanderbilt Mansion** (Phone: 229-9115), a fine example of Beaux Arts architecture built in 1896–98 by Frederick Vanderbilt, grandson of "The Commodore."

5. THE ARTS

   ▪ The **Julia I. Butterfield Memorial Library** (Morris Avenue, Route 9D; phone: 265-3040) has a small collection of important Hudson River paintings. Open Monday, Wednesday, Friday, and Saturday from 2 to 5; weekday evenings from 7 to 9; and Saturday from 10 to 3.

   ▪ Ninety outdoor sculptures by such masters as Noguchi and

David Smith are on display in the gardens and open fields of the
Storm King Art Center (Old Pleasant Hill Road, Mountainville, six
miles south of Newburgh; phone: 914/534-3115). Open late May
through October, Wednesday to Monday from 2 to 5:30.

- The **River Cultural Center of the Arts** (50 Main Street;
phone: 265-3613) sponsors a year-long program of music and dance.
Phone for a schedule of upcoming events.

- **Hand to Mouth Players** (Garrison's Landing; phone: 223-
3801) gives community theater productions in the Garrison Railroad
Station.

- **Boscobel Restoration** (Garrison, Route 9D, one mile south of
Cold Spring; phone: 265-3638) is an ideal setting for a series of four
Sunday afternoon classical concerts in July and August. Concerts are
included in the $4 admission fee to the estate.

- **Hyde Park Festival Theater** (Vanderbilt Lane, Hyde Park;
about 40 minutes north of Cold Spring; phone: 229-9335) recently
produced such shows as Imogene Coca in *The Gin Game* and Jo
Sullivan in *Songs of Frank Loesser.*

6. ANTIQUES AND CRAFTS

- There are more than two dozen antique dealers on either side
of Main Street from Route 9D down to the railroad tracks. Most
offer an eclectic (and somewhat uneven) collection of Victorian oak
furniture, clothing, jewelry, and accessories. **Mycroft Holmes Antiques** specializes in Sherlock Holmes memorabilia. **The Sampler** (91
Main St.; phone: 265-3122) sells handcrafted works by Hudson Valley artisans.

- Jay Lindsay *is* **The Garrison Art Center** (Garrison's Landing;
phone: 424-3960). His pottery is sold here and throughout the States.

- Early Hudson River engravings are sold next door to the
Golden Eagle Inn at the **Dock House Gallery.**

7. TOURS

- **PROCO** (Preservation and Revitalization of Cold Spring
Area, 73 Main Street; phone: 265-2111) gives free weekend tours and
slide shows on historic Cold Spring.

- **West Point Tours,** Inc. (Box 268, Highland Falls, NY 10928;
phone: 446-4724) offers daily guided bus tours of the military
academy from May through October. Buses depart from the Visitor's
Information Center.

8. WALKS

▪ **Manitoga** (Garrison, Route 9D; 2½ miles north of Bear Mountain Bridge; phone: 424-3812) is a peaceful woodland preserve created by famed industrial designer Russell Wright on his estate overlooking a nineteenth-century quarry. Influenced by Japanese design, but using only native species, Wright transformed the barren hillside into a delight of running water, cathedrallike forest rooms, and unexpected glimpses of the Hudson River below. Open Wednesday through Sunday for picnics, walks, and guided tours, by reservation. Self-guided tours cost $2 for adults, 50 cents for children. Guided tours are $3 for adults, $1 for children.

▪ **Hudson Highlands State Park** (Route 9D, Cold Spring) has scenic hiking trails and undeveloped beaches.

▪ **Fahnestock State Park** (Route 301, Carmel; 8 miles from Cold Spring; phone: 225-7207) has miles of trails, including a section of the Appalachian Trail.

▪ **Constitution Marsh Sanctuary** (Garrison, Route 9D to Indian Brook Road) is a public wildlife sanctuary with self-guided nature trails and boardwalk. For guided tours by foot or canoe, phone the resident warden, Jim Rod, at 265-3119.

▪ **The Bird & Bottle Inn** is a great starting point for walks down winding gravel roads, past stone walls and colonial farmhouses. Ask for directions to the swimming hole.

9. BIKING

▪ **The Hudson House** (2 Main Street; phone: 265-9355) rents bikes.

10. BOATING AND FISHING

▪ For guided canoe tours of the **Constitution Marsh Sanctuary** just south of Cold Spring, contact the warden, Jim Rod, at 265-3119.

▪ You can combine a visit to West Point with a two-hour Hudson Highlands cruise aboard the M/V *Commander.* Contact **Hudson Highlands Cruises & Tours Inc.,** P.O. Box 265, Highland Falls, NY 10928; phone: 446-7171.

▪ Jackie Ring, director of the Four Winds Hospital in Katonah, has her Coast Guard captain's license and both owns and operates the 32-foot *Claddagh,* which she charters to groups up to six for breakfast or sunset cruises, trips to West Point, or two-hour cruises through the Hudson Highlands. Contact the Hudson House (phone: 265-9355).

11. SWIMMING

- **Fahnestock State Park** (Route 301, Carmel; 8 miles from Cold Spring; phone: 225-7207) has a delightful lake with a sandy beach.
Stop at the Bird & Bottle Inn and ask the manager for directions to a very local swimming hole, a 15-minute walk from the Inn.

14. TENNIS

- You can play at the **Highlands Country Club** (Route 9D; phone: 424-3727) if you're willing to take a lesson from the pro, Biff Danza.
- **The Haldane School** in Cold Spring has two public courts.

15. GOLF

- **Garrison Golf and Country Club** (Route 9 and Travis Corner Road, Garrison; phone: 424-3604) has an 18-hole Robert Trent Jones course open to the public on weekdays.
- **Highlands Country Club** (Route 9D, near Route 403, Garrison; phone: 424-3727) is open to the public. Golfers can lunch here at Xavier's, the former ninth-hole club house, today one of the finest restaurants in the region.

17. DINING

- Ask local residents where to go for a consistently first-rate meal and the answer is invariably Plumbush or **Xavier's** (Highlands Country Club, Route 9D, Garrison; phone: 424-4228). The chef at Xavier's is Peter Xavier Kelly, a self-taught chef from Wappingers Falls who has worked at Laurent in New York and The Arch in Brewster. The 12 tables are dwarfed beneath the 25-foot ceilings with their bare blue walls, creating the feeling of a banquet hall owned by a somewhat impoverished Kashmiri maharaja. A harpist and violinist play on weekends. The menu, printed on a glass mirror, is seasonal, and includes such specialties as breast of duckling with green peppercorns, sweetbreads, and soft-shell crabs. Entrées range from $14 to $17.50. Dress is casual. Dinner reservations are required. No credit cards are accepted.

▪ If you're planning to visit Garrison, drop in at lunch or brunch time and soak up the atmosphere of the **Verandah Café** in the Golden Eagle Inn (phone: 424-3067). An inexpensive lunch of salads and quiches is lovingly prepared on the porch or under the stamped tin ceiling on Thursday through Sunday from 11 to 3. Garrison also has a very small, very local bar attached to the general store—a great spot for a beer on a hot summer afternoon.

▪ Both owners of **The Plumbush Restaurant** (Route 9D, Cold Spring; phone: 265-3904/9764) are Swiss, but you won't find Bratwurst on their continental menu, which several years ago won three stars in *The New York Times*. Before opening their Cold Spring restaurant, Hans Benderer and Gieri Albin spent ten years at the Stonehenge Restaurant in Ridgefield, working under Alfred Stockli, the original chef at the Four Seasons in New York. Specialties include duck with plum sauce and trout from the kitchen's own tanks. Apple fritters are a must for dessert. Entrées on the à la carte menu cost from $14.95 to $17.50. The fixed-price dinner costs $24.50. Sunday brunch is served from 11:30 to 2:30. Dress is informal. The Victorian mansion has five dining rooms. The darkest and most intimate is the Oak Room. The largest, with piano, has less charm than the others. Reservations are recommended. All major credit cards are accepted.

▪ No one could complain about the atmosphere at **The Bird & Bottle Inn** (Nelson's Corner, Route 9, Garrison; phone: 424-3000), one of the most intimate and tasteful dining spots in the Northeast. Nothing is cute, self-conscious, or overdone in this tastefully and lovingly restored pre-Revolutionary inn, although area residents feel that the food sometimes falls short of expectations aroused by the high prices charged. Dining is leisurely, so bring someone you like. The Map Room, with only three tables, is the most intimate of all. Favorite appetizers are spinach and shrimp soufflé and Bird & Bottle Festive Pie (omelet with tarragon, prosciutto, red pepper, fresh spinach, imported Swiss cheese, and smoked ham layered inside a pastry shell). Two popular entrées are roast pheasant and fresh sautéed baby salmon covered with sesame seeds. For dessert, try the homemade chocolate rum torte. The fixed price is $30. There is live folk music on Friday nights in season. A $12.95 Sunday brunch, with eggs Benedict and chicken liver sauté is served from 11:30 to 2:30. Dress is informal. All major credit cards are accepted.

▪ If you're wandering around Cold Spring and care more about a good, quick, inexpensive meal than a leisurely dining experience, head for **45 Fair Street** (phone: 265-3166), two blocks north of Main Street. Lunches range from $3.95 to $6.95.

▪ **Hudson House** (2 Main Street; phone: 265-9355) serves very honest American fare, such as country pork chops and Putnam pot roast. Entrées range from $9.95 to $16.95. All major credit cards accepted.

18. AFTER HOURS

▪ The only serious after-hours spot is the 40-seat **Olde Post Taverne** (43 Main Street; phone: 265-2510), which features live jazz by such artists as Junior Mance.

▪ The under-25 crowd heads for **Briar's** (Route 9, Cold Spring), which advertises "three levels of entertainment" and "multi-screen video."

19. LODGING

▪ At the foot of Main Street, at the water's edge, sits the **Hudson House** (Cold Spring; phone: 265-9355), a multi-million-dollar restoration that some say sparked the recent renaissance of Cold Spring. Rooms are very tastefully decorated with pine furniture, small-flower-print wallpaper, brass or iron beds, ceiling fans, cookie-cutter wall decorations, and lacquered wine decanter bed lamps. Front rooms have breathtaking views of Storm King Mountain and Crow's Nest Mountain across the Hudson, but also the noise and fumes of weekend traffic. The Hudson House is the center of whatever weekend activity there is in Cold Spring—which will attract some visitors and frighten others away.

▪ **The Bird & Bottle Inn** (Nelson's Corners, Route 9, Garrison 10524; phone: 914/424-3000) may be one of the most romantic inns anywhere in the country. The pre-Revolutionary yellow clapboard house sits beside a babbling brook. The smoky blue wainscoting, the woodburning fireplaces, low-beamed ceilings, and beautiful wide plank floors all capture the ambience of colonial America. The four rooms cost $155 a night for two, including dinner and breakfast ($180 for the suite). A European plan is sometimes available. All credit cards are accepted.

▪ The 137-year-old **Golden Eagle Inn** (Garrison's Landing, NY 10524; phone: 424-3067) sits at the edge of the Hudson in the tiny town where *Hello, Dolly* was filmed in 1968. You'll soon be on a first-name basis here with hosts Stephanie and George Templeton, both former designers from New York. Rooms are "decorated," with the sorts of warm fabrics Bloomingdale's went in for before it succumbed to chrome and brass. The second floor veranda is a perfect place to watch the ebb and flow of the river, and succumb to cocktails as the sun sets behind the hills of West Point. Six rooms, four with private bath, cost $60 to $70, including continental breakfast. There's a two-night minimum on weekends. All major credit cards accepted.

■ For bed and breakfast, try the centrally located **Olde Post Inn** (43 Main Street, Cold Spring; phone: 265-2510). The four rooms in this modernized 165-year-old building are cheerful, unpretentious, and country-comfortable.

■ **Plumbush Restaurant** (Route 9D, Cold Spring; phone: 265-3904) will have four Victorian guest rooms open this summer, priced at $75.

20. EMERGENCIES

■ **Butterfield Hospital** (phone: 265-3642)
■ **Ambulance:** Garrison (phone 424-3131); Cold Spring (phone 265-9500)

21. HOW TO GET THERE

BY CAR. *To Garrison:* George Washington Bridge to the Palisades Parkway. At the end of the Parkway, follow signs to the Bear Mountain Bridge. Cross bridge, turn left (north) on Route 9D for 4½ miles to the junction of Route 403. Turn left (west). *To Cold Spring:* for the scenic route, follow directions to Garrison, but continue north on Route 9D. Otherwise, take the West Side Highway or New York Thruway to the Saw Mill River Parkway. Go north on the Taconic Parkway to Route 202, Peekskill Exit. Take Route 202 west to Route 9 North. Turn left onto Route 403 and north on Route 9D.
BY TRAIN. The Hudson Division of the Metro-North Railroad (phone: 212/532-4900) makes regular stops at Garrison and Cold Spring. Anthony Limousine (Cold Spring; phone: 265-9283) will take you from the train station to your hotel.

22. FOR FURTHER INFORMATION

■ Write the **Cold Spring Area Chamber of Commerce,** Box 71, Cold Spring, NY 10516. Ask for the "Guide to Cold Spring," the "Restaurant and Lodging Guide," and the "Hudson River Valley Guide."

23. RECOMMENDED READING

■ A quarterly newspaper called *The Historic Cold Spring & Gar-*

rison Guide (50 cents) is available in local stores or by mail from The Putnam County News & Recorder, 84 Main Street, Cold Spring, NY; phone: 914/265-2468.

• Jeffrey Simpson's *The Hudson River: 1850–1918. A Photographic Portrait* is one of several books on the area published by Sleepy Hollow Press, 150 White Plains Road, Tarrytown, NY 10591.

• Other books on the region include Robert H. Boyle's *The Hudson River: A Natural and Unnatural History* (Norton, $6.95); William T. Howell, *The Hudson Highlands* (Walking News, $12.95); John Howat, *The Hudson River and Its Painters* (Penguin, $14.95), and *The Hudson River School: American Landscape Painting from 1821 to 1907* (Norton).

Greene County (the Northern Catskills), New York

(Area Code, 518)

1. DISTANCES

BY CAR. *From New York,* 2¾ hours; *from Boston,* 4 hours.

BY BUS. *From New York,* 3 hours.

2. MAJOR ATTRACTIONS

- A wealth of outdoor sports, including golf, tennis, horseback riding, and the best fly fishing in the northeast.
- Miles of downhill and cross country ski trails.
- Miles of scenic mountain trails; 200 waterfalls with pools for swimming.

- Ethnic festivals and fairs.
- One of the best northern Italian restaurants in the country.
- Antiques at last year's prices.

3. INTRODUCTION

A local woman explained to me the difference between Greene County, where she lives, and the "other" Catskills to the south: "Those are the foothills, these are the mountains," she said. "The difference is that down there at Grossinger's they're wearing mink coats in summer. Here we don't even wear mink coats in winter, we leave 'em on the animals."

The name Catskills conjures up images of borscht simmering on stoves in Sullivan County or of flower children coming of age in Woodstock. But there's another Catskills to the north, with such towns as Hunter and Windham, which is just being discovered by New York professionals fashionably seeking unfashionable places to spend their summers.

Except for a few hotels and restaurants run by expatriate New Yorkers, there's nothing slick, smart, or sophisticated about Greene County; *New York Magazine* is unlikely to recommend it for a weekend escape. It is a region of startling contrasts; of rich and poor, mansions and shacks, scenic splendors and squalid eyesores. I have no doubt that the gourmet deli is on its way, and some of you may wait till then to pay a visit. But others will insist on going now—for the same reasons that you prefer old Levis to designer jeans.

Jeans would have been out of place in Greene County a century ago, when Presidents, governors, and the elite of New York summered at the 1,200-room Hotel Kaaterskill or the elegant Catskill Mountain House, a "palace in the clouds," with its glistening façade of 13 classic columns. The train and then the car first increased the summer traffic, and then reduced it, as summer visitors packed their trunks and headed farther north. The grand hotels were soon replaced by 100-room boarding houses, and farmers, finding it easier to change sheets than harvest wheat, opened their homes to working-class guests. The Irish came, and so did the Germans, the Italians, and the Poles. Jews summered in the Catskills too, but because they were not always welcome in the north, they staked their claim in Sullivan County.

Greene County, like the rest of the Catskills, suffered from its proximity to the population centers of a growing nation. The mountains were stripped of hemlocks and fractured into paving stones for the sidewalks of New York. Pines were felled for Philadelphia shipbuilders; white ash for oars; balsam for Christmas trees. In 1963 the empty, vandalized Catskill Mountain House was razed and turned into a campsite.

From 1945 to the emergence of the Hunter Mountain ski resort in 1959, the northern Catskills stood abandoned. The gilded hotels were gone, the boarding houses in disrepair. Then, in response to the needs of skiers, a transformation began. New Yorkers fed up with the pace and price of city life, and attracted by the low cost of real estate, began moving in and turning old homes into quality restaurants and inns. The owners of a northern Italian restaurant—one of them from Brooklyn—have just opened a 24-room Victorian inn on their property in Windham. Plans are underway for a 200-room hotel complex at Hunter Mountain. The process is just beginning.

And all the while, nature's scars continue to heal. The Hudson River School of painters, who began here, could still take their inspiration from the spectacular falls and awesome gorges of Greene County. Oaks, hickories, and chestnuts fill the forests again; beech, yellow birch, and hemlock carpet the mountains, beneath the balsam and the red spruce. Count it a blessing that Lilly Pulitzer and Laura Ashley have not yet made their way to Greene County; that there are Hummel figurine look-alike contests and four-day polka fests highlighted by the election of a national polka queen and the songs of the Polish Prince, Bobby Vinton. This ethnic celebration, against a backdrop of awe-inspiring scenery and fresh mountain air, is what Greene County is all about.

4. WHAT TO SEE AND DO

• Works by the Hudson River School of artists seem hopelessly romantic till you've seen the actual landscapes that inspired their art. If you don't mind seeing this world framed by a car window, drive west along Route 23A from Palenville to Tannersville. **Bastion Falls** drops through a rocky glen at a hairpin turn on Route 23A just below the town of Haines Falls. **Upper Kaaterskill Falls,** one of the most frequently painted scenes of America's early landscape artists, drops 180 feet; the lower falls drop 80 feet. To view the falls from the top, follow the green sign marked North Lake off Route 23A in Haines Falls and park in North Lake State Park. It's a fairly level 30-minute walk along marked trails. To view Kaaterskill Falls from the bottom, follow the trail off Route 23A from the hairpin turn called Horseshoe Curve, about one mile north of the hamlet of Palenville. It's a steep 10-minute climb. Another lovely walk begins at the bridge at the north end of Palenville. **Fawn's Leap Waterfall** is hidden here behind foliage, but you can see the break in the rock where the water flows. Take your shoes off and walk about 100 feet through the creek to the falls. For a more ambitious walk, follow the falls up the mountain. The trail takes you past numerous other falls and swimming holes. There are dozens of other mountain trails that take you past waterfalls—some 200 of them—and numerous scenic overlooks. Trails are described in the *Guide to the Catskills* (Walking News), available in various sporting goods stores in the Hunter area, or in Manhattan at Hammond Map Center (57 West 43 Street) and at various local camping and sporting goods stores.

▪ Route 23A will take you to the town of Hunter, where in summer you can ride up to 3,200 feet on the **Hunter Mountain Sky Ride** (phone: 263-4223), the highest chairlift in the Catskills. Open late June through Labor Day daily, and on fall weekends. Tickets are $4.50 for adults, $2.50 for children 6 to 12. *See #8, Walks* for trails leading down the mountain.

▪ You don't have to be Polish to enjoy the National Polka Festival, and you don't have to know who the Oak Ridge Boys are to enjoy the Country Music Festival—both part of a summer-long series of ethnic celebrations at Hunter Mountain. Those of you who have kept your cynical distance from this side of America owe it to yourselves to find what it's all about; go with an open mind and it won't be long before you're signing up for polka lessons, learning how to allemande left and right, stamping your foot to the country beat of Box Car Willie, or swigging Dinkelacker beer to the sounds of the 35-piece Blaichacher Musikanten brass band from the Allgauer Alps. For details, contact **Exposition Planners,** Bridge Street, Hunter 12442; phone: 263-3800.

▪ **The Thomas Cole House** (218 Spring Street, Catskill; phone: 943-6533) is the former residence and studio of the English-born, self-taught artist, Thomas Cole, founder of the Hudson River School of painting. Works by Cole, his student Frederic Church, and other nineteenth-century painters are often on display.

▪ More than 300 years of Upper Hudson Valley history are reflected in the complex of buildings that comprise the **Bronck House Museum** (Route 9W, Coxsackie; phone: 731-8862). Of particular interest are the Thomas Cole paintings, a Victorian horse barn, and an unusual 13-side barn constructed around a center pole.

▪ The iridescent blue morpho butterfly is only one of thousands of butterflies on display in the **Butterfly Museum and Farm** (Wright Street, East Durham; phone: 634-7759). If dead butterflies don't make your heart flutter, try the **Little Ole Museum** in back of the A. J. Cunningham Funeral Home (Route 81, Greenville; phone: 966-

8313), where early nineteenth-century hearses, caskets, and burial items are on display.

▪ In summer you'll want to bring home some fresh fruits and vegetables. Farm stands include: **Albright Brothers** (one mile northwest of Athens; phone: 945-1716); **Hamilton Farm Stand** (Route 145, two miles west of Cairo; phone: 622-3713); **Kaatskill Cider Mill** (Route 32, Catskill; phone: 678-5529); **Mountain Top Produce** (Route 23A, Haines Falls); **Story Farm** (Routes 32 and 23A, Catskill; phone: 678-9716); **Sunflower** (Route 32, Cairo).

▪ *The River Queene* (388 Main Street, Catskill; phone: 943-4450) is a steam paddle-wheel vessel that takes 150 passengers on three-hour Hudson River cruises from Catskill Marina on Sunday and Monday.

▪ See the Catskills by plane. Contact Cairo Airport (phone: 622-9736) and Freehold Airport (phone: 634-7626 or 622-3307).

▪ *See #16, For Kids* for descriptions of the Catskill Reptile Institute and the Catskill Game Park.

Woodstock is, in spirit, halfway between Greene County and Columbus Avenue (Manhattan). You may want to stop here on your way home to window shop, or to take in a Sunday afternoon concert, dance, or play *(See #5, The Arts).*

5. THE ARTS

▪ **The Art Awareness Gallery** (Route 42, Lexington; phone: 989-6433) exhibits works by New York State artists and craftspeople. Recent music and theater events include a Dadaesque review and a performance by jazz guitarist Kenny Burrell.

▪ On your way to Lexington, stop at the **Stone House Gallery** (six miles west of Hunter, off Route 23A; phone: 989-6755) for quality antiques and the work of some very talented local artists.

▪ **The Pine Orchard Artists Festival** (Palenville; phone: 678-9286) may continue in 1985 with chamber music and dance. Performances are held in the same hamlet where America's first artist's colony began, attracting the likes of Washington Irving and James Fenimore Cooper.

▪ The Greene Council on the Arts (phone: 943-3400) runs both the **Catskill Gallery** (398 Main Street, Catskill; phone: 943-3400) and the **Mountain Top Gallery** (Main Street, Windham; phone: 734-3104), both of which exhibit the work of local and national artists.

▪ **Athens Photographic Workshop** (Athens Promotion Center, 44 Second Street, Athens 12015) has weekend workshops with New York City professionals.

• *Mass Appeal* and *Ten Little Indians* were among recent productions at the **Woodstock Playhouse** (Mill Hill Road, Woodstock; phone: 914/679-2436). Performances run from mid-June to late September. You may want to stop here on your way home for a Sunday show at 2 or 7. Tickets are $10 and $13. The Playhouse also hosts a summer dance festival with Joffrey II and other professional companies.

Also in Woodstock in July and August are the **Maverick Concerts** (phone: 914/679-8746/7558), featuring such groups as the Emerson String Quartet. Sunday performances begin at 3.

6. ANTIQUES

• The Greene County Promotion Department (see #22, *For Further Information*) has a useful map locating 53 antique dealers in the area. Though you have to look for quality antiques, prices tend to be lower than in other resort areas, which attract a more affluent summer crowd. There are Saturday night auctions at the **Durham Auction Barn** (Route 145, Durham; phone: 239-8475). Auctions are also held at the **Cairo Auction Mart** (Main Street, Cairo; phone: 622-3547); **Sterling's Auction Arena** (Route 9W, Coxsackie; phone: 731-8563); and **Red Barn Auction Sales** (Route 9W, Coxsackie; phone: 731-8525).

• **Open Gates Antiques** (Route 23A, three miles west of Catskill; phone: 943-3806) has five rooms with English bric-a-brac, crystal, furniture, and clocks.

• **Stone House Antiques** (six miles west of Hunter, off Route 23A; phone: 989-6755) has a small but quality collection of early American primitives, folk art, and jewelry. Open weekends by chance, or by appointment.

7. TOURS

• **George Greiner** (PO Box 64, Athena 12015; phone: 945-1411) leads individuals, families, or groups on drives, hikes, or fishing trips in the northern Catskills. This is a great way to discover hidden waterfalls or learn about the area from someone who has lived here all his life.

8. WALKS

• The Catskills rise from 600 to 4,200 feet. Of 34 peaks over 3,500 feet, 20 have trails to the summit. The walk to Kaaterskill Falls is described in *#4 (What to See and Do)*. Walking News publishes both a *Guide to the Catskills* and a series of regional trail maps. The Appalachian Mountain Club also publishes a map pack called *Catskill Trails*. Trail maps and topographical maps are sold at various sporting goods stores in Hunter. The Greene County Promotion Department *(see #22, For Further Information)* will send on request a booklet describing the most popular trails in the region.

▪ If walking down is more appealing than climbing up, take the chairlift to the top of 4,040-foot Hunter Mountain, the second highest peak in the Catskills, and walk down any of four trails, varying in length from 2.02 to 3.35 miles.

▪ The historic **Escarpment Trail** goes north from Kaaterskill Creek off Route 23A to East Windham on Route 23, a distance of 23 miles. The trail follows the escarpments of both North and South Mountains, with almost continuous overlooks 1000 feet above the deep gulfs of Kaaterskill Clove and the Hudson River Valley.

9. BIKING

▪ There are no bike rental stores in the county. One popular bike route is along Route 23A from Hunter to Lexington, a distance of about six miles.

10. BOATING AND FISHING

FISHING

▪ Largemouth bass, pickerel, yellow perch, and panfish can be found at the headwaters of the Kaaterskill in the **North & South Lakes Campsite** (phone: 589-5058 or 943-4030) in Haines Falls (there are canoes and rowboats for rent here). Downstream, the Kaaterskill plunges through a spectacular gorge or clove where you can fish for rainbow trout. As the Kaaterskill descends to the Hudson, brown trout become more plentiful; downstream from High Falls, the Kaaterskill supports bass and panfish. The Catskill Creek and its major tributaries, Ten Mile Creek, Basic Creek, and Shingle Kill, are excellent for brown trout. Rainbow trout are found in the Catskill Creek upstream from Oak Hill. The Hudson River supports striped bass, herring, smallmouth bass, sturgeon, and white and yellow perch. The shad season runs from mid-April to early June. The Hudson is accessible from boat ramps in Athens, Catskill, Coxsackie, and New Baltimore. There are Hudson River boat rentals at **Riverview Marine Services** (Main Street, Catskill; phone: 943-5311) and **Shady Harbor Marina** (Route 144, New Baltimore; phone: 756-

8001). The **River Basin Sports Shop** (Catskill; phone: 943-2111) has tide tables and fishing tips for the Hudson.

▪ The Greene County Promotion Department *(see #22, For Further Information)* has free fishing maps of the region.

▪ The **Glen Durham Fishing Preserve** (Morrison Road, off Route 23, South Durham; phone: 622-9878) has two large ponds stocked with trout, bass, and pickerel. The charge is $2.50. Tackle is available.

▪ Go for a para sail ride at **Water Sports Unlimited** (Hagar's Harbor, Athens; phone: 622-8280).

▪ Take a three-day sail between Catskill and Kingston aboard the 33-foot, gaff-rigged ketch *Old Friend.* The cost is $385 for two, including all meals. Contact Norman Bauman at 943-5311 or 518/346-4997.

11. SWIMMING

▪ Swim in the mountain streams or in the pools beneath most of the 200 waterfalls. Popular swimming holes include **North Lake** in Haines Falls; **Clarence D. Lane Park** in Maplecrest; the **Schoharie Creek** in Lexington or Hunter; **Colgate Lake** in East Jewett; the **Woodstock Dam** on Route 32 in Cairo.

12. SKIING

▪ Snowmaking equipment covers 99% of the 37 slopes and trails at **Hunter Mountain Ski Bowl** (Hunter; phone: 263-4223; 212/683-4933).

▪ Snowmaking covers 95% of the 25 trails at **Ski Windham** (Windham; phone: 734-4300; 800/342-5111 in NY State; 800/833-5051 outside NY State).

▪ **Cortina Valley** (Haines Falls; phone: 589-5361) is a less crowded family downhill ski area.

▪ There are 15 miles of groomed cross-country ski trails at **White Birches Ski Touring Center** (Windham; phone: 734-3266). Other cross-country ski areas include **Hyer Meadows** (Tannersville; phone: 589-5361) and **Winter Clove** (Cairo; phone: 622-3267).

13. RIDING

▪ Explore the woodlands and meadows from an English or Western saddle. Stables that rent horses include: **Bailwick Ranch** (Lawrenceville; phone: 678-5665); **Corley's Saddlesaw Ranch**

(Cairo; phone: 622-9287); **Hunter Mountain Resort Ranch** (Haines Falls; phone: 589-6430); **Ponderosa Ranch** (Route 32, Catskill; phone: 678-9206); **Ravine Farm** (East Durham; phone: 678-9206); **Roda's Top Hat Resort** (Round Top; phone: 622-3804); and **The Shapanack Resort** (Oak Hill; phone: 239-4626).

14. TENNIS

▪ **Crest Park Tennis Club** (South Street, Windham; phone: 734-3258); **Windham Ridge Club** (Windham; phone: 734-3600); **Premier Tennis** (Goshen Street, Jewett; phone: 734-3388).

15. GOLF

▪ The only 18-hole course is the **Windham Country Club** (Windham; phone: 734-9910/9917). Nine-hole courses are: **Sunny Hill Golf Club** (Greenville; phone: 634-7642/7698); **Catskill Golf Club** (Catskill; phone: 943-2390/9728); **Colonial Country Club** (Tannersville; phone: 589-9807/5031); **The Glenwood** (Round Top; phone: 622-3100/8440); **Rainbow Golf Club** (Greenville; phone: 966-5343); **Rip Van Winkle Country Club** (Palenville; phone: 678-9779); **Schmollinger's Golf Club** (Freehold; phone: 634-2523).

16. FOR KIDS

▪ You can touch and feed the animals at the very special **Catskill Game Park** (Catskill, off Route 32; about 13 minutes from Catskill, 30 minutes from Hunter; phone: 678-9595), with its large breeding herds of rare and vanishing animals. Admission is $6.50 for adults, $3.50 for children 4 to 11. Open mid-April through October.

▪ Pet a python or make eyes at an Egyptian cobra at the **Catskill Reptile Institute** (south of Cairo on Route 32; two miles north of the Game Park; phone: 678-5590). Open mid-May to mid-September daily from 10 to 6; off-season, weekends from 12 to 5.

▪ Slide down the **Zoom Flume** (Shady Glen Road, off Route 145, East Durham; phone: 239-4559) or drive down the **Junior Speedway** (Route 32, Cairo; phone: 622-3330).

▪ *See #4, What To See and Do* for the ethnic festivals at Hunter Mountain and the Hunter Mountain Sky Ride.

17. DINING

▪ I've been adding garlic to food for the past six months, trying to recapture the experience of dining at **La Griglia** (Route 296,

Windham; phone: 734-4499), one of the best northern Italian restaurants this side of Milan. Begin with a choice of 18 appetizers brought to your table on the antipasto cart. Vito Radelich, a native of Veneto province (once part of Italy but now part of Yugoslavia), has been experimenting with Italian Renaissance dishes that blend Italian staples such as citrus fruits with spices brought to Europe by the crusaders and the Arabs. Pork Michelangelo is a pork dish served with braised apples, apple sauce, tomatoes, and garlic. Other dishes include *osso buco* (braised veal shanks) with risotto; *crostina di polenta;* and pesto (fresh basil sauce) with a variety of homemade pastas. Entrées range from $12.50 to $14. Dress is casual. Reservations are recommended. All major credit cards are accepted.

- **La Rive** (Old Kings Road, Catskill; phone: 943-4888) is a traditional French restaurant, with a charming French country ambience. Meals are served in a 100-year-old farmhouse tastefully paneled with old barnwood, or on a narrow enclosed porch with bowls of fresh fruit on every table. Popular appetizers include codfish mousse, and thin slices of veal in an avocado sauce. Entrées include Beef Wellington with a truffle sauce, veal breast with green peppercorn sauce, and *bouillabaise* (served on Friday). The veal is brought in fresh from Utica; the fresh trout from Phoenicia. For dessert, how about a frozen kiwi soufflé or homemade raspberry ice cream? The complete dinner costs from $19.75 to $21.25. No credit cards are accepted. Dress is casual. Reservations are recommended. Open early May through October.

- The food at **The Redcoat's Return** (Platte Clove Road, Tannersville; phone: 589-9858) may not be up to La Griglia's level, but it still enjoys an excellent reputation, and the intimate English pub atmosphere is in a class by itself. British-born chef Tom Wright learned his art as a chef for Cunard. Appetizers include country paté, baked stuffed clams, and mussels vinaigrette. Entrées, ranging in price from $12 to $16, include frogs' legs, broiled scallops, and beef steak and kidney pie. All major credit cards are accepted. Reservations are advised.

- **Chez Marcel** (Route 23A, Hunter; phone: 263-3722) may be short on atmosphere, but enjoys a good reputation for its Swiss/continental menu that includes cheese fondue, and veal steaks in a light cream sauce. Entrées range in price from $9 to $11. All major credit cards are accepted. **Marie's Dream House** (Route 42, Westkill; phone: 898-6565) has a cute "yodelly" atmosphere that may turn some people off, but the freshly prepared Austrian dishes (tender crispy schnitzel, beef *rouladin*, homemade soups, and Viennese pastries) are highly recommended by area residents.

• A place you could easily miss is a roadside restaurant called
The Fish Market (Route 23, Windham; phone: 734-3055). Since the
owner is a wholesaler who supplies the whole region with fish, meals
are always fresh and inexpensive. The self-service lunch costs about
$5.

18. AFTER HOURS

• The ethnic festivals at Hunter Mountain often continue till 10
or 11 at night, and in the late evening you can enter the grounds
without charge.

• For the under-30 crowd, nightlife centers on the Tannersville-
Hunter area, along Route 23A. **Scruples** (Tannersville; phone: 589-
6623), with its DJs and its giant video screen, probably leads the
pack. Anyone over 30 should come to the northern Catskills with a
friend and/or be prepared to go to bed early.

19. LODGING

• The huge, turn-of-the-century hotels, with rooms for 1,000 or
more guests, gave way in the 1930s to the more modest 50- to 100-
room boarding houses. Most of these are either abandoned or in a
state of disrepair. The region finds itself today with one of the largest
ski resorts in the northeast and less than a handful of comfortable,
quality places for people to stay. The situation is changing as expatriate New Yorkers, fed up with life in the city and attracted by low
real-estate prices, move to Greene County and transform homes and
farmhouses into country inns. Both the Eggery and The Redcoat's
Return have the advantage of being within 30 minutes of both Hunter
and Woodstock. The Albergo has the advantage of being in Windham, the most sophisticated area of the northern Catskills.

• **The Redcoat's Return** (Platte Clove 12427; phone: 589-9858)
was taken over in 1972 by two refugees from New York, English-
born Tom Wright and his wife Peggy. The Wrights converted the 62-
year-old four-story boarding house into an English country inn,
complete with old prints and paintings and a 2,000-book library. It
sounds contrived, but nothing is overdone, and the inn is as charming
and as full of character as Peggy herself, talking to her guests across
the Victorian bar. Rooms are tastefully decorated with brass or iron
beds, Victorian oak dressers, and country fabrics. The only problem
with the Redcoat's Return is the absence of spectacular views and the
smallness of the rooms. Doubles, some with private bath, cost $65 to
$75, including a full breakfast.

▪ **The Eggery** (SR 1, Box 4, Country Road 16, Tannersville; phone: 589-5363/9882) lacks some of the character of The Redcoat's Return, but the views of the northern Catskills are absolutely spectacular. Decorations are homey and unpretentious. The Victorian parlor has lovely wood wainscoting, a wood-burning Franklin stove on a brick hearth, an antique player piano, and Mission Oak furnishings. Rooms have sweet country curtains and tattersall spreads. The owners—from, where else? New York—are a young, friendly couple who have invested their dreams in The Eggery and are working hard to make those dreams come true. Doubles in winter cost $85 to $95 per person for two nights, including two breakfasts and one dinner; summer rates are $10 less. Visa and Mastercard are accepted.

▪ **The Albergo** (Route 296, Windham; phone: 734-4499) was still under construction when we went to press, but since this Victorian inn ("Albergo" is Italian for "inn") is being built by the owners of La Griglia *(see #17, Dining)*, I can only assume the atmosphere and the furnishings will be first-rate. The inn, decorated with period antiques, is being constructed from two nineteenth-century cottages. Doubles, all with private bath, will cost about $70, including breakfast. All major cards are accepted.

▪ The 95-year-old **Greenville Arms** (Route 32, Greenville 12083; phone: 966-5219) began life as one of William Vanderbilt's summer retreats; today it's a 20-room Victorian inn on seven acres, with swimming pool, lawn games, and many third-generation guests.

▪ **Christman's Windham House** (Windham 12496; phone: 734-4230) began as a dairy farm; today it's a Greek Revival boardinghouse with swimming, tennis, and its own nine-hole golf course. Rooms have modern furnishings and TV. Best bet are the rooms in cottages surrounding the original farmhouse. Doubles cost $36.50 to $44 per person, including three meals.

▪ If you must stay in a motel near Hunter, try **Scribner Hollow** (Route 23A, Hunter 12442; phone 263-4211). One of the theme rooms, Future World, has its own private waterfall; another is called The Playmate because of—or in spite of—the fact that it has two double beds on the driveway level. Best bet are upstairs rooms facing the mountains. Doubles cost $42 to $135 off-season, $55 to $200 during the ski season.

▪ For other accommodations, contact **Hunter Mountain Reservation Center** (phone: 263-3827; 201/371-4075; 800/631-7811).

20. EMERGENCIES

▪ **Memorial Hospital** (159 Jefferson Heights, Catskill; phone: 943-2000).

▪ **Columbia Memorial Hospital** (71 Prospect Avenue, Hudson, NY; phone: 828-7601).

21. HOW TO GET THERE

BY PLANE. The nearest airport is the **Albany County Airport.** You can arrange for limousine service from the airport to your hotel by contacting: **Classic Taxi Service** (34 West Bridge Street, Catskill; phone: 943-6626); **Decker's Taxi Service** (Palenville Road, Catskill; phone: 943-4530); **Mountain View Coach Lines,** Route 9W, Coxsackie; phone: 945-1404); or **Hudson Valley Airporter** (139 Partition Street, Saugerties; phone: 914/246-6612).

BY TRAIN. Take Amtrak to Hudson, New York, and then one of the taxis listed above.

BY BUS. **Adirondack Trailways** (212/947-5300) goes from Port Authority in Manhattan to Palenville and Hunter. **Mountain View Coach Lines** (945-1404) goes from Port Authority to East Durham, Cairo, and Catskill during the summer months.

BY CAR. *From New York:* take the New York Thruway north to exits 20, 21, or 21B. *From Boston:* take the Mass. Turnpike (I-90) to the New York Thruway, then south to exits 21 or 21B.

22. FOR FURTHER INFORMATION

▪ **Greene County Promotion Department,** Box 467, Catskill 12414; phone: 518-6559.

▪ There's a county information booth on Route 23B, across from New York Thruway Exit 21, open Monday to Thursday from 11 to 5, Friday from 10 to 8, Saturday from 10 to 7, and Sunday from 11 to 5.

23. RECOMMENDED READING

▪ **Hope Farm Bookshop** (Strong Road, Cornwallville, NY 12418; phone: 239-4745) has an extraordinary collection of books on the Catskills, with separate sections on art, architecture, history, and so on.

- *Greene County, New York: A Short History* by Mabel Parker Smith is available on request from the Greene County Promotion Department *(see #22, For Further Information)*.
- Other books include: *The Catskills* by Alf Evers (Overlook Press); *The Catskills: Land in the Sky* by John G. Mitchell (Viking); *The Hudson River School: American Landscape Painting from 1821 to 1907* (Norton); and *The Hudson River and Its Painters* (Penguin).

Essex, Connecticut

(Area Code, 203)

1. DISTANCES

BY CAR. *From New York,* 2¼ hours; *from Boston,* 2½ hours; *from Hartford,* 45 minutes.

BY TRAIN (to Old Saybrook). *From New York,* 2½ hours; *from Boston,* 2¼ hours.

BY BUS (to Old Saybrook). *From New York,* 3½ hours; *from Boston,* 3¾ hours.

2. MAJOR ATTRACTIONS

   • A Gothic castle with sweeping views of the Connecticut River Valley.
   • A refurbished Victorian opera house where Broadway hits such as *Annie* and *Man of La Mancha* were born.
   • River cruises and an old-fashioned steam engine train ride.
   • A colorful, seventeenth-century New England river town, with antique and gift shops, art galleries, and a venerable old inn.

223

3. INTRODUCTION

The Connecticut River flows down the Vermont-New Hampshire border, across Massachusetts and Connecticut, past Springfield and Hartford. It winds past the front door of the Goodspeed Opera House in East Haddam; under the Gothic ramparts of Gillette Castle in Hadlyme, and along the coves and boatyards of Essex. And then it passes between Old Lyme and Old Saybrook and empties into Long Island Sound.

Old Saybrook—an Amtrak stop along Route I-95—has kept pace with the twentieth century. But Essex and the other river towns along the lower Connecticut remain essentially as they were hundreds of years ago, when the river was the main trade route to markets in New England. A visit here is a trip back to an age when America traveled by water and fortunes were made from the sea.

The story of Essex goes back to one of the earliest settlements in the New World. King James I, grateful to the Earl of Warwick for his role in the founding of the Massachusetts Bay Colony, rewarded him with a land grant that included all of present-day Connecticut. When Charles I came to the throne in 1625, Warwick and other Puritan sympathizers—Lord Brooke, Viscount Saye, Oliver Cromwell, and others—felt that their lives were in jeopardy. They formed a syndicate to colonize Warwick's holdings in the New World, and called it the Saybrook Colony in honor of the noblemen Saye and Brooke. In 1635, John Winthrop, younger son of the governor of Massachusetts Bay Colony, was sent to colonize the land at the head of the Connecticut River.

Cromwell eventually came to power, and the noblemen, no longer threatened, stayed home. Only one of the original group—George Fenwick—ever reached America.

The town of Essex, known then as Potapaug or Pettipaug (the Indian word for "bulging out of the land"), was settled in the 1640s by farmers from the Saybrook Colony, who used the river for food and the islands and marshes as a source of hay for their animals. In time, the original 40,000-acre settlement was divided up, and each of the original areas, including Essex, Chester, Lyme, and Deep River, became a town in its own right.

Essex was a distribution center for goods from the West Indies as early as the 1660s. The goods were carted overland in horse-drawn wagons or shipped upriver in small boats as far north as Springfield. Ships laden with rum and molasses sailed from Essex to the east coast of Africa and returned with ivory, from which the first combs in America were made. (In the 1840s, several local manufacturers of

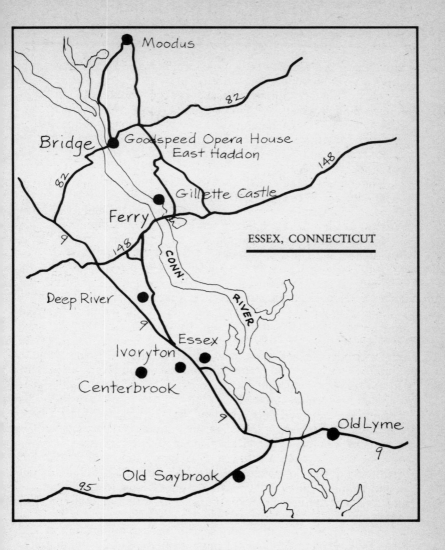

Moodus

82

Bridge
Goodspeed Opera House
East Haddon

148

82

Gillette Castle

Ferry

9

148

CONN.

RIVER

ESSEX, CONNECTICUT

Deep River

9

Essex

Ivoryton

Centerbrook

9

Old Lyme

9

Old Saybrook

95

ivory products combined to form Pratt, Read and Company, now
headquartered in Ivoryton, which became the largest maker of organ
and piano keyboards in the world.)

By the time of the American Revolution, the village of Essex was
a recognized shipbuilding center, and the yard of Uriah and John
Hayden, near the foot of present-day Main Street, was chosen to
build the Continental Navy's first man-of-war, the twenty-four-gun
Oliver Cromwell. The British, appreciating Essex's strategic impor-

tance during the War of 1812, raided the town and destroyed from twenty-two to forty seagoing vessels.

The many sea captains Essex produced eventually returned home with their wealth and built attractive homes along Main Street. Ships were then small enough to sail over the sandbar at the mouth of the Connecticut. But by the 1840s, iron steamboats had begun to replace wood, and the river became too shallow for navigation by oceangoing vessels.

The lower Connecticut River Valley continued to enjoy a lively steamboat trade between Hartford and New York. Fleets of schooners carried deckloads of brown stone quarried at Portland (near Middletown) to New York, and returned with holds full of coal.

In the 1870s, the Hartford Steamboat Company, managed by a man named William H. Goodspeed, operated three palatial side-wheel steamboats on a daily freight and passenger run between Hartford and New York. Boats left about four in the afternoon, and arrived early the next morning in New York.

East Haddam, upriver from Essex, was then a popular Victorian summer resort. Most visitors arriving by steamer disembarked at the lower landing, which was conveniently located near the theater at Maple Seminary. Goodspeed, who owned the upper landing, decided to build a rival attraction. A practical businessman, he put his passenger and freight terminal in the basement—at river level—and a general store and offices above. The top two floors were turned into an opera house. Featured performers of the day included Effie Ellsler, Josh Billings, and Henry Ward Beecher. Sometimes complete Broadway shows were brought to East Haddam by steamboat.

The curtain continued to rise at the opera house until 1902, but the coming of the Connecticut Valley Railroad in 1871 eventually put an end to most commercial traffic on the Connecticut, and villages such as Essex and East Haddam returned to obscurity as sleepy river towns.

The main roads south from Hartford headed to New Haven and New York, leaving the lower Connecticut River Valley tranquil in neglect. Farmers continued to gather crops and cut the salt marshes for hay. Great quantities of shad, which found markets in the cities, were caught each spring.

One man who fell in love with this undeveloped river valley was the Hartford-born actor and playwright William Gillette. In 1913, at the height of his career, he decided to build a home in Greenport, Long Island. But sailing home one evening on his 144-foot houseboat, *Aunt Polly*, he passed beneath the tree-lined mountains towering above the Connecticut and decided to build his castle atop the loftiest peak.

Patterned after a Rhenish castle, complete with crenellated battlements and three-foot-thick granite walls, it took five years to build. The view from the terrace is as dramatic as any in the lower Connecticut River Valley. In his will, Gillette instructed his executors "to see to it that the property does not fall into the hands of some blithering saphead who has no conception of where he is and with what surrounded." His wish was carried out, and his property, with three-quarter miles of waterfront, is today part of a state park enjoyed by tens of thousands of visitors each year.

In the 1940s the six-story Goodspeed opera house, the tallest building along the Connecticut River, was turned into a state highway garage for trucks and plows. The Highway Department was about to demolish it in 1959 when the newly formed Goodspeed Opera House Foundation purchased it for one dollar. A refurbished theater, in full High Victorian splendor, opened on June 18, 1963, and has since introduced the world to such Broadway hits as *Man of La Mancha* (1965), *Shenandoah* (1974), and *Annie* (1977).

Essex today is a year-round yachting and tourist center with strong roots in the past. The sea captains have been replaced by suntanned yachtsmen in topsiders, and the great steamers, by yachts and pleasure boats, scurrying in and out of the coves or swaying at anchor at the foot of Steamboat Dock. A steam engine train takes visitors from Essex to Deep River, where they board an excursion boat for cruises to Gillette Castle and the Goodspeed Opera House. Antique shops and boutiques line the streets, but the venerable Griswold Inn still serves ale to visitors as it did in 1776, and the river still looks as it did when Captain Adrian Bloch first sailed upriver aboard his ketch *Onrust* in 1614.

An old-fashioned steam engine train ride, a river cruise; theater in a Victorian opera house; a walk through a Gothic castle and along the streets of a three-century-old New England river town with shops and first-class restaurants—what more could one want from a weekend escape?

4. WHAT TO SEE AND DO

THE VILLAGE OF ESSEX

▪ The Town of Essex includes the villages of **Essex, Ivoryton,** and **Centerbrook.** Most shops are in the village of Essex. Begin your walk at Essex Square, at the head of Main Street. The better antique shops are there *(see #6, Antiques and Crafts)*, as well as **Talbots, Airlooms Stained Glass,** and **The Sheared Sheep** (selling yarns and custom hand knits). Walk past a few shops down North Main Street to the **Clipper Ship Book Shop** and buy the $1 self-guided walking tour map of Essex; then return to Essex Square and continue along Main Street to the river. The 15-minute walk will take an hour if you stop at all the attractive craft and clothing stores along the way. Near the harbor, on the right, is the **Griswold Inn,** where you can enjoy a pint of ale. The street ends at **Steamboat Dock,** the commercial center of old Essex, which has lovely views of the harbor.

▪ To your left at Steamboat Dock (facing the water) is the **Museum of the Connecticut River Foundation** (phone: 767-1564). The museum houses a life-sized model of the first submarine built in the U.S. (1775); it has a hand-cranked propeller. Also on view are ship models, tools, and memorabilia that relate to the maritime history of the lower Connecticut River Valley. Open April through December Tuesday through Sunday, from 10 to 5. Admission is $1.50 for adults, 50¢ for children under 16.

▪ Head back up Main Street and turn right on Ferry Street. The **Essex Boat Works,** where yachts are still being constructed, may let you look inside. Turn left up Pratt Street. **The Gull** (Dauntless Boat Yard; phone: 767-0916), is Essex's only waterfront restaurant and a good bet for lunch. Continue past Main Street to Prospect Street and West Avenue. The **Pratt House** (20 West Avenue; phone: 767-8987) is the home of the Essex Historical Society and a museum of early Connecticut furnishings and accessories. Open June 1 to October 1, Tuesday, Wednesday, Thursday, and Sunday from 1 to 5. Admission is $1.50.

▪ Return to North Main Street and continue north to the **Essex Art Gallery,** which has exhibits in summer. Turn right after Little Point Street and walk through the **Riverview Cemetery,** with panoramic views of North Cove and the river.

GILLETTE CASTLE

▪ If you take Route 9A north from Essex to Gillette Castle (a five-mile drive), you can stop midway at the **Old Stone House** (Deep River; phone: 526-2609). Maintained by the Deep River Historical Society, it contains oil paintings of ships commanded by local captains, rare early photos of the shipyards, old costumes, and Indian artifacts. Particularly noteworthy are collections of cut glass made here at the turn of the century, a display of more than 200 walking sticks, and examples of ivory products made in local factories in the

1800s. Open June through September, Tuesday and Thursday from 2 to 4. Admission is free.

▪ There are two ways to reach **Gillette Castle** (Hadlyme; phone: 526-2336): by ferry from Chester to Hadlyme, or across the bridge at East Haddam. The ferry trip affords the most dramatic view of the castle—the same one that inspired William Gillette to build his home there. To reach the ferry from Deep River, continue north on Route 9A for about two miles and turn right on Route 148. This is the second oldest ferry in continuous operation in Connecticut. It runs from April 1 to November 30 and costs 75¢ for car and driver, and 25¢ for each additional passenger. If you enjoy strenuous walks, and if there's a wait for the ferry, leave your car on the west bank, ferry across, and climb about one-fifth of a mile to the castle. To the left of the ferry landing is a popular picnic spot along the water.

▪ Don't tour Gillette Castle without first reading the *Gillette Castle Guide*, on sale in the souvenir shop for $1. It's beautifully written, and points out things to see you would otherwise miss on your self-guided tour. The flagstone porch offers dramatic three-mile views up and down the river. In June and after Labor Day visitors are allowed in the tower, which affords an even more breathtaking, 360-degree view of the lower Connecticut River Valley. One upstairs room is decorated to look like 221-B Baker Street in London, Sherlock Holmes's address. (From 1899 to 1932, Gillette portrayed Holmes on stage over 1,300 times.) Gillette loved cats and had 15 of his own: see how many of the 60 cat doorstops, mantle decorations, and ceramics you can find. Ask yourself what sort of man would build himself a castle with such a splendid view and then live in a small bedroom facing away from the river. Study the peculiar locks on the doors, the built-in furniture, the foolproof locking device on the bar, and the unique oak light switches. Gillette designed the castle and its furnishings himself, which is why no two of the 47 hand-carved doors are alike. A carved oak "icicle" hangs from the ceiling at one end of the balcony over the living room; pulling it activated a system of valves that threw the entire 7,000-gallon water system on to the main pipe line to produce a 1½-inch stream of water under pressure, in the event of fire. The dining room table was built on rollers so that it could be pushed back while guests seated themselves. The arm chair in Gillette's study also glides back on metal rollers on an oaken track. Gillette built his own narrow-gauge railroad on his property, complete with switches, trestles, and stations. His rolling stock included two miniature locomotives, one steam and one electric, two small Pullman cars that held seven passengers, and a 21-passenger observation car. Top speed was 20 mph. Gillette would entertain guests by taking them on a three-mile run from "Grand Central" to "125th Street." The old train bed is now a series of scenic trails where visitors are free to wander before or after their tour of the castle. Open daily, May 22 through Columbus Day, then weekends only through October from 11 to 5. Admission is $1 for adults, 50¢ for children aged 6 to 11. The park itself, which has three picnic grounds, is open throughout the year from 8 to sunset. Admission is free.

EAST HADDAM

▪ From Gillette Castle, drive north on Route 82 to East Haddam for a look at the **Goodspeed Opera House** (phone: 873-8668) and a tour of the many craft stores between East Haddam and Moodus *(see #6, Antiques and Crafts).* The opera house has tours from early June through August on Mondays from 1 to 3. Admission is $1 for adults and 50¢ for children. The **Tea Caddy** (phone: 873-8371) sells elegant box lunches for picnics. The porch overlooking the river at the **Gelston House** (phone: 873-8257 and 873-9300) is a lovely spot for lunch.

BOAT AND TRAIN RIDES

▪ For a bit of nostalgia, take a 55-minute steam engine train ride on the **Valley Railroad** (Essex; phone: 767-0103) from Essex Junction to Chester and back to Deep River; and then board a 200-passenger river boat for an hour's sail up the Connecticut, past Gillette Castle and the Goodspeed Opera House. The two steam engines were built in the 1920s, and the five Pullman cars were built between 1915 and 1925. First-class service is available in the 1927 **Wallingford Parlor Car** with plush red mohair swivel seats. (For the best view, sit on the right side of the train.) There are no advance train reservations except for groups, so arrive 30 minutes before departure time. If you want to skip the train and take only the boat cruise, contact the **Deep River Navigation Co.** (phone: 526-4954). Tickets for the train trip only cost $4.95 for adults and $3 for children aged 3 to 11. The combination train and boat ticket costs $7.95 for adults and $5 for children. For information on evening cruises, *see #18, After Hours* for details.

▪ **Saybrook Point Cruises** (Old Saybrook; phone: 767-1440) are 1½- to 2-hour trips upriver from Old Saybrook to Essex in a 150-passenger boat. Cruises leave four times daily from July to Labor Day. Call for rates and schedules.

▪ **Yankee Clipper Cruises** (New England Steam Boat Lines, Marine Park, Haddam; phone: 345-4507) are daily cruises between Haddam and either Sag Harbor or Greenport on a 500-passenger excursion boat. The M/V *Yankee Clipper* sails by Gillette Castle and Essex on its way past Old Saybrook into Long Island Sound. Passengers have three-hour stopovers in either of the two Long Island ports. Trips run from June 6 through Labor Day, leaving at 9 A.M. and returning at 6. Greenport cruises are Monday through Wednesday; Sag Harbor cruises are Thursday through Sunday. Tickets cost $14.50 for adults and $7.25 for children under 12.

- The *Yankee Clipper* and the *Eastern Clipper* also have (1) evening musical excursions with live Dixieland jazz or "oldies but goodies" from July to Labor Day, Friday and Saturday at 7:30 and 10:30. Adults, $12, children $6; and (2) Connecticut River cruises with live music from June to Labor Day, Tuesday through Sunday at 1:30. Adults, $7; children, $4.

OLD LYME

- On your way to or from Essex, visit **Elizabeth Tashijan's Nut Museum** (303 Ferry Road; phone: 434-7636). Two rooms of Ms. Tashijan's sprawling nineteenth-century mansion pay homage to the lore of the nut and of its archenemy, the nutcracker. Nut masks and headdresses, nut collages and nut sculptures, even a table with nutcracker legs are on display. Ms. Tashijan, who has appeared on the Mike Wallace and Johnny Carson shows, is a talented painter who has been exploring the aesthetic potential of nuts since she was a teenager. "My family liked nuts and we had bowls and bowls of nuts to eat and play with," she explains. "And one day they became more than edible delights but paintable subjects." The Nut Museum is open May to November, Wednesday, Saturday, and Sunday from 2 to 5. Admission is $2 and a nut.

5. THE ARTS

- The 1985 season at the **Goodspeed Opera House** (East Haddam; phone: 873-8668) runs from late March through mid-November. Tickets cost from $18 to $20. There are occasional last-minute cancellations, but most weekend performances are sold out weeks in advance. Be sure to make reservations before you arrive. Check with the Opera House for new musicals at **Goodspeed at Chester,** 15 minutes away.
- **Ivoryton Playhouse** (Ivoryton, two miles from downtown Essex; phone: 767-8348) is getting more professional all the time, with a six-show season that runs from July to mid-September. Recent productions include *Sleuth* and *Ain't Misbehavin'* with members of the original Broadway cast. Tickets cost $12 to $15. Order a $7.50 picnic supper from Fine Bouche when you place your ticket orders.

6. ANTIQUES AND CRAFTS

ANTIQUES

▪ Within a block of each other in Essex are three top-quality antique stores. **Francis Bealey** (3 South Main Street; phone: 767-0220) deals in American furniture and the Old Lyme School of Impressionist paintings.

▪ Visitors with a serious interest in pewter should make an appointment to see **June and Ben Cardé** (Main Street, Centerbrook; phone: 767-0022). Their collection is a reminder that pewterware is not limited to mugs and tankards, but includes basins, bowls, teapots, demijohns, creamers, inkwells, and ladles. **Charles and Patricia Thill Antiques** (Main Street, Centerbrook; phone: 767-1696 or 767-0590) is located nearby and also open only by appointment.

▪ Visitors to the Goodspeed Opera House in East Haddam can stop at **Howard and Dickerson Antiques** (Main Street, East Haddam; phone: 873-9990), which specializes in eighteenth- and nineteenth-century English and American antiques and accessories.

CRAFTS

▪ A walk down Main Street in Essex takes you past several attractive craft stores, including **Airlooms Stained Glass** (2 South Main Street; phone: 767-0534), **Limited Editions** (59 Main Street; phone: 767-1071), and **Connecticut Mariner** (Griswold Square, across from the inn; phone: 767-8198).

▪ The craft stores in East Haddam and Moodus are in themselves worth a visit to the area. A few blocks behind the Goodspeed Opera House is the **Connecticut River Artisans Cooperative,** (Goodspeed Landing, East Haddam, phone: 873-1661), selling pottery, jewelry, woolen ponchos, belts, reproduction folk art animals, and other sophisticated goods handcrafted by 30 local artisans. Open April through December from 11 to 6, and January through March from 1 to 5. Closed Monday.

▪ From the Opera House, turn north on Route 149, and drive about four miles to Moodus. At the caution light, turn left on North Moodus Road. On your right is **A Touch of Glass** (North Moodus Road, Moodus; phone: 873-9709). The former Methodist Church had been a Jewish community center before Michael Axelrod bought it in 1972 for $12,500 and converted it into his studio and home. The main church area, 28 feet by 60 feet, is now Michael's living room. The stage, where the altar once stood, is the bedroom. A side Sunday school classroom is the main showroom, which carries the work of some 12 talented artists. Stained glass windows, lamps, wall hangings, and pill boxes sell from $12 to $300.

▪ Further down the road is **Finally!** (phone: 873-1111), where you can buy yarns homespun from the owner's two Angora goats. Goats may also be for sale, "depending on how it goes."

▪ Make a left turn, just past **Finally!**, and visit **Down on the Farm** (Banner Road, Moodus; phone: 873-9905). Housed in this converted chicken coop is the work of some 300 craftspeople from across the country. Two glass blowers and a woodworker have permanent studios on the premises. The "farm" is open April to mid-January, Tuesday through Sunday from 1 to 5.

8. WALKS

▪ The **Museum of the Connecticut River Foundation** (near the foot of Main Street, Essex; phone: 767-1564) sells a self-guided walking tour map of Essex for $1. The walk takes from 60 to 90 minutes. The map is also sold at the Griswold Inn and at the Clipper Ship Book Shop.

▪ After visiting Gillette Castle *(see #4, What to See and Do)*, explore 190 acres of wooded trails in the **Gillette Castle State Park.** Three miles of trails follow the old train bed of Gillette's private railroad. About one-quarter mile from the castle the trail passes through a 150-foot train tunnel. The park, open year-round from 8 A.M. to sunset, has four picnic areas.

▪ The dramatic falls at **Devils Hopyard State Park** (about seven miles northeast of Gillette Castle; phone: 873-8566) are located near the parking area. A better bet is the scenic trail along **Eight Mile River.** But if you prize solitude, stay away on summer weekends.

▪ A favorite spot for quiet walks is the **Cockaponset State Forest** (about 11 miles north of Essex, off Route 9; phone: 345-4449). You can walk around **Cedar Lake** or swim at spring-fed **Pataconk Lake.**

▪ Few out-of-towners know about two protected areas owned by the Nature Conservancy. **Turtle Creek Wildlife Sanctuary** (Watrous Point Road, off Route 9A, less than two miles south of Essex) is an 89-acre tract with trails leading to a pond, a swamp, and a wooded area with some fine old beech, oak, hemlock, and hickory. The sanctuary borders the South Cove and the Connecticut River. **Meadow Woods Natural Area** (off Dennison Road, less than two miles northwest of Essex) is a 97-acre tract with spectacular views of the Connecticut River from its rocky ridges.

10. BOATING AND FISHING

BOATING

▪ The **Dauntless Marina, Windsurfer** (37 Pratt Street, Essex; phone: 767-0743) rents windsurfers and gives lessons. The **Inflatable Boat Center** (phone: 767-8101)—also known as **Offshore Rentals**—rents small four-passenger inflatable boats with or without motors. You can take one upriver and enjoy dramatic views of Gillette Castle and the Goodspeed Opera House. You can also explore beautiful **Seldon's Creek** and some of the river islands. The same company has a 38-foot sloop available for day charters along the river. **Windsurfing of Essex** (1 Essex Square; phone: 767-2343) rents sailboards for $10 an hour, $35 a day.

▪ Canoes can be rented from **North American Canoe Tours** (Hadlyme, near Gillette Castle; phone: 526-5492) and **Down River Canoes** (P.O. Box 265, East Haddam; phone: 388-4175). Both outfitters offer a variety of trips and can arrange to transport your canoe upstream. The lower Connecticut can be a problem for beginners because of tricky winds, fast currents, and heavy motor boat traffic. Paddlers may prefer to canoe down the **Salmon River.**

FISHING

▪ First stop for fishermen should be the **Pataconck Trading Post** (Route 9A, Deep River; phone: 526-3378), where Charley Castelli will sell you bait and a fishing license, along with a net full of free advice. He also organizes escorted fishing trips to **Cedar Lake.**

▪ **Devils Hopyard State Park** (phone: 873-8566) has trout-stocked streams.

▪ According to Castelli, motor boats drive fish out of the river, into **Chapman's Pond,** below Haddam Bridge. You need a boat to get there or permission from the Goodspeed Airport (phone: 873-8632) to walk across their property.

▪ Fishing gear is also for sale at **Davis Bait and Tackle** (Falls Road, East Haddam; phone: 873-9952).

11. SWIMMING

▪ **Banner Lodge** (Moodus, 14 miles north of Essex; phone: 873-8652 or 873-9075) has an Olympic-sized pool nonguests may use. The $7.50 fee includes use of the tennis courts, basketball court, and other sports facilities. For an additional $8, you can rent a cabin for daytime use.

▪ Swimming is permitted in **Pataconk Lake** in the **Cockaponset State Forest** (about 11 miles northwest of Essex; phone: 345-4449).

12. SKIING

▪ **Powder Ridge** (Middlefield, off Route 147, about 25 miles northwest of Essex; phone: 349-3454) is the nearest ski area. Five lifts lead to 14 trails. There is also a three-quarter mile loop for cross-country skiing. Lifts are open weekdays until 10:30 and on weekends from 6:30 A.M. to 3 A.M.

▪ **Mt. Southington** (Southington, Exit 30 off I-84, about 35 miles northwest of Essex; phone: 628-0954 or 628-0955) has six lifts leading to 12 trails. There is night skiing until 10:30.

▪ Skis can be rented from **Action Sports** of Old Saybrook (1385 Boston Post Road, Old Saybrook; phone: 388-1291).

▪ There are eight miles of cross-country skiing trails in the **Cockaponset State Forest** (about 11 miles north of Essex, off Route 9; phone: 345-4449).

13. RIDING

▪ **Cave Hill Stables,** (Moodus, 14 miles north of Essex; phone: 873-8347 in summer, 873-8476 off-season) offers one-hour trail rides throughout the year.

14. TENNIS

▪ **Banner Lodge** (Moodus, 14 miles north of Essex; phone: 873-8652 or 873-9075) has four outdoor courts open to nonguests. A $7.50 admission fee entitles you to free use of the lodge's courts, pool, and other sports facilities.

▪ Essex has free municipal courts in back of the Town Hall on West Avenue.

▪ **Centerbrook Elementary School** (Centerbrook, two miles west of Essex) has public courts.

▪ **Old Saybrook Racquet and Swim Club** (6 Springbrook Road, Old Saybrook; phone: 388-5115) has four indoor courts. Courts remain open until 11 P.M.

▪ **Nathan Hale High School** (Town Street, East Haddam) has courts open to the public.

15. GOLF

▪ **Banner Lodge** (Moodus, 14 miles north of Essex; phone: 873-8652 or 873-9075) has a championship 18-hole, par-72 course.

▪ **Fenwick Golf Course** (Fenwick, about 8 miles south of Essex; phone: 388-2516) is a nine-hole town course.

▪ **Lyman Meadow Golf Club** (Middletown, junction of Routes 147 and 157, about 22 miles north of Essex; phone: 349-8055) is an 18-hole championship course designed by Robert Trent Jones.

16. FOR KIDS

▪ Look under *#4, What to See and Do* for **Gillette Castle.** Kids with excessive energy can walk the steep one-fifth mile trail from the ferry landing to the castle, while adults make the one-mile trip by car. Don't miss the trail that goes under the old railroad tunnel. A trip to the castle will be a richer experience if children read some Conan Doyle before their arrival.

▪ Look under *#4, What to See and Do* for **Elizabeth Tashijan's Nut Museum** in Old Lyme, the **Valley Railroad, Yankee Clipper** cruises, and the **Goodspeed Opera House.**

▪ Older children can rent inflatable boats near **Steamboat Landing** in Essex *(see #10, Boating and Fishing).*

▪ *See #18, After Hours* below for evening music cruises on the Connecticut River.

▪ The best restaurant for families is the **Griswold Inn,** where children will enjoy listening to sea chanteys and singing along with an unlikely assortment of instruments, ranging from harmonicas to tubas.

17. DINING

Ask local people where they dine and most will say "The Gris"—not because the food is exceptional, but because the atmosphere is. For a more imaginative menu, in a more relaxed setting overlooking the river, they head for The Gull. And for special occasions, when they can afford the price of a serious French restaurant, they dine at the Copper Beach Inn in Ivoryton, Fine Bouche in Centerbrook, or the Old Lyme Inn in Old Lyme.

▪ Everyone in Essex loves the **Griswold Inn** (Main Street, Essex; phone: 767-0991). It's the social heartbeat of the community—an American answer to the British pub. To fully appreciate it, arrive on a cold winter weekend when the fireplaces are roaring, and the taproom is filled with old friends. The inn opened for business in 1776, and has been adding rooms and memorabilia ever since. The bar was a 1738 schoolhouse, moved here on rolling logs by a team of oxen. The back dining room was built in the 1940s from the wood of an abandoned New England bridge. The walls are filled with a happy confusion of Currier and Ives steamboat prints (one of the most important collections in the country), firearms dating back to the fifteenth century, turn-of-the-century marine paintings, and steamboat memorabilia. There's music throughout the year: sometimes a piano or a Scottish folk singer; other times a banjo, harmonica, piano, and tuba. Visitors are encouraged to sing along. The inn's approach to food is summed up in a note on its brochure: "We have no pretenses. Our menu is printed in English. We call fish fish and beef beef. No tenderizers. No chemicals. The real thing." The popular Hunt Breakfast, served on Sunday from 11:30 to 2:30, includes fried chicken, lamb kidneys, creamed chipped beef, Maine smelts, grits, and of course thick slab bacon and eggs. Dinner entrées cost from $9 to $15, and include roast duckling with orange sauce; roast prime ribs of beef with freshly grated horseradish; fried chicken with biscuits and honey; and fresh fish. Favorite homemade desserts include pecan pie and hot deep-dish apple pie. Reservations are advised. Dress is casual. All major credit cards are accepted.

▪ The **Copper Beech Inn** (Ivoryton, two miles from Essex; phone: 767-0330) has for five years been voted "best restaurant" by readers of *Connecticut* magazine. Waiters in starched white jackets and black ties wander through a world of candlelight and crystal. Diners can choose between the restrained elegance of the Ivoryton room or the less formal Comstock Room, a former billiard parlor with rich, dark mahogany paneling. Popular appetizers include boned chicken stuffed with lobster, served with a sauce of red currants, port wine, orange rinds, and ginger; poached oysters wrapped with spinach leaves, flavored with lemon butter and garnished with caviar and diced pimentos; and paté of wild rabbit with a pumpkin sauce. Entrées, priced from $14.95 to $23, include fillet of salmon prepared with crème fraîche, layered with puff pastry, and served with a sauce of chablis, shallots, cream, and butter; and roast leg of veal garnished with braised cabbage, buttered chestnut sauce, bacon, and pearl onions. Reservations are advised. Jackets are required. All major credit cards are accepted.

▪ **Fine Bouche** (28 Main Street, Centerbrook, about two miles from Essex; phone: 767-1277) opened in 1979. It is smaller and less well known than the Copper Beech Inn or Old Lyme Inn, but enjoys a similar reputation as a first-class French restaurant. The turn-of-the-century farmhouse has three small dining rooms that together seat only 45. The menu leans toward nouvelle cuisine. The five-course fixed-price dinner costs $29. Popular appetizers are poached oysters served in a shell on a bed of spinach topped with herb sauce, and warm duck paté surrounded by puff pastry dough. A la carte entrées, priced from $10.50 to $14.50, include ragout of sweetbreads and veal tenderloin with mushrooms in a madeira and tarragon sauce; and sautéed duck with leeks, green peppercorns, and a cream sauce. A favorite dessert is three-layer hazelnut and almond meringue cake, with layers of chocolate praline and crème fraîche. Reservations are advised. Ties are recommended. Visa and Mastercard are accepted.

▪ **The Gull** (Dauntless Boat Yard, Pratt Street, Essex; phone: 767-0916), now run by the owners of the Cooper Beech Inn in Ivoryton, is Essex's only waterfront restaurant, with a wide view of the harbor. The specialty is fresh seafood, such as steamers and broiled swordfish with herb butter. Dinner entrées range from $9 to $16. Reservations are advised. Dress is casual. All major credit cards are accepted.

▪ **The Restaurant du Village** (Chester, phone: 526-5301) serves traditional French meals that have won three stars in *Connecticut Magazine* and two stars in *The New York Times*. Entrées range from $15 to $20. Visa and Mastercard are accepted.

▪ **Old Lyme Inn** (Lyme Street, Old Lyme; phone: 434-2600) offers sophisticated, formal dining in an 1850 house restored with period furnishings. A single rosebud adorns each spacious table in the Empire room, where yellow swag curtains hang from high French windows. Entrées, priced from $14 to $17.50, include poached salmon in a red wine, cream, and béarnaise sauce; braised game hen with a pear brandy and madeira sauce; and scallop mousse with a saffron and watercress cream sauce. A favorite dessert is Queen of Sheba cake—a thick chocolate cake made with buttercream frosting and nuts. Reservations are advised. Ties are optional, but most guests dress up. All major credit cards are accepted. (*See #19, Lodging* for more information.)

▪ Area residents have nothing but praise for the new menu and ambience at the **Bee and Thistle Inn** (100 Lyme Street, Old Lyme; phone: 434-1667). The atmosphere here is more informal and relaxed than at the Old Lyme Inn. The main dining room has only seven tables, with country flower-print tablecloths, fresh flowers, and lanterns. Dinner guests listen to soft classical music, or to innkeeper Barbara Bellows singing ballads and accompanying herself on dulcimer or guitar. Sophisticated seasonal dishes, priced from $12 to $17, include linguine, mussels, clams, and shrimp in a fresh pesto sauce;

and veal sweetbreads. Don't miss the homemade scones with honey. Reservations are advised. Jackets are recommended for Saturday dinner. All major credit cards are accepted.

▪ The historic **Gelston House** (East Haddam; phone: 873-8257 or 873-9300), located next door to the Goodspeed Opera House, is under new management and the food, according to all reports, has improved markedly. The porch overlooking the river is a lovely spot for lunch. The beer garden behind the restaurant, also overlooking the river, is fine for steamers or for Cajun or Creole specialties. Visitors who are attending a performance at the Goodspeed Opera House will appreciate the convenience of the Gelston House, which is less than a minute's walk away. The dinner menu, with entrées priced around $10, includes such regional specialties as Chesapeake veal and crab casserole, and San Francisco Cioppino (a fish stew with garlic, tomatoes, and herbs). Reservations are advised, particularly before performances. Dress is casual. All major credit cards are accepted.

▪ The new owner of the Gelston House also runs the new 47-room **Inn at Chester** (ten minutes from Essex, 13 minutes from the Goodspeed Opera House; phone: 526-4961). The Inn, used midweek as an executive retreat, has six elegant dining rooms serving regional American food. The Connecticut edition of *The New York Times* gave it 2½ stars. Entrées cost from $10 to $20. All major credit cards are accepted.

18. AFTER HOURS

▪ After dark, couples and singles head for the **Griswold Inn** (Main Street, Essex; phone: 767-0991). *See #17, Dining* and *#19, Lodging.*

▪ **Willy J.'s** (Ferry Road, Old Saybrook; phone: 388-1441) has an outdoor porch with dixieland music and an indoor lounge with disco music and dancing.

▪ The **Valley Railroad** (Essex 06426; phone: 767-0103) offers evening train and boat rides on Saturday nights, May 15 to October 16, from 7:30 to 10:30. The steam engine train takes you from Essex Junction to Deep River, where you board an excursion boat for a two-hour music cruise on the Connecticut River. The 165 passengers dance to live jazz or country music. July 17 is classical music night; August 14 is Polish night. The $12 tickets must be prepaid.

▪ Upstream at Haddam, two cruise ships (New England Steamboat Lines, Marine Park, Haddam 06438; phone: 345-4507) take passengers on three-hour Friday and Saturday night Connecticut

River cruises, featuring live music and dancing. The choice is yours, either a ship with a live dixieland band or a band playing rock and roll from the fifties and sixties. Cruises run from July to Labor Day, from 7:30 to 10:30. Tickets cost $12 for adults and $6 for children under 12.

  ▪ **Old Saybrook Racquet and Swim Club** (Old Saybrook; phone: 388-5115) has night indoor tennis. **Powder Ridge** and **Mount Southington** have night skiing in season *(see #12, Skiing)*.

19. LODGING

  ▪ **Bishopsgate** (Goodspeed Landing, East Haddam; phone: 873-1677) is a six-bedroom colonial house within walking distance of the Goodspeed Opera House. The recently renovated rooms are furnished with family heirlooms and antiques, and the wide pine floorboards are covered with oriental rugs. Four rooms have working fireplaces; one has a Jenny Lind spool bed with a fishnet canopy. Each floor has its own comfortable sitting room. Guests gather for breakfast at the long harvest table for homebaked apple crisps or freshly baked scones. Doubles, two with shared bath, cost $60 to $85, including a light breakfast. No credit cards are accepted.

  ▪ The atmosphere upstairs in the **Griswold Inn** (Main Street, Essex 06246; phone: 767-0991) is a mixture of Sears and age-old charm. Classical music is piped into loudspeakers; with switches to regulate the sound. Some mattresses are very soft. Second-floor rooms are preferable to those on the third. Some rooms have Victorian furnishings—marble-topped night tables, four-poster beds, and the requisite white chenille spreads. Staying here, in the center of Essex, guests can shop or explore the waterfront without using their cars. They can also wander through town in the early morning and at dusk, when the summer crowds are gone. Doubles, most with private bath, cost $52 to $75, including a continental breakfast. All major credit cards are accepted.

  ▪ **The Gelston House** (East Haddam; phone: 873-8257) is expected to have six upstairs suites this summer for $80 to $250 a night.

  ▪ **Copper Beach Inn** (Ivoryton 06442, two miles from Essex; phone: 767-0330) is much more formal and elegant than the Griswold Inn. "The Gris," built in 1776, is a rambling old building, with creaky stairwells and a down-home, somewhat salty Yankee tang to it. The meticulously restored Copper Beach Inn was the former residence of a prosperous nineteenth-century ivory merchant. It has beautifully carved solid oak doors and paneling, and is the home of one of the finest French restaurants in Connecticut. The room with white wicker furniture and limegreen bedspreads may seem excessively decorated to some. The room with queen-sized canopied bed seems more in keeping with the spirit of a New England seaport. All five rooms have private bath. Doubles cost $55 to $85. All major credit cards are accepted.

• Rooms in the **Old Lyme Inn** (Lyme Street, Old Lyme, about seven miles south of Essex; phone: 434-2600) are as elegant and comfortable as those in the Copper Beach Inn, but don't have quite the same personality. The wainscoted rooms have deep blue carpets, four-poster beds with chenille spreads, and plush velvet couches. Bed tables have magazines like *Bazaar, Signature,* and *Business Week.* Room #4 is a large, attractive corner room. The five rooms are located upstairs in an 1850 farmhouse that was restored with Empire and Victorian furnishings. The restaurant is considered one of the best in Connecticut. Doubles, all with private bath, cost $60, including a continental breakfast. All major credit cards are accepted.

• Rooms in the **Bee and Thistle Inn** (100 Lyme Street, Old Lyme, about seven miles south of Essex; phone: 434-1667) have been tastefully redecorated, two with antique canopy beds and wingback chairs. The Old Lyme Inn has the atmosphere of a formal hotel; the Bee and Thistle, of a country home. Doubles, most with private bath, cost $49 to $70. All major credit cards are accepted.

• The nearest motel is **Howard Johnson's Motor Lodge** (exit 69 off I-95, then Route 9, north to exit 2; phone: 388-5716 or 800/654-2000). Facilities include an indoor pool. Doubles cost $55. Other motels are the **Baldwin Bridge Motel** (I-95, exit 68 from Providence or exit 67 from New York; phone: 388-5776); **The Admiral House Motor Inn** (exit 66 off I-95 south; phone: 399-6273); and **Old Saybrook Motor Hotel** (Route 1, Main Street, Old Saybrook; phone: 388-3463).

20. EMERGENCIES

• **Middlesex Memorial Hospital's Shoreline Clinic** is located on Route 153, Essex. Phone: 767-0107. Hours are from 8 A.M. to midnight.

• The hospital nearest to Essex and East Haddam is the **Middlesex Memorial Hospital,** Middletown. Phone: 347-9471.

• For emergency medical service in the Essex area, dial 911. For emergency service in the East Haddam area, dial 537-3411.

• The nearest hospital to Old Saybrook and Old Lyme is the **Lawrence Memorial Hospital,** New London. Phone: 442-0711.

21. HOW TO GET THERE

BY CAR. *From New York:* I-95 north to exit 69, then Route 9 north to exit 3. Follow signs to Essex. *From Boston:* I-95 south to exit 69. Then Route 9 north to exit 3. Follow signs to Essex. *From Hartford:* Route 91 south to Route 9 south. Take exit 3 and follow signs to Essex.

BY TRAIN. Take Amtrak *from New York* (phone: 212/736-4545) or *from Boston* (phone: 617/482-3660) to Old Saybrook. During the summer, the Valley Railroad (phone: 767-0103) takes passengers from the Amtrak station in Old Saybrook to Essex Junction. The 20-minute trip is made in a single passenger car behind a diesel engine. If you plan to take a taxi from Old Saybrook to Essex, be sure to reserve a cab in advance. Phone: 388-2101.

BY BUS. *From New York:* take Greyhound (phone 212/635-0800) to Old Saybrook. *From Boston:* take Bonanza Bus Lines (phone: 617/423-5810) to Providence, then switch to Greyhound to Old Saybrook. (*See By Train* above for travel from Old Saybrook to Essex.)

22. FOR FURTHER INFORMATION

▪ **Essex Township Board of Trade** (G.P.O. Essex 06426; phone: 767-1666).

▪ East Haddam is represented by the **Northern Middlesex Chamber of Commerce** (100 Riverview Center, Middlesex 06457; phone: 347-6924).

▪ General information on the lower Connecticut River Valley is available from the **New England Tourist Information Center** (Olde Mistick Village, Mystic 06335; phone: 536-1641).

23. RECOMMENDED READING

▪ Marie Moore's *Portrait of Essex* (Globe Pequot Press, $5.95) is for sale in the Clipper Ship Book Shop, North Main Street, Essex. Phone: 767-1666.

▪ "The Innkeeper's Log," distributed by the Griswold Inn, is filled with useful information on the history of Essex.

Mystic, Connecticut

(Zip Code, 06355; Area Code, 203)

1. DISTANCES

BY CAR. *From New York,* 2½ hours; *from Boston,* 2 hours; *from Hartford,* one hour.

BY TRAIN. *From New York,* 3 hours; *from Boston,* 2 hours.

2. MAJOR ATTRACTIONS

- America's largest maritime museum, with a recreated nineteenth-century seaport village, the last remaining wooden whaling ship, craft demonstrations, and an exciting collection of figureheads, ship models, and scrimshaw.
- An $8 million aquarium, with trained porpoises, white whales, sea lions, sharks, and displays of 2,000 fish from around the world.
- A nearby fishing village (Stonington) with antique stores and a first-class French restaurant.
- Sailing; swimming; submarine tours; river cruises aboard one of the country's last coal-fired steamboats.

243

3. INTRODUCTION

Only the sea is equal to our imagination. It awakens a sense of possibilities, and a fearful yearning for the unknown. Our heroes today are drawn from comic books, but the nineteenth-century sea captains, pitting their wits against the elements, were heroes from real life. The values they prized were resourcefulness and discipline. Life aboard their ships was essentially medieval, with well-defined roles and responsibilities and a common respect for the awesome forces that control our lives.

It is this lost world of the nineteenth-century whalers and clipper ships that most landlubbers try to recapture when they visit Mystic today. Wandering along the waterfront in the recreated seaport, they can travel back in time to the days when Mystic produced more noted captains and a greater tonnage of fine ships and steamers than any place of comparable size in the world.

Carl Cutler, the museum's founder, has described Mystic during its heyday from 1850 to 1870: "The little port was a veritable hive of industry. Blunt bowed old whaleships lay side by side with lofty clippers, whose slender towering spars and exquisitely modeled lines gave no suggestion of the massive timbering below. Clumsy coasters, steamboats, smacks and packet sloops appeared and vanished in endless procession.

"From early morning until dusk the village resounded with the clatter of axes and mauls and the incessant scream of power saws, mingled with the shouts and cries of sailors, riggers and stevedores, loading and outfitting the ships. Boiler factories and forges added to the clamor. Ox and horse drawn timber gears, trucks loaded with casks and crates, hand carts piled high with coils of rigging or sailors' dunnage streamed through the narrow streets. Men hurried back and forth on feverish errands as though life itself depended on speed.

"During the four years of the Civil War alone, Mystic launched 56 steamships, the largest of which was 250 feet in length. This, in addition to six schooners, three brigs, two barks and three ships, the smallest of which measured over 300 tons and the largest, 1,500 tons.

"From whatever angle the record is viewed, it stands as one of the notable human achievements in American history. No shipbuilding center on the Atlantic Coast with three times the population of Mystic ever approached it."*

Mystic's history really begins with the arrival of the Pilgrims, who stepped ashore on what they assumed was the rich farmland of

*Reprinted with permission from Carl C. Cutler's *Mystic: The Story of a Small New England Seaport.*

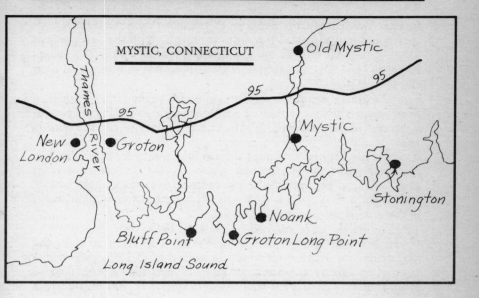

"Northern Virginia," and found themselves in a "howling wilderness." Fish and timber were the only natural resources. Since their survival depended on goods imported from abroad, the settlers became fishermen, boat builders, and sailors.

To build ships, Cutler explains, two things were necessary: gently sloping banks on deep channels, where ships could be laid down and safely launched, and broad tidal rivers stretching inland to tap the forests, with their stands of hardwood.

One of these rivers, which the Indians called "Mistick," was only five miles long, yet had probably more natural shipbuilding sites than any other similar stretch of water in America. There was a big sandbar halfway up—the original village of Mystic was established here—but beyond that, the river was navigable to the head.

Until 1800, the Mystic River had few permanent shipyards, and only a dozen farms spread along its banks. Vessels were built by itinerants who went wherever their services were in demand, or by farmers and fishermen who needed small coastal fishing vessels for their work. Long voyages were the exception.

Mystic developed as a major seaport essentially because of the purchase of Florida in 1819, the economic development of the south, and the rapid rise of the seal and whaling trades.

When the U.S. purchased Florida, Mystic sailors began trading at southern ports. As the cotton crop increased in value, southern farmers needed Mystic shippers to transport manufactured goods they could now afford to buy from the north. With the development of the steamboat in 1820, goods were brought down the Mississippi River to New Orleans, where Mystic men were waiting with their ships.

The great demand for seal fur and oil led to the mass slaughter of these animals along the coast of South America, in the Pacific Northwest, and in the Antarctic. Mystic sailors actively joined the hunt in 1819.

The need for oil for lamps and for lubricating the new industrial machinery sparked the search for whales. In 1815, whale oil sold for $1.50 a gallon. Though Mystic's population never exceeded 1,500, in 1840 it had a fleet of 18 whaleships. Mystic men often bought shares in these ships, or signed on as crew.

The whale trade reached its peak in 1845, then gradually declined. Whales became scarce, and the price of whale oil so expensive that people turned to turpentine and kerosene. In 1859, oil was discovered in Pennsylvania and the price of whale oil dropped to 10 cents a barrel. Mystic's last whaler was sold shortly after the outbreak of the Civil War.

Both the war and the migration of Americans to California prompted the need for fast-sailing clipper ships. Mystic's shipyards experienced their greatest activity between 1850 and 1870, when the little village produced 22 clippers, and a large number of packets, brigs, and schooners. During the Civil War, when 56 steamships were constructed, the population never exceeded 3,600.

Mystic's "day" ended with Appomattox. As the supply of local timber dwindled, boat manufacturing costs went up and builders of wooden ships moved north to Maine, where hardwoods were still plentiful. The war taught the nation a respect for iron steamers, and iron boat construction shifted to regions near the coal and ore centers—along the Delaware, in Philadelphia, Chester, and Wilmington. Mystic's last full-rigged ships were launched in 1869; thereafter, construction shifted to small craft, commercial fishing boats, and yachts. Today only one shipyard still functions on the Mystic, building small boats. The others have turned into marinas, which repair and store boats for the summer traffic. The famous Greenman and Mallory yards are now part of the Mystic Seaport Museum.

The concept of a Seaport Museum began with three men: Carl Cutler, a Michigan-born lawyer who grew up along the Rhode Island coast and experienced life at sea aboard the bark *Alice* to New Zealand; Dr. Charles K. Stillman, a doctor, artist, and descendant of local shipbuilders; and Edward E. Bradley, a local businessman who had gone to sea as a boy. Meeting on Christmas Day 1929, they decided to pool together what artifacts they could find—sea chests, blubber hooks, lanterns—and to go in search of more. They incorporated as the Marine Historical Association with the purpose of preserving America's maritime heritage.

In 1941, the association acquired the *Charles M. Morgan*, the last wooden whaling ship afloat. A second ship, *Joseph Conrad*, was presented to the Museum by an act of Congress. Homes of shipbuilders were donated by their descendants, and a nineteenth-century coastal community was recreated along the waterfront. Attendance in 1935, which cost 25 cents, was 184. In 1943 it was up to 7,050. By the museum's fiftieth anniversary in 1979, attendance had reached 434,059.

Along the Atlantic coast today, most of the great nineteenth-century shipyards are empty or gone. A few have turned into marinas, or are busy launching atomic submarines and fiberglass sailboats. The Mystic Seaport Museum stands alone as a tribute to the Age of Sail. Visitors who walk in the shadows of the tall ships will recognize this period as a vital part of their American heritage. Many will find themselves pulled by the ageless magic of the sea, and hear themselves repeating John Masefield's familiar lines:

> *I must down to the seas again, to the lonely sea and the sky,*
> *And all I ask is a tall ship and a star to steer her by,*
> *And the wheel's kick and the wind's song and the white sail's shaking*
> *And a gray mist on the sea's face and a gray dawn breaking.**

NOTE: Mystic is really two villages connected by a drawbridge across the Mystic River. It is no more than a mailing address, and has no government of its own. The area on the west bank is part of the Township of Groton. Until 1890 it was known as Portersville. Most of the downtown shops are here, on East Main Street and Water Street. The area on the east bank, which includes the aquarium and the Seaport Museum, is part of Stonington Township. Until 1890 it was known as Mystic Bridge. The *Borough* of Stonington is a small, charming seaside village within the township. The Lighthouse Museum is here, and the elegant Harbor View Restaurant, and the last commercial fishing fleet in Connecticut.

Confused? There's more. When people refer to "Old Mystic," they may have three places in mind. The first is an area in downtown

---

*"Sea Fever" by John Masefield from *Poems* (New York: Macmillan, 1953). Reprinted by permission of Macmillan Publishing Co., Inc.

Mystic, on the Groton side, where many of the nineteenth-century sea captains lived. You may want to walk there, along Gravel Street, and admire their homes.

Old Mystic is also the original colonial trading center, near the head of the river. It was situated there, near a sandbar, because of the difficulty of crossing the river farther south. The lower Mystic developed rapidly in the first quarter of the nineteenth century, with the rise of the shipbuilding industry and the construction of a wooden drawbridge in 1819; and Old Mystic today is no more than a post office, a church, a general store, and a post office. Oldtimers who do not take kindly to tourists have been known to send them to Old Mystic when they ask to go there. Nine times out of ten, the visitors are trying to find Olde Mistick Village—a relatively new, mock-colonial village with some 40 specialty shops. The village is located on Route 27, just south of Exit 90 on I-95. The Information Center is part of the complex, and the aquarium is nearby.

4. WHAT TO SEE AND DO

▪ A visit to Mystic is incomplete without trips to the **Marinelife Aquarium** and the Mystic **Seaport Museum.** The two attractions are within a mile of each other along Route 27, just south of exit 90 of I-95. Both are run by nonprofit organizations, which have nothing in common but an interest in attracting the largest share of visitors. The aquarium will take at least two hours, the Seaport Museum, four. Of course, you could spend a week in the museum and not see everything. Visitors who get upset by crowds should restrict their visits to weekdays and off-season. Mystic is particularly lovely and unrushed in late spring and fall. If you must come on a summer weekend, get an early start. Both the seaport and aquarium open at 9. Begin at the seaport, since crowds are more objectionable there, and in the morning you'll have more energy to tour the 17-acre site. In the aquarium, you can sit and enjoy the show.

THE SEAPORT MUSEUM

Mystic Seaport Museum (phone: 572-0711) is open from late April to late November from 9 to 5; December through April from 9 to 4. Admission in season is $8.50 for adults and $4.25 for children aged 5 to 15. Two-day passes in-season cost $9 for adults and $4.50 for children.

Parking lots are located opposite both the north and the south entrances. The tour proposed below begins at the north entrance. The driver of your car may want to leave passengers here, and then park at the south entrance so that the car will be waiting at the end of the trip. The driver can walk back and meet others in the **Stillman Building.**

Large families may save money and help a good cause by purchasing a $30 family membership ticket, which entitles them to free admission and to a 10-percent savings on purchases in the **Museum Store.** When buying your tickets, get a copy of the list of daily activities, which includes sail setting and furling; whaleboat rowing; fish splitting, salting, and drying; and dory trawling. The $1 guidebook provides useful background information on each of the exhibits. Some of the highlights are described below, but there is much more to see and do, depending on your time and interests.

▪ The **Stillman Building** has a first-floor exhibit that traces the maritime history of New England. This is a sensible place to begin your visit. If you thought scrimshaw was a form of turnpike gift shop art, don't miss the extraordinary scrimshaw collection on the second floor. The carved whalebone would be the pride of any major museum collection in the country. Children of all ages love ship models, and the second and third floors have some fine examples, some of them made from bone, glass, and silver.

▪ Across the street from the Stillman Building, to the north, is the **Packard Cabin Exhibit.** Odds are you'll feel a bit seasick as you wander through the actual mess quarters and captain's stateroom of a late nineteenth-century cargo-carrying sailing ship.

▪ Across the street, to the south, is the **Figurehead Exhibit.** Some of these wooden figures look as though they had just seen an apparition; others look just plain seasick.

▪ Continue south along the waterfront to the fishing schooner *L.A. Dunton,* now moored at **Chubb's Wharf.** This 123-foot Gloucester fisherman was launched from Essex, Massachusetts, in 1921, and was fitted out as a dory trawler for netting cod and halibut in the Grand Banks off Newfoundland, and in the Georges Banks off Cape Cod. Standing below deck, you can imagine what it was like to live on board for two or three long winter months. (It must have felt like home after seven hours of fishing in an open 18-foot dory!)

▪ To the east of **Chubb's Wharf,** away from the river, is **Buckingham House,** a typical Connecticut dwelling of the pre-Revolutionary period. The main house was built in Old Saybrook between 1758 and 1768. In the early 1950s, it was brought to Mystic Seaport by barge in two sections, and restored with period furniture.

▪ From Buckingham House, continue west along the river, through the recreated nineteenth-century seaport village. The ship carver, blacksmith, boat builder, and weaver demonstrate their crafts.

In other village buildings—the grocery store, drug store, chandlery, and cooperage—interpreters describe how these businesses were operated a century ago.

▪ The **Mystic River Diorama** shows how Mystic looked in 1853. Keep the diorama in mind later as you wander through downtown Mystic, past the homes of sea captains on Gravel Street.

▪ The *Charles W. Morgan*, the only surviving wooden whaling ship left in America, is at her permanent berth now at Chubb's Wharf. From 1841 to 1921, she earned more for her owners than any other whaling ship on record. In September 1980, Seaport workers removed the *Morgan's* masts and standing rigging and raised her on the lift dock at the shipyard to restore her hull.

▪ Just outside the south entrance (so that visitors may enter without an admission ticket to the Seaport Museum) is the **Museum Store** (phone: 536-9688). This two-story white clapboard house is your best bet for gifts and mementos in the Mystic area. Browsers and serious shoppers will have no trouble spending several hours among the model ship kits, the nautical placemats, and just about every imaginable object related to the sea. The range of goods varies from jellybeans and Navy crewneck sweaters to $2,800 limited-edition bronze sculptures of whales. Upstairs is an art gallery with nautical prints and exhibits by living artists, and a bookstore with one of the country's largest collections of new, rare, and out-of-print books on sailing. If time is limited, do your shopping in the store catalogue.

▪ The **Seaport Planetarium** (phone: 572-0711, ext. 255) has 30-minute shows throughout the day that show you how sailors navigate by the positions of the stars. Hours are posted on the door. The cost is 75¢. The planetarium also offers concentrated weekend seminars for adults and seriously interested teenagers on piloting and dead reckoning, practical celestial navigation for the offshore sailor, and advanced training in dead reckoning, piloting, and celestial navigation.

THE MARINELIFE AQUARIUM

▪ The **Marinelife Aquarium** (Route 27, just off exit 90 of I-95; phone: 536-3323 or 535-9631) is as fascinating for adults as for kids; there is no age barrier to enjoyment of a snorting seal or the graceful double backflip of a dolphin. The young guides and trainers are seriously committed to their work, and their enthusiasm is contagious. Try to visit the sea lions and other pinnipeds in **Seal Island** at feeding time (ask a guide for hours); they usually give impromptu performances before lunch. Inside the building, some 2,000 fish and invertebrates, from the ugly spider crab to the iridescent permit fish, swim peacefully about in 30 display tanks. Sharks swim by only inches from your nose. The main show is upstairs in the 1,400-seat marine theater. The two white whales don't seem to mind when their 350,000-gallon tank is taken over by performing dolphins, who jump 21 feet in the air, execute triple somersaults, even walk on their tails. Visitors can watch the show in the theater, and then enjoy an unusual underwater performance by standing outside the same glass-enclosed tank on the first floor. The aquarium is open daily at 9. From July 2 to Labor Day, the admission window closes at 6, the last marine show begins at 6, and the building closes at 7:30. Off-season the admission window closes at 4:45, the last marine show begins at 4:45, and the building closes 6. Admission is $5.75 for adults and $2.75 for children aged 5 to 17.

BOAT TRIPS

- The 1908 *Sabino,* one of the few remaining coal-fired passenger steamboats in America, takes 100 passengers on half-hour trips along the museum's waterfront, where they have a unique view of the seaport, its historic buildings and sailing ships. From the main cabin, you can see the original Paine compound steam engine in operation, with the engineer shoveling coal into the furnace. The 57-foot vessel served Newburyport, Massachusetts, and the Casco Bay islands in Maine before the Seaport Museum acquired it in 1973. Cruises run from May to October, every hour on the half-hour from 11 to 4. Tickets, which cost $2 for adults and $1.25 for children, are sold at the *Sabino* booth on the museum grounds.
- The *Sabino* also takes 90-minute evening cruises past downtown Mystic, through the drawbridge and the railroad swing bridge, past historic **Fort Rachel** and the village of **Noank,** to **Fishers Island Sound,** and back. Tickets cost $5 for adults and $3 for children aged 5 to 15. On certain evenings, dixieland bands, barbershop quartets, and chanteymen perform on board. Tickets are $5.50 for adults and $4 for children aged 5 to 15.

OLDE MISTICK VILLAGE

- Olde Mistick village (just off exit 90 of I-95) is a collection of more than 40 specialty shops constructed to look like an old New England village. Inveterate shoppers and browsers will enjoy themselves here. Paris fashion dolls, Toni dolls, Shirley Temple dolls—these and hundreds more are on view or for sale in the **Memory Lane Doll and Toy Museum** (phone: 536-6001). Admission is 50¢ for adults, $2.25 for children. **The Toy Soldier** (phone: 536-1554) has some well-made puppets. **Green Onion** (phone: 536-6001) sells quality kitchenware. **Sturbridge Yankee Workshop** (phone: 572-0529) sells reproduction early American furniture.

DOWNTOWN MYSTIC

The village of Mystic is less than a five minutes' drive south of the Seaport. It has dozens of crafts, antique, and clothing shops, lovely restaurants, and some back streets with historic houses from Mystic's heyday in the late nineteenth century.

▪ From the Seaport Museum, continue south on Route 27 (away from I-95) and turn right on Route 1. On your right, before the bridge, is **Second Impression Antiques.** In the old train depot across the street are **Nanna's Handcrafts** and the **Chamber of Commerce,** where you can pick up a self-guided walking map of historic Mystic. The depot, built in 1905, was used by the Lionel Company as the model for its toy railroad stations. Cross the drawbridge (which goes up at quarter past the hour) and park. You're now on Main Street (Route 1), on the Groton side of Mystic. The first right after the bridge takes you up Gravel Street. The walking tour map lists 43 homes worth seeing on a 20-minute loop up Gravel Street, left on Clift Street, left on High Street, and back to West Main. If you don't have a map, you can read the signs attached to each of the historic houses. Gravel Street borders the Mystic River, and as you walk along you can imagine the nineteenth-century sea captains and ship-builders living here, watching the great ships sailing by their windows. House #13 was a "spite house," deliberately built into the street to block the neighbor's view. House #29 is a handsome Greek Revival house built in 1837 for John Appleman, captain of the *Neptune* and the *Hero.* More recently the house was owned by Captain Edward L. Beach, captain of the *U.S.S. Triton* on its historic underwater circumnavigation of the globe, and author of *Run Silent, Run Deep.*

▪ Bear left along Water Street to **The Emporium** (15 Water Street; phone: 536-3891), which has three floors of gifts. Across the street, at Factory Square, are 12 shops.

▪ The Mystic Art Association Gallery (Water Street; phone: 536-7601) has a national reputation, and is well worth a visit. Admission is free *(See #6 The Arts* for details.)

▪ End your tour of downtown Mystic with a drink or snack at **Margaritaville** (phone: 536-4589), which is part of the restored factory complex.

STONINGTON TOWNSHIP

▪ **Denison Homestead** (Pequotsepos Road, about two miles from the Seaport Museum; phone: 536-9248) gives visitors an opportunity to compare styles and furnishings of five eras, from the colonial period to the early 1920s. The 1717 house was occupied by 11 generations of Denisons. The furniture each successive generation stored in the attic and barn is now back in place, and visitors can wander through time, from a colonial kitchen to a Revolutionary-era bedroom, a Federal parlor, a Civil War–era bedroom, and an early nineteenth-century living room. The Homestead is open May 15 to October 15 from 1 to 5 (closed Monday). Admission is $1.25 for adults and 25¢ for children under 16. Across the street is the **Denison Pequotsepos Nature Center** (see #8, Walks).

▪ **Whitehall** (Route 27, just north of exit 90 of I-95; phone: 536-2428) was built in the early 1770s by Dr. Dudley Woodbridge, a prosperous physician of Old Mystic. It was moved to its present location in 1962 to make way for Route I-95. Most of the paneling is original, and the huge fireplace in the kitchen has a rare brick "trimmer arch" supporting the hearthstone of the fireplace in the room upstairs. The attic worksroom contains spinning wheels. The **Stonington Historical Society** uses this restored, authentically furnished building as its headquarters. The mansion is open daily except Saturday, May 1 to October 31, from 2 to 4. Admission is $1 for adults and 50¢ for children aged 6 to 12. Across Route 27, near the Mystic River, is the **Whitehall Burying Ground,** with some handsomely carved gravestones of early settlers and the markers of freed slaves.

▪ Many people consider **Stonington Borough**—a ten-minute drive east of Mystic—the loveliest coastal village in Connecticut. Surely it's one of the wealthiest, with an impressive list of resident celebrities (Peter Benchley, Sergio Franchi, Pulitzer Prize-winning poet James Merrill), two fine restaurants (**Harborview** and **Noah's**), and the last commercial fishing fleet in the state. Visitors who plan to dine here will want to spend an hour before dinner exploring the town. The **Stonington Historical Society,** located in the Whitehall mansion, has a self-guided walking tour map of the borough that you may also be able to pick up at antique shops. The walking tour takes you down Water Street to the **Lighthouse Museum,** and back up Main Street. **Water Street** has a half-dozen antique shops within three blocks of each other, and a few boutiques. Below Wall Street is the **Arcade.** Built in the 1830s, with a long, low Doric colonnade, it is one of the few Greek Revival commercial buildings in America. The

Lighthouse (phone: 535-1440), at the end of Water Street, was built in 1823 and remained in service until 1889. It now houses a display of locally made stoneware, firearms, ship models, whaling gear, early portraits, and toys. The museum is open July 4 through Labor Day, daily except Monday from 11 to 4:30. From **The Point** you have a splendid view of **Watch Hill** to the east and **Fishers Island** to the west.

▪ Heading back from the Lighthouse, turn right on Omega, left on Hancox, left on Diving, and right on Main. On the corner of Main and Wall Streets is the **Colonel Amos Palmer House** (1780), with its graceful double row of steps. James McNeill Whistler lived here as a child; the house was later owned by Stephen Vincent Benet. Across the street is the gambrel roof of a West Indies trader's house (1761). On the next corner, note the Ionic columns of a wealthy sailmaker's house (1820). Continue north to Broad Street and turn left toward the harbor. Behind a high stone wall is the **Robinson Burying Ground.** Turn left down Gold Street named after the jeweler's shop, then right down High Street to the docks, where the Stonington lobster boats and dragger fleet are moored.

▪ Visitors who love trains will make tracks to **Jim Bradley's Pullman Museum** (Cheeseboro Road, Stonington; phone: 535-1021). Bradley loves trains so much that he bought six railroad cars, dating back to 1914, and installed a track in his backyard. Bradley uses one of the cars as a summer home, and from the observation deck you can see Montauk on a clear day. Other cars include a parlor car with plush seats and old brass lamps, and a sleeping car. Admission is free.

GROTON

▪ For a taste of life aboard a World War II submarine, drive about 10 minutes west of Mystic and tour the 312-foot diesel-powered *U.S.S. Croaker* (359 Thames Street, Groton; phone: 448-1616). The *Croaker* is permanently moored near the **Electric Boat Company,** where she was built in 1944 for duty in the Pacific. Among her victims were a cruiser, four tankers, two freighters, two escort craft, a minesweeper, and an ammunition ship. The 30-minute tours take you to the torpedo room, the engine room, and the crew's living quarters. Tours run April 14 to October 15, daily from 9 to 5; and October 16 to April 13 daily from 9 to 3. Tickets cost $3 for adults and $1.50 for children over 12.

▪ The *Croaker* looks impressive until you compare it to the Trident submarine under construction some 500 feet to the south. The nuclear-powered submarine is in dry dock for all to see.

▪ Visitors can see some of the naval submarines on a one-hour cruise aboard the *River Queen* (Thames Botel and Harbour Inn, 193 Thames Street; phone: 445-8111). Trips run in May and September on weekends, and daily mid-June through Labor Day. The cost is $4.75 for adults, $2.50 for children 12 and under.

▪ **Project Oceanology** (Thames Street, near the *U.S.S. Croaker*, Groton; phone: 448-1616) takes you aboard an oceanographic boat, where you will pull a trawl net filled with fish, study lobster, and use oceanographic equipment with the help of marine scientists. Trips are run by a nonprofit marine education association, which uses proceeds to support its educational programs during the school year. The 2½-hour trips run mid-June to Labor Day, on Saturday and Sunday at 9, 12, and 3; and on Monday and Wednesday at 10 and 1. Tickets cost $9 for adults and $7 for children under 12.

▪ The **U.S. Naval Submarine Base** (Groton; phone: 449-3393), the largest in the Western Hemisphere, is visible only by guided bus tours. The one-hour trips take you along the waterfront, close to nuclear-powered submarines, floating drydocks, rescue vessels, and Polaris and Poseidon missiles. Trips run from the end of June to Labor Day. Phone for an updated schedule and fees.

▪ **Fort Griswold State Park,** the scene of the only Revolutionary War battle in Connecticut, is only a five minutes' walk from the *U.S.S. Croaker.* It was here in 1781 that colonial defenders were slaughtered by British troops under Benedict Arnold. Today it is a lovely, quiet spot for walks and picnics. From on top of the **Memorial Tower** you can see downtown **New London** and the ships under construction in the shipyard.

▪ Another "undiscovered" spot for picnics and dramatic views is **Avery Point** on the campus of the University of Connecticut. The lawn rolls down from an old Newport-type mansion to the water's edge, where you can sit and enjoy the view of the **Thames River** and **Fishers Island Sound.** Avery Point is only a five-minutes' drive from the *U.S.S. Croaker.* Continue south on Thames Street, which turns into Eastern Point Road and leads to Avery Point.

NEW LONDON

▪ **Connecticut Arboretum** (Williams Street, New London, about 20 minutes west of Mystic; phone: 447-1911) is one of the finest nature preserves in the East. Located on the Connecticut College Campus, it has more than 350 acres to explore, including a three-quarter mile self-guided nature trail, and a jogging path around the lake. Open Monday to Saturday from 9 to 5 and Sunday from 1 to 5.

Admission is free. TO GET THERE, take exit 83 on I-95 and drive north on Williams Street.

- South of the arboretum, on Williams Street, is the **Lyman Allyn Museum** (625 William Street, New London; phone: 443-2545). Children will love the display of dollhouse furniture. There are also permanent displays of Egyptian, Greek, and Roman antiquities; medieval and Renaissance art; Oriental and primitive art; and American and European paintings. Open Tuesday through Sunday from 1 to 5.

- **Joshua Hempsted House** (11 Hempstead Street; phone: 443-7949), built in 1678, is one of the few remaining seventeenth-century homes in Connecticut. It is open from May 15 to October 15, Tuesday through Sunday from 1 to 5. Admission is $1 for adults, and 25¢ for children.

- The **Eugene O'Neill House** (325 Pequot Avenue; phone: 443-0051 or 443-5378), known as the Monte Cristo Cottage, was the home of the Eugene O'Neill family and the setting for *Long Day's Journey into Night.* Open Monday to Friday from 1 to 4 or by appointment. Admission is by donation.

5. THE ARTS

- **Eugene O'Neill Theater Center** (305 Great Neck Road, Waterford, about 30 minutes from Mystic; phone: 443-5378) is a must for anyone seriously interested in contemporary theater. A dozen manuscripts of the hundreds received each year are given staged readings by professional actors. Audiences can "play" critic and decide which works are destined for Broadway. Playwrights who got their start here include Israel Horovitz, John Guare, Christopher Durang, and Lanford Wilson. Performances run from July to mid-August, Monday through Saturday, evenings at 8:30, and Saturday at 2. Tickets cost $6 on weekdays, $7 on weekends. Picnic dinners are available at the box office.

- **Connecticut College** (Palmer Auditorium, New London; phone: 447-1911 or [box office] 447-7610) has an ongoing series of classic films, plays, and concerts during the academic year. Phone for details.

- **R. F. Schaefer Gallery** is a museum of maritime paintings located within the Seaport Museum.

- The **Mystic Maritime Gallery,** located on the second floor of the Seaport Museum Store (phone: 536-9688), has changing exhibits of maritime paintings. Prints, paintings, and photographs on maritime themes are for sale.

▪ The **Mystic Art Association Gallery** (Water Street, downtown Mystic, on the Groton side; phone: 536-7601) features changing exhibits by nationally known artists. The gallery was built in 1931 to exhibit the work of such well-known local artists as Robert Brackman, Kenneth Bates, and Lars Thorsen. Openings were the social event of the season, with full-page reviews in *The New York Times*. The gallery is open daily in summer from 10 to 5. There is no admission charge.

▪ **Stone Ledge Studio and Art Galleries** (59 High Street, Noank, about four miles southwest of Mystic; phone: 536-7813) exhibits the work of local painters and members of the **Mystic Art Association School of Painting.** Open daily except Wednesday and Sunday, from 9 to 5.

6. ANTIQUES AND CRAFTS

▪ **Olde Mistick Village** (Route 27, just south of I-95) has several shops that might qualify as craft or antique stores. **Thomas J. SCoughlin, Ltd.** (phone: 572-0529) specializes in marine antiques. **Sturbridge Yankee Workshop** (phone: 572-0529) manufactures reproductions of early American furnishings. The **Memory Lane Doll and Toy Museum** (phone: 536-3450) has a museum full of antique American and European dolls, some of which are for sale. Admission to the museum is 50¢ for adults and 25¢ for children under 12.

▪ **Craft Land** (Olde Mistick Village; phone: 572-9494) holds regular classes and demonstrations in macramé, needlepoint, découpage, and other crafts.

▪ From Olde Mistick Village, continue south on Route 27, and turn right at the intersection with Route 1. On your right is **Second Impression** (phone: 536-4424), which carries everything from old sleds to wicker. Cross the drawbridge and continue down Main Street in downtown Mystic. On the right, at **Dexter & Company,** John Dexter sells his fine handcrafted gold and silver jewelry. Across the street, **The Company of Craftsmen** has a tasteful display of pottery, quilts, hand-woven tablemats, and other locally made crafts.

▪ The **Seaport Museum Store,** just outside the south entrance to the museum, sells original scrimshaw and one-of-a-kind or limited-edition model boats ranging in price from $875 (for a New England whaleboat) to $6,200 (for the 1910 brigantine whaler *Viola*).

▪ The Borough of Stonington, about 4 miles east of Mystic, has several antique stores along Water Street, all within a minute's walking distance of each other. **Stonington Antique Shop** (148 Water Street; phone: 535-1458) has an eclectic collection of Victoriana. At

141 Water Street you can buy English enamels and a complete set of Quimperware. **Victoria Station** (109 Water Street; phone: 535-3258), sells everything from early eighteenth-century brass candlesticks to Victorian mantle clocks.

7. TOURS

▪ **Out o'Mystic Tours** (phone: 572-0070) runs numerous trips through southeastern Connecticut in nine-passenger minibuses.

▪ **Mystic Valley Bicycles** (26 Williams Street, one half-mile east of the drawbridge on Route 1; phone: 536-4767) runs guided bike tours of the Mystic area.

8. WALKS

▪ Self-guided walking tour maps of downtown Mystic are available at the Chamber of Commerce and at the Information Center *(see #4, What to See and Do)*.

▪ Visitors to **Groton** (about 15 minutes west of Mystic) will enjoy a 1½-mile walk to the 50-foot cliffs at **Bluff Point.** Drive west on Route 1 to the Groton Town Hall. Take the first left, Depot Road, and park at the end. The path follows the Poquonnock River to Bluff Point. Numerous side trails lead to the shore, where you can swim and picnic away from the crowds.

▪ **Denison Pequotsepos Nature Center** (Pequotsepos Road, about two miles from the Seaport Museum, Mystic; phone: 536-1216) is a 125-acre wildlife sanctuary with four miles of hiking trails, a museum, and a wildflower garden. Trails go through various habitats, including a wooded area, a meadow, and a swamp. There is also a 1200-foot trail for the blind, with handrails, guide ropes, and signs in Braille. Two picnic tables sit on a knoll above the wildflower garden. The center is open daily from 8 to 5 and Sunday from 1 to 5; and December through March daily from 10 to 4 and Sunday from 1 to 5. The **Denison Homestead** *(see #4, What to See and Do)* is located across the street. Admission is $1 for adults and 50¢ for children.

▪ The **Connecticut Arboretum** on the **Connecticut College** campus (Williams Street, New London; phone: 447-1911) is a 350-acre nature preserve with a three-quarter-mile nature trail and a lovely walking or jogging path around the edge of a lake. The mountain laurel is at its colorful best in June. Admission is free.

▪ Leave your car in **Watch Hill**, Rhode Island, a 20-minute drive east of Mystic, and walk 1½ miles along a narrow spit of land to

Napatree Point. Across Little Narragansett Bay, to your right, is the borough of Stonington. Ahead is Fishers Island. The farther you go, the more alone you will be. The beach is a fine and private place for swimming and sunbathing. Picnicking is not allowed.

9. BIKING

▪ Cyclists will enjoy easy four-mile bike trips either west to Noank and Groton Long Point, or east to the village of Stonington.

▪ **Mystic Valley Bicycles** (26 Williams Avenue, Route 1, one-half mile east of the bridge; phone: 536-4767) rents both three-speed and ten-speed bikes. The store has self-guided tour maps, free advice, and escorted bike trips for groups of 10 to 20 persons.

▪ **Bicycle World** (5 West Main Street, near the bridge; phone: 536-4819) rents bikes.

10. BOATING AND FISHING

BOATING

▪ **Spicer's Marina Boat Rental** (93 Marsh Road, Noank, about three miles southwest of Mystic, on the Groton side; phone: 536-4978) rents 14-foot and 16-foot outboard motorboats for fishing.

▪ **Spicer's Marina** is also located in Groton (916 Shennocossett Road, about eight miles west of Mystic, phone: 445-9729). You can rent boats here to fish or to visit Bluff Point, where you should be able to find some privacy for swimming or picnicking.

▪ **Brower's Cove Marina** (Mason's Island Road, Mystic; phone: 536-8864) rents 14-foot motorboats and 16-foot cat boats for sailing on the sound or on the Mystic River.

▪ **Shaffer's Boat Livery** (Mason's Island Road, Mystic; phone: 536-8713) rents fiberglass skiffs with or without engines.

▪ **Windsurfing of Mystic** (13 West Main Street; phone: 536-7121) rents sailboards for $10 an hour or $35 a day.

▪ **Mason's Island Marina** (Old North Road, Mystic; phone: 536-9615) rents 16½-foot Tanzer sailboats by the half-day or full day, and sunfishes by the hour or day. Sailing lessons are available for adults and for children who can swim.

▪ For training programs on the *Joseph Conrad* and the *Brilliant*, see #16, *For Kids*.

▪ For cruises on the steamboat *Sabino*, see #4, *What to See and Do*.

▪ The **Inn at Mystic** (Junction of Routes 1 and 27, Mystic; phone: 536-9604) has a canoe nonguests may rent for a lovely 1½-

mile paddle up Pequotsepos Cove. **Charley's Harbour Guest House** (Edgemont Street, Mystic; phone: 572-9253) also rents a canoe you can paddle up the Mystic River, past the *Joseph Conrad* and dozens of smaller boats moored along the Seaport Museum.

▪ Visitors who have dreamed of sailing overnight on a schooner can sign up for one-, two-, or three-day trips aboard the 65-foot *Voyager* or the 62-foot *Pipe Dream*. The *Voyager*, launched in 1978, has 10 first-class double cabins. The packet schooner sets sail at 9 A.M. and returns two or three days later at 4 P.M., with such ports of call as Newport, Block Island, and Sag Harbor. Trips run from June 1 through mid-October. The summer 1984 prices were $200 per person for two days, $280 per person for three days. The schooner/yacht *Pipe Dream* offers only half-day cruises, but passengers may choose to sleep on ship the night before departure. The summer 1984 price was $40 per person, including lunch, and an additional $15 to $20 for an overnight berth. Reservations can be made from **Voyager Cruises** (Steamboat Wharf, Mystic, on the Groton side, near the drawbridge; phone: 536-0416 or 800/243-0882).

▪ The *Mystic Whaler* (7 Holmes Street, Mystic; phone: 536-4218), is a 15-year-old replica of a two-masted, gaff-rigged nineteenth-century schooner. The diesel-powered 100-foot ship takes up to 44 passengers on two-day, two-night sails from Mystic to Shelter Island, Block Island, Sag Harbor, and Essex, Connecticut. Trips run from May 1 through August and cost from $139 to $195 per person. The *Whaler* also has one-day "sneak-away" cruises every weekday from early May through July 4, and on Wednesday from July 4 through late August. The one-day trips sail from Whaler Wharf, Mystic, at 9:15 and return at 4:15. The cost is $49, including breakfast and lunch. Passengers on the one-day cruises can pay an additional $20 to $30 to sleep aboard ship the night before departure.

FISHING

▪ Fishermen can rent 16-foot skiffs with or without motors from **The Fisherman's Hideout** (Route 1, Stonington; phone: 535-1950) or **Don's Dock Rentals** (North Water Street, Stonington; phone: 535-0077).

▪ **Hel-Cat** (181 Thames Street, Groton, about eight miles west of Mystic; phone: 535-2066, 535-3200, or, for a recording, 445-5991) is a steel catamaran that goes on fishing trips from 6 A.M. to 4 P.M. The twin hulls reportedly reduce the ship's roll—a plus for landlubbers with weak stomachs. Cod, pollack, and blacks are caught in spring; fluke, sea bass, and mackerel from Memorial Day to midsum-

mer; and blues from midsummer to mid-November. Hot snacks are
sold aboard ship.

▪ Two deep-sea fishing charter boats, each holding up to six
people, are *Anna R* (52 Riverview Avenue, Noank; phone: 536-
8372); and *Seaweed Too* (Noank; phone: 536-1665). *The Majestic* (27
Main Street, Mystic; phone: 536-1943) may be rented for sailing.

11. SWIMMING

▪ Ask local people where they swim and nine out of ten will tell
you Rhode Island—either at **Watch Hill** or **Misquamicut,** about 13
miles east of Mystic. Watch Hill gets an older, quieter, family crowd.
Misquamicut is a mile long, the longest state beach in Rhode Island.
Families come here, but most of the 30,000 bathers on a hot summer
weekend are singles, who wander between the beach and the clam
shacks, roller rink and amusement park.

▪ **Williams Beach** (Mason Island Road, Mystic) is a 175-yard
community beach on the river—fine for sunbathers and for people
who are determined to get wet. The bacteria count in the water can
get high in August.

▪ **Esker Point** (Noank, three miles southwest of Mystic) is
another local beach. Located on the sound, it has no surf, but a better
flow of water than Williams Beach.

▪ **Bluff Point** (Groton, about seven miles south of Mystic) must
be reached by foot, which eliminates the crowds. Drive south on
Route 1 and turn left on Depot Road, just past Groton Town Hall.
The town beach is adjacent to the parking area, but you can follow
the path for 1½ miles to the 50-foot cliffs at Bluff Point. Before you
reach the point, you'll see a barrier beach—a spit of land between the
river and the ocean—on your right. The beach is a lovely, quiet place
to swim and picnic. An alternative way to reach Bluff Point is by
motorboat, which can be rented at **Spicer's Marina** in Groton *(see
#10, Boating and Fishing).*

▪ **Howard Johnson's Motor Inn** and **Ramada Inn** have indoor
pools. **Day's Inn,** the **Inn at Mystic,** and **Seaport Motor Inn** have
outdoor pools.

▪ If you enjoy long walks and a degree of solitude, drive about
20 minutes east to Watch Hill, Rhode Island, and walk 1½ miles
along a narrow spit of land to **Napatree Point.** On one side is Little
Narragansett Bay, on the other, the sound. The ocean beach is fine
for swimming and sunbathing.

12. SKIING

Denison Pequotsepos Nature Center (Pequotsepos Road; phone: 536-1216) is popular for cross-country skiing. So is **Bluff Point,** in Groton.

Cross-country skis can be rented from **Mystic Valley Bicycles** (26 Williams Avenue, Route 1; phone: 536-4767).

13. RIDING

Wintechog Ranch (86 Wintechog Hill Road, North Stonington; phone: 535-3171) offers riding lessons at $10 an hour.

14. TENNIS

- **Williams Beach** (Mason Island Road, Mystic) has two community courts.
- **Fitch High School** (Route 1, Groton, about 10 minutes west of Mystic) has courts open to the public.
- **Pond View Racquet Club** (Route 1A, between Watch Hill and Weekapaug, 20 minutes east of Mystic; phone: 401/322-1100) has four outdoor courts.
- The **Inn at Mystic** (Junction of Routes 1 and 27, Mystic; phone: 536-2621) has a court nonguests may rent.

15. GOLF

- **Pequot Golf Club** (Wheeler Road, Stonington; phone: 535-1898) has an 18-hole, par-71 course.
- **Elmridge Golf Club** (Elmridge Road, Pawcatuck; phone: 599-2248) has an 18-hole, par-70 course.
- **Shennecoossett Municipal Golf Course** (Plan Street, Groton, off I-91) is a championship 18-hole course.

16. FOR KIDS

- There is very little in Mystic area that is not for kids. The **Aquarium** and the **Mystic Seaport Museum** are musts. At the seaport, check the calendar of daily events, given to all ticket holders, for demonstrations of special interest to children. These would include sail setting, chantey singing, and fish splitting. See the 30-minute orientation film, *Whales, Whaling and Whalemen.* On the second floor of the **Stillman Building** are models of trawlers that show how fish are caught in nets. Nearby is a push-button demonstration of how a ship's propeller works, and a whale's eyeball. The third floor has a fascinating assortment of model ships.

▪ Children left on their own would probably head directly for the three ships moored along the Mystic River. Best bets are the schooner *L. A. Dunton* and the *Morgan,* where visitors are allowed below decks. Since the *Joseph Conrad* is used in a training program, the crew's quarters are off limits to visitors.

▪ The **Children's Museum** will give young visitors a sense of what it was like to live aboard ship as the son or daughter of the captain. The **Planetarium** show demonstrates how sailors navigate by the stars.

▪ Wander through the re-created nineteenth-century seaport village and visit the shipcarver's shop, the ship chandlery, the one-room schoolhouse, and other exhibits of special interest to children. Kids will be fascinated by the **Mystic River Diorama**—a birds' eye view of Mystic as it looked in 1853.

▪ The more a child knows beforehand about shipbuilding and whaling, the more rewarding his experience will be. *Captains Courageous* should be required reading. Richard Dana's *Two Years Before the Mast* is recommended for older students. The **Seaport Store,** located just outside the southern entrance to the museum, has an imaginative collection of children's books about the sea. Families who arrive in Mystic in the early evening can buy some bedtime books here without paying an admission fee to the museum. In summer the store closes at 8.

▪ See entries under *#9, Biking* and *#10, Boating and Fishing.*

▪ *See #4, What to See and Do* for cruises on the steamboat *Sabino* and for visits to the submarine U.S.S. *Croaker* in Groton; the **U.S. Naval Submarine base** in Groton; the **Pullman Museum** in Stonington; the dollhouse collection in the **Lyman Allyn Museum** in New London; and the **Memory Lane Doll and Toy Museum** in Olde Mistick Village.

▪ Boys and girls aged 12 to 17 may spend a week aboard the 103-foot ship *Joseph Conrad,* permanently berthed at Mystic Seaport. The young sailors take guided tours of the seaport, participate in maritime crafts, and study small boat handling, weather, and piloting. Sailing is taught in nine-foot fiberglass dinghies on the Mystic River. Ten-oared seine boats are used for rowing instruction. Evening programs include planetarium shows, whaling lectures, and sea chantey singing. Programs run mid-June through August, from 4 P.M. Sunday to 3 P.M. Friday. The $210 fee covers meals, accommodations, and instructions.

■ Four-day and six-day training cruises on the 61-foot auxiliary schooner *Brilliant* are given to boys and girls aged 15 to 20. The young sailors handle the sails, cook, clean, wash down the decks, polish the brass, and learn to live and work together on a small ship. Four-day cruises run in May, September, and October from 9 A.M. Friday to 5 P.M. Monday. The cost is $260. Six-day cruises run June through August from 4 P.M. Sunday to 5 P.M. Friday. The fee is $340.

17. DINING

■ The **Harbor View Restaurant** (Cannon Square, Stonington, about four miles east of Mystic; phone: 535-2720) offers the most elegant and expensive dining in the area. What was once a chowder/ fish restaurant was gutted three years ago and replaced by shiplapped pine stained a dark mahogany, brass wall sconces, and prints of nineteenth-century sailing ships. The three dining rooms can seat 176 people, but the dim lights and dark paneling create the mood of a formal but intimate Victorian dining room. Tables are set with blue linen and fresh flowers, waiters wear white shirts and black ties, and a strolling violinist plays music so thick with schmaltz you could cut it with a knife. Most diners will prefer the two rooms with bay windows overlooking Stonington harbor. The menu is traditional French, with heavy sauces and an emphasis on fish and veal. A special appetizer is huîtres Ainslie—oysters with green peppers, onions, herbed crumbs, bacon, and a sauce of horseradish and tomatoes. The 20 entrées, ranging in price from $10 to $17, include sole Marguery (poached sole sauced with shrimp, mushrooms, and mussels); escalopes Normande (veal lightly sauced with apples and Calvados); and riz de veau du Guesclin (creamed veal sweetbreads with a vol-au-vent pastry). For dessert, try the walnut roll (sponge cake with walnuts, spiced apples, and fresh whipped cream). Reservations are advised. Ties are not required, but most men wear them anyway. All major credit cards are accepted.

■ **Kitchen Little** (Route 27, Mystic, between the aquarium and the Seaport Museum; phone: 536-2122) is hardly more than a shack, with seven tables and a counter; but local people love the low prices and imaginative menu. Popular breakfasts include an oyster omelet with apples, celery, clams, onions, and mushrooms; and raisin French toast with a sour cream and strawberry topping. Expect a 20-minute wait on summer weekends. No credit cards are accepted.

■ Many locals will tell you that when they can't afford the Harbor View, they dine at **Noah's** (115 Water Street, Stonington; phone: 535-3925). Visitors will be happy here in anything from corduroy to black tie. The informal atmosphere is softened by locally made linens and candles. The menu is divided between fish and meat dishes. Entrées are priced from about $6 to $11. Fresh fish specials include flounder and cod (no lobster). Also on the menu are homemade clam chowder, steamers, and pasta. Popular desserts are homemade pecan pie, apple brown betty, and a ball of bittersweet chocolate with nuts and cream. Reservations are advised. No credit cards are accepted.

▪ **Abbott's Lobster in the Rough** (Pearl Street, Noank, about 3 miles southwest of Mystic; phone: 536-7719) is the in spot for lobster. The restaurant's own watermen bring in from 600 to 1000 pounds of lobster a day, and store them in 21 tanks. The restaurant has room for 400, most of whom sit outside on gaily colored picnic tables overlooking the sound. Bring your own wine and expect up to 30-minute waits on summer weekends. Lobster dinners range from $9.75 for a 1¼-pound lobster to $40 for a six-pounder. The shrimp plate costs $5.25. Two pounds of steamed clams or mussels cost $4.50. Dress is informal. All major credit cards are accepted. No reservations are accepted.

▪ **Seaman's Inne** (Route 27, at the north entrance to the Seaport Museum; phone: 536-9649) was built in 1965 as part of the museum complex. The cozy Tap Room, paneled with old wood imported from England, is the loveliest of the three dining areas; unfortunately, no reservations are accepted, so whether you end up here or in River Room, which seats 400, is a question of luck. (If you're willing to wait, stand at the front of the line until a table opens up in the Tap Room.) In summer, you can add your name to the waiting list, spend an hour or two exploring the seaport (which remains open until 8), and then return to the inn in time to be seated. Light lunches include quiche, salads, baked scrod, hamburgers, and salads. The 17 dinner entrées, priced from $8 to $18, include several breaded fish dishes. Specialties include the Fisherman's Platter (shrimps and filet of flounder, lightly breaded and baked); Seafood Fantasy (baked stuffed shrimp, stuffed filet of sole, scallops, clams, and Alaska king crab baked in a casserole and served with lemon and butter; and fillet of sole layered with spinach and topped with cheddar cheese. Dress is casual. No reservations are accepted for groups under eight. All major credit cards are accepted.

▪ **The River Room,** part of the Seaman's Inne, serves light lunches, including clam chowder. Expect to wait in line up to an hour in summer, unless you arrive after 9 P.M.

▪ **Steamboat Café** (73 Steamboat Wharf, Mystic, on the Groton side; phone: 536-1975) offers lovely views of the boats waiting for the drawbridge to open on the Mystic River. Entrées, priced from $7.95

to $14.95, include lobster bisque and chicken teriyaki. A favorite dessert is grasshopper pie. Dress is casual. Reservations are accepted only off-season. All major credit cards are accepted.

18. AFTER HOURS

▪ **Margaritaville** (12 Water Street, Mystic; phone: 536-4589), located upstairs in a former tool-and-die factory, is the favorite local nightspot for the 20- to 35-year-old set. There's rock music and a small dance floor that no one uses.

▪ **Rhana Pippins** (Lighthouse Square, Long Hill Road, Groton; phone: 445-9731) is a New York-style disco for anyone able to keep up with the music.

▪ **Howard Johnson's Motor Lodge** (phone: 536-2654) and **Ramada Inn** (phone: 536-4281), both near the intersection of I-95 and Route 27, have live bands on weekends.

▪ **Steamboat Café** (73 Steamboat Wharf; phone: 536-2661) has a lovely upstairs bar overlooking the river and the draw bridge.

▪ **"The Beach"** is a strip of land along the Rhode Island shore, near Misquamicut, which the under-25 make for after dark.

▪ The **Planetarium** in the Seaport Museum (phone: 536-2631) has a "Sky Watcher's Program" on Wednesday night at 8:30.

▪ For live music and special attractions, look in the entertainment section of the *New London Day* newspaper.

19. LODGING

The Mystic area has friendly guest houses and comfortable motels, but none of the small, beautiful old inns one associates with quaint New England villages. All lodgings listed below are within a five minute's drive of the Seaport Museum, except for ones in Stonington and Groton Long Point, which are no more than 15 minutes away. Prices are for the summer season; off-season rates drop as much as 40 percent. Be sure to make reservations in advance; after 6 on a summer weekend you'll be lucky to find a room anywhere between Providence and New Haven.

INNS AND MOTELS

▪ Visitors who can afford the price should stay in the colonial-style mansion in back of the motel complex at the **Inn at Mystic** (Junction of Routes 1 and 27, Mystic; phone: 536-9604). The imposing three-story white building sits on a hilltop overlooking Mystic harbor. It was built by a sea captain in 1904 and purchased and restored by the Inn at Mystic in 1980. The five upstairs rooms are furnished with period antiques. Some have excellent views, Jacuzzis, and working fireplaces. The Pine Room has English paneling and canopied beds. Before it acquired this eight-acre estate, the Inn at Mystic was called the Mystic Motor Inn. The original motel units have weathered cedar shingles and blue shutters. The more expensive rooms have porches with views of the harbor. This is the only motel in Mystic that tries to remain faithful to the spirit of a nineteenth-century seaport. Facilities include a canoe, a 10-foot sailboat, a tennis court, and a swimming pool. Doubles in the motel cost $75 to $80. Doubles in the colonial-style mansion cost $90 to $125. All major credit cards are accepted.

• **Whaler's Inn Hotel and Motor Court** (20 East Main Street, Route 1, Mystic, on the Groton side; phone 536-1506) has three buildings surrounded by a courtyard. Two of the buildings are less than five years old. The complex is conveniently located in downtown Mystic, near the shops and the historic walks along Gravel Street. Doubles cost $41 to $85. Packages are available both in-season and off-season that include two nights' lodging, breakfasts, and admission to the museum and aquarium. All major credit cards are accepted.

• The **Ramada Inn** (junction of I-95 and Route 27; phone: 536-4281 or 800/228-2828) has an indoor pool and sauna. Doubles cost $75.

• **Howard Johnson's Motor Lodge** (junction of I-95 and Route 27; phone: 536-2654 or 800/654-2000) has an indoor pool and sauna. Doubles cost $75 to $82.

• Doubles at **Days Inn** (one-quarter mile north of Exit 90 on I-95; phone: 572-0574) cost $62. All major credit cards are accepted. Doubles at the **Taber Motel** (near the junction of Routes 1 and 27; phone: 536-4904) range from $54 in the guest house to $70 in the motel. Visa and Mastercard are accepted on bills over $100. **Days Inn** has a pool.

GUEST HOUSES

There is nothing slick or elegant about the guest houses in Mystic. The ambience is Sears modern—plain and comfortable, in a wholesome, all-American way.

• The **1833 House** (33 Greenmanville Avenue, Route 27; phone: 572-0633) is the best bet because it's only a short walk from the Seaport Museum, and its owner, Joan Smith, is a former volunteer at the Information Center and knows everything about Mystic. Visitors who have enjoyed B & B (bed and breakfast) in Great Britain will appreciate the friendly, unpretentious atmosphere here. Doubles, some with private bath, cost $44 to $48, including a continental breakfast. A two-room suite for four people costs $65. No credit cards are accepted.

▪ **Harbour Guest House** (Edgemont Street, Mystic; phone: 572-9253) is a modest house with lovely views of the harbor. A canoe and rowboat are available for guests. All rooms have private baths. No credit cards are accepted.

▪ **Pleasant View Guest House** (92 Water Street, Stonington, about four miles east of Mystic; phone: 535-0055) is the only place to stay in the tiny Borough of Stonington. The front downstairs room is small but attractive. Guests will enjoy sitting in the garden—sunbathing, reading, or watching the sun set over the harbor. Doubles, some with private bath, cost $40 to $48. No credit cards are accepted.

▪ Guest rooms are also available at the **Taber Motel** (junction of Routes 27 and 1, Mystic; phone: 536-4904) and at the **Shore Inn** (54 East Shore Avenue, Groton Long Point, about five miles southwest of Mystic; phone: 536-1180).

20. EMERGENCIES

▪ For immediate treatment, drive to the **Pequot Medical Center,** just off Exit 88 of I-95, five minutes south of the Information Center. Phone: 446-8265, or contact the Information Center at 536-1641.

▪ Nine miles to the east is **Westerly Hospital** (phone: 401/596-4961). Nine miles to the west is **Lawrence Memorial Hospital** (New London; phone: 442-0711).

21. HOW TO GET THERE

BY CAR. *From New York:* I-95 north to exit 90, then south on Route 27. *From Boston:* I-95 south to exit 90, then south on Route 27.

BY TRAIN. Amtrak goes *From New York* (phone: 212/736-4545) and *from Boston* (617/482-3660). More trains stop in New London than in Mystic. If your train stops in New London, you will have to take a 15-minute bus trip on Southeast Area Transit (phone: 886-2631) from the New London train station to Groton, and another 15-minute trip on bus #10 from Groton to Mystic.

BY PLANE. **Allegheny Commuter** (phone: 800/428-4253) flies *from*

Washington and *from Philadelphia* to the New London/Groton Airport. **Pilgrim Airlines** (phone: 203/446-1212) flies to the New London/Groton Airport *from Boston* (phone: 617/569-1414), *from Hartford* (phone: 203/547-1711), *from New York* (phone: 212/995-2230), and *from Washington* (phone: 202/638-7948).

BY FERRY. **Cross Sound Ferry Service,** Box 33, New London 06320 (phone: 516/323-2415 or 203/443-5281) has car-ferry service from Orient Point, Long Island, to New London. In summer, the 90-minute trip runs between 7 A.M. and 9 P.M.

22. FOR FURTHER INFORMATION

▪ **New England Tourist Information Center,** Olde Mistick Village, Mystic 06355. Phone: 536-1641. Take exit 90 of I-95 and follow signs.
▪ **Mystic Chamber of Commerce,** Route 1, Mystic (in the train depot). Phone: 536-8559. Open weekdays from 9 to 12.
▪ **Mystic Seaport Museum,** Mystic 06355. Phone: 203/572-0711.
▪ **Mystic Marinelife Aquarium,** Mystic 06355. Phone: 203/536-9631.

23. RECOMMENDED READING

▪ The **Mystic Seaport Museum Store** (phone: 536-9688), outside the south entrance, has one of the country's largest collections of new and out-of-print maritime books. A catalog is available on request. Children's books—all related to the sea—range from *The Story of Ping* to *Michael and the Merry Day* (an updated version of *Captains Courageous,* set in Gloucester).
▪ Eleanor B. Read's *Mystic Memories,* sold both in the museum store and in the Tourist Information Center, is the best history of Mystic.
▪ Carl C. Cutler's *Mystic: The Story of a Small New England Seaport* is the best short history of the rise of Mystic as one of the nation's great seaports.
▪ To whet your appetite for the sea, read Kipling's *Captains Courageous,* Richard Dana's *Two Years Before the Mast,* and Melville's *Moby Dick.*

Litchfield Hills, Connecticut

(Area Code, 203)

1. DISTANCES

BY CAR. *From New York*, 2 hours to New Preston, 2½ hours to Norfolk. *From Boston*, 3 hours.

BY BUS. *From New York*, 2½ hours to Cornwall Bridge.

2. MAJOR ATTRACTIONS

Sugar maples, village greens, country inns, and covered bridges—everything you expect from Vermont, but an hour or two closer to home.

Music festivals and mountain lakes, apple orchards and antiques, national landmarks and nouvelle cuisine—all within two hours of Times Square.

3. INTRODUCTION

Northwestern Connecticut has just about everything the Berkshires has to offer, minus the weekend crowds. It may not have the majestic peaks or the untamed wilderness of New Hampshire or

Vermont, but it has an equal amount of fresh air and at least as many first-rate inns and restaurants.

What used to be called "the foothills of the Berkshires" is now, with the wave of a Tourist Board wand, "Litchfield Hills." It's a good hour's drive from one corner to another, and unless you're in love with your car, you'll need at least three weekends to discover all that the region has to offer. The Lake Waramaug/Washington Depot/ Litchfield area deserves one weekend; the Kent/Cornwall region, a second; and Lakeville/Salisbury/Riverton/Norfolk, a third.

"Rediscovered" is the word for Litchfield Hills; the area was a popular summer retreat back in the 1890s. The train ride to New Milford took 2½ hours then; when the route was discontinued in 1968, the trip took two hours and 45 minutes.

There were 12 inns on Lake Waramaug in 1900; today there are four. The region's decline began in the 1920s with the construction of Route 7, which sent summer visitors scurrying north to Massachusetts and Vermont. The decline continued in the Motel Years after World War II, when Americans put a greater premium on wall-to-wall carpeting than on low-beamed ceilings and wide pine floors.

The region was rediscovered about a decade ago when country inns became fashionable and bleary-eyed New Yorkers sought weekend retreats close to home. Expatriate New Yorkers opened boutiques selling clothes that New Yorkers who moved to Connecticut liked to wear. Delicatessens began selling chicken with grapes and wild rice; restaurants turned from ham steaks to paillard of veal.

Litchfield Hills today is *People* magazine country. Eugene Fodor lives near Litchfield; Arthur Miller and Calvin Klein are neighbors in Roxbury. Within a 15-mile radius live Dustin Hoffman, Milos Forman, Susan St. James, Mia Farrow, Bill Blass, and Henry Kissinger, all of whom have moved here in the past five years or so.

In the sixties the sandal set moved to Vermont and New Hampshire with their palettes and easels; the craftsmen who moved to Litchfield Hills were potters like Todd Piker, who sells to Saks; or Stephen Fellerman, whose $400 hand-blown glass lamps are exhibited in museums across the country.

This is a land of golf carts and horses. Every village worth its salt has a bookstore, an art association, and an antiquarian book dealer. The butcher in the Marbledale Market has a special antenna to pick up WQXR so he can listen to Mozart while he reduces cattle to porterhouse and filet mignon.

Somehow, even the oaks and maples in Litchfield Hills seem a bit more gentrified than the oaks and maples further north. And yet the fall show here is as splendid as anywhere in New England. You can still find an occasional wild turkey strutting across Route 45, and if you can't afford to buy a house from the David L. Bain Real Estate Agency in Kent, you can always buy a dozen eggs, because David sells them too. Few of the 39 towns here have more than 2,500 people, and you can reach them by back roads known only to cows and local farmers. The inns are as charming, the houses as historic, the steeples as white as anywhere in the northeast. If you're looking for a New England weekend escape, why go further?

4. WHAT TO SEE AND DO

▪ Towns you'll not want to miss include **Washington, Washington Depot, Kent, West Cornwall, Riverton, Litchfield, Salisbury,** and **Lakeville.** The **Litchfield Hills Travel Council** *(see #22, For Further Information)* will send on request a brochure with five driving tours in northwest Connecticut. Among the most scenic drives, particularly in the fall, are (1) around Lake Waramaug; (2) Route 209 around Bantam Lake; (3) Route 7 along the Housatonic River; and (4) Route 67 through Roxbury, then Route 199 to Washington, Route 47 to Washington Depot, Route 109 to Morris, Route 209 around Bantam Lake, and Route 202 to Litchfield; (5) from Route 4 through the Mohawk State Forest to the top of 1,683-foot Mohawk Mountain. (There's an observation tower 2½ miles into the forest with breathtaking 360-degree views.)

The **Inn at Lake Waramaug** publishes (for guests only) a useful guide to weekly events, including auctions, theater, and concerts. The patio overlooking the lake at the **Boulders Inn** is ideal for 4 P.M. tea on summer weekends.

▪ **Kent** is the only town with a Main Street bustle. You'll find antiques here—the greatest concentration of dealers outside of Woodbury—as well as smart country clothes, crafts, and jewelry from around the world. There's a **covered bridge** off Route 7 (the other one, also across the Housatonic, joins Routes 7 and 128 at West Cornwall). A butter churn operated by a dog running on a treadmill is one of the early-American implements and tools on display in the **Sloane-Stanley Museum** (Route 7; phone: 566-3005). Grounds include a replica of an early New England log cabin built by Eric Sloane. Open May through October, Wednesday through Sunday from 10 to 4:30. Adults $1.25, children 50 cents.

▪ **Litchfield,** like Deerfield, Massachusetts, is a living museum, with one of the finest collections of colonial mansions in the country, all conveniently located along two streets radiating out from the village green. In 1790 Litchfield was the third largest town in the

U.S., after New York and Philadelphia. The entire town center, settled in 1720, is a National Historic Landmark. The **Information Center** on the Village Green distributes free walking tour maps. The **Cobble Court Bookshop** sells for $1 a useful booklet on Litchfield. There are some 41 buildings worth seeing on either side of the Green, almost all of them built before 1790. Walk down South Street to the Y, and return on the other side of the street; then walk down South Street to the Y and back, passing the house where Ethan Allen lived and the elm marking the homestead where Henry Ward Beecher and his sister Harriet Beecher Stowe were born. If I could live in an eighteenth-century home, it would be the **Tapping Reeve House** (South Street; phone: 567-6862), which became the first law school in America. Judge Tapping Reeve opened his home to law students in 1773. His brother-in-law Aaron Burr was his first pupil. The original students lived with the family and studied in the downstairs parlor. Open mid-May to mid-October on Tuesday to Saturday from 11 to 5, and Sunday 2 to 5. Litchfield also has several sophisticated shops, such as **The Kitchen Works** and the **Workshop of Litchfield.** Best bet for a quick lunch is the **Village Restaurant,** off the Green. For picnics, try the **Litchfield Food Company.**

▪ Near Litchfield is the **Haight Vineyard and Winery** (Chestnut Hill Road, off Route 118; phone: 567-4045). There are tastings and tours, too, at the **Hopkins Vineyard** (New Preston; phone: 868-7954).

▪ Look down on Litchfield from a hot air balloon (**Adventure Rides, Inc.,** Route 61, Bethlehem; phone: 266-5260).

▪ Ten minutes south of Litchfield is **White Flower Farm** (Route 63; phone: 567-0801), an internationally known horticultural center with eight acres of exotic display gardens (peak blooms in May and June) and a greenhouse with tuberous begonias (mid-July to mid-September). Open daily from mid-April to late October.

▪ In **New Milford,** 15 miles west of Litchfield, is **The Silo** (Upland Road, off Route 202; phone: 355-0300), a former stable and dairy barn where Skitch and Ruth Henderson sell the work of hundreds of craftspeople and unusual kitchenware.

▪ **Woodbury** is noted for its antique stores—almost 40 of them along Route 6—and the **Glebe House** (Hollow Road; phone: 263-2855), an authentic colonial home dating from the late 1600s, with gardens, an escape tunnel used during the American Revolution, and a curator whose enthusiasm is contagious. Open Saturday through Wednesday from 1 to 5 (or dusk). Admission is a $1 donation for adults.

▪ One great way to appreciate the fall foliage, or to come to rest after a full day of sightseeing, is to take a 30- or 60-minute predinner showboat cruise across **Lake Waramaug,** near **New Preston.** Contact the Inn at Lake Waramaug; phone: 868-0563. Trips cost $2.50 and $3.50.

▪ **Washington** is a wonderful example of a colonial village, with exquisite white houses around a small green flanked by elms. At **Plumb Hill Studio** (Plumb Hill Road; phone: 868-2938) you can watch Priscilla Porter and her workers at their six kilns, firing just about anything you can make from glass. The **American Indian Archaeological Institute** (Route 199; phone: 868-0518) is doing for the American Indian what Mystic has done for the clipper ship. Displays include a 12,000-year-old mastodon, a life-size reconstructed Indian longhouse, an Indian garden, an authentic wigwam, and dioramas of early Indian life. The gift shop sells tasteful reproductions of items in the collection. Open daily from 10 to 4:30, Sunday from 1 to 4:30. Adults $2, children $1. Also in Washington is the **Gunn Historical Museum** (Route 47; phone: 868-7756) with military and local memorabilia, including gowns and dollhouses. Open Tuesday and Thursday from 1 to 4 and Saturday from 12 to 3. Admission is free.

▪ In the northwest corner of the northwest corner of the state are **Salisbury** and **Lakeville,** each with its share of country boutiques and crafts and antique shops. **Undermountain Weavers** is in Salisbury *(see #6, Antiques and Crafts);* **Settings Ltd.** is in Lakeville (Route 44), selling designer fabrics and French hand-painted porcelain. Salisbury is a colonial town with huge historic estates and more than 300 homes at least a century old along Route 41. The **Holley-Williams House** (Upper Main Street, Lakeville; phone: 435-2878) is a fine example of Classical Revival and Federal architecture. Family furnishings include silver, china, and fine furniture. Guided tours July to mid-October on Thursday and Saturday from 2 to 4. Admission is $2 for adults, $1.50 for children.

▪ Paul Newman races at **Lime Rock Park** (Route 112, just south of Salisbury; phone: 435-2572), which bills itself as the road-racing center of the east. Races are scheduled from July through October.

▪ North of Salisbury on Route 44 is the town of **Canaan,** where you can board the newly restored **Housatonic Valley Railroad** for a scenic hour-long round-trip voyage to Falls Village to view the Great Falls. It's a spectacular trip along the Housatonic, through several state parks. The six-mile journey will eventually be expanded to 35, as the train makes its way south to West Cornwall. The nonprofit organization that runs the railroad did not have a phone when we went to press; call the Litchfield Hills Travel Council at 868-2214 for information.

▪ At **Norfolk,** drive through **Great Mountain Forest** (Wangum Mountain Road; phone: 542-5422), an experimental 6,000-acre forest preserve with Oriental spruces and huge hemlocks and black maples.

▪ **Riverton** was originally named Hitchcockville by Lambert Hitchcock, who built the **Hitchcock Chair Factory** here (Route 20; phone: 379-4826) so that housewives could have stenciled furniture at Yankee prices. Today you can watch reproductions being made, and buy them at factory prices. You'll want to compare these modern reproductions to the originals, and to other painted furniture on display in the **John Kenney Hitchcock Museum** (Old Union Church; phone: 379-1003). The factory is open June through October, Tuesday to Saturday from 10 to 5. Admission is free. The museum is open June through October, Wednesday to Saturday from 11 to 4 and Sunday from 1 to 4. **Seth Thomas** (Main Street; phone: 379-1077) is a factory outlet with good buys on wall and grandfather clocks from America's oldest clockmaker.

▪ The family that picks together, sticks together. The strawberry season usually runs from mid-June to July; the blueberry season through July and August; the raspberry season from July 20 to August 7. Among the farms that let you pick your own are **Swanson's** (Baldwin Hill Road, just south of **New Preston**); **Ellsworth Hill Farm** (Route 4, **Sharon;** phone: 364-0249), and **Terekook Farm** (Kielwasser Road, **New Preston;** phone: 868-2648).

▪ Experience the sweetest of all New England's traditions, the making of maple sugar, during the early spring months of March and April at **Laurel Brook Farm Sugar House** (Route 44, East Canaan); **Atwood Sugar House** (off Route 219, New Hartford; phone 379-2625); **Coolwater Maple Sugar House** (Norfolk; phone: 542-5266 or 542-5090); **Northeast Audubon Center** (Route 4, Sharon; phone: 364-0520); or **The Inn at Lake Waramaug** (New Preston; phone: 868-0563).

5. THE ARTS

▪ The most professional summer theater in the region is the **Sharon Playhouse** (Route 343, Sharon; phone: 364-0559; 364-3733; 800/223-0120). Tickets cost $8 and $12. Shows run in July and August, Tuesday to Saturday at 8 P.M., and Wednesday and Saturday at 2 P.M.

▪ Manhattan's 13th Street Repertory Theater is in summer residence at the **Thomaston Opera House** (Thomaston; phone 283-9268). Recent productions include *Little Women* and *You're a Good Man, Charlie Brown.* The season runs from mid-June to early September. Tickets cost $8 and $10.

▪ A 200-year-old barn is the home of the **Southbury Playhouse** (near the junction of Route 6 and Route 67, one mile from I-84; phone: 264-8215), a professional summer stock theater whose recent productions include *Agnes of God* and *Crimes of the Heart.* Performances run from Wednesday through Sunday. Tickets are $7.50 and $10.

▪ **The Little Theatre** (Brookside Avenue, New Milford; phone: 354-7853) is a community theater performing mysteries, comedies, and musicals at $5 a ticket.

▪ **Music Mountain Chamber Music Series** (Falls Village; phone: box office, 824-7126; information, 496-1222; New York City: 212/355-3720) is the oldest continuous chamber music series in the U.S., featuring the Manhattan String Quartet and other well-known groups. Concerts run from mid-June to mid-September. Admission is $6.

▪ The Yale School of Music has summer concerts in the Music Shed at the **Norfolk Chamber Music Festival** (Norfolk; phone: box office, 542-5537; information, 436-3690; Chargit, 800/223-0120 or 212/944-9300). Concerts run from mid-June through early August on Friday and Saturday at 8:30 and Sunday at 3:30. Bring your own picnic supper and dine alfresco by a brook before the concert.

▪ Tanglewood is a bit far; closer to Litchfield Hills is the **Berkshire Choral Festival** (Berkshire School; Sheffield, MA; off Route 41, about ten minutes north of Salisbury; phone: 413/229-3522), where you'll hear the Springfield Symphony Orchestra led by such famous conductors as Richard Westenberg. Tickets cost $7 and $12.

▪ **The Washington Chamber Music Society** (Washington Club Hall, Route 47, Washington; phone: 868-0065) has a series of five Saturday evening concerts from late May through September.

▪ **The Washington Art Association** (Washington Depot; 868-2878) has ongoing exhibits by nationally known artists.

6. ANTIQUES AND CRAFTS

▪ Though there are antique stores scattered throughout the region, the greatest number are clustered along Route 7 between Kent and Gaylordsville, and in Woodbury, along Route 6. A list of stores in the Kent and Woodbury area is available from any of the dealers. The stores along Route 6, on either side of Woodbury, are not inexpensive, but the quality—particularly for early American, English, and Canadian furniture—is in a class by itself.

▪ At **Bull's Bridge Glass Works** (Route 7, Kent; phone: 927-3302), in a renovated barn on the banks of the Housatonic, you can watch the nationally recognized master craftsman Stephen Fellerman blow glass. Open Tuesday through Sunday from 1 to 5:30.

▪ The **Cornwall Bridge Pottery Store** (Route 7, West Cornwall; phone: 672-6545) sells hand-blown glassware, Pierre Deux fabrics, hand-wrought fireplace accessories, Dansk flatware, and pottery that is also sold in Bloomingdale's.

▪ **Connecticut Woodcarver's Gallery** (Route 44, East Canaan; phone: 824-0883) features the work of 14 professional woodcarvers. Open Wednesday through Sunday from 10 to 5.

▪ **Contemporary Crafts Gallery** (Route 30, Riverton; phone: 379-2964) sells original work in blown glass, pottery, graphics, and pewter.

▪ **Undermountain Weavers** (Undermountain Road, Route 41, four miles north of Salisbury; phone: 435-2321) sells rare Chinese cashmere wools and lightweight hand-loomed fabrics.

▪ The **J. Hoffman Gallery** (Main Street, Kent; phone: 927-4104) sells and exhibits limited-edition prints by Eric Sloane and others.

▪ There are regularly scheduled weekend auctions at the **Litchfield Auction Gallery** (Route 202, three miles west of Litchfield).

▪ **Rawburn Hall Antiques** (Route 341, Warren; phone: 868-7173) has a large collection of estate silver, china, furniture, and paintings.

▪ **Lisa C, Inc.** (Route 44, West Canaan; phone: 824-7952) sells period clothing (1900–1950), unusual wedding dresses, and Edwardian whites.

▪ **Charisma** (Railroad St., New Milford; phone: 355-2459) has a wide variety of clothes from the turn of the century to the 1950s, from everyday dresses to one-of-a-kind glamorous gowns.

8. WALKS

▪ The **Audubon Center** (Route 4, Sharon; phone: 364-0520) is a 684-acre sanctuary with 11 miles of self-guiding trails. The 2.35 mile Woodchuck Trail has great views to the west. The Bog Meadow Trail is a 1.6 mile loop trail. Adults $1, children 50 cents. Open daily 9 to 5, Sunday 1 to 5.

▪ **White Memorial Foundation** (Route 202, Litchfield) is the state's largest nature center, with 4,000 acres of trails, including one with Braille signs for the blind. The Museum has an imaginative touch-and-see exhibit, where kids of all ages can peek into the gruesome but fascinating core of a working beehive, feel the skull of a young deer, or touch the wing of a great horned owl. Does touching a toad really cause warts? Here's the place to find out. You can also sit at peepholes in the bird observatory or wander through the Catlin Wood with 20 acres of massive deciduous trees, notably hemlocks, untouched by man's ax for at least 100 years. Photographers and bird lovers will want to follow the raised boardwalk through the marsh around Little Pond. There are guided nature walks on Saturday at 2. The Museum is open daily from 9 to 5, Sunday from 11 to 5. Closed Monday.

▪ For splendid views that include the Catskills and the Berkshires, hike to the top of 1,683-foot **Mohawk Mountain,** through the Mohawk Mountain State Forest (off Route 4, northwest of Litchfield).

▪ **Kent Falls State Park** (Route 7, Kent) has steps up the side of a 200-foot waterfall. Views are spectacular, but don't expect to have them to yourself.

▪ The **Appalachian Trail** runs through the Macedonia Brook State Park (Route 341, Kent).

▪ In the Lake Waramaug area, climb **Pinnacle Mountain** in Steep Rock Reservation for a panorama that includes New York and Massachusetts. The trail is lined with laurel blossoms in June.

▪ In the Canaan area, head north into Massachusetts to **Bartholomew's Cobble** (off Route 7A, Ashley Falls; phone: 413/229-8600), a 200-acre rock garden with some 500 species of wildflowers, 100 species of trees and shrubs, and 40 species of ferns.

▪ **Topsmead State Forest** (off Route 118, one mile east of Litchfield) has a 40-acre nature trail and wildflower preserve.

9. BIKING

▪ The Litchfield Hills Travel Council *(see #22, For Further Information)* has a free booklet, *Bicycle Touring in the Litchfield Hills,* which recommends (a) biking around Lake Waramaug, (b) biking around Bantam Lake on Route 209, and (c) a back-road trip north on Route 67 to Roxbury, Route 199 to Washington, Route 47 through Washington Depot, Route 109 to Morris, Route 209 around Bantam Lake to Bantam, and Route 202 to Litchfield.

▪ The Inn at Lake Waramaug (New Preston; phone: 868-0563) rents bikes for a lovely 8-mile ride around Lake Waramaug. It's a scenic ride, but the road is narrow; watch out for traffic.

10. BOATING AND FISHING

▪ Locals say the best fishing is **Lake Wononscopomuc** (Salisbury; 1500 feet south of the junction of Routes 41 and 44), which is stocked with trout. Boat rentals are available.

▪ **Mt. Tom State Park Pond** (Route 202, Litchfield) is also stocked with trout. There's a public launch, and shore fishing is permitted in the park. Many other state parks have streams and ponds for fishing, including **Burr Pond State Park** (Torrington), **Campbell Falls** (Route 272, Norfolk), **Housatonic Meadows State Park** (Route 7, Cornwall Bridge), **Housatonic State Forest** (Route 7, Canaan), **Kent Falls State Park** (Route 7, Kent), **Lake Waramaug** (New Preston), **Macedonia Brook State Park** (Route 341, Kent), **Mohawk Pond** (Route 4, Cornwall).

▪ There are boats for rent at **Bantam Lake** (four miles south of Litchfield), the largest natural lake in the state. Ice fishing is popular here, in the lake at **Mt. Tom State Park,** and on **Lake Waramaug** (near New Preston) in winter.

▪ **Riverrunning Expeditions,** Ltd. (Main Street, Falls Village; phone: 824-5579) rents canoes for the Housatonic River.

▪ **White Creek Expeditions** (9 Myanos Road, New Canaan; phone: 966-0040) organizes trips down the Housatonic and Farmington Rivers.

▪ **Clarke Outdoors** (Route 7, West Cornwall, one mile south of the covered bridge; phone: 672-6365) rents canoes for a portion of the Housatonic River that's good for beginners anxious to try some easy rapids.

11. SWIMMING

▪ There's swimming in **Hall Meadow State Park** (Torrington); **John Minetto State Park** (off Route 272, Torrington); **Lake Waramaug** (New Preston); **Lake Wononscopomuc** (Lakeville); and O'Hara Beach at **Twin Lakes** (off Route 44, Salisbury). **Mt Tom State Park** (Woodville, off Route 202) has a spring-fed pond with a beach and individual changing rooms. **The Inn on Lake Waramaug** has an indoor pool.

12. SKIING

▪ **Mohawk Mountain** (Cornwall; Route 4, 20 minutes northeast of Litchfield; 672-6100/6464) is Connecticut's largest ski area. The slopes are 90 percent covered by snowmaking equipment. **Ski Sun-**

down (New Hartford, 30 minutes from Litchfield; phone: 379-9851) has a good variety of trails.

▪ **Riverrunning Ski Touring Center** (Falls River; phone: 824-5579) has cross-country ski rentals and 15 miles of trails over gently rolling countryside, with warming huts along the way.

▪ **Blackbeard Cross Country Center** (Norfolk; phone: 542-5455) has cross-country ski rentals and 20 miles of trails. Open for moonlight skiing.

▪ **Woodbury Ski and Racquet Area** (Woodbury; about 15 miles south of Litchfield; phone: 263-2203) has 60 miles of cross-country trails, 20 of them groomed, and a family downhill ski area.

13. RIDING

▪ **A-Bar-A** (Route 202, New Milford; phone: 355-1039); **Rustling Winds Stable** (Lakeville; phone: 824-7634); **Sunny Ray Farm** (Route 202, Bantam; phone: 567-0522); **Lee's Riding Stable, Inc.** (East Litchfield Road, off Route 118, Litchfield; phone: 567-0785); **Sugarbush Farm** (Washington; phone: 868-2317/7085).

14. TENNIS

▪ **Pinewoods Racquet Club** (104 Pinewoods Road, Torrington; phone: 482-9424); **Woodbury Ski & Racquet Club** (Woodbury; 263-2203).

15. GOLF

▪ **Hotchkiss School Golf Course** (Lakeville; phone: 435-9033); **Litchfield Country Club** (Litchfield; phone: 567-8383); **Stonybrook Golf Club** (Litchfield; phone: 567-9977); **Norfolk Country Club** (Norfolk; phone: 542-5582); **Sharon Country Club** (Sharon; phone: 364-5964); **East Lawn Country Club** (Torrington; phone: 489-9102).

16. FOR KIDS

▪ *See #4, What To See and Do* for the American Indian Archaeological Institute and the Housatonic Valley Railroad. *See #8, Walks* for the White Memorial Foundation (check out the Florida king snake that eats other snakes, and a boa constrictor named Pugsley).

▪ *See #6, Arts* for the Sharon Playhouse (Sharon, phone: 364-

0559), which has an afternoon children's theater featuring such plays
as *The Hobbit* and *The Wind in the Willows* (tickets are $2.50); and
the Thomaston Opera House Summer Theatre, which has a children's theater on summer weekends at 1 P.M. (tickets are $3).

- *See #8, Walks* for the Northeast Audubon Center (Sharon;
phone: 364-0520), which has guided family walks on Wednesdays at
9:30.

17. DINING

- Each of the four inns on Lake Waramaug has its own restaurant open to outside guests. Each has an indoor dining room and an
outdoor patio that catches the views and breezes from the lake below.
All can be recommended. Reservations are always advised on summer and fall weekends. Jackets are advised at dinner, if only because
the temperature can drop quickly, even in August. My own favorite
for lunch, dinner, or afternoon tea is **The Boulders Inn** (Route 45,
New Preston; phone: 868-7918). The imaginative luncheon menu
includes curried chicken salad with slices of fresh mango. The sophisticated dinner menu features such dishes as Kashmiri lamb in a sauce
of tomatoes, ground almonds, yogurt, and curry; and boned breast
of duck in a sauce of red wine and shallots. Entrées range from $11 to
$14. Visa and Mastercard are accepted.

- It's fitting that the waitresses wear dirndls at the **Hopkins Inn**
(Hopkins Road, New Preston; phone: 868-7295), for the owner/chef
is Austrian, and the menu features Austrian and continental specialties such as duck à l'orange, veal piccata, wienerschnitzel, and sweetbreads. Entrées range from $9.50 to $14. Dress is informal. No credit
cards are accepted.

- **The Inn at Lake Waramaug** (New Preston; phone: 868-0563)
is for people who like homemade soups; fresh, hot rolls; and big
portions of good, honest food such as steak, veal, and fresh fish. All
major credit cards are accepted.

- **The Birches** (West Shore Road, New Preston; phone: 868-
0229) is less known than the other three, in part because it's farthest
away from New Preston, but some residents claim it serves the best
food on the lake. The menu and the ambience, like the owner Heinz
Holl, are decidedly Austrian. Entrées, ranging in price from $8 to
$13, include wienerschnitzel and *zwiebelrostbraten.* The apfelstrudel
is in a class by itself. All major credit cards are accepted.

- The feeling is contemporary in the thoroughly renovated 1844
factory now called **Holley Place** (Pocketknife Square, Lakeville;
phone: 435-2727), which enjoys a good reputation among area resi-

dents. Specialties include sliced calves' liver and thinly sliced veal charcoaled with lemon and butter. Entrées range in price from $10 to $15. All major credit cards are accepted.

▪ **The Ragamont Inn** (Route 44, Salisbury; phone: 435-2372) has a fine reputation for its Swiss/German menu, which includes bratwurst and sauerbraten. Entrées range in price from $10 to $15. No credit cards are accepted.

▪ The atmosphere is almost Japanese-modern in **The Woodland** (Route 41, Lakeville; phone: 435-0578), which specializes in fresh fish, such as swordfish, squid, soft-shell crabs, and tuna. This is a good bet for lunch. Visa and Mastercard are accepted.

▪ The $12 brunch at the **Mayflower Inn** (Route 47, Washington; phone: 868-0515) was one of the best I've ever had, with champagne, poached salmon, raw oysters, and crabmeat crepes. The dinner menu, with entrées priced from $14 to $19, features classical French dishes from Escoffier recipes. The Inn was up for sale when we were going to press; check to see who's in the kitchen.

▪ **Fife 'N' Drum** (Main Street, Kent; phone: 927-3509) is, like its name and like its pewter plates stamped with the Kent insignia, a bit more deliberately old-fashioned than some would like. The restaurant has a solid reputation, however. The French and Italian menu, with entrées priced from $11.50 to $19, features mussels marinara and duck flamed in raspberry brandy.

▪ Also recommended are the **Blackberry River Inn** (Route 44, Norfolk; phone: 542-5100); the **White Hart Inn** (Salisbury; phone: 435-2511); the romantic **Toll Gate Hill** (Route 20, Litchfield; phone: 482-6116); and **Yankee Pedlar Inn** (93 Main Street, Torrington; phone: 489-9226).

▪ For ice cream cones on sultry summer afternoons, those in the know give three licks to **Depot Ice Cream** in Washington Depot and **Sweet Creams** in New Milford.

18. AFTER HOURS

▪ **Interlake Inn** in Lakeville and the **White Hart Inn** in Salisbury attract an over-30 crowd. **Holly Place** in Lakeville gets a 22–35 bar crowd.

19. LODGING

If you want to be on a lake with swimming and water sports, stay at one of the inns on Lake Waramaug, which is only two hours from Times Square. The area has been compared to the Salzkammer-

gut or Lake District of Austria, because the lake is surrounded by
mountains and two of the innkeepers are Austrian. Each of the inns
has its own private beachfront. To stifle impossible expectations, I
should point out that the lake is encircled by a road, and that the
sounds of cars compete with the sounds of motorboats. On the other
hand, Lake Waramaug is one of the least developed lakes in the state,
with no marinas or other "attractions," except for the private homes
nestled among the trees along the shore. In summer you can swim,
sail, or paddle a canoe around the lake; in winter, you can go ice
fishing or skating. A steady breeze cools off even the most sultry
summer day. Nearby are miles of trails for autumn walks or cross-
country skiing.

　• **The Inn at Lake Waramaug** (New Preston 06777; phone:
868-0563 or 212/724-8775) is more a friendly four-season resort than
a country inn. Rooms have TVs and air conditioning, and, except for
a few rooms in the main building, are essentially motel units with a
comfortable country feel to them. With an indoor pool, tennis, game
room, bikes, stable, canoes, sailboats, and winter sleigh rides, the Inn
is ideal for active couples or for families with children. Doubles cost
$60 to $89 per person, including breakfast and dinner, and free use of
facilities. All major credit cards are accepted.

　• The ambience at the 90-year-old **Boulders Inn** (Route 45,
New Preston 06777; phone: 868-7918) is more that of a comfortable
old house or a small English hotel than of a fabled New England
inn—but it is still more "innish" than any of the other establishments
on the lake. The winterized cabins behind the inn have modern conveniences and not much character; best bet are the six rooms in the
main house. Facilities include tennis and the use of various boats on
the lake. Doubles are $60 to $68 per person, including breakfast and
dinner. Call for winter rates.

　• The **Hopkins Inn** (New Preston 06777; 868-7295) is a 138-
year-old Federal-style summer guest house with wide pine floors and
simple area rugs. All is clean and cheerful, with a sampler quality.
The most popular rooms are on the second floor, facing the lake.
Doubles cost $31 to $38. Open May through October.

　• The **Toll Gate Inn** (Route 202, Litchfield 06759; 2¼ miles
north of the Green; phone: 482-6116) is a 240-year-old restored
tavern listed in the National Register of Historical Places. The
character of the inn, with its beautiful pine floors and low-beamed
ceilings, survives, despite some of the more modern furnishings.
Doubles cost $80. All major credit cards are accepted.

　• Your other choice in the Litchfield area is the **Litchfield Inn**
(Route 202, Litchfield 06759; phone: 567-4503), a new building that

tries hard and sometimes succeeds in capturing the charm of an old inn. The grounds need landscaping, but once you're safely inside you'll find that no expense has been spared to make guests comfortable. The 32 spacious rooms (some reached by elevator) all have TVs and private bath and are tastefully decorated with chenille spreads, soft, salmon-colored walls, and reproduction antique furniture. Doubles cost $65. All major credit cards are accepted.

▪ The **Ragamont Inn** (Main Street, Salisbury 06068; phone: 435-2372) has lots of character, with wide, warped pine floors, squeaky stairs, and low ceilings. If modern comforts mean more to you than age-old charm, stay in the motel units in back, complete with air conditioning and TV. Doubles cost $42 to $62. No credit cards are accepted.

▪ The Victorian **Mountain View Inn** (Route 272, Norfolk 06058; 542-5595) and the colonial **Blackberry River Inn** (Route 44, Norfolk 06058; phone: 542-5100) are ideal places to stay for the Yale chamber music concerts, or for proximity to cross-country ski trails. (It's about 10 degrees cooler here than in southern Litchfield Hills.) Also recommended are the **White Hart Inn** (Village Green, Salisbury 06068; phone: 435-2511), with 14 rooms and seven motel units; and the **Riverton Inn** (P.O. Box 6, Route 20, Riverton 06065; phone: 379-8678). You'll enjoy the **Interlaken Inn** (Route 112, Lakeville; phone: 435-9878) if you like modern resorts with lots of facilities and the smart, slate-and-leather ambience of an executive retreat. The **Yankee Pedlar Inn** (93 Main Street, Torrington 06790; phone: 489-9226) is charming and within 30 minutes of most everything you'll want to see and do in Litchfield Hills, but it has the disadvantage of being located in the middle of a town.

▪ If you like Laura Ashley, you'll love **Flanders Arms** (Route 7, Kent; phone: 927-4224). Every room in this private 235-year-old home is lifted from a Laura Ashley Decorator's Book, from the pillows to the matching ceiling trim. Doubles cost $55 to $65, including continental breakfast. For other bed and breakfast accommodations, contact **Covered Bridge Bed & Breakfast**, West Cornwall 06796; phone: 672-6052.

20. EMERGENCIES

- **New Milford Hospital** (21 Elm Street; phone: 335-2611).
- **Sharon Hospital** (West Main Street; phone: 364-5511).
- **Winsted Memorial Hospital** (115 Spencer; phone: 379-3351).

21. HOW TO GET THERE

BY CAR. *From New York to Litchfield:* the Saw Mill River Parkway or the Hutchinson River Parkway to Route 684 north, then Route 84 east to Route 7 north. In New Milford take Route 202 north to Litchfield. *From New York to New Preston:* Interstate 684 to Exit 9, I-84 east to Exit 7, Route 7 North, then Route 202 to New Preston. *From New York to Lakeville and Salisbury:* New York Thruway to Route 287 east to Route 684 north to Route 22 north to Route 343 east to Route 41 north to Lakeville. *From Boston to Lakeville:* take the Mass. Turnpike to Exit 2, then west on Route 102, south on Route 7, and west on Route 44 to Lakeville. *From Boston to New Preston:* I-86 and 84 through Hartford to Exit 39 to Route 44 and 202 west to Cherry Brook and Route 202 to New Preston.

BY BUS. **Bonanza Bus Lines** (212/564-8484) makes three scheduled trips daily from New York City to Cornwall. **Connecticut Transportation Co.** (phone: 203/435-2083) has daily round-trip transportation between Lakeville, Salisbury, or Sharon and New York City. The cost is $25 one-way. Credit cards are accepted.

22. FOR FURTHER INFORMATION

Litchfield Hills Travel Council, P.O. Box 1776, Marbledale, CT 06777; phone: 203/868-2214.

23. RECOMMENDED READING

The *250th Anniversary Guide to Litchfield, Connecticut* (sold in the **Cobble Court Bookshop,** Litchfield) is a useful guide to the town. Other bookstores with materials on Litchfield Hills are **Atticus Books** (Heritage Village Bazaar, Southbury) and the **Hickory Stick Bookshop** (Washington Depot).

Newport, Rhode Island

(Area Code, 401; Zip Code, 02840)

1. DISTANCES

BY CAR. *From New York*, 4 hours; *from Boston*, 1½ hours; *from Providence*, 45 minutes.

BY BUS. *From New York*, 4½ hours; *from Boston*, 1½ hours; *from Providence*, 1 hour.

BY TRAIN AND BUS (via Providence). *From New York*, 5 hours; *from Boston*, 2 hours.

2. MAJOR ATTRACTIONS

▪ A pride of mansions—Rhine castles, Italian palaces, French chateaux—from the Gilded Age, when families like the Vanderbilts and Astors summered here.

- One of the largest collections of pre-Revolutionary homes in the country.
- A restored waterfront with dozens of quality shops and first-class restaurants.
- Theater and music festivals.

3. INTRODUCTION

If you expect to be intimidated by the smart, lime-green wealth of Newport, relax. Newport attracts the same summer crowds that weekend in the Hamptons and on Fire Island.

The super-rich keep a low profile these days, preferring to party in their sumptuous homes on Bellevue Avenue and Ocean Drive. They avoid the tourist spots, and venture down to the waterfront only long enough to board their yachts and sail out to sea.

The rich here weren't always so private. Newport in the nineteenth century was a playground for high society, for people like the Astors and the Vanderbilts, who outdid each other with glittering displays of wealth. For about six weeks each summer they entertained in their modest 30-room "cottages" on the cliffs overlooking the sea. They played polo, sailed yachts, rode thoroughbreds, and played tennis on the grounds of the gingerbread casino designed by Stanford White.

"During its heyday," David Riley writes in *Country Journal*, "Newport was a freak show of excesses. Mrs. Clews set aside $10,000 every summer for 'mistakes in my clothes'; Mrs. Belmont never wore the same article of clothing twice; and during the depression of the 1890s, Mrs. Stuyvesant Fish and Mrs. Lehr gave a dinner (stewed liver, rice, and fricassee of bones) for a hundred dogs in fancy dress, during which Mrs. Dyer's dachshund fainted from overeating and had to be carried home."

The Gilded Age came to an end, of course, and mansions became museums and the main attraction for some three million visitors each year.

What visitors tend to ignore is Newport's other heritage as a colonial seaport with one of the largest collections of pre-Revolutionary buildings in the country. These early American houses recall a time when Newport's wide, well-protected harbor made it the nation's third largest seaport, after Boston and Philadelphia. Fortunately, a restoration project funded by tobacco heiress Doris Duke has been buying up and restoring these old properties. Visitors can see them along the narrow streets in the Point section and in the area surrounding Washington Square.

As for the downtown area, it had been reduced to boarded-up tenements and sailor's dives when the waterfront development program began in the mid-1960s. Little remains that is salty today—the lobstermen have all scurried away, chased by crowds of Lacoste alligators—but the area does have a restful weathered-pine-and-shingle look and a tasteful assortment of quality shops and restaurants that are the delight of weekend visitors.

On Sunday nights, while these visitors are thinking of the long drive home, a few of the families of old Newport leave their mansions and arrange themselves around the piano bar at The Inn at Castle Hill. There is an easy mingling of generations, a quiet sense of place. Young and old seem to wear the same clothes and expressions, and to drink the same drinks. Radiating confidence, they take turns singing show tunes like "Hello, Dolly," then join together in a rousing chorus of "God Bless America." The evening over, they head back to their mansions on the cliffs, while a few remaining visitors—reluctant to let go of a fun-filled weekend—gather around the blinking harbor lights below.

4. WHAT TO SEE AND DO.

A first trip to Newport is unthinkable without a visit to one or more of the mansions. The sheer size and opulence of these summer "cottages" staggers the imagination; nothing comparable will ever be seen again.

▪ **The Preservation Society** (phone: 847-1000) owns six of them—Kingscote, Chateau-sur-Mer, Marble House, The Breakers, The Elms, and Rosecliff—and a seventh building, the Hunter House, built in 1748. All are open May 1 through October, from 10 to 5. In April, The Breakers, The Elms, Marble House, and Rosecliff are open daily from 10 to 5; other mansions are open weekends only from 10 to 5. In winter, Marble House, The Elms, and Chateau-sur-Mer are open on weekends from 10 to 4, and Hunter House (phone 847-6543) is open by appointment. At least one mansion is open each summer night until 8; call the Preservation Society for details.

A visit to two or more mansions will cost less with a combination ticket sold at any of the seven properties. Single tickets cost $4.50 for The Breakers and Marble House, and $3.50 for all others. Individual tickets for all properties cost $1.25 for children aged 6 to 11. For adults, combination tickets cost $6 for two properties, $8 for three, $10 for four, $12 for five, and $18 for six. For children aged 6 to 11, combination tickets cost $1.75 for two properties, $2.50 for three, $3.25 for four, $4 for five, and $4.75 for six.

- Visitors with limited time are usually advised to head for **The Breakers,** the most extravagant mansion of all, built in 1895 for Cornelius Vanderbilt. Poor Cornelius must turn in his grave at the crowds stalking through his halls, or at the guides reeling off information with the enthusiasm of dusty tapes. If you go in summer, stick to early mornings or weekdays.

- For a similar sense of opulence, visit **Rosecliff, The Elms,** or **Marble House.** *The Betsy* and *Great Gatsby* were filmed at Rosecliff, which was designed by Stanford White after the Grand Trianon at Versailles. The Elms, modeled after the Chateau d'Asnières near Paris, has the loveliest gardens. Marble House, built in 1892 for William K. Vanderbilt, was designed by Richard Morris Hunt and retains most of its original furnishings.

- Visit one of these three and then, for an interesting counterpoint, turn to **Kingscote,** the oldest of the mansions, built in 1839. Kingscote is unique in that it bears no resemblance to a baroque bordello. A fine example of Gothic Victorian architecture, it was built to be lived in, not just to present a face to the world.

- **Belcourt Castle** (phone: 846-0669), a privately owned mansion, must have the largest collection of priceless art and antiques in Newport. The Tinney family lives here, and visitors are given tea and made to feel like guests. The castle was designed in 1891 by Richard Morris Hunt, in the style of Louis XIII's palace in France. There is a Gothic ballroom, a Louis XV salon-boudoir, a Versailles dining room, an Italian banquet hall that seats 300, and a host of other architectural conceits attesting to the wild eclecticism of a lost age. Open April 1 to December 1, from 10 to 5. Admission is $4.50 for adults and $1.25 for children.

- At **Beechwood** (phone: 846-3774), another private mansion, a woman in long Victorian skirt greets you at the gate and instructs you to "leave your carriage to the right." "Here is your calling card," she says. "Give it to Mr. Skiffington at the door." Mr. Skiffington stands very erect in footman's livery and accepts your $4.50 calling card on a silver tray. Neither he nor a half dozen other actors ever steps out of role as they tour you about the former summer palace of Mrs. Caroline Astor. The novelty, unfortunately, lasts about 10 minutes, when it dawns on you that there is almost nothing to see. Dialogue becomes repetitious and rambling, and descends to *Upstairs/ Downstairs* clichés about life in Victorian Newport. Kids under 12 will enjoy at least the first half of the show, but unaccompanied adults should get in their carriages and drive way. Open daily from 9:30 to 7.

- While visiting the mansions be sure to stroll along **Cliff Walk,** an oceanside trail that literally runs past the back door of many mansions, with dramatic views over the Sound.

Blinded by the glitter of the mansions, visitors tend to forget that Newport has one of the largest collections of colonial buildings in the country. Wander along the narrow streets back from the harbor and visit:

▪ **Touro Synagogue** (72 Touro Street; phone: 847-4794), built in 1763, is the oldest synagogue in America and one of the most beautiful of America's early houses of worship. Open late June through Labor Day on weekdays from 10 to 5, and Sunday from 10 to 6. Off-season open Sunday from 2 to 4 or by appointment. The historic Jewish cemetery is one block up Touro Street.

▪ **Trinity Church** (corner of Spring and Church streets), was built in 1725–26, probably from designs by Sir Christopher Wren. It has the only extant three-tiered wineglass pulpit in America. Handel played the organ before it was shipped here in 1773, a gift of English philosopher-bishop George Berkeley. George Washington's pew was Number 81. Open early May to late June from 1 to 4; late June through August from 10 to 4; off-season, on Sunday, following morning service.

▪ **The Old Colony House** (Washington Square), built in 1739, is the nation's second oldest capitol building. The acceptance of the Declaration of Independence was proclaimed from its second-story balcony. Open July through Labor Day from 9:30 to 4; off-season, weekdays from 9:30 to 12 and 1 to 4, and Saturday from 9:30 to 12. Admission is free.

▪ **Redwood Library** (Bellevue Avenue) is a National Historic Landmark built in 1748 by Peter Harrison. It is the country's oldest continuously functioning library building. Open Monday through Saturday from 10 to 6.

▪ **The 1811 Samuel Whitehorne House** (416 Thames Street; phone: 847-2448) is a fine example of architecture from the Federal period, with furniture made by Newport craftsmen. Open May through October daily from 10 to 5; April weekends from 10 to 5; other times, by appointment. Admission is $2.

▪ The 1748 **Hunter House** (54 Washington Street, near Goat Island Causeway; phone: 847-7516) is considered the finest pre-Revolutionary house in Newport. Furnishings were built by famous nineteenth-century Newport cabinetmakers. Open May 1 through October daily from 10 to 5; April weekends from 10 to 5; other times, by appointment. Admission is $3.50 for adults; $1.25 for children aged 6 to 11.

▪ **Quaker Meeting House** (Marlborough and Farewell streets;

phone: 846-0813) was built in 1699 as a center for yearly meetings for
the oldest congregation of Friends in New England. It is an outstanding example of colonial architecture. Visits include a taped slide show
on early Quaker history. Admission is $1 for adults, 50¢ for children.

▪ **St. Mary's Church** (Spring Street) is the oldest Roman Catholic parish in Rhode Island. Jacqueline Bouvier was wed to John Kennedy here on September 12, 1953. Open daily from 9 to 4, except
Sunday and holidays.

▪ On your first trip to Newport, you will want to drive or bike
the ten scenic miles along **Ocean Drive**. Bring a picnic for one of the
beaches or stop for lunch or drinks at The Inn at Castle Hill or
Shamrock Cliff Hotel (*see #19, Lodging* for details).

▪ **Hammersmith Farm** (phone: 846-0420 or 846-7346) lies
along Ocean Drive. Built in 1887 by John W. Auchincloss, this 28-
room farm served as the summer White House for John Kennedy
from 1961 to 1963. Open Memorial Day to Labor Day, daily from 10
to 8; in April, May, and October daily from 10 to 5; March and
November on weekends from 10 to 5. Admission is $3.50 for adults,
$1.50 for children aged 6 to 15.

▪ For shopping, wander along **Bellevue Avenue** and along the
wharves in the restored waterfront area. Many waterfront restaurants
do not accept reservations, so leave your name with the hostess and
spend an hour or two shopping while you're waiting for a table.

▪ The **International Tennis Hall of Fame** (194 Bellevue Avenue;
phone: 849-3990) is housed in part in the famed Newport Casino,
designed in 1880 by Stanford White. Visitors watch an 8½-minute
slide show on the history of the casino, and tour one of the country's
largest collections of tennis memorabilia, including paintings, cups,
costumes, and early racquets. The Miller Hall of Fame Tennis Cham-
pionships are held here in July. Open daily in summer from 9:30 to
5:30; off-season, weekdays from 10 to 4:30 and weekends from 11 to
4. Admission is $4.50 for adults, $1.75 for children under 14.

5. THE ARTS

▪ Jazz is not the only music in Newport. Newport mansions are
the setting for a series of chamber concerts by internationally known
musicians in late July. Contact the **Newport Music Festival** (50
Washington Square; phone: 846-1133).

▪ The **Rhode Island Shakespeare Theater** has summer productions at the Swanhurst Theater (Bellevue Avenue and Webster Street;
phone: 849-7892).

▪ **Christmas in Newport** (P.O. Box 716, Newport; phone: 849-

6454) is a nonprofit organization offering candlelight tours of historic houses, organ recitals, and other cultural events daily through December.

- The **Incredible Far-Off Broadway Ensemble** (phone: 846-8259 or 847-1996) present modern plays in an outdoor theater.
- **Newport Casino Theater** (phone: 846-1984) has a summer program of plays and readings by professional actors during July and August. Phone for details.
- For information on the **Newport Jazz Festival,** contact the Chamber of Commerce (phone: 847-1600).
- For information on art exhibits, contact the **Art Association of Newport** (76 Bellevue Avenue; Phone: 847-0179).
- **Brass Tacks** (Washington Square; phone: 849-6291) has an ongoing festival of classic films, free with drinks or meals.

6. ANTIQUES AND CRAFTS

- There are more than 20 antique shops along Spring Street and Franklin Street (between Thames and Spring streets), including **Ramson House Antiques, Old Fashion, Ruskin Antiques,** and **John Larner Antiques.**

7. TOURS

- **Viking Tours** (128 Thames Street, phone: 847-6921) has 1½-hour and three-hour bus tours of Newport from April through November 13. The longer trip includes a stop at a mansion. Buses leave from various hotels and from the Chamber of Commerce. The 90-minute trip costs $7.50 for adults and $4.50 for children aged 6 to 11. The three-hour trip costs $10.50 for adults and $5.50 for children aged 5 to 11.
- **Viking Tours** (128 Thames Street; phone: 847-6921) offers hour-long shoreline cruises aboard the 140-passenger *Viking Queen* and the 49-passenger *Viking Princess.* Boats leave from the Goat Island Marina from May through October. Tours cost $4 for adults and $2 for children aged 5 to 11.
- **Oldport Marine Services** (Newport Yachting Center, America's Cup Avenue; phone: 849-2111) runs narrated hour-long harbor cruises in a 42-passenger, 40-foot boat. Trips run June through September, between 10:30 and 7:30.
- **Arthur P. Mattos** (6 Barney Street; phone: 846-7880) offers private taxi tours of Newport.
- Auto cassette-tape tours of Colonial Newport, Ocean Drive, and Cliff Walk are available from the **Chamber of Commerce.**

8. WALKS

▪ The three-mile **Cliff Walk** along the Atlantic Ocean passes many of the most famous mansions.

▪ The restored waterfront is the place to go for shops and restaurants, but to appreciate the colonial city, walk down the narrow streets in the **Historic Hill Area,** around Trinity Church and Touro Park. The area is bounded roughly by Thames Street, Bellevue Avenue, Memorial Boulevard, and Washington Square. There are also many lovely restored homes on Washington Street, north from Hunter House. The Chamber of Commerce sells maps for self-guided walking tours.

▪ The 450-acre **Norman Bird Sanctuary** (Third Beach Road, Middletown; phone: 846-2577) has ten miles of trails.

9. BIKING

▪ Cyclists will enjoy biking down Bellevue Avenue, stopping for a mansion or two, then following the spectacular ten-mile **Ocean Drive** around the coast. The coastal road has beaches for swimming and picnics, and two hotels (The Inn at Castle Hill and Shamrock Cliff Hotel) for drinks or lunch.

▪ Rent bikes or mopeds by the day or hour at **Ten Speed Spokes** (79 Thames Street; phone: 847-5609). Open daily from May to October. Bike-route maps are available for self-guided tours.

10. BOATING AND FISHING

▪ **J. C. Myles Standish** (4 Smithfield Drive, Middletown; phone: 846-7225) has party boats for sport fishing (sea trout, blues, mackerel) and bottom fishing (tautog, fluke, flounder, cod).

▪ **Oldport Marine Services, Inc.** (Newport Yachting Center; phone: 847-9109) rents sailboats and rowboats.

▪ **McMichael Newport** (Bannister's Wharf; phone: 849-4327) rents sailboats, motorboats, and yachts.

▪ **Island Windsurfing, Inc.** (375 Thames Street; phone: 846-4421) rents windsurfers at Third Beach and Fort Adams Beach.

▪ **Newport Sailing School and Cruises** (5 Beaver Road, Barrington; phone: 246-1595) offers two-hour, half-day, and full-day cruises aboard 25-foot and 30-foot auxiliary sloops. Boats leave from Goat Island Marina from April through October.

11. SWIMMING

▪ To escape the crowds and the high cost of parking, the small beach in **Fort Adams State Park** (phone: 847-2400) is your best bet. Windsurfers can be rented here from **Island Windsurfing, Inc.**

▪ **Bailey's Beach,** (junction of Bellevue and Ocean avenues) has no parking facilities; you must arrive by foot or bike. (Drivers can park nearby at Belcourt Castle.) Bailey's is the most exclusive beach in Newport, but has no lifeguards or beach facilities. Picnic along the pasture to the right. Climb the rocks to Cliff Walk for a great view of the mansions.

▪ **First Beach** (Memorial Boulevard) has lifeguards and concessions near the east parking lot, where surfboards can be rented at the **Straight Arrow Surf Co.** To avoid crowds, leave cars at the far end of the beach, away from downtown Newport.

▪ **Second Beach, Middletown** (follow Memorial Boulevard to Purgatory Road [Second Beach Ave.]) is the area's most popular beach, famous for its body-surfing waves. Climb the hill to Purgatory Chasm, a 160-foot fissure. Scenery from the top is tops.

13. RIDING

▪ **Middletown Stables** (phone: 846-0904) offers evening trail rides along the beach.

14. TENNIS

▪ **International Tennis Hall of Fame** (194 Bellevue Avenue; phone: 849-3990) has grass courts open from June through November.

▪ **Casino Racquet Club** (on grounds of the Hall of Fame; phone 849-4777) has indoor courts open year-round.

15. GOLF

▪ **Newport Country Club** (phone: 846-0461) is open to nonmembers if they call ahead and space is available.

▪ **Wanumetonomy Country Club** (Middletown; phone: 847-3420) is also open to nonmembers if they call ahead and space is available.

16. FOR KIDS

▪ Tour a child's playhouse at **The Breakers** (phone: 847-1000).

▪ Enjoy the dramatic tour of **Caroline Astor's Beechwood** (phone: 846-3774). *See #4, What to See and Do.*

▪ *See entries in #9, Biking; #10, Boating and Fishing; #11, Swimming; #14, Tennis.*

17. DINING

Newport is blessed with more than a half-dozen first-class restaurants. Those along the waterfront are, on summer weekends, noisy and crowded, which to some is part of their charm. Two-hour waits are not unusual. Menus are posted outside, so come early, find a place that fits your budget and taste, leave your name with the hostess, and squander a lovely hour or two among the many shops. You can also drink the time away at lounges upstairs at The Chart House or Le Bistro. The latter has soft classical music.

The two most popular, elegant, and expensive waterfront restaurants are:

▪ **The Black Pearl** (phone: 846-5264) has a formal dining room jutting out over the sea, with food as good as any in Newport. Popular appetizers include snails Narbonnaise (snails in cognac, ham, walnuts, and tomato sauce) and fondue parmesan (Gruyère cheese batter-dipped and deep-fried). Entrées, prices from $11 to $22, include filet of beef with a port and truffle sauce, and veal Black Pearl (medallions of veal sauteed with sliced artichoke bottoms and fresh mushrooms in a dry sherry sauce). A popular dessert is pears Pernod (halves of pears flambé in a Pernod and cream caramel sauce). Reservations are required in summer in the formal Commodore's Room. Jackets are required. All major credit cards are accepted.

▪ **The Clarke Cooke House** (phone: 849-2900) is as elegant as its hors d'oeuvres, which include roasted pharaoh quail stuffed with foie gras in a pecan sauce. Entrées, priced from $14 to $22, include sole poached in Chardonnay wine with asparagus and lemon saffron cream, and tenderloin rolled in mustard seed and cooked with Cabernet Sauvignon. Jackets are requested. Reservations are required in summer. All major credit cards are accepted.

For intimate surroundings away from the frenetic pace of the waterfront, try:

▪ **The Inn at Castle Hill** (Ocean Drive; phone: 849-3800) is popular among the old Newport set—which is, after all, what many visitors come to see. The inn sits on a lonely promontory overlooking the ocean. Ask for a table with a view. The nonsmoker's room is also attractive. Entrées, priced from $12.50 to $19, feature beef Wellington with a Madeira sauce. Jackets are required. ("No jeans, designer or any other kind," the innkeeper told me.) Reservations are advised. Visa and Mastercard are accepted.

▪ My own favorite Newport restaurant is the **White Horse Tavern** (Marlborough Street; phone 849-3600), housed in a seventeenth-century colonial building. One of the oldest operating taverns in the country, the White Horse is a place of rustic elegance, perfect for couples who appreciate candlelight, classical music, and meaningful conversation. Entrées on the continental menu range from $15 to $22 and include roast duckling and beef Wellington. Jackets are required. Reservations are required. All major credit cards are accepted.

▪ **La Petite Auberge** (19 Charles Street; phone: 849-6669) is a small country French restaurant, built in 1714. Bright blue tablecloths and Piaf-vintage accordian music make the Auberge a trifle more cheerful than the White Horse Tavern. The largest room has only five tables. Entrées, prices from $15 to $22, include white fish served on fennel, flambé with Pernod, and filet mignon in a pastry crust and truffle sauce. Jackets are requested. Reservations are advised. All major credit cards are accepted.

▪ Visitors on low budgets will find solace at **Salas'** (343 Thames Street; phone: 846-8772). Locals are willing to wait up to two hours for a $4.25 spaghetti dish with red clam sauce or a $13.95 "lobster" clambake served up on red and white plastic tablecloths. There's also a raw bar. The stamped-tin walls are painted a deep green and covered with Italian movie posters. Dress is casual. No reservations. All major credit cards are now accepted.

▪ Local people have kind words for the reasonable prices and large portions at **Courtney's** (65 Long Wharf; phone: 846-5004). Piped music is only a note above Muzak, but there's a friendly brick-pine-and-hanging-plant ambience, and porch tables overlook the harbor. Entrées, priced from $7.50 to $14.50, include broiled scrod and broiled filet mignon. Dress is informal. Reservations are advised. All major credit cards are accepted.

▪ **Frick's** (673 Thames Street, Groton; phone: 846-5830) is a popular German/Viennese restaurant featuring sweetbreads, escargots and veal and fresh fish dishes. Entrées range from $12 to $22. Jackets are required. All major credit cards are accepted.

18. AFTER HOURS

▪ The under-30 crowd hangs out under the blinking harbor lights on **Bannister's Wharf**, particularly at **The Landing** and in front of **The Black Pearl.** Another "in" spot is **The Mooring** on **Sayer's Wharf.**

- The over-30 singles crowd moves indoors to **Courtney's** (65 Long Wharf), upstairs at **Le Bistro** (Bowen's Wharf), the lounge at the **Chart House** (Bowen's Wharf), the Daisy at the **Clarke Cooke House** (Bannister's Wharf), and the tavern at **The Black Pearl** (Bannister's Wharf).

- **Harry's Harbour Front Club** (109 Harbour Front; phone: 846-3660) features live jazz on summer weekends.

- Bars are open until 1 A.M. weekdays, 2 A.M. on weekends.

19. LODGING

Taped to the window of the Chamber of Commerce (10 America's Cup Ave.) is a list of 67 hotels, motels, guest houses, and inns in the Newport-Middletown area. But don't arrive on summer weekends without a reservation. I once did, and had to convince an all-night gas attendant 30 miles out of town to rent me his room while he worked.

Most rooms and furnishings capture (or parody) the somewhat fussy elegance of Victorian Newport, with none of the simple rustic charm one associates with the city's rich colonial past. That is not meant as criticism; not everyone is into simple rustic charm. But you will look in vain for the equivalent of an old New England inn. Large floral-pattern wallpapers have taken over like kudzu vines down south. More elegant inns—the one at Castle Hill, for instance—have Greef and Old Stone Mill papers, and more modest establishments like the Brinley have fabric from Sears. But all are Decorated. "I've given up on primitives," a Franklin Street antique dealer told me; "all local people want now are comfortable twentieth-century furnishings."

Note: Prices quoted below are in the high season, from Labor Day to mid- or late October. Off-season rates drop as much as 35 percent.

HOTELS AND INNS.

- Reservations can be made through the **Newport Reservation Service** (270 Main Street; phone: 846-1825).

- A room at **The Inn at Castle Hill** (Ocean Drive; phone: 849-3800) is as close to expensive Newport as weekend folk can come, which is why rooms are often booked up to a year ahead. George Bush tried to stay here one summer, but was turned away. Paul Newman had no better luck, and was sent to The Inntowne (owned by the innkeepers at Castle Hill).

The inn was built in 1874 as a summer home for the scientist and explorer Alexander Agassiz. Thornton Wilder visited frequently and in *Theophilus North* described one bedroom (where guests can stay) as "the pentagonal room in a turret above the house: from that magical room I could see at night the beacons of six light houses and hear the booming and chiming of as many sea buoys." Two favorite rooms are #5 and #9. Doubles run from $45 in the old servants' quarters, with shared bath, to $140. A continental breakfast is included. Facilities include a private beach and tennis rights at the nearby Shamrock Cliff Hotel. Visa and Mastercard are accepted.

- When The Inn at Castle Hill is booked, visitors are sent to **The Innetown** (Mary and Thames Street; phone: 846-9200), which is considerably more modest but under the same management. Guests in the 1980 inn may use the private beach at Castle Hill and tennis facilities at the Shamrock Cliff Hotel. Doubles, with private bath, cost $85 to $110, including a continental breakfast. One considerably less expensive room has an outside bath. Visa and Mastercard are accepted.

- **Admiral Benbow Inn** (93 Pelham Street; phone: 846-4256) is only two blocks from the waterfront. The 130-year-old inn has been recently restored with black marble fireplaces, canopy and brass beds, wingback chairs, and other antiques. The 15 rooms, all with private bath, cost $60 to $85 or $45 to $55 off-season.

- **The Wayside** (Bellevue Avenue; phone: 847-0302) was recommended by *New York* magazine as a "great weekend getaway." Here's your chance to stay in one of the smaller summer "cottages," once owned by people actively involved in the glittering social life of turn-of-the-century Newport. Rooms are huge, with 15-foot ceilings, fireplaces, and French windows. Doubles, with private bath, cost $59, including continental breakfast. All major credit cards are accepted.

- **The Queen Anne Inn** (16 Clarke Street; phone: 846-5676) was built in 1890 and was recently redecorated. Rooms are clean and cheerful, some with antiques and bay windows. More expensive rooms are worth the extra price. Doubles, with shared bath, cost $35–$50, including continental breakfast. No credit cards are accepted.

- **Yankee Peddler Inn** (113 Touro Street; phone: 846-1323) is very decorated, with matching everything, and lovely wide pine floors. Doubles with private baths, cost $75 to $95; without bath, $55. No credit cards are accepted.

GUEST HOUSES.

For a list of guest houses, call the Newport Chamber of Commerce at (800) 343-4511. Homes offering bed and breakfast for $40-$60 a night are listed with **Castle Keep** (44 Everett Street; phone: 846-0362).

- **Waterview Guest House** (10 Cliff Terrace; phone: 847-4425) is a small, unpretentious private home, and the best buy in town. It sits at the foot of Cliff Walk, a few minutes from the beach. Doubles, some with private bath, cost $30 to $35, including continental breakfast. No credit cards are accepted.

- **Woodbine Manor** (82 Mill Street; phone: 846-3538) is an 1832 Greek Revival-style summer home. All the furniture belonged to the present owner's grandmother. The dark entranceway has stuffed birds of paradise, buffalo antlers, a Chinese peacock scroll, a large Japanese satsume, and buckling Eastlake wallpaper. A real period piece that some will love. Doubles, some with private bath, cost $40 to $50. No credit cards are accepted.

- **The Ailinas Inn** (27 Mann Avenue; phone: 847-3909) is a clean, shingled Victorian house on a quiet residential side street. Doubles, with shared bath, cost $35 to $40. No credit cards are accepted.

MOTELS.

- **Treadway Inn** (Newport Harbor; phone: 800/631-0182) is closest to the waterfront, but noise can be a problem for light sleepers. Facilities include an indoor pool and saunas. Weekend packages are available. Doubles cost $110 to $125. All major credit cards are accepted.

- **Sheraton-Islander Inn** (Goat Island; phone: 849-2600 or 800/325-3535) has indoor and outdoor pools, a sauna, and a marina. Weekend packages are available. Doubles cost $130 to $170. All major credit cards are accepted.

- **Viking Hotel and Motor Inn** (1 Bellevue Avenue; phone: 847-3300 or 800/556-7126) has an indoor pool and sauna. Weekend packages are available. Doubles, some with shared bath, cost $49-$119.

- **Easton's Inn on the Beach** (30 Wave Avenue, Middletown; phone: 846-0310) is more a comfortable motel than an inn. Doubles cost $95. All major credit cards are accepted.

20. EMERGENCIES

- **Police** (phone: 847-1212).
- **Newport Hospital** (phone: 846-6400).

21. HOW TO GET THERE

BY CAR. *From New York:* Route I-95 north to Route 138 east. Follow blue road signs for Newport Bridge into Newport. *From Boston:* Route 128 south to Route 24 south via Sakonnet River Bridge to Route 114 south into Newport. *From Providence:* Route I-95 south to Route 2 south and Route 1 south. Follow blue road signs to Route 138 and the Newport Bridge into Newport. *Also from Providence:* Route 195 east to Route 114 south via Mt. Hope Bridge into Newport.

BY BUS. *From New York:* Greyhound (212/635-0800). *From Boston:* Bonanza Lines (617/423-5810). *From Providence:* Bonanza Bus Station (401/781-9400).

BY TRAIN. *From New York:* Amtrak (212/736-4545) to Providence, then a five-minute walk to the Bonanza Bus Station (401/781-9400). *From Boston:* Amtrak (617/482-3660) to Providence, then a five-minute walk to the Bonanza Bus Station (401/781-9400).

22. FOR FURTHER INFORMATION

- **Newport County Chamber of Commerce,** P.O. Box 237 MS, 10 America's Cup Avenue, Newport, RI 02840. Phone: 847-1600.
- In New York City: **New England Vacation Center,** 630 Fifth Avenue, New York, NY 10020. Phone: 212/757-4455.
- For additional information on the mansions: **The Preservation Society of Newport County,** 118 Mill Street. Phone: 847-1000.

23. RECOMMENDED READING

- Thorton Wilder's *Theophilus North* (Avon, $1.75) captures the flavor of the Gilded Age in Newport.
- *Architectural Heritage of Newport, Rhode Island, 1640–1915,* by A. F. Downing and V. J. Scully, Jr. (Potter, $25) is a serious and comprehensive architectural study.
- Richard O'Connor's *The Golden Summers* and Consuelo Vanderbilt Balsalm's *The Glitter and the Gold* are available in libraries.

Windham County, Vermont

(Area Code, 802)

1. DISTANCES (TO BRATTLEBORO)

BY CAR. *From New York*, 4 hours; *from Boston*, 2 hours; *from Hartford*, 1¾ hours.

BY BUS. *From New York*, 5 to 6½ hours; *from Boston*, 3½ hours; *from Hartford*, 1¾ hours.

BY TRAIN. *From New York*, 5½ hours.

2. MAJOR ATTRACTIONS

- Corncribs and covered bridges, red barns and village greens—all the best New England has to offer, only four hours from Times Square.
- The restfulness of old inns.
- Three-star dining in a setting of rustic elegance.
- Crafts, music, theater. A heady mixture of cows and culture.
- Some of New England's most popular downhill and cross-country ski trails.

3. INTRODUCTION

Brattleboro. Marlboro. Wilmington. West Dover. Newfane. Grafton. Putney. Saxtons River.

The towns lie between the Connecticut River and the Green Mountains, and each has its own character and charm. But wherever you stay you will find a venerable old inn with elegant country dining, and a list of outdoor activities four seasons long. Ski trails, antique stores, music festivals, farmers' markets, fall foliage—everything you hope to find in Vermont is here in Windham County.

What makes the southeast corner of the state so culturally fascinating is the mixture of old-timers—the Foxfire folk—and the urban expatriates with their looms and their frogs' legs Provençale.

Cows and culture; farmers' markets and anti-nuke foundations; pig sales and seminars in psychodrama—the two worlds coexist in Windham because they are a universe apart and because Vermonters respect each person's right to be himself. Isn't that why they moved here in the first place?

Craftspeople discovered Windham in the late nineteenth century, but the real influx began in the 1960s, when people seeking alternative life-styles filtered up from the cities. Many, turning in their sandals, are back in law school or studying for their MBAs. But the serious ones remain; you can buy their crafts on Main Street, Brattleboro, and in dozens of studios and shops throughout the county. The Putney area alone has more than 40 craftspeople who moved here with their lifetime savings and set about making a living at what they loved to do. You will meet some of them in the Common Ground Restaurant in Brattleboro, munching on Veggieburgers and scrambled tofu.

Many young professionals and retired couples came to Windham, too, and discovered that they could support their country lifestyle by catering to the expensive tastes of other expatriates from Boston and New York. Old inns, restaurants, antique stores—almost every place you visit on weekends is run by out-of-staters. If you want to meet a Grade A Vermonter—and no one who was not born here is a Grade A Vermonter—then you must visit private homes selling bread or honey, and strike up a conversation.

Newcomers have transformed Brattleboro, the commercial center of the region, into a little Cambridge, with Indian print dress shops, boutiques, and craft stores. When I last visited Brattleboro 25 years ago it was a sleepy country town; after dark one night, the only sign of life came from a downtown restaurant where farmers stood on wooden tables, chasing bats with brooms.

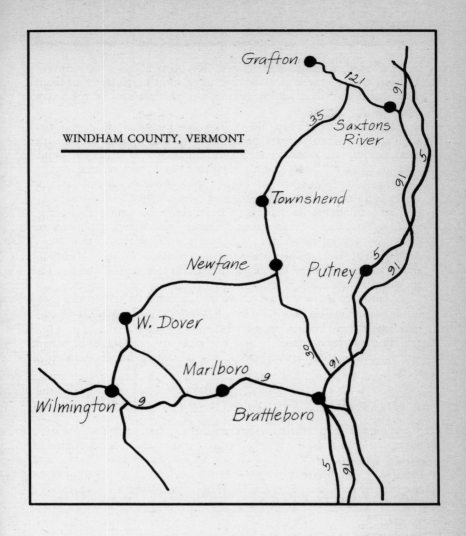

WINDHAM COUNTY, VERMONT

Grafton

121

91

35

Saxtons
River

5

91

Townshend

5

Newfane

Putney

5

91

91

W. Dover

30

91

Marlboro

9

Wilmington

9

Brattleboro

5

91

Victorians would have been horrified by the decline of their thriving river town, which in the late nineteenth century had a 900-seat opera house, Italianate villas, and a number of factories shipping Estey organs, books, tools, and furniture to the four corners of the globe.

The town's progress toward nowhere continued through the 1960s. Wreckers smashed the frescoed halls of the town hall where Mark Twain and Oliver Wendell Holmes had lectured. The building where Rutherford B. Hayes's father worked was carried clapboard by clapboard to Sturbridge Village "for purposes of preservation." The inn where Hayes himself lived after refusing to serve a second term was demolished and is now the site of a parking lot for a state liquor store.

Renovation began in the 1970s when Brooks House, modeled after a seventeenth-century palace, was turned into an office complex. You can see it today, dominating Main Street. Other old buildings on Elliott Street were converted into homes and shops. Craftspeople provided a market for sophisticated book and clothing stores and for a year-long program of music, dance, and theater.

So fashionable have parts of Brattleboro become that the Performing Arts Center was recently chased out by high rents and replaced by several boutiques. Weekend visitors will love the "new" Brattleboro; the question is whether too much "newness" will force artists to pack up their brushes and head for northern Vermont. The answer for now is no.

Windham is still a place where the Chamber of Commerce publishes pamphlets on how to watch beaver ponds at dusk, and where innkeepers leave latches open for late-night guests.

The county remains a land of farms and rolling hills, where visitors can stretch, breathe deep, and fall asleep under a crowd of stars.

4. WHAT TO SEE AND DO

The following route is one of the loveliest in New England, particularly in the fall. It takes you past farmers' markets, antique stores, and quaint New England villages—past brooks, barns, and brindled cows. Some of the most scenic backroads are listed only on the official state map available at Vermont Information Centers (see #22, For Further Information).

Brattleboro

▪ **L. J. Serkin** (Elliot Street; phone: 257-7044) is a top-quality hand-weaving studio and weaving supply store, with jewelry, batik, pottery, etc., from more than 80 craftspeople.

▪ **Brattleboro Museum and Art Center** (phone: 257-0124) is a stately 65-year-old former railroad station with imaginative displays of local art and memorabilia.

Route 9 west from Brattleboro to Marlboro and Wilmington

▪ Some very local people sell home-grown produce, baked goods, and crafts at the **Brattleboro Farmer's Market** (phone: 257-

7967 or 257-1568), just outside of town, past the Creamery Covered
Bridge. Open Wednesday and Saturday in season, from 10 to 2.

▪ In **Marlboro**, visit Lucy Serkin's weaving studio (phone: 257-
0181), open Saturday afternoons in summer or by appointment; Mal-
colm Wright's pottery studio (phone: 254-2168), with wood-fired
stoneware inspired by classical Oriental forms; and David and
Michelle Holzapfel's woodworking studio (phone: 254-2908), selling
sculptural furnishings for the home and office made from rare Vermont hardwoods.

▪ Drive to the top of **Hogback Mt.** for a breathtaking three-state
view.

▪ At the **Craft-Haus** (Wilmington; phone: 464-2164), Ursula
and Ed Tancrel sell enameled copper bowls and plates, stained glass,
silver, and jewelry. Lilias MacBean Hart sells pottery, Scottish
woolens, etc. at the **Quaigh Design Center** (Wilmington; phone:
464-2780).

▪ **Coombs Beaver Brook Sugar House** (Wilmington; phone:
464-5232) sells maple products from the state's largest sugar house.

North on Route 100 from Wilmington to East Jamaica.
This is a particularly scenic route through the foothills of the
Green Mountains.

▪ About two miles north of Wilmington, turn left on Coldbrook
Road toward Mountain Snow. Dine at the **Hermitage** (phone: 464-
3759) or stop there for homemade maple sugar and jams.

▪ **Mount Snow** (nine miles north of Wilmington; phone: 464-
3333) has a 7,000-foot gondola ride to the summit. Ride back down
or take the 2½-mile Thompson Nature Trail.

▪ Stop for drinks or dinner at the **Inn at Saw Mill Farm** (West
Dover; phone: 464-8131).

*Alternative route: drive west from West Dover to South Newfane and
West Dummerston, then head north on Route 30 to Newfane. This is a
small country road not listed on gas station maps.*

▪ **Newfane** is a lovely green and white clapboard village with
several buildings in the Greek Revival style of 1825. The county
courthouse stands on the village green beside the church, surrounded
by two famous inns, antique shops, and a country store.

▪ Dine in Newfane at either the **Four Columns Inn** (phone:
365-7713) or the **Newfane Inn** (phone: 365-4427).

▪ **Newfane Country Store** (phone: 365-7916) is a 150-year-old
store with dollhouse miniatures, calicos, cheeses, penny candies, and
a large selection of locally made quilts.

- **Lawrence Smoke House** (Route 30; phone: 365-7751) sells corncob-smoked hams, bacon, salami, and cheese.

Drive north on Route 100 from West Dover to East Jamaica. Go south on Route 30, then north on Route 35 to Grafton.

- Some consider Grafton the loveliest village in New England because its restored eighteenth- and nineteenth-century buildings are lived in, not roped off as museums. Dine at the **Old Tavern** (phone: 843-2231), where Kipling went for his honeymoon, then spend a delightful hour strolling down to Saxtons River and back. The town has two art galleries and seven antique stores, including **Grafton Antiques** and the **Village Pump.**

- A short stroll from the tavern takes you to the **Grafton Village Cheese Company** (phone: 843-2221), which makes a tasty, aged Vermont cheddar. Next door is a covered bridge.

From Grafton drive southeast on Route 121 to the town of Saxtons River. This is a particularly attractive ride on a winding road along the river.

- The town of Saxtons River has four antique stores, a crafts cooperative, and an orchard (1½ miles from town on Route 121) where you can pick your own apples in season.

- **Saxtons River Inn** (phone: 869-2110) is noted for its good food.

Take Route 121 east to Route 5, then head south through Putney to Brattleboro.

- If you're into igloo pancake houses, Arabian camels, iceberg slides, and the largest collection of Christmas decorations this side of the North Pole, stop at **Santa's Land** (Route 5, five miles north of Putney; phone: 387-5550).

- **Harlow's Sugar House** (Route 5, three miles north of Putney; phone: 387-5852) sells maple sugar products.

- **Dwight Miller & Son Orchards** (Route 5, three miles north of Putney; phone: 254-9158) lets you pick your own fruit—apples, peaches, pears, strawberries—in season.

- **Carol Brown's** (turn left at the general store in Putney; phone: 387-5875) has a large, tasteful collection of Irish tweeds, London bobby capes, batiks, Italian silks, and Aran sweaters. Not a synthetic stitch in sight.

- Up from Carol Brown's on West Hill Road is **Green Mountain Orchards,** where you can buy or pick your own berries and apples.

- Back in Putney, **The Sawmill** (phone: 387-4688) sells Vermont-made crafts and food.

▪ **Putney Woodshed** (Putney; phone: 387-4481) sells wooden toys, locally made shawls, pottery, prints, and rugs.

▪ **Basketville** (Route 5, Putney; phone: 387-5509) has thousands of white ash and red oak baskets. Look out for the imports!

▪ **Putney Nursery** (Route 5, Putney; phone: 387-5577) offers a wide selection of unusual wildflowers, ferns, perennials, and herbs.

▪ To reach Kipling's house **Naulahka,** continue south on Route 5, past Exit 3 on I-91 north. Turn right on Black Mountain Road, then on to Kipling Road. The house is not open to the public. Kipling and his bride arrived in 1892 in a 30-below-zero snowstorm, an experience that exhilarated him, since he had never seen snow before. Naulahka, where he wrote *The Jungle Books,* is built in the shape of a boat. Kipling's study, looking to the south and east, was in the bow.

▪ On your way south from Putney to Brattleboro, turn right on the road to West Dummerston and cross the longest covered bridge in Vermont.

5. THE ARTS

▪ At the **Marlboro Music Festival,** an extended family of some 70 talented musicians come together for seven weeks each summer on the campus of Marlboro College. Pablo Casals spent 13 summers here. Rudolf Serkin has been the artistic director since 1952. What makes the festival so special is the fact that it is run not for audiences but for the artists themselves, who are given a unique opportunity to study and rehearse together in ideal surroundings. Of the hundreds of compositions rehearsed each week, only a half-dozen or so are chosen for public performance. Audiences tend to take their music more seriously than at Tanglewood, since programs are rarely selected more than a day ahead, and most works are for chamber orchestra and ensembles. Tickets are usually gone by May, though last-minute seating is available in a canopied area outside the 670-seat concert hall, with an obstructed view and restricted sound. The festival runs from July 10 to August 15. Performances are Friday and Saturday nights at 8:30 and Sunday afternoons at 2:30. Picnic facilities are available. For tickets, contact the Marlboro Music Festival, 135 South 18th Street, Philadelphia, PA 19103. Phone: 215/569-4690. After June 10 contact the Marlboro Music Festival, Marlboro 05344. Phone: 254-8163 or 254-2394.

▪ Emerging artists from major conservatories and world-renowned artists perform at the **Yellow Barn Music Festival** (Putney; phone: 387-6637) from July through August. Chamber concerts are performed in a rambling 150-seat barn.

▪ The **Brattleboro Music Center** (15 Walnut Street, Brattleboro; phone: 257-4523) presents a wide variety of classical music concerts year-round. During foliage season the Center sponsors the New England Bach Festival, with concerts around New England. Winter programs include chamber music series with artists such as the Concord String Quartet, Rudolf Serkin, and Pina Carmirelli.

▪ **Actor's Theater** at the Latchis Ballroom (2 Flat Street, Brattleboro; phone: 257-1129) performs plays (from musicals to Greek tragedy) and sponsors an art film series.

▪ Contra dances are held on Sunday night throughout the year at the **Green Street School** (Green Street, Brattleboro; phone: 387-5544 or 387-4644).

▪ International folk dances are held on Monday nights at **The Red Barn,** formerly the Chelsea House (Route 9, West Brattleboro; phone: 254-2040 or 257-0126).

▪ Classical music lovers will want to turn their radios to **WVPR,** 89.5 FM in southern Vermont.

6. ANTIQUES AND CRAFTS

There are many antique stores along Routes 30, 9, and 100. Among the best in the county are:

▪ **Family Additions** (Cross Town Road, Route 100, West Dover; phone: 464-2244) has a quality collection of seventeenth-, eighteenth-, and early nineteenth-century furniture and accessories.

▪ **Deerfield Valley Antiques** (three miles east of Wilmington on Route 9; phone: 464-8221) specializes in European furniture and clocks.

▪ **Ed Jaffe Studio** (Shearer Hill Road, Wilmington; phone: 464-8516) sells antiques and contemporary wood and bronze sculpture.

▪ **Grafton Antiques** (Route 121, Grafton, one-half mile east of the Old Tavern; phone: 843-2254) specializes in highboys and eighteenth- and early nineteenth-century furniture and accessories.

▪ **Smith's American Antiques** (Route 30, Townshend; phone: 365-4027) has mostly unfinished period and early country furniture and accessories.

9. BIKING

Most of the region is hilly, except for the area between Chester and Grafton. To rent bikes:

▪ **West Hill Shop** (Exit 4 of I-91, across from the Putney Inn; phone: 387-5718) rents bikes from used stock; call ahead to see if any are available. The shop owners are happy to recommend routes suited to your skill and temperament.

- **Gretchen's Bicycle Rentals** (Grafton; phone: 843-2234) has three-speed bikes for rent.
- **Vermont Bicycle Touring** (Bristol; phone: 388-4011) organizes weekend bike trips, from inn to inn.
- **Valley Cyclery** (Main Street, Wilmington; phone: 464-2728).
- **Grafton Bike Vermont Weekends** (Grafton; phone: 843-2259) rents bikes and runs weekend bike tours.
- **Red Circle's Vermont Gift Center** (Brattleboro; phone: 254-4933).

10. BOATING AND FISHING

- Fishermen hooked on trout (brown, lake, rainbow), smallmouth bass, or yellow perch have a choice of winding brooks, placid lily ponds, tumbling mountain streams, rivers, and isolated backcountry beaver ponds. For details, ask at your inn or at one of the sporting goods stores listed below. *The Atlas of Vermont Trout Ponds* ($4.95) is available at most bookstores, including the Green Mountain Book Store, High St., Brattleboro.
- **Galanes Sporting Goods** (116 Main Street, Brattleboro; phone: 254-5677) has fishing equipment and free advice.
- **Parmerless & Howe** (Main Street, Wilmington; phone: 464-5169) has equipment, bait, and advice.
- For a free guide to fishing in Vermont, write to **Vermont Fish and Game Department,** I. & E. Section, Montpelier 05602.
- **Harriman Reservoir** is a lovely boating lake with no commercial development *(see #11, Swimming).* Sailboats and canoes can be rented at **Wilmington Canoes** (Lake Front Restaurant, Route 9, Wilmington; phone: 464-5838).

11. SWIMMING

- **Harriman Reservoir** is a local favorite—11 miles long, with no commercial development. Rent a sailboat or canoe at **Wilmington Canoes** (Lakefront Restaurant; phone: 464-5838) and paddle to your own private beach. To reach **Mountain Mills Beach,** drive one mile from Wilmington on Castle Hill Road and follow signs. To reach **Wards Beach,** take Route 100 south from Wilmington for 1½ miles; turn right at Flame Stables, and follow signs. A 1½-mile walk along the shore will take you to **The Ledges,** an unauthorized nudist beach.
- **West River,** along Route 30.

12. SKIING

DOWNHILL

Larger resorts—Stratton, Bromley, Mount Snow, and Magic Mountain—all have extensive snow-making equipment. Budget-minded families with no need for expert slopes should head for smaller resorts—Maple Valley and Hogback—which have shorter lift lines and lower prices. Wherever you go, holiday weekends will be crowded. Many skiers consider March the ideal month to take to the slopes. Lines disappear and temperatures rise to nearly 30 degrees.

- **Bromley** (phone: 824-6915) and **Stratton** (phone: 297-2200) are both under the same management and constitute the largest skiing complex in the area. A single lift pass is honored at both resorts, which are connected by a free, 20-minute shuttle bus ride. Bromley is called the "sunshine ski area" because of its southern exposure.
- **Mount Snow** (phone: 464-3333), with its wide, ego-boosting trails, is the second-largest resort. An excellent children's program is helping to erase its image as Mascara Mountain. Nationwide Ski Trails (212/596-4227) has weekend ski packages from New York City. For room reservations in the area, call the Mount Snow Lodging Bureau (phone: 464-8501).
- **Magic Mountain** (phone: 824-5566) is smaller than Bromley, Stratton, and Mount Snow, and thus has fewer trails and shorter lines. Snowmaking equipment reaches the summit now, so advanced skiers are guaranteed a challenging day on the slopes.
- **Maple Valley** (phone: 254-6083) has some snowmaking equipment and is recommended for families that want to avoid the crowds.
- **Hogback** (phone: 464-5656) has low prices and short lines, but no snow-making equipment. The Skyline Lodge on the summit has an impressive five-state view.
- **Haystack Ski Area** (phone: 464-2776) has opened this winter with family-type trails.
- **Timber Ridge Ski Area** (Route 121; Windham; phone: 875-2103).

CROSS-COUNTRY

No inn is far from cross-country ski trails. Ask your innkeeper for the best ones in your area.

- **Jud and Gretchen Hartmann** (Grafton; phone: 843-2234) have rentals and instruction on 25 miles of marked trails.
- **Sitzmark Ski Lodge** (East Dover Road, Wilmington; phone: 464-3384) has equipment and miles of trails.

- **Brattleboro Country Club** (Brattleboro; phone: 257-7380).
- **Haystack Mountain** (Wilmington; phone: 464-5321) has rentals and miles of trails.
- **The White House** (Route 9, Wilmington; phone: 464-2135) has rentals and 18 miles of trails.
- **Hermitage Ski Center** (Coldbrook Road, Wilmington; phone: 464-3759) has rentals, instruction, and 25 miles of trails. The Hermitage Rental Shop sells wine and cheese for picnics.

13. RIDING

- **Homestead Farm and Riding Stables** (Newfane; phone: 348-7834).
- **Horseshoe Stables** (South Newfane Road, Marlboro; phone: 464-5891).
- **Flame Stables** (Wilmington; phone: 464-8329).

14. TENNIS

Many inns and resorts have their own courts *(see #19, Lodgings)*. Public school and municipal courts are open to the public.

- **Brattleboro Memorial Park** (West Brattleboro, 1½ miles from downtown Brattleboro) has public courts operated by the Battleboro Park and Recreation Department.
- **Andirons** (Route 100, West Dover; phone: 464-2114) has four courts.
- **Sitzmark Ski Lodge** (East Dover Road, Wilmington; phone: 464-3384) has eight all-weather courts.
- **Tater Hill** (Windham; phone: 875-2517).
- **Wishing Well Village** (West Townshend; phone: 874-4108).

15. GOLF

- **Mount Snow Country Club** (Mount Snow; phone: 464-3333) has an 18-hole championship course at a cool 2,000 feet.
- **Sitzmark** (East Dover Road, Wilmington; phone: 464-3384) has a par-3, 18-hole course.
- **Brattleboro Country Club** (Brattleboro; phone: 254-9864 or 257-7380) has a nine-hole course open to nonmembers.

16. FOR KIDS

- **Mount Snow** (phone: 464-3333) has a special children's ski program.
- Visit a maple sugar house in March or April. For a brochure on Vermont sugar houses open to the public, contact **Vermont Travel Division**, 61 Elm Street, Montpelier 05602. Phone: 828-3236.
- Pick berries and apples in season. For a list of farms and orchards, contact **Vermont Travel Division**, 61 Elm Street, Montpelier 05602. Phone: 828-3236.
- Gravestone rubbing is a fun, free lesson in history. Bring a waxed lumber crayon; architect's detail paper (or other thin, strong white paper) and masking tape—all available in art stores.

17. DINING

Most inns serve meals to outside guests. For more information on the Four Columns Inn, Saxtons River Inn, The Inn at Saw Mill Farm, Newfane Inn, and The Hermitage, *see #19, Lodging.*

- The name Rene Chardain was synonymous with his restaurant, **Four Columns Inn** (Newfane; phone: 365-7713), until he moved to South Salem, Connecticut, in 1981 and started a new restaurant. The kitchen is now run by two of his former acolytes, who bill their fare as "beyond *nouvelle*" (light sauces, fresh crunchy vegetables, and local produce that changes with the seasons). The new owner, Jack Allembert, ran Le Chateau restaurant in Tenafly, New Jersey. Entrées, priced from $15 to $22, include trout from the Inn's own pond sautéed with hazelnuts, and double breast of duck with rhubarb and peppercorns. Visa and Mastercard are accepted. Jackets are requested. Reservations are advised.
- **Newfane Inn** (Newfane; phone: 365-4427) has a smaller, more intimate dining room than the Four Columns Inn, but enjoys a comparable reputation as one of the finest restaurants in New England. Entrées, priced from $20 to $40, include breast of capon cordon bleu and rack of lamb. No credit cards are accepted. Jackets are usually worn. Reservations are advised.
- **Saxtons River Inn** (Saxtons River; phone: 869-2110) has a Victorian dining room with an excellent reputation among knowledgeable locals. Prices are lower than at both the Newfane Inn and the Four Columns Inn and the atmosphere is more informal. Try the West African peanut soup and the chicken breasts in cheese sauce with artichoke hearts. No credit cards are accepted. Reservations are advised. Ties are optional.
- **The Hermitage** (Wilmington; phone: 464-3511) has four inti-

mate candle-lit rooms with fresh flowers and smoky blue tablecloths. Pheasant, duck, and other game birds are raised on the grounds. Entrées, ranging in price from $11 to $19, include boneless trout from the inn's own pond, wienerschnitzel, and frogs' legs Provençale. A favorite dessert is cherries jubilee (cherries flamed in brandy and Cointreau and served on vanilla ice cream). The wine cellar has more than 1,000 labels. All major credit cards are accepted. Jackets are optional. Reservations are advised.

▪ **The Inn at Saw Mill Farm** (West Dover; phone: 464-8131) attracts a slightly older, more country-clubbish set than **The Hermitage** and enjoys a reputation for consistently high quality meals. Popular appetizers are coquille of crabmeat in a cream and sherry sauce with peppers and mushrooms and red Spanish shrimps in a meunière sauce. Entrées, priced from $15.50 to $20, include rack of lamb and roast sliced duck. The pastry chef's specialties include coconut cake, made from Godiva chocolates and fresh coconut milk; and ice cream with a homemade butternut sauce. No credit cards are accepted. Reservations are advised. Jackets are requested.

▪ **The White House** (Route 9, Wilmington; phone: 464-2135) is a 68-year-old Victorian mansion with three dining rooms. The new chef has drawn favorable reviews. Entrées on the continental menu are priced from $10 to $16.50 and include broiled scallops and saltimbocca (sautéed medallions of white veal topped with prosciutto, cheese, wine, and mushrooms); and Cornish hen with fresh peaches and brandy sauce. A favorite dessert is chocolate almond pie. All major credit cards are accepted. Ties are requested. Reservations are advised.

18. AFTER HOURS

Windham comes alive at night in winter for the ski crowd on the western, Green Mountain side of the county. Leave it to Vermont to close bars at 2 A.M. on weekdays and 1 A.M. on Saturday.

▪ For the over-30 crowd, the best bet is **The Hermitage** (Coldbrook Road, Wilmington; phone: 464-3759).

▪ Popular among visitors under 30 are **North Country Fair** (Route 100 north, Wilmington; phone: 464-5697); **Snow Lake Lodge at Mount Snow** (phone: 464-3333); **Deacon's Den** (West Dover; phone: 464-9361); and **Sitzmark** (East Dover Road, Wilmington; phone: 464-3384).

▪ In Brattleboro a mixed crowd heads for **The Tavern** (Putney Road; phone: 257-1481). A younger crowd gathers at **Flat Street** (phone: 254-8257) for disco and rock.

19. LODGING

▪ **The Whetstone Inn** (Marlboro 05344; phone: 254-2500) is less known than other New England hostelries, but many visitors consider it the top choice. Like its owners, Jean and Harry Boardman, the 1787 inn radiates character and charm. The living room piano is piled with books: *Sonnets from the Portuguese, The Ascent of Man,* Kafka's *The Trial.* The original kitchen is now the dining room, where breakfast is served whenever you're ready. ("What would you like?" asks Jean. "Fresh blueberries? Strawberries? Pineapple? Eggs or waffles? With the eggs you get popovers.") The five rooms upstairs are decorated to be lived in, with wide pine floors, L. L. Bean blankets, rocking chairs, and old jug lamps. Through lace curtains you can see the curve of a stone wall lined with purple and yellow iris, and beyond, a pond bordered by rushes, cattails, and white birch. The town of Marlboro has only three buildings: a post office, a church, and the inn. It is about as "country" as you can get. The Boardmans moved here in 1979 from California, where Harry worked for the Salk Institute. Overnight guests include Jean-Pierre Rampal, James Galway, and other performers at the Marlboro Festival, only two miles away. Doubles, some with private bath, cost $35 to $55. Breakfast is available for $4.50 to $5.50. No credit cards are accepted. TO GET THERE: I-91 north to Exit 2 (Brattleboro, Route 9). Drive west to Marlboro.

▪ **Saxtons River Inn** (Route 121, Saxtons River; phone: 869-2110) is a five-story turn-of-the-century building with rooms for people who appreciate flamboyance. Each is a decorator's conceit, and no two are alike. Floral, William Morris–type wallpaper leads upstairs to the Jonquil Suite and the Bill Blass room. No woman will feel comfortable in the Rose Room without a corselette and a French memoir. More subdued is the popular Painted Bedroom in the Calvin House across the street. It includes a sitting room with two 7 × 9 rugs. The breakfast room in the main building is papered with Oriental cockatoos. Doubles with bath cost from $40 to $50. No credit cards are accepted. TO GET THERE: I-95 to Exit 5 (Bellows Falls). Take Route 121 west to the inn, in the center of town.

▪ **Newfane Inn** (Route 30, Newfane 05345; phone: 365-4427) has 10 rooms with antiques, and a restaurant with an excellent reputation *(see #17).* Doubles, with bath, cost $65 to $85. No credit cards are accepted. TO GET THERE: I-91 to Brattleboro Exit 2, then Route 30 north for 12 miles to Newfane. The inn is to the left, on the town square.

▪ **Four Columns Inn** (Newfane 05345; phone: 365-7713), like the Newfane Inn next door, is noted more for its food than for its lodging. However, the 12 rooms have recently been redecorated with early American antiques and four-poster, brass, or canopied beds. Rooms are clean and comfortable, with wide pine floors and area rugs. Doubles with private bath cost $50 to $70, including a continental breakfast. Visa and Mastercard are accepted. TO GET THERE: I-91 to Brattleboro Exit 2, then Route 30 north 12 miles to Newfane. The inn is to the left, on the town square, behind the Newfane Inn.

▪ **Old Tavern** (Grafton; phone: 843-2231). A stolid, "sampler" quality hangs over this 1801 tavern, which may explain why visitors tend to be on the far side of 40, and why devotees make reservations up to a year in advance. It is not a small, intimate inn where guests gather around the fire, but a place for people who enjoy privacy and quiet. Hallways are decorated with American eagle wallpaper and prints of hog hunts. The hunters wear top hats and carry spears. Chairs silently face each other in rooms of muted Williamsburg colors, with canopied beds, hooked rugs, and Sheraton bureaus. The 36-room tavern was a social and intellectual way station on the Boston-Montreal stagecoach route and entertained such notables as Hawthorne, Emerson, Thoreau, Oliver Wendell Holmes, and Daniel Webster. Kipling brought his wife here on their honeymoon in 1892. Facilities include a sand-bottom pond for swimming, and tennis courts. The restored town of Grafton is one of the loveliest—and most proper—towns in New England. No credit cards are accepted. Doubles cost $45 to $85, some with private bath. TO GET THERE: I-91 to Exit 5 (Bellows Falls). Take Route 121 west through Saxtons River to Grafton.

▪ **The Hermitage** (Wilmington 05363; phone: 464-3511) is a century-old inn on nearly 600 acres at the foot of Mount Haystack, a few minutes drive from Mount Snow. The owner, Jim McGovern, is a self-styled maverick who attracts a sophisticated, urban crowd that is both formal and offbeat. McGovern's interests seem to fill whatever space he's in. His sugarhouse turns out more than 700 gallons of syrup a year. In summer the kettles are fired for homemade jams and jellies. It's unclear which is stronger, his passion for wines—the wine cellar has over 1,000 labels—or for game birds. Wild turkeys, wood ducks, pheasants, and quails are only a few of the birds raised on the premises. Many appear on the menu in the fall. Irregularly shaped rooms under the eaves are simply and smartly decorated with quality antiques. Rooms with private bath cost $70 to $80 per person, including breakfast and dinner. All major credit cards are accepted. TO GET THERE: I-91 to Exit 2 (Brattleboro, Route 9). Follow Route 9 west to Wilmington, then Route 100 north toward West Dover. Turn left on Coldbrook Road, following signs to Mount Snow.

▪ **The Inn at Sawmill Farm** (West Dover 05356; phone: 464-

8131) consists of an old barn and outbuildings that the owners, an architect and a designer, have converted into a conversation piece. The 20-room inn is a mixture of Newport and New England. Some may prefer to see the past less tampered with; others will appreciate the way the past and present have been incorporated into an architect's single vision. Some will find the matching fabrics on waitresses and chairs too studied; others will appreciate this loving attention to detail. Each room is different. Some are Victorian, some early American. All are carpeted, with potted floor plants, Godiva chocolates, fresh fruit, and magazines like *Vogue* and *Town and Country*. The grounds are exquisite. Over the tops of maple and apple trees rises the spire of West Dover Church. Mount Snow can be seen to the north. Facilities include a swimming pool, tennis courts, and a two-acre pond for boating, trout fishing, and skating. Jackets are required in all public areas after 6 P.M. Doubles, with private bath, cost $140 to $200 including breakfast and dinner. No credit cards are accepted. TO GET THERE: I-91 to Brattleboro Exit 2. Take Route 9 west for 21 miles to Wilmington and Route 100 north for six miles to West Dover. The entrance is just north of town center on the left.

▪ **Nutmeg Inn** (Route 9, Wilmington 05363; phone: 464-3351) is a clean, wholesome farmhouse where people can rest up from a day in the sun or snow. Rooms are friendly, with patchwork-patterned quilts and bright blue walls. No credit cards are accepted. Doubles, some with private baths, cost $50 to $60 in summer and $60 to $70 in the fall. Rooms in winter cost $39 to $59 per person, including breakfast and dinner. TO GET THERE: I-91 to Brattleboro Exit 2. Take route 9 west, one mile past the traffic light in Wilmington.

▪ **Brook Bound Lodge** (Coldbrook Road, Wilmington 05363; phone: 464-5267), now managed by The Hermitage, is a 26-year-old lodge with a knotty-pine ambience—the perfect setting for people who want to unwind and make new friends. Relationships develop quickly among the Monopoly boards, or at the long wooden dining room tables, where wholesome meals are served on platters. Couples dependent on candlelight and privacy should roll the dice again. Facilities include a heated outdoor pool and tennis court. No credit cards are accepted. Doubles, some with private bath, cost $50 to $70, including breakfast. TO GET THERE: I-91 to Brattleboro Exit 2. Take Route 9 west to Wilmington. At the traffic light turn north on Route 100 for 2.5 miles. At the traffic island, turn left on Coldbrook Road for 2.2 miles. The driveway is on the right.

▪ **Putney Inn and Motor Lodge** (P.O. Box 181, Putney 05346; phone: 387-5517) is as close to an inn as a motel can be. It is also conveniently located just off I-91. The menu includes maple mousse and Indian pudding—a very "country" dessert of corn meal and molasses. Doubles cost $42. All major credit cards are accepted. TO GET THERE: I-91 to Exit 4.

20. EMERGENCIES

▪ For the western half of the county (the Mount Snow area): **Deerfield Valley Health Center** (phone: 464-5311) or **Deerfield Valley Rescue Squad** (phone: 464-5335).

▪ For the eastern half of the county (Brattleboro area): **Brattleboro Memorial Hospital** (phone: 257-0341).

21. HOW TO GET THERE

See #19, Lodging, for directions to specific inns and hotels.

BY CAR. *From New York to Marlboro, West Dover, Wilmington, and the Mount Snow area:* take I-95 to I-91 north. At Brattleboro Exit 2 take Route 9 west. To reach West Dover, turn right (north) on Route 100. *To Saxtons River and Grafton:* I-95 to I-91 north. At Bellows Falls (Exit 5) take Route 121 west. *To Newfane:* I-95 to I-91 north. At Brattleboro Exit 2 take Route 30 north.

From Boston: west on Route 2 to Greenfield, Mass, then north on I-91 and follow directions above.

BY BUS. *From New York:* Greyhound (212/635-0800) to Bennington (for the Mount Snow area) or to Brattleboro (for eastern parts of the county). New England Shuttle Service (464/8660-2276) has a 45-minute service from bus terminals to the Mount Snow area. The New England Shuttle Service will also drive four persons round trip from Boston to the Mount Snow area. Nationwide Ski Trails (212/596-4227) has ski buses to Mount Snow leaving Port Authority, New York City, on Friday evening and returning Sunday evening, December through March.

From Boston: Peter Pan Bus Co. (617/482-6620) goes to Brattleboro, via Springfield. Greyhound/Vermont Transit (617/423-5810) goes to Brattleboro, via Keene. New England Shuttle Service (464/8660-2276) has a 45-minute taxi service from Brattleboro to the Mount Snow area.

BY TRAIN. *From New York:* Amtrak (212/736-3967) leaves New York at 9 P.M. and arrives in Brattleboro at 2:32 A.M. Trains leave Brattleboro at 1:10 A.M. and arrive in New York at 6:45 A.M.

BY PLANE. Precision Airlines (800/451-4221) flies from Boston and New York to Keene. New England Shuttle Service (464-8660 or 464-2276) has a taxi service from the airport to the Mount Snow area.

22. FOR FURTHER INFORMATION

- For information on Windham County and Brattleboro: **Brattleboro Chamber of Commerce,** 180 Main St., Brattleboro, 05301. Phone: 254-4565.
- For information on Vermont: **New England Vacation Center,** 630 Fifth Ave., New York, NY 10020. Phone: 212/399-4905.
- For information on the Mount Snow area: **Mount Snow Region Chamber of Commerce,** Box 3, Wilmington 05363. Phone: 464-8092.
- For ski information: **Vermont Ski Area Association.** Phone: 223-2439.
- For 24-hour-a-day ski conditions, from November through April, phone: 229-0531.
- There is a **Welcome Center** at the Vermont-Massachusetts border on I-91. Phone: 254-4593.

23. RECOMMENDED READING

- John Freidin. *20 Bicycle Tours in Vermont* (NH Publishing Co.).
- Madeleine Kunin and Marilyn Stout. *The Big Green Book: A Four-Season Guide to Vermont* (New York: Crown).

Monadnock Region, New Hampshire

(Area Code, 603)

---

1. DISTANCES

BY CAR. *From New York,* 4½ hours; *from Boston,* 1½ hours.

BY BUS. *From New York,* 5 to 6½ hours; *from Boston,* 2 hours.

2. MAJOR ATTRACTIONS

- One of the most frequently climbed mountains in the world, with 100-mile views from the summit.
- Dozens of antique and craft stores.
- A rich cultural life, with a year-round program of concerts and theater.
- Hundreds of miles of groomed cross-country-ski trails.

3. INTRODUCTION

Proper Bostonians know all about the southwest corner of New Hampshire—they've been summering here since the Monadnock Railroad came through in 1871. The town of Dublin, at the foot of Mount Monadnock, was once a small edition of Newport or Bar Harbor. The woods are full of fifty-room "cottages" owned by families like the Firestones and the Marshall Fields, who entertain behind closed doors and are perfectly willing to let the beauty of their region remain unsung.

That the area has never attracted much of a weekend crowd is, of course, one of its greatest charms. Unlike the more developed resort areas of New England, the Monadnock region is neither elegant nor aggressively old-fashioned. Visitors who return year after year tend to appreciate things that are softened, sometimes worn with age. They love the outdoors and have the resourcefulness to entertain themselves and the patience to slow down and get back in touch.

Not that there aren't things to do. Dozens of top-quality craft and antique stores cater to expensive city tastes. Some two hundred lakes and ponds in the region are ideal for fishing, boating, swimming, and skating. No other area in New England has as many groomed cross-country ski trails—so many that you could ski for a week without ever crossing your tracks. And not a summer weekend goes by without a first-rate concert, dance, or lecture.

New Yorkers who think of southern New Hampshire as cow country may be shocked to know that the world's first free, tax-supported public library was established here. Willa Cather loved the area so well she asked to be buried in Jaffrey Center. Joyce Kilmer wrote "Trees" while summering in Swanzey. Amy Lowell lived in Dublin, where Mark Twain spent his last years. Edward MacDowell, America's first internationally known composer, lived in Peterborough, and, with his wife, established the MacDowell Colony, a retreat for artists and writers. E. A. Robinson, Elinor Wylie, Thornton Wilder, William Rose Benet, Aaron Copland, and Leonard Bernstein are only a few of these Colonists, who, over the years, have won more than 37 Pulitzer Prizes.

Defining and dominating the landscape is Mount Monadnock. There are much taller mountains—it rises only 3,165 feet above the sea—but its splendid isolation makes it the symbol and focal point of the area. Emerson called it the most beautiful mountain in America and began his famous poem "Monadnoc" while sitting near the summit one morning before dawn. Kipling, who lived just across the Vermont border with his bride, called Monadnock "A wise old

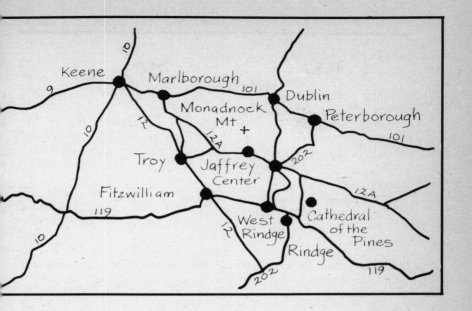

giant." To Richard Burton, it was "an Anak of the hills"; to E. A. Robinson, the emblem of permanence and calm; to J. E. Nesmith, "A Titan fallen from the stars."

From the shores of Walden Pond, Thoreau could see Monadnock looming against the sky. He paid one of his three visits on August 4, 1860, and stayed on the summit for six days. Those who plan an afternoon walk to the top will appreciate Thoreau's list of provisions:

I carried on this excursion the following articles (beside what I wore), *viz.:*—

One shirt.
One pair socks.
Two pocket-handkerchiefs.
One *thick* waistcoat.
One flannel shirt (had no occasion to use it).
India-rubber coat.
Three bosoms.
Towel and soap.
Pins, needles, thread.
A blanket (would have been more convenient if stitched up in the form
    of a bag).

Cap for the night.
Map and compass.
Spy-glass and microscope and tape.
Saw and hatchet.
Plant-book and blotting-paper.
Paper and stamps.
Botany.
Insect and lichen boxes.
Jack-knife.
Matches.
Waste paper and twine.
Iron spoon and pint dipper with handle.
    All in a knapsack.
Umbrella.

N.B.—Add to the above next time a small bag, which may be stuffed with moss or the like for a pillow.

For provision for one, six days, carried:—

2½ lbs. of salt beef and tongue.	Take only salt beef next time, 2 to 3 lbs.
18 hard-boiled eggs.	Omit eggs.
2½ lbs. sugar and a little salt.	2 lbs. of sugar would have done.
About ¼ lb. of tea.	⅔ as much would have done.
2 lbs. hard-bread.	The right amount of bread, but
½ loaf home-made bread and a piece of cake.	might have taken more home-made and more *solid* sweet cake.

N.B.—Carry salt (or some of it) in a wafer box. Also some sugar in a small box.

Thoreau discovered that the mountain, like the region it dominates, is for people who travel light, and who have the time to explore and look into the heart of things. Emerson wrote from the summit:

Bookworm, break this sloth urbane;
A greater spirit bids thee forth
Than the grey dreams which thee detain . . .

'Happy,' I said, 'whose home is here!'
Man in these crags a fastness finds
To fight pollution of the mind.

4. WHAT TO SEE AND DO

▪ Winter visitors will want to ski down **Crotched Mountain,** cross-country ski on hundreds of miles of groomed trails, and skate on dozens of lakes and ponds *(see #12, Skiing).* Visitors in summer and fall can follow in the footsteps of Emerson and Thoreau to the top of **Mount Monadnock**—an easy, 3½-hour walk round trip, with spectacular views as far away as Boston and the White Mountains *(see #8, Walks).*

▪ **The Rhododendron State Park** (2½ miles west of Fitzwilliam, on Old Richmond Road) was placed on the National Register of Historic Places in 1980. In mid-July, some 16 acres of wild *Rhododendron maximum* burst into bloom, like pink and white stars, against the green of sheltering pines. Visitors can walk around the entire glen, and picnic in shaded pine groves.

▪ Visitors who don't want to work for their scenic views can drive to the top of **Pack Monadnock Mountain** (off Route 101, about five miles east of Peterborough). The 2,280-foot summit has picnic sites and walking trails.

▪ No trip to the region is complete without a visit to the **Cathedral of the Pines** (Rindge, about four miles southeast of Jaffrey; phone: 899-3300). You don't have to belong to any particular religious persuasion to be moved by the spiritual beauty of this shrine to America's war dead. The Memorial began as a family tribute to a son who hoped to build his home there, but was killed in World War II. In 1957 Congress unanimously voted to recognize the Altar as a memorial to all Americans who have sacrificed themselves for their country. The Bell Tower, dedicated in 1967, is the nation's only war memorial for women. Some 50 different faiths have held services here, and more than 100 couples choose to get married on the site each year. Crude wooden benches squat on a floor of pine bark and wood chips, beneath a natural roof of towering pines. The Altar has a simple stone cross overlooking the entire Monadnock region. During sunrise services, the deep tones of the organ mix with bird songs and the sighing of the wind through the trees—a very moving experience. To keep the site clean and uncommercial, the state has developed the **Annett Wayside Area** for picnics and cookouts, one mile north of the shrine.

▪ **Boston University's Sargent Camp** (Peterborough; phone: 525-3311) is an environmental education center that caters mostly to groups, but individuals or families can also use the facilities on weekends. Programs are offered in rock climbing, white-water canoeing, wilderness survival, and so on. The 850-acre property has an 80-acre lake for canoeing; a dining hall, and cabins where couples can stay for $28 a night.

▪ **The Harris Center for Conservation Education** (Hancock; phone: 525-4073) is a nonprofit organization with natural history and conservation programs almost every weekend in the winter, spring, and fall. Saturday lectures and field trips focus on everything from lichens and wildlife to acid rain.

▪ **Sharon Arts Center** (Route 123, Sharon; phone: 924-7257) offers day or weekend lessons in such crafts as glass blowing, Japanese pottery techniques, bookbinding, early American stenciling, photography, and painting.

▪ Maple sugaring time is March to mid-April, when nights are cold and days warm. To watch the process and taste the results, contact in Jaffrey: **Bacon's Sugar House** (Dublin Road; phone: 532-8836); **Chadwick Farm** (Chadwick Road; phone: 532-8811); **Dan's Sugar House** (phone: 532-7379); **Ed's Sugar House** (phone: 532-7019); **Kay's Sugar House** (Fitzwilliam Road; phone: 532-7913).

▪ A 40-mile drive—28 if you miss Hancock—will take you to most of the main sights and shops in the southern Monadnock area. (For recommended antique and craft stores along the route, *see #6, Antiques and Crafts.*) The triangular route begins in the beautiful village of **Fitzwilliam.** The **Congregational Church** here has a magnificent four-story steeple, each deck surrounded by a carved balustrade. The Rhododendron State Park is nearby, and a dozen antique shops. Take Route 119 east about two miles past Rindge, turn left at the sign to Cathedral of the Pines. Picnic facilities are available in the **Annett State Forest,** one mile farther north. Continue north and turn right on Route 124. If you're interested in contemporary crafts, turn left on Route 123 to the Sharon Arts Center. Return to Route 124 east and at the town of Temple, turn left (north) on Route 45. Turn left again on Route 101 west, and drive to the summit of Pack Monadnock Mountain. Continue west on Route 101, then turn north (right) on Route 202 to **Peterborough.** This is the cultural and commercial center of the region, with many craft and antique stores to visit. The **Unitarian Church,** built in 1826, is attributed to one of the greatest architects of the post-colonial period, Charles Bulfinch. The exhibit at the **Historical Society** (Grove Street; phone: 924-3235) includes antique furniture, clocks, pewter, a colonial kitchen, an early nineteenth-century mill house, and a fine collection of early tools. The people of Peterborough like to believe their town is the model for Thornton Wilder's mythological New Hampshire village, Grover's Corners, since the author of *Our Town* began his Pulitzer Prize-winning play as a guest at the nearby **MacDowell Colony.**

Visitors who hear about this artists' retreat hope to get a sight (or photo) of artists at work, but only the library, which includes some 300 books written by Colonists, is open to the public. The Colony was the inspiration of America's first internationally known composer, Edward MacDowell, who dreamed of converting his farm into a retreat for artists. The writers, painters, sculptors, and photographers who are accepted work rent-free in private studios in the woods, out of sight of each other. So that the artists won't be disturbed, lunches are left in baskets by their doors, and phone messages are delivered only in emergencies. Since 1907, more than 37 Pulitzer Prizes have been won by Colonists. Leonard Bernstein completed his *Mass* here, and Aaron Copland composed parts of *Appalachian Spring*.

After not seeing the MacDowell Colony—which after all exists to protect artists from the public eye—head north on Route 202 to **Hancock,** one of the loveliest towns in the region. The **John Hancock Inn** is a popular spot for lunch. From Hancock, head south on Route 137 to **Jaffrey,** another quaint New England town. The **Monadnock Inn** is a good bet for lunch. Many visitors will be surprised to discover that Willa Cather (1876–1947) is buried here in the **Old Burying Ground.** The author of *O Pioneers!, My Antonia,* and *Death Comes to the Archbishop* visited the region in 1917 at the urging of a friend who was living at the nearby Shattuck Inn. Inscribed on her gravestone are the words, "That is happiness, to be dissolved into something complete and great." The quote is from *My Antonia,* which she wrote in part while living here.

5. THE ARTS

The Monadnock region has the richest cultural life of any area in the state. Visitors have a choice of plays, concerts, and lectures throughout the year. For information on upcoming events, contact the **Grand Monadnock Arts Council** (31 Central Square, #9, Keene 03431; phone: 357-3906).

▪ Free Monadnock Music Concerts are given about four times a week, from July 19 to September 6, in the Jaffrey Center Meeting House, the Peterborough Unitarian Church, and other local settings. The professional ensemble also presents the Peterborough Town House Series, with operas and orchestral works. Contact: **Monadnock Music,** Box 255, Peterborough 03458; phone: 924-7610.

▪ If you missed the **Apple Hill Chamber Players** in their concert series at New York's Lincoln Center, you can hear them in their summer home in Nelson (Phone: 847-3371), about 35 minutes northeast of Peterborough. Free concerts are given most Tuesday nights from mid-June through August.

▪ A talk by B. F. Skinner on behaviorism is indicative of the quality of lectures and concert programs sponsored by the **Monadnock Summer Lyceum** at the Unitarian Church, Peterborough. Programs take place on various Sundays at 11 A.M., from early July through August.

▪ **Peterborough Players** (Stearns Farm, Middle Hancock Road, Peterborough; phone: 924-7585) is a professional summer stock theater that performs such plays as Steinbeck's *Of Mice and Men* and Wilde's *The Importance of Being Earnest.* Performances run from late June to the end of August on Tuesdays through Saturdays at 8:30 P.M.; and on Sundays at 2 and 7 P.M.

▪ **American Stage Festival** (Milford, about 30 minutes east of Peterborough; phone: 673-7515) offers musicals, comedies, classics, and world premières May through September daily at 8, Sunday at 2 and 7, and Wednesday at 2. Closed Monday.

▪ **Keene Summer Theater** (Keene State College Fine Arts Center, Keene; phone: 357-4041) performs such works as *Vanities, Oklahoma!* and *Grease.* Performances are at 8:30 P.M., Wednesday through Sunday, from June 24 to August 20.

6. ANTIQUES AND CRAFTS

There are so many first-rate craft and antique stores in the southern Monadnock area that you could spend an entire weekend exploring nothing else. Fitzwilliam alone has 11, listed on a brochure distributed locally. Hours often depend on an owner's whim. Many live nearby, and you can usually get them to open up if you call ahead. Shops listed below can be reached by following a triangular route from Fitzwilliam east on Route 119 to West Rindge; north past the Cathedral of the Pines to Route 124 east; north on Route 123 to Sharon and Peterborough; then south to Jaffrey on Route 136. Visitors willing to travel farther afield can head north from Peterborough on Route 202 to Hancock, and then return to Fitzwilliam via Marlborough. Anyone with an itch for flea markets should drive about 16 miles east of Peterborough to the town of Amherst *(see below).* **The Directory of New Hampshire Antique Dealers** is available on request with a self-addressed, stamped, legal-size envelope from Lois Meredith, Box 942, Hillsboro, NH 03244.

▪ **William Lewan Antiques** (Route 119, Old Troy Road, 4.5 miles west of Fitzwilliam; phone: 585-3365) features early country and primitive furniture, copper, brass, and iron.

- **Bloomin' Antiques** (junction of routes 12 and 119, Fitzwilliam; phone: 585-9092) is a group of shops under a single roof, with some quality New England primitives. Some pieces need repair, others are refinished.
- **Rindge Country Auctions** (West Rindge; phone: 899-6654) are held on Saturdays, in summer at 10 A.M., and in winter at 6 P.M.
- **Baskets, Inc.** (Main Street, West Rindge; phone: 899-2231) makes and sells baskets of ash, oak, and birch. Open Monday to Thursday from 7 to 5:30.
- **Sharon Arts Center** (Route 123, Sharon; phone: 924-7257) is a respected handcraft shop and gallery, featuring the work of many of the state's leading artists. Weekend visitors can spend a day here taking lessons in glass blowing, Japanese pottery techniques, bookbinding, early American stenciling, photography, and painting.
- **The Game Preserve** (110 Spring Street, Peterborough; phone: 924-6710) is a fascinating museum and store of antique board games dating back to 1820. Admission is $1.50 for adults, $1 for children.
- **Cobbs** (83 Grove Street; phone: 924-6361) specializes in formal and painted eighteenth- and nineteenth-century American furniture, folk art, porcelain, and rugs. Open daily except Sunday.
- **Strawberry Hill Antique Shop** (3 Elm Street, Peterborough; phone: 924-6443) features fine china and early American glass.
- **Peterborough Brookstone** (Vose Farm Road, Peterborough; phone: 924-7181) gained a national reputation through its catalog of hard-to-find tools. The show room is open daily, July through December, from 9 to 5; off-season, closed Sundays.
- **Peterboro Basket Co.** (Grove Street, Peterborough; phone: 924-3861) has been selling handmade split oak baskets since 1854. Open weekdays only from 9 to 4.
- **David L. O'Neal** (263 Elm Hill road, Peterborough; phone: 924-7489) is an antiquarian bookseller, with everything from fifteenth-century manuscripts to modern first editions. Open daily from 9 to 5.
- **The Depot Antique Shop** (Depot Street, Hancock; phone: 525-3518) specializes in seventeenth- and eighteenth-century American furniture and early lighting and iron. Open "when we're here," including Sundays.
- **Top o' the Meadow Herbs and Crafts** (Old Antrim Road, Hancock; phone: 525-4072) stocks a large line of culinary herbs and spices. Open from 10 to 5; closed Sundays and Mondays.
- **Petticoat Junction** (Route 101A, going east from Amherst to Nashua, about 16 miles east of Peterborough) is a large outdoor antique market open on Sundays, late April through October, from 8 to 4. About four miles away, within walking distance of each other,

are the **Amherst Flea Market** and the **Hollis Market** (Route 122, about six miles past Milford). These flea markets, also open on Sundays, tend to offer less quality goods than Petticoat Junction, but browsing is fun, and there's always an occasional buy.

7. TOURS

▪ **The Monadnock Region Association** (see #23, For Further Information) distributes a booklet with five recommended fall foliage tours, ranging from 63 to 150 miles.

▪ For bike tours, see #9, Biking.

8. WALKS

▪ Mount Monadnock is so completely identified with the region that it's almost disrespectful to leave the area without a pilgrimage to the summit. The mountain rises 3,165 feet above sea level and about 2,000 feet above the surrounding hills and countryside, with spectacular one-hundred-mile views on clear days. There are at least 10 trails to the summit, some steep, some long and gradual, taking from 3½ to 8 hours, round trip. The most scenic route, along the 4½-mile Pumpelly Ridge Trail (beginning on the east side of Dublin Lake), is also the longest. The White Cross trail and the White Dot trail, each about 2.3 miles, are two of the most direct routes. Both begin in the **Monadnock State Park** (Jaffrey Center, on the road to Dublin; phone: 532-8862). At the Ecocenter here you can buy the useful "Monadnock Guide," and obtain information on trails and hiking conditions. Bear in mind that Monadnock is one of the most climbed mountains in the world, and solitude—as Thoreau discovered in 1860—is one of the few pleasures you will *not* enjoy on the summit, particularly on summer weekends. If you want to be alone, climb Monadnock on weekdays or early in the morning, and avoid picnicking on the summit.

▪ Those who march to Thoreau's drum will appreciate these comments from Volume XIV of his *Journals*, describing his six-day trip up Monadnock in 1860:

> There were a great many visitors to the summit, both by the south and north, i.e. the Jaffrey and Dublin paths, but they did not turn off from the beaten track. One noon, when I was on the top, I counted forty men, women, and children around me, and more were constantly arriving while others were going. Certainly more than one hundred ascended in a day. When

you got within thirty rods you saw them seated in a row along the gray parapets, like the inhabitants of a castle on a gala-day; and when you behold Monadnock's blue summit fifty miles off in the horizon, you may imagine it covered with men, women, and children, in dresses of all colors, like an observatory on a muster-field. They appeared to be chiefly mechanics and farmers' boys and girls from the neighboring towns. The young men sat in rows with their legs dangling over the precipice, squinting through spy-glasses and shouting and hallooing to each new party that issued from the woods below. Some were playing cards; others were trying to see their house or their neighbor's. Children were running about and playing as usual. Indeed, this peak in pleasant weather is the most trivial place in New England. There are probably more arrivals daily than at any of the White Mountain houses. Several were busily engraving their names on the rocks with cold-chisels, whose incessant clink you heard, and they had but little leisure to look off. The mountain was not free of them from sunrise to sunset, though most of them left about 5 P.M.

They who simply climb to the peak of Monadnock have seen but little of the mountain. I came not to look *off from* it, but to look *at* it. The view of the pinnacle itself from the plateau below surpasses any view which you get from the summit. It is indispensable to see the top itself and the sierra of its outline from one side. The great charm is not to look off from a height but to walk over this novel and wonderful rocky surface. Moreover, if you would enjoy the prospect, it is, methinks, most interesting when you look from the edge of the plateau immediately down into the valleys, or where the edge of the lichen-clad rocks, only two or three rods from you, is seen as the lower frame of a picture of green fields, lakes, and woods, suggesting a more stupendous precipice than exists. There are much more surprising effects of this nature along the edge of the plateau than on the summit. It is remarkable what haste the visitors make to get to the top of the mountain and then look away from it.

▪ **Rhododendron State Park** is a 294-acre tract near Fitzwilliam, where 16 acres of wild rhododendron explode into pink and white blossoms in mid-July *(see #4, What to See and Do)*.

▪ Hikers who want to picnic in style can pick up supplies at the **Worldwide Cheese Company** (3 School Street, Peterborough; phone: 924-6365).

▪ The "Monadnock Guide," topographical maps, camping equipment, and free advice are available at **Eastern Mountain Sports** (Route 202, two miles north of Peterborough; phone: 924-9571). Open daily.

9. BIKING

▪ **Freewheel Tours** (33 Thorndike Street, Beverly, Massachusetts; phone: 922-1228) runs weekend foliage biking tours in the Monadnock region.

▪ There are no bike rental stores in the region. Roads are quite hilly, so 10-gear bikes are advisable. Bike stores with equipment and trip suggestions are:

▪ **Roy's Bike and Photo Shop** (Jaffrey; phone: 532-8800).

▪ **Sun Cycle** (Peterborough; phone: 924-7656).

10. BOATING AND FISHING

Anglers hooked on bass and trout have their choice of dozens of lakes, ponds and streams in the Monadnock area. Favorite spots include:

▪ Dublin: Dublin Lake (bass); Frost and Thorndike ponds (bass).

▪ Hancock: Nubanusit Pond (salmon, lake trout); Halfmoon, Hunts, and Norway ponds (bass).

▪ Jaffrey: Contoocook Lake (bass); Front, Gilmore, and Thorndike ponds (bass).

▪ Rindge: Contoocook and Monomonock lakes (bass); Hubbard Pond (bass).

▪ Greenfield: Stoney Brook (brook trout).

▪ Wilton: Souhegan River (rainbow trout).

▪ Canoes can be rented from **Eastern Mountain Sports** (Route 202, two miles north of Peterborough; phone: 924-9571). Fishing licenses are available from town or village clerks and from most sporting goods stores.

11. SWIMMING

Many inns have their own pools, but the Monadnock area is a special delight for visitors whose idea of happiness is a plunge into a cool, clear pond or mountain lake. Favorites include:

▪ Dublin: Dublin Lake; Frost and Thorndike ponds.

- Fitzwilliam: Laurel Lake.
- Jaffrey: Contoocook Lake; Frost, Gilmore, and Thorndike ponds.
- Rindge: Contoocook and Monomonock lakes; Hubbard Pond.

Contoocook Lake is the largest, most developed lake and the only one with a supervised waterfront.

12. SKIING

DOWNHILL.

- **Crotched Mountain Ski Area** (Francestown, about 20 minutes northeast of Peterborough; phone: 588-6345) is the largest ski area in southern New Hampshire. The former Bobcat Ski Area is now under the same management, and a single lift ticket is valid at both centers. A ticket to all seven lifts, leading to 27 trails, costs $12 during the week, $18 on weekends. Night skiing is Wednesday through Saturday from 4:30 to 10:30.
- **Temple Mountain** (Route 101, Peterborough; phone: 924-6949) is a family ski area with 13 trails, one chair lift, and two T-bars. Night skiing began this winter.

CROSS-COUNTRY.

- **Woodbound Lodge,** (Jaffrey; phone: 532-8341) has 15 miles of particularly picturesque trails, and equipment rentals.
- **Temple Mountain Touring Center** (Route 101, Peterborough. Phone: 924-6949) has 35 miles of trails, equipment rentals, and guided tours on request.
- **Sargent Ski Touring Center** (Peterborough; phone: 525-3311) has trails on 850 acres, and equipment rentals.
- **Tory Pines Resort** (Francestown, one mile from Crotched Mountain Ski Area; phone: 588-6352) has 24 miles of trails—some with double tracks—on 600 acres, and both rentals and lessons.
- **Windblown** (New Ipswich, 15 minutes southeast of Jaffrey; phone: 878-2869) has 18 miles of trails—some steep for advanced skiers—and equipment rentals.
- **Fitzwilliam Inn** (Fitzwilliam; phone: 585-9000) maintains five miles of cross-country trails. No rentals.
- **Eastern Mountain Sports** (Route 202 two miles north of Peterborough; phone: 924-9571) is a skiing, camping, and mountaineering store that also rents cross-country equipment and offers free advice on the best trails in the area. Open daily.

- **The Inn at East Hill Farm** (Troy, about eight miles west of Jaffrey; phone: 242-6495) has miles of trails, and equipment rentals.

13. RIDING

- **Silver Ranch** (Route 124, Jaffrey; phone: 532-7363) has 500 acres of trails.
- **The Inn at East Hill Farm** (Troy, about eight miles west of Jaffrey; phone: 242-6495) has western riding on trails through wooded areas, with views of Mt. Monadnock.
- **Honey Lane Riding Stable** (Goldmine Road, Dublin, five miles west of Peterborough; phone: 563-8078) has a spring and fall riding program for adults and families. The cost per person for two nights, including meals and lessons, is $95.

14. TENNIS

- **Monadnock Country Club** (Peterborough; phone: 924-7769) has courts open to the public.
- There are four public courts behind the high school in Jaffrey.
- **Woodbound Lodge** (Jaffrey; phone: 532-8341) has courts open to nonguests.
- **Peterborough Recreation Area** (west on Main Street, Peterborough) has several public courts.

15. GOLF

- **Brentwood Golf Course** (Keene; phone: 352-7626) is a championship 18-hole, par-72 course.
- **Keene Country Club** (West Keene; phone: 352-0135) is an 18-hole, par-72 course open to nonmembers.
- **Tory Pines,** Hall of Fame Golf Course (Francestown, 20 minutes northeast of Peterborough; phone: 588-6352) is a par-71 course patterned after the best 18 holes from famous courses around the world.
- **The Monadnock Country Club** (High Street, Peterborough; phone: 924-7769) has a nine-hole, par-29 course.
- **Woodbound Inn** (two miles off Routes 119 and 202, Jaffrey; phone: 532-8341) has a nine-hole, par-3, 1200-yard course.

16. FOR KIDS

- Parents who dread children's theater have a happy surprise waiting for them at **Andy's Summer Playhouse** (Wilton Center Community Hall, Wilton, about 20 minutes east of Peterborough; phone: 654-2613 in summer, 924-3048 in winter). Children ages 8 to 17 perform plays such as *Dracula, Harriet the Spy,* and *The Phantom Tollbooth.* Performances are delightfully professional and a real must for anyone, child or adult, interested in theater.

▪ Sunrise services at the **Cathedral of the Pines** *(see #4, What to See and Do).*

▪ Square and contra dances are held on Saturday nights in Fitzwilliam and Francestown (about 10 miles northeast of Peterborough). *See #18, After Hours,* for details.

▪ Children aged 12 and over can play golf on the par-3, nine-hole golf course at the Woodbound Inn (Jaffrey; phone: 532-8341).

17. DINING

The most highly regarded restaurant in the region is a bit out of the way. Maplehurst Inn in Antrim is 12 miles north of Peterborough. For a meal closer to home, try the Monadnock Inn in Jaffrey Center.

▪ **Maplehurst Inn** (Main Street, Antrim [Route 202]; phone: 588-2891) has been serving guests since the late eighteenth century. Two of the three intimate dining rooms are in the original building, with low ceilings and hand-hewn beams. The smaller room has a fireplace. The fare, which could be called "elegant New England," includes veal Oscar, baked stuffed shrimp, coquilles St. Jacques, and beef Wellington. Entrées range in price from $9 to $15. Jackets are optional. Reservations are advisable on weekends. Visa and Mastercard are accepted.

▪ **Monadnock Inn** (Jaffrey Center, Route 124; phone: 532-7001) was recommended by *Gourmet* magazine as one of the top restaurants in the area. The 130-year-old inn has three dining rooms that seat 60. Entrées, ranging in price from $6 to $12, include gratin of scallops in white wine sauce, and steak Diane—slices of beef in a brown sauce with brandy and cream. Save room for the chocolate mousse. Dress is optional. Reservations are recommended on weekends. Visa and Mastercard are accepted.

▪ **The Hancock Inn** (Main Street, Hancock; phone: 525-3318) is the oldest continuously operating inn in New Hampshire. Visually it's as charming as the town of Hancock, and can be recommended as a fine place for lunch while you're touring the area. Luncheon entrées, from roast beef sandwiches to broiled haddock, cost under $5. Dinner entrées are priced from $8 to $12 and include prime ribs of beef with freshly baked popovers; roast duckling with an orange and pineapple sauce; and a seafood casserole of lobster, shrimps, and scallops in a Newburg sauce. Homemade pumpkin bread comes with all meals. Dress is optional, but ties are usually worn. Reservations are advisable on weekends. Visa and Mastercard are accepted.

18. AFTER HOURS

▪ Monadnock is square dance country. Dances are held every Saturday night at 8:30 during the summer in Fitzwilliam's historic **Town Hall** (phone: 585-2200). Dances are also held from Labor Day to Christmas at the **Inn at East Hill Farm** (Troy, about eight miles west of Jaffrey; phone: 242-6495). Contra dances are scheduled monthly throughout the year from 8:30 to 12 P.M. at the **Francestown Town Hall,** about 10 miles northeast of Peterborough.

▪ **Crotched Mountain Ski Area** (Route 47, Francestown, about 10 miles northeast of Peterborough; phone: 588-6345) has night ski-ing, Tuesday through Saturday, from 4:30 to 10:30.

▪ **The Folkway Restaurant** (85 Grove Street, Peterborough; phone: 924-7484) hosts folk music concerts and occasional classical music concerts throughout the year.

19. LODGING

The inns in the Monadnock area are slightly frayed at the edges, which to some visitors is part of their character and charm. Rooms tend to be plainly decorated with few serious antiques—like rooms in comfortable old homes. New Hampshire's exquisite old inns are found farther north in the mountain resorts around Franconia or in the lake regions around Winnipesaukee. Monadnock inns have their own loyal following, however, and guests checking out at the end of one vacation usually make reservations for the next. So what if the wallpaper is buckled—it's *their* room, different from all others, and they would be unhappy staying anywhere else.

Here as elsewhere in New England, rooms within the same inn can vary drastically in size and furnishings. If you're fussy, discuss rooms on the phone with the innkeeper until you've found one that seems right for you. Do the same on arrival. In any case, your best bet in the Monadnock area is to view your inn not as the central experience of your weekend, but as a warm, comfortable place to put your head at night while exploring one of the loveliest and least known areas of southern New England.

▪ **The Monadnock Inn** (Jaffrey Center 03454; phone: 532-7001) was built in 1830 as a private home, and has been accepting overnight guests since 1870. Furnishings are a mixture of early American and Victorian. Downstairs is a large, comfortable living room with fireplace and piano; and an old-fashioned bar lounge. Many of the 14 rooms are carpeted, with white lace curtains and simple but honest furnishings. A few rooms have four-poster beds. Doubles, some with private bath, cost from $30 to $45. Visa and Mastercard are accepted. TO GET THERE: *From New York:* I-91 to Route 10 to Route 119. Follow Route 119 to West Rindge, then go north on Route 202 to Jaffrey and left on Route 124 to Jaffrey Center. *From Boston:* Route 2 to Route 119 north to West Rindge. Go north on Route 202 to Jaffrey, and left on Route 124 to Jaffrey Center.

▪ The venerable **Fitzwilliam Inn** (Fitzwilliam 03447; phone: 585-9000), with its tall chimneys and double porch overlooking the town common, was built in 1796. The parlor has pink walls outlined with 200-year-old hand-painted stencils. A portrait of the Earl of Fitzwilliam—an eighteenth-century nobleman whose name was bestowed on the village he never visited—hangs near the baby grand, where informal classical concerts are given on Sundays. Some will say the rooms, which vary dramatically in quality, have "character"; others will simply call them run-down. Back rooms tend to be darker. There's a swimming pool in back and five miles of cross-country trails. Doubles, some with private bath, run from $26 to $30. TO GET THERE: *From New York:* I-91 to Route 10 east. Then Route 119 east to Fitzwilliam. *From Boston:* Route 2 to Route 119 north to Fitzwilliam.

▪ **The John Hancock Inn** (Hancock 03449; phone: 525-3318) was built in 1789, and is today the oldest continuously operating village inn in New Hampshire. The village of Hancock is charming and a visit here is worth the extra few minute's drive. More attention has been given to antiques at the John Hancock Inn than at most other places in the region. Some of the 10 rooms, for instance, are furnished with canopied beds and dry sinks. The Mural Room has Rufus Porter's original 1825 wall paintings. The Carriage Lounge has tables made from giant bellows from an old foundry in Nova Scotia. Doubles, all with private baths, cost $49.50. TO GET THERE: *From New York:* I-91 north to Route 9 east. Continue east on Route 101, past Keene, to Route 137 north, to Hancock. *From Boston:* Route 2 to Route 119 north. At West Rindge, go north on Routes 202 and 137 to Hancock.

▪ **Woodbound Inn** (Rindge, P.O. Jaffrey 03452, phone: 532-8341) is listed in *Back Roads and Country Inns,* but it is really a family camp/resort. It is located on the shores of Lake Contoocook, with 200 acres of woodlands for hiking and cross-country skiing. Facilities include sailboats, canoes, tennis courts, a stocked trout pond, a lighted skating pond, a nine-hole, 3-par golf course, and babysitting services. Rooms cost $46 to $65 per person, including free use of most facilities and two meals. Children ages 6 to 12 pay two-thirds the daily rate. Mastercard and Visa are accepted. TO GET THERE: *From New York:* I-91 to Route 10 east. Then Route 119 east to Rindge. From Rindge, follow signs. *From Boston:* Route 2 to Route 119, then north to Rindge.

20. EMERGENCIES

▪ **Monadnock Community Hospital** (Peterborough; phone: 924-7191).

21. HOW TO GET THERE

BY CAR. *From New York and Hartford:* I-91 north to Brattleboro, then Routes 9 and 101 east to Peterborough. To reach Jaffrey, turn south (right) off Route 101 in Marlborough and follow Route 124. To reach Fitzwilliam, take I-91 north to Route 10 east. At Winchester, go east on Route 119. *From Boston:* Route 3 north to 101 west to Peterborough. To reach Jaffrey Center from Peterborough, take Route 202 south and 124 west. To reach Fitzwilliam from Peterborough, take Route 202 south and Route 119 west.

BY BUS. *From New York:* Vermont Transit (212/635-0800) has service to Fitzwilliam and Troy via Keene. For additional information on service from Keene, phone Vermont Transit at 800/451-3292. To reach Peterborough, take Greyhound (212/635-0800) to Albany, and change to People's Bus Line (802/254-9455). *From Boston:* Vermont Transit (617/423-5810) has service to West Rindge, Fitzwilliam, Troy, and Keene.

BY AIR. Precision Airlines (800/451-4221) flies from Boston and New York to Keene.

22. FOR FURTHER INFORMATION

▪ **Monadnock Region Association,** Box 269, Peterborough 03458. Phone: 603/924-3611. Ask for the *Monadnock Regionnaire,* a local guide.
▪ **Greater Keene Chamber of Commerce,** 12 Gilbo Avenue, Keene 03431. Phone: 603/352-1303.

23. RECOMMENDED READING

- Ralph Waldo Emerson's famous poem "Monadnoc" is included in most collections of his work. It was inspired by his trip up the mountain on May 4, 1845.

- Henry David Thoreau's *Journal*, Volume XIV, includes lengthy descriptions of his six-day visit to Monadnock in early August of 1860.

- The "Monadnock Guide" ($3.50) is available at the Monadnock State Park and at all local bookstores. The *Monadnock Regionnaire* is a local paper with descriptions of all the activities in the area.

Newburyport, Massachusetts

(Area Code, 617; Zip Code, 01950)

1. DISTANCES

BY CAR. *From New York*, 5 hours; *from Boston*, 45 minutes.

BY BUS. *From New York*, 6 hours; *from Boston*, 1 hour.

2. MAJOR ATTRACTIONS

- A restored seaport town with four lovely inns and dozens of craft shops.
- Outstanding examples of eighteenth- and early nineteenth-century American architecture.
- A wildlife refuge on nearby Plum Island with fascinating nature trails, dunes, and miles of ocean beach.

338

3. INTRODUCTION

Seven of ten people living in Newburyport today did not live there a decade ago. The newcomers are mostly young professionals from Boston and Cambridge, who are happy to trade in the suburbs for a 350-year-old seaport town less than 45 minutes from work.

Only 15 years ago the town was cursed by high unemployment and a dilapidated waterfront. The urban development people wanted to level the area and begin again, but preservationists had their way. Beautiful nineteenth-century houses were renovated and turned into craft shops, inns, and boutiques. Market Square became a pedestrian mall. Sidewalks were widened, trees and shrubs planted, and gas lamps installed. Visitors who like Faneuil Hall in Boston or the restored Newport harbor will love Newburyport, for it has the same clean, natural brick-and-cobblestone feel to it, the same architectural integrity of an earlier age.

Newburyport offers something else, too—a wildlife refuge on nearby Plum Island with six miles of clean sandy beaches. Wander a few hundred yards away from the access points and the only footsteps will be your own. The inland side of the refuge is filled with marshes and estuaries, where shorebirds come to nest and feed. More than 300 species of birds have been identified, and as many as 25,000 ducks and 6,000 geese can be seen in a single day during spring and fall migrations.

The Hellcat Swamp Trail within the refuge offers one of the most fascinating introductions to shore life anywhere in the country. The raised boardwalk takes you over dunes and through forests of Japanese black pine. Yellow-rumped warblers feed on bayberries along the walk, and tree swallows darken the sky.

Warblers and swallows were probably making the same commotion back in the early eighteenth century, when Newburyport was the clipper ship capital of the world. Between 1680 and 1740 more than 100 ships were launched from the town's shipyards. In Newburyport's heyday, from the Revolution to the War of 1812, the ship owners and sea captains built their stately mansions on a three-mile stretch of land along High Street. These Federal-style homes, which sold for $10,000 a decade ago, are now going for $100,000 and up. Late Georgian, Federal, Greek Revival, shingle style, colonial revival—almost every late eighteenth- and early nineteenth-century architectural style can be seen by visitors along High Street today.

Toward the end of the nineteenth century, Newburyport's seagoing trade foundered against heavy tariffs and embargoes. The advent of steam put an end to the shipbuilding industry. "Newburyport became a kind of New England Pompeii, buried intact under the ash of eruptive change in New England's economy," wrote the late author John P. Marquand. The town's decline continued through the 1960s, when it was officially designated "a persistent unemployment area."

It was the artists and craftspeople who first rediscovered the possibilities of Newburyport in the late sixties. They were given homes and warehouses virtually rent-free in return for fixing them up. As happens wherever artists go, the wealthy followed; and many of the artists were forced to relocate on side streets or to follow the poor to Amesbury and Seabrook. Those who remained established the galleries and studios that give Newburyport much of its present character and charm.

Young blood is pouring into Newburyport and giving the town a new energy and life. An old waterfront building has been turned into a theater. Four old houses, including a captain's mansion on High Street, have been transformed into lodgings for weekend guests. Unlike other tourist towns that depend on the vagaries of the weekend trade, Newburyport has a year-round population of bright, affluent people who are giving their community an integrity of its own. It won't be long before the summer crowds discover quaint shops and the unique ocean beach. Visitors who hope to discover an area before it becomes too established should head for Newburyport today.

4. WHAT TO SEE AND DO

- **The Cushing House** (98 High Street; phone: 462-2681) is home of the Historical Society of Old Newburyport. The 21-room 1808 mansion was for many years the center of Newburyport's high society. Today it is partly an historic house, partly a museum, with exhibits that tell the story of the seaport town and the industries that flourished there. Open May through October, daily from 10 to 4; Sundays from 2 to 5. Closed Mondays. Admission is $1.50.
- **Custom House Maritime Museum** (25 Water Street; phone: 462-8681) is an 1835 Greek Revival building that houses exhibits of the shipbuilder's craft, local decorative arts, and exotic souvenirs of the China trade. Slide shows on Newburyport's architecture are shown hourly from 10 to 3. Open April to October daily; October to April, weekdays only.
- **Coffin House** (16 High Road), circa 1654, was the home of Tristram Coffin, the first governor of Nantucket Colony. Of particular interest are the parlor, which retains its early nineteenth-century

American wallpaper, and the buttery. A tour of the house takes you through various architectural styles up to 1929, when the house was purchased by the Society for the Preservation of New England Antiquities. Open from June 1 to October 15, Tuesday, Thursday, and weekends from 12 to 5. Admission is $1.50.

- **Old South Presbyterian Church** (corner of Spring and Federal streets), built in 1756, has a famous whispering gallery. George Whitfield, the evangelist, is buried in a crypt. The steeple bell was cast by Paul Revere.

- No trip to Newburyport is complete without a walk along **High Street,** where sea captains built their homes in the eighteenth and early nineteenth centuries, and a trip through the wildlife refuge on **Plum Island** *(see #18, Walks).* Shoppers should head for the restored area around Market Square and along State Street.

- **The Historical Society** (phone: 462-2681) has information on historic houses open to the public.

- Trained naturalists will take you to the feeding grounds of humpback whales aboard a 70-foot vessel. Contact **New England Whale Watch** (Box 825, Hampton, NH 03842; phone: 603/926-0952 or 617/465-7165).

5. THE ARTS

- **Newburyport Art Association** (67 Water Street; phone: 465-8769) has frequent exhibits of work by local artists and information on local art events.

- **Inn Street Gallery,** a cooperative of local artists and craftspeople, was still looking for new headquarters at the time of publication. Two members, Lois Gerrish and Joe Blackburn, can be reached at Another Atmosphere (19 Market Square; phone: 462-8029). Lois's home number is 363-2944.

- **Edward Piel** (307 High Street; phone: 462-7012) has a national reputation for his handmade model ships, selling for $40 to $350.

- Silversmithing has been practiced here since the seventeenth century. **Towle Silversmiths,** the oldest corporation in the country, has a factory outlet store in the 1690 House at 262 Merrimack Street. (Phone: 465-8430.)

- **The Theatre of Newburyport** (75 Water Street; phone: 462-3332) is a repertory group with productions for both children and adults. Recent productions include an original musical based on the works of e. e. cummings. Tickets cost $6 to $7.

- **Amesbury Playhouse** (15 minutes from downtown Newburyport; phone: 388-9444) is a dinner theater presenting drama, comedy, and musicals. Recent productions include *Damn Yankees*. Dinner and show cost $12.50 to $17.50.

- **Castle Hill Festival Concert Series** (Box 283, Ipswich 01938; phone: 356-4070) is a summer outdoor classical music festival with performances on Friday and Saturday at 8:30 and Sunday at 5:30. Tickets cost $8 to $12.

6. ANTIQUES AND CRAFTS

- **Christopher L. Snow** (37 Forrester Street; phone: 465-8872).

7. TOURS

- **Air Plum Island** (Plum Island Turnpike; phone: 462-2114) offers 15-minute antique and open-cockpit biplane rides over Newburyport and Plum Island. Flights in a three-passenger Piper Cherokee 140 cost $8 to $10. Flights in a two-passenger 1927 open-cockpit Curtis Travelair 4000 biplane cost $15 for one person, $25 for two.

8. WALKS

HISTORIC NEWBURYPORT

- The Chamber of Commerce distributes a free brochure called "Historic Newburyport" that includes a self-guided walking tour. The more detailed 75¢ guide, "A Walking Tour of Newburyport," is sold at the Chamber of Commerce and at bookstores on State Street. The "Walking Tour" suggests two hour-long walks and includes comments on the architecture and history along the route.
- **The Historical Society** (phone: 462-2681) has information on houses open to the public.
- For a taste of early nineteenth-century Newburyport, take a 40-minute walk along High Street from the Short House (1717) at Rolfe's Lane to the Old Hill Burying Ground behind the Chamber of Commerce information booth. In the late eighteenth century, shipbuilding and foreign trade generated great wealth in Newburyport. Ship owners and sea captains built their homes on a three-mile stretch along High Street, which today offers one of the finest displays of Federal architecture in the country.

On this route you will see the Coffin House (1653), one of the oldest houses in the region, and the Cushing House (1808), home of the Historical Society. Both buildings are open to the public *(see #4,*

What to See and Do). The courthouse, just beyond the information booth, was originally designed in 1805 by Charles Bulfinch, who left his elegant imprint on the state houses in Boston and Hartford. The rear of the building, which retains the original Bulfinch design, is best seen by walking behind the Frog Pond. The **Old Hill Burying Ground** contains the graves of Revolutionary War veterans and various merchants and sea captains.

Return down High Street and turn left on State Street to **Market Square,** through the shopping center of the town. If it's lunchtime, Steake & Steinn (corner of State Street and Threadneedle) is a good bet. All major credit cards are accepted. As the "Walking Guide" points out, the rows of brick commercial buildings at Market Square are virtually unique in America, since they were all built at one time, after the Great Fire of 1811. This was one of the first examples of urban renewal in America—one of the first attempts to make an attractive urban environment with a completely unified downtown setting.

After shopping in the many craft and speciality shops around the Square, follow Water Street to the Custom House, built in 1835 by Robert Mills, who also designed the U.S. Treasury and the Washington Monument. Continue to the Art Association (65 Water Street) to view the work of local artists. Follow Independence Street up from the harbor. At Middle Street turn left. Across Federal Street is the Old South Presbyterian church (1756), with its whispering gallery and monument to the great evangelist George Whitfield. Just beyond the church, on School Street, is the Garrison House, where the abolitionist William Lloyd Garrison was born in 1805.

PARKER RIVER NATIONAL WILDLIFE REFUGE ON PLUM ISLAND

▪ The six miles of sandy ocean beach are ideal for long walks. Wander away from the areas adjacent to the parking lots and you will have the beach to yourself.

Because access is limited, be sure to arrive before 9 A.M. on a summer Saturday or Sunday. An eight-mile road runs the length of the refuge, with dunes and sandy beach on one side and marshland on the other. The seven parking lots are located near nature trails, observation towers, and raised boardwalks leading to the ocean. Though you may pull over in designated areas and observe the wildlife through your car window, you get little sense of the wild beauty of the refuge unless you leave your car and follow one of the self-guided nature trails. The green-head fly season usually lasts from mid-July to mid-August. Insect repellent, long pants, and long-sleeved shirts are necessary precautions against both the flies and the gnats, which arrive in the early morning, at dusk, or when the wind dies down.

▪ Most visitors stop at parking lot 4 only long enough to climb the observation tower. This is a terrible mistake, for the two-mile **Hellcat Swamp Trail** is one of the most fascinating introductions to shorelife anywhere in the country. Self-guided tour maps are available at the entrance to the trail. No one, not even young children, will get bored here, for the view is always changing. The raised boardwalk takes you over dunes and through forests of Japanese black pine. The highlight of the walk is the observation blind at the edge of the swamp, where muskrats build their home and mallards glide silently by.

The Hellcat Trail runs on both sides of the service road. The oceanside walk is more rigorous, as the path winds in and out of the dunes. There is a lovely picnic spot on top of a sandy rise overlooking the ocean, swamps, marshes, and dunes.

▪ **The Refuge Headquarters** are closed on weekends, so for detailed maps, fact sheets on fishing and wildlife, and bird identification charts, write ahead to the Manager, Parker River National Wildlife Refuge, Northern Boulevard, Plum Island 01950. Phone: 465-5753.

▪ If you plan to picnic, stop at **Esbensen's Danish Bakery** (127 Water Street), a local favorite in downtown Newburyport.

9. BIKING

▪ A three-mile bike ride along High Street will give you a strong sense of Newburyport in the eighteenth and early nineteenth centuries. Weekend traffic, however, may be a problem.

▪ It is an easy four-mile ride to **Plum Island** and another eight miles through the Wildlife Refuge. The refuge road may be a bit bumpy and dusty, since sections are not paved.

▪ There are no bike rental stores in Newburyport. Check with **Elan Ski and Bike Shop** (151 State Street; phone: 462-7753) or **Country Hearth—Tenth Speed** (143 State Street; phone: 462-9500) to see if they have any used bikes they may be willing to rent for the day.

10. BOATING AND FISHING

▪ **Hilton's Fishing Dock** (54 Merrimack Street; phone: 465-9885 or 465-0858) can arrange for private charters, half- or full-day group fishing parties, or hour-long historic harbor tours. The harbor boat makes several stops, including the dock at **Michael's Harborside Restaurant** (Phone: 462-7785).

- **Captain's Fishing Parties** (Plum Island Point; phone: 465-7733 or 462-3141) offers half- and full-day fishing trips.
- **Clipper Marine Deep Sea Fishing** (Route 1, Salisbury; phone: 465-7495) has half- and full-day fishing trips.
- Both **Hilton's Fishing Dock** (see above) and **Clipper Marine** (see above) offer six-hour trips to observe whales and sharks.
- **Captain Fred Littlefield** (Hilton's Fish Dock, 54 Merrimac Street; phone: 465-9885) runs half-day fishing trips.
- Most boat charters go for tuna, mackerel, and bass. There is also surf-casting along Plum Island for striped bass, cod, winter flounder, pollack, and an occasional bluefish blitz. Boardwalks are available from most parking lots for easy access to the beach. When striped bass have migrated into the area, some of the best catches are taken around Emerson's Rocks and the deep areas around parking lot 5.

11. SWIMMING

- The **Parker River National Wildlife Refuge** on Plum Island—about four miles from downtown Newburyport—has six miles of unbroken sandy beaches. This is the longest stretch of beach anywhere north of Cape Cod. There are no lifeguards and access is limited; on a warm summer weekend all visitors, either on foot or by car, are usually turned away after 9 A.M.
- The northern third of **Plum Island** has public beaches.
- There is a public beach and a large parking area in **Salisbury State Park,** a 10-minute drive from downtown Newburyport.

13. RIDING

- **Beech Tree Riding Stables** (just south of route 133, Rowley, about eight miles from Newburyport; phone: 948-2896) has wooded trails on the owner's property.

14. TENNIS

- There are public courts in **Moseley Pines Park** (at the crossroads of Moseley Avenue and Spofford and Merrimack streets) and in **Atkinson Common** (just north of Plummer Avenue at Three Corners). Moseley Pines Park has playgrounds for children and a lovely view of the Merrimack River.
- The **Racquet Club of Newburyport** (178 Low Street; phone: 462-3121) has four courts, sometimes open to nonmembers.

15. GOLF

▪ **Ould Newbury Golf Club** (Route 1A, four miles from downtown Newburyport; phone: 465-9888) is a championship 18-hole course sometimes open to the public. Call ahead for reservations.

▪ **Rowley Country Club** (Route 133, Rowley, seven miles from downtown Newburyport; phone: 948-2731) is a nine-hole course open to the public.

16. FOR KIDS

▪ Bike the length of the **Wildlife Refuge on Plum Island** and climb the observation tower at parking lot 7. Access is limited so on summer weekends be sure to enter the refuge before 9 A.M.

▪ Swim along six miles of sandy beach in the refuge and walk the two-mile **Hellcat Swamp Nature Trail** at parking lot 4. Bring along a checklist of the hundreds of birds seen in the refuge and see how many you can identify.

▪ The **Theatre of Newburyport** (75 Water Street; phone: 465-9051) has productions for children.

▪ Take a one-hour boat tour of the harbor or a six-hour trip to observe sharks and whales *(see #10, Boating and Fishing)*.

17. DINING

There are really no celebrated eating places in Newburyport, though three-star restaurants are bound to appear as Bostonians continue to pour into the area.

▪ **Scandia** (25 State Street; phone: 462-6271) is the best bet for elegant dining in an intimate setting. The limited menu, with entrées priced from $10 to $14, includes baked yellowtail sole stuffed with lobster, scallops, and clams; and seafood linguine, a blend of scallops, clams, and lobster in a white wine and lobster sauce. Ties are optional. Reservations are advised on weekends. All major credit cards are accepted.

▪ **Ten Center Street** (one block from Market Square, off Water Street; phone: 462-6652) has an outdoor patio in summer, where the mood is louder and more casual than at Scandia. Entrées, priced from $9 to $17, include broiled sole with white grapes, vermouth, and lemon; and chicken cutlets layered with prosciutto, mushrooms, artichoke hearts, and cheese. Ties are optional. All major credit cards are accepted. Reservations are advised.

▪ **Michael's Harborside** (Tournament Wharf; phone: 462-7785) has your standard seafood restaurant ambience, but a lovely view over the river, particularly from the open porch in summer. Entrées, priced from $6 to $12, include baked stuffed shrimp and haddock. Dress is informal. No reservations are accepted; expect a 60- to 90-minute wait on summer weekends. Visa and Mastercard are accepted.

▪ **Starboard Galley** (55 Water Street; phone: 465-9005) has reasonable prices. Entrées are reasonably priced from $7 to $11 and include a seafood platter and a 14-ounce sirloin steak. Dress is casual. No credit cards or reservations are accepted. Expect a 30-minute wait on summer weekends.

▪ **The Grog** (13 Middle Street; phone: 465-8008) is great for light, inexpensive meals. Nothing on the menu is over $8.50.

▪ **Arriba** (13 Middle Street; phone: 465-8008) is an inexpensive Mexican restaurant.

18. AFTER HOURS

▪ Bars in surrounding towns close at 2. Newburyport's close at 1.

▪ Summer evening cocktail cruises from 7 to 11 P.M. leave from **Hilton's Fishing Dock.** Phone: 465-9885.

▪ **The Grog** (13 Middle Street) has music downstairs for the under-30 set. The upstairs bar is for an older crowd.

▪ **Michael's Harborside** (Tournament Wharf; phone: 462-7785) has live music on weekends for those young enough to appreciate it.

▪ **Ten Center Street** (one block from Market Square, off Water Street; phone: 462-6652) has an indoor bar and an outdoor patio in summer for couples and singles in the 25- to 35-year-old range.

19. LODGING

▪ Newburyport has four inns or lodging houses, each with its own sophistication and charm. All can be recommended.

▪ **Morrill House** (209 High Street; phone: 462-2808) is on its way to becoming one of the great inns of the Northeast. Rose Ann Hunter, former owner of the Benjamin Choate House, took over the property three years ago and is working tirelessly to restore the 1806 Federal period mansion to its former glory. Early owners include three sea captains, hence the rooftop widow's walk. Henry W. Kinsman, a junior law partner of Daniel Webster, bought the 20-room house in 1836, and Webster was a frequent visitor. Kinsman's room today has a queen-sized four-poster canopied bed. Webster's room has a lithograph of the American statesman over the fireplace, staring down on guests in the hand-carved mahogany bed. Upstairs hallways are hand-stenciled. Third-floor rooms—the former servant quarters—have exposed beams, rockers by the windows, and candles by the bed. No wonder Hallmark used one for a Christmas card. Ms. Petunia Buns, the resident cat, likes to sleep in the music room, where professional musicians are invited to give concerts on the baby grand. Doubles with shared bath cost $45 to $70, including continental breakfast, and afternoon tea.

▪ **The Essex House Inn** (7 Essex Street; phone: 465-3148) has the character and comfort of a small, first-class European hotel. What makes it particularly unique is the wonderful mixture of motellike comforts—color TVs, Jacuzzis, and thick wall-to-wall carpet—and old-world charm. Doubles cost $34 to $100, most with private bath. All major credit cards are accepted.

▪ **The Windsor House** (38 Federal Street; phone: 462-3778) is a restored 1796 brick home, once a chandlery and a butcher shop, located some 200 yards from the banks of the Merrimack River. Spacious rooms are decorated with antique furnishings, and the 14-inch pine floors are as lovely as any you will ever see. The Chandler Suite, with back stairs leading to the old scullery, is the most fully decorated. Third-floor rooms are most private. Doubles, with private bath, cost $60 to $80, including an English breakfast. Visa and Mastercard are accepted.

▪ **Benjamin Choate House** (25 Tyng Street; phone: 462-4786) is a three-story 1794 mansion decorated with modern lithographs. The Leonard Baskin room is one of five rooms named after contemporary artists and decorated with their works. Rooms are tastefully furnished with fine antiques. The innkeeper, Herbert A. Fox, is a Boston lithographer who teaches at the Rhode Island School of Design. Doubles, some with private bath, cost $40 to $56, including breakfast. Visa and Mastercard are accepted.

20. EMERGENCIES

▪ The **Anna Jaques Hospital** has 24-hour emergency service. (Phone: 462-6600.)

21. HOW TO GET THERE

BY CAR. *From New York:* I-95 to I-91 north. At Hartford take I-86 to I-90 east. At Worcester, take I-290 to I-495 north. (When traffic is heavy, avoid 290 and continue east on I-90 to I-495). Take I-495 north to Salisbury exit, Route 110 east. Take Route 1 south into

Newburyport. *From Boston:* I-95 to Route 113 east into Newburyport.

BY BUS. *From New York:* Greyhound (212/635-0800). *From Boston:*
Greyhound (617/423-5810) or Kinson Bus lines (465-8333 or 352-
8787). **C&J Limo** (603/692-5111 or 800/258-7111) has regular
limousine service from Boston's Logan Airport to Newburyport.

22. FOR FURTHER INFORMATION

▪ **Chamber of Commerce,** 29 State Street, Newburyport 01950.
Phone: 462-6680.

▪ **Information Booth** on High Street at the Mall (one block
from the corner of High and State Streets). Open June through October.

▪ Manager, **Parker River National Wildlife Refuge,** Northern
Boulevard, Plum Island 01950. Phone: 465-5753.

23. RECOMMENDED READING

▪ *A Walking Tour of Newburyport,* 75¢, includes commentary
on the architecture, history, and legends of nineteenth-century Newburyport. Available from the Chamber of Commerce (29 State Street)
or from book stores on State Street.

▪ Peter Randall. *Newburyport and the Merrimack.* Pictures and
commentary. Available in local book stores.

Historic Deerfield, Massachusetts

(Area Code, 413; Zip Code, 01342)

1. DISTANCES

BY CAR. *From New York,* 3½ hours; *from Boston,* 2 hours.

BY BUS. *From New York,* 4 to 6 hours; *from Boston,* 2¾ hours.

2. MAIN ATTRACTIONS

▪ A trip through New England's past along a mile-long eighteenth-century village street with some 30 early American houses.

▪ Guided tours through 12 museum houses displaying one of the nation's finest collections of Connecticut Valley furniture, American and English silver, textiles and needlework, English and Chinese ceramics, and household objects from colonial days to the early National period.

• An elegant 98-year-old inn with antique furnishings and a first-class restaurant.

• Concerts, antique stores, ski trails, wildlife areas for hikes and picnics.

3. INTRODUCTION

When the Reverend William Bentley of Salem, Massachusetts, rode on horseback through Deerfield in the spring of 1782, he remarked, "The Street is one measured mile running North & South. . . . There [are] about 60 houses in the Street in better style, than in any of the Towns I saw."

Twenty-five of these houses still stand on "The Street." Another 27 eighteenth- and nineteenth-century buildings also survive, and are admired by visitors who search for the beauty of America's past.

Most of the homes are lived in—by descendants of the earliest settlers, by the staff of Historic Deerfield, and by the faculty of Deerfield Academy. But 12 buildings are open to the public, restored with exquisite collections of early American furniture, textiles, and ceramics. The entire collection is almost always on display, so you won't find yourself searching for objects stowed away for future exhibits.

It's hard to believe that these venerable old buildings were not assembled to satisfy some commercial whim, but stand on their original sites, many of them with their original furnishings.

Unlike Williamsburg and Sturbridge Village, Historic Deerfield does not turn into a ghost town when weekend visitors head back to the cities. "The Street" has a life, an integrity of its own, rooted as much in the present as in the past. There are no stores, no supermarkets or gas stations, to assault you with a sense of the present, but people do live here, just as they did 300 years ago. Working farms still touch the street, with their stands of cows and corn. Boys still shout in the playing fields of Deerfield Academy, along the banks of the Deerfield River.

The town began as an outpost on the frontier and in a sense it remains one today: a tiny community isolated against the tawdriness of modern life. A glimpse of a vanishing America is what Deerfield offers; a privileged view into a safe, homogeneous, small-town world, light-years away from tenements, split-levels, and shopping malls. Deerfielders like to point out that Williamsburg attracts as many visitors in a day as Deerfield gets in a year. This is just fine with them, for hordes of tourists would pose a threat as serious as the

French and Indians posed in 1704, when the "heathens" poured in over the walls and destroyed the town.

A sense of external threat has always given Deerfielders a feeling of unity and communal pride, and helps explain their infatuation with their past.

The town was settled in 1669 as a wilderness outpost of colonial America in the upper Connecticut River Valley. The settlement was abandoned after the Bloody Brook Massacre of 1675. Several venturesome men returned two years later, but were captured and carried off to Canada. In 1704, Queen Anne's War between England and France spread to their colonies in America. To prevent English settlers in Massachusetts from moving farther north and establishing outposts near the Canadian border, the governor of New France persuaded the Indians to join with the French in raids of the English settlements. Deerfield was attacked on February 9, 1704. Two hundred French regulars and 142 Abenaki and Caughnawaga Indians crept across the frozen Deerfield River, scaled the high snowbanks against the stockade wall, and dropped silently inside. Half the settlers were killed. Help from surrounding settlements came too late, and 112 settlers were taken captive and marched 300 miles to Canada through deep snow and bitter cold. Twenty perished. Many were later returned; a few stayed in Canada and married into French and Indian families. Deerfield remained a military outpost until a treaty was negotiated with the six Iroquois nations in 1735. The town then regained its former prosperity as the commercial center of a rich agricultural region. Settlers began to build substantial homes with the refined furnishings of an established and well-to-do society.

Go to Memorial Hall today and you will see the actual door that was hacked through by the tomahawks during the Massacre of 1704. The door, all that remains of what is now called the Indian House, is the symbol of a town that has struggled to maintain its identity ever since. As a writer from the Federal Writer's Project put it: "The wonderful ghostliness of this mile-long 'Street' of grave and ancient houses, the strange air of unreality that hangs over it, arises precisely from the fact that the little town is saying two things at once. It is saying, 'I dared to be beautiful, even in the shadow of the wilderness; but it is also saying, 'And the wilderness haunts me, the ghosts of a slain race in my doorways and clapboards, like a kind of death.' "

A sense of death may still hover over Historic Deerfield, but so does life, ever since Henry Flynt and his wife set about preserving and restoring "The Street" in 1952. Flynt, whose son attended Deerfield in 1936, later became chairman of the academy's board of trustees. It was the academy's illustrious headmaster, Frank Boyden, who convinced Flynt to buy the Deerfield Inn and open it year-round for visiting parents and guests. A New York attorney, Flynt had always dreamed of opening an inn.

In time, what began as a hobby became a passionate lifetime commitment. Moving into the Allen House, the Flynts began buying up properties, restoring them, and filling them with antiques. A few buildings such as Hall Tavern and the Dwight-Barnard House were returned to their original site. By the time their work was completed, 22 properties had been bought and refurbished. Twelve are open to the public today—12 museum homes that capture a quality of life still alive and well in Deerfield today.

4. WHAT TO SEE AND DO

HISTORIC DEERFIELD

- "The Street" has 12 museum houses open to the public. Except during the busy fall foliage season, you can hurry through five of them in a day. Three would allow you a more leisurely pace. First stop is the **Information Center** in **Hall Tavern,** diagonally across from the **Deerfield Inn.** Here you can buy combination tickets, and arrange to see a 25-minute orientation film. You should also pick up a copy of the *Valley Advocate*, a weekly paper listing local events. The homes are open year-round except Christmas and Thanksgiving. Hours are Monday through Saturday from 9:30 to 6, and Sunday from 11 to 4:30. (For personal guides *see #7, Tours*.) The cost for visiting all 12 buildings is $15. The three-house ticket costs $4.50. Individual admissions may be purchased for **$2** or **$3** at each house. Guided tours last 30 to 45 minutes per house, and are limited to six visitors.

- The **Wells-Thorn House** (included in the Deerfield Sampler) is the recommended first stop, not only because it is the oldest building, but because it was built in two stages (1717 and 1751), and visitors will enjoy contrasting the different styles. The house has a bit of everything: Federal architecture, English ceramics, a lawyer's office, a pantry, a buttery, and so on. The older part has high windows and an indoor well—precautions against a repetition of the Indian Massacre, which took place only 13 years before the house was built.

- The **Frary House** (also on the Sampler) has a "touch it" room that is ideal for children. The enormous, L-shaped, 2½-story building has an elegant ballroom in the half of the house that was used as a tavern.

- The **Wright House** (1824) is particularly worthwile for Oriental porcelain and furniture that is not of New England origin.
- For an overview of Connecticut Valley furnishings, visit the **Sheldon-Hawks House** (1743).
- **The Dwight-Barnard House** (c. 1725) is particularly fine for ceramics and painting.
- Though not included on any of the combination tickets, the **Allen House** is worth the $3 admission price. The Flynts lived here from 1944 to 1975, and left behind one of the country's finest collections of Connecticut Valley furniture, textiles, prints, and decorative accessories.
- The **Ashley House** (c. 1730) shows the elegant life-style of the Reverend Jonathan Ashley, an early New England minister. Over his desk hangs a portrait of George III, a reminder of his Tory sympathies during the American Revolution.
- **Asa Stebbins House** (1799), Deerfield's first brick house, was built for the wealthiest landowner in Franklin County and today features French wallpapers, freehand wall painting, and fine New England furniture of the Federal period.
- **Helen Geier Flynt Fabric Hall** features a fine collection of American, English, and European needlework, textiles, and costumes. Admission is $2.
- Visitors can call 772-0241 and arrange for free tours of **Deerfield Academy,** established in 1797 and today one of the leading small preparatory schools in the country. The main buildings are within walking distance of "The Street."
- **Memorial Hall** (on the corner of Memorial Street and Routes 5 and 10; phone: 773-8929 or 773-5206) contains the famous **Indian House Door**—gashes and all—that survived attacks on the 1698 homestead of Ensign John Sheldon. Designed in 1798 as the first home of Deerfield Academy, the hall is now a museum with period rooms (an old family kitchen, parlor, and bedroom); a replica of a 1797 schoolroom; and collections of early carved and painted chests, Indian artifacts, musical instruments, tools, pewter, paintings, embroidery, and ceramics. Also on display is a collection of photos by the Allen sisters, among the country's most gifted early glass-plate camerawomen, which records nineteenth-century Deerfield life and landscapes. Open May through October, weekdays from 10 to 4:30, and weekends from 12:30 to 4:30; open off-season by appointment. Admission is $2 for adults, 75¢ for children 12 and under.
- **The Old Burying Ground** (*see #16, For Kids*), a short walk from "The Street" along Albany Road, is a moving tribute to Deerfield's past. There are many eighteenth-century stones, with

some memorable and somber epitaphs ("Death is a debt to nature due/ which i have Paid & so must you").

IN THE DEERFIELD AREA

▪ If you've never seen maple sugar being made, or tasted hot, pure maple sugar on cold, clean snow, visit one of the local maple farms from mid-March to early April. Three of the best known in the area are **Highland Bush** (Ashfield, about 16 miles west of Deerfield; phone: 628-3268); **Gould's Sugar House** (Route 2, Shelburne, about 9 miles from Deerfield; phone: 625-6170); and **Davenport's Sugar House** (Shelburne, off Route 2, about 15 miles from Deerfield; phone: 625-2866). Other sugar houses include: **Beaver Meadow Farm** (Ashfield; phone: 625-6559); **Howes Sugar House** (Ashfield; phone: 628-3296); **Roger Scott** (Ashfield; phone: 625-2250); **Burnett's Sugar House** (Conway; phone: 369-4626); **Hickory Ridge Farm** (Conway; phone: 369-4447); and **R. Carlyle Field & Sons,** (Leverett; phone: 549-1788).

▪ The 44-foot, 60-passenger cruise boat *Quinnetukut II* (the Indian name for the Connecticut River) takes visitors on a 90-minute ride on a 12-mile stretch of the river. The crew describes the ecological and geographic features along the way. Advance reservations are recommended from the **Northfield Recreation and Environmental Center** (Northfield, off Route 63, about 18 miles northeast of Deerfield; phone: 659-3714.) Tickets must be picked up at least 30 minutes before departure. The cruise runs from June through the fall foliage season, Wednesdays through Sundays. The boat trip, picnic areas, and miles of cross-country trails here were developed by Northeast Utilities in return for the right to build a pumped storage generating plant deep within the mountain. Water from the Connecticut River is pumped into a 320-acre reservoir on top of the mountain and released during periods of high electrical demand. Underground bus tours to the hydroelectric station can be arranged in conjunction with a 30-minute film on the station's construction. Write to R.R.I., Box 377, Northfield 01360.

Visitors who appreciate a lovely country ride past antique stores, farm stands, and colorful villages can follow a rectangular route that starts and ends in Deerfield. Take Routes 5 and 10 south to Route 116 west. At Ashfield, turn north on Route 112 to Shelburne Falls. Drive east on Route 2, back to Routes 5 and 10, and continue south to Deerfield. Along the route you will pass:

▪ **Deerfield Antiques and Lighthouse Antiques** on Routes 5 and 10 *(see #6, Antiques and Crafts).*

• Conway, on Route 116, is home of the **Conway House,** one of the best antique stores in the area, and of **Robert Merriam's** rare book store *(see #6, Antiques and Crafts).* The **Conway State Forest** and the **South River State Forest** are lovely for walks, fishing, and picnics. The monumental **Field Memorial Library** seems out of place in such a rural setting. It was donated in 1906 by Marshall Field, who grew up on a nearby family farm. Inside, the floor is a richly colored marble mosaic. The rotunda is surrounded by Ionic columns of solid Brescia Violet marble. Over the fireplace in the south reading room hangs a portrait of Marshall Field.

• Ashfield, in the midst of maple sugar country, is a beautiful little town with double-porch homes, an 1812 town hall that was once a church, and an old folks' home, **Ashfield House,** that was formerly a summer hotel for prominent visitors attracted by the high elevation and the cool summer temperatures. The 128-acre **Chapel-brook Reservation** has streams, waterfalls, and sheer rock faces—a dramatic site for walks and picnics.

• The County Chamber of Commerce distributes a brochure on **Shelburne Falls** warning visitors to slow down as they pass through because "the town is so small that they had to widen the main street to paint a white line down the middle, and politicians have to stick their hands in their own pockets." So tiny is Shelburne Falls that "you can't get drunk because there's no room to fall down," and "there isn't enough room for people to change their minds."

Visitors will slow down on their own, however, to walk across the famous **Bridge of Flowers.** The five-arch concrete span was originally built in 1908 to carry a trolley line across the Deerfield River. It became an eyesore with the passing of the trolley in 1928, and community groups converted it into a pathway for flowers; it's lit from dusk to 11 P.M. during the summer months.

• Just downstream from the Bridge of Flowers is **Salmon Falls.** The river bottom has the largest selection of glacial potholes in the country. (New York City drivers may not agree.) The holes were ground out of granite during the glacial age and vary in size from six inches to 39 feet in diameter.

• To buy or pick your own fruit, stop at **Mohawk Orchards** (Shelburne; phone: 625-2874), one-quarter mile north of Route 2 on the Colrain-Shelburne Road. At **Valley View Orchards** (Peckville Road, Shelburne) you can pick your own apples in the fall.

• Returning to Deerfield on Routes 5 and 10, you will pass **The Antique Center of Old Deerfield,** a collection of 12 shops.

5. THE ARTS

▪ **Mohawk Trail Concerts** (Charlemont, Route 2, about 22 miles northwest of Deerfield; phone: 774-3690) are performed in the **Charlemont Federated Church** from mid-July to early October. Small ensemble groups featuring such artists as Jaime Laredo give public rehearsals Friday nights at 7:30 and performances Saturdays at 8. Tickets cost from $2.50 to $5.50. Mailing address: Box 843, Greenfield 01302.

▪ The **Arena Civic Theatre** (Box 744, Greenfield 01302; phone: 773-9891) offers musicals and comedies from mid-June through August. Tickets are $3.50 to $6.

▪ **"Music in Deerfield"** (phone: 773-8929) presents a series of quality concerts in the fall, winter, and spring in the **Historic Brick Church Meeting House of The First Church of Deerfield** (located on **The Commons**, along "The Street.") Tickets are $6. The **Memorial Hall Museum** (at the same number) also holds a series of chamber music concerts on Sunday afternoons from the end of June through the fall foliage season.

6. ANTIQUES AND CRAFTS

▪ **Leverett Craftsmen and Artists** (Leverett, about 12 miles southeast of Deerfield; phone: 549-6871) is located in an 1875 box factory, where the work of 200 New England weavers, painters, potters, silversmiths, etc. are on sale. Fifteen artists have studios on the premises, which may be visited by appointment. Open daily from 12 to 5; Saturdays from 10 to 5. TO GET THERE: Routes 5 and 10 south to Route 116 east. Past the Sunderland apartment complex, turn left on Bull Hill Road to Route 63. Turn left and after about 500 feet, turn right on Depot Road to Leverett Center. Follow the signs.

▪ **Ken Miller** (Warwick Avenue, Northfield, about 18 miles northeast of Deerfield; phone: 498-2749) holds auctions on Monday nights at 6:30 in the summer and fall, and on Saturdays from 10 to 5 during the off-season. He also runs a flea market on Sundays, April 15 through October, from 7 to 3. Everything from antiques to fruits and plants is on sale.

▪ **Deerfield Pottery** (phone: 772-0345), located behind the reconstructed **Indian House** on "The Street" in Historic Deerfield, sells pottery, quilts, and hand-crafted lampshades. Open daily from 9 to 5 during the summer and fall foliage season.

▪ There are several antique dealers on Routes 5 and 10. South of Greenfield is **The Antique Center of Old Deerfield** (phone: 773-

3620), a collection of 16 shops. Just off the South Deerfield exit of I-91, are **A Antiques** and **Lighthouse Antiques** (phone: 665-2488 or 665-4554), selling New England furniture and accessories.

▪ Visitors who take Route 116 to Ashfield *(see #4, What to See and Do)* will pass the **Conway House** (Route 116, about 11 miles southwest of Deerfield; phone: 369-4660), where furniture and eighteenth- and nineteenth-century accessories, including samplers, quilts, early lighting, glass, and china, are sold. On the same route is **Robert L. Merriam's** rare book store (Newhall Road, Conway; phone: 369-4052 or 773-5021), open on Sundays from 1 to 5 or by appointment.

▪ A list of 42 antique shops in the county is available from the **Chamber of Commerce** *(see #22, For Further Information)* or from Mrs. Frederick Pugliano, Secretary, **Pioneer Valley Antique Dealers Association,** P.O. Box 244, Westfield, Massachusetts 01085.

7. TOURS

▪ Guides will take you on 30- to 45-minute tours of each of the 12 museum houses. Visitors who want to tour at their own pace and focus on their own special interests should arrange at least one week in advance for **Tours-by-Appointment** (phone: 774-5581.) Groups of two to six persons can spend an entire morning in the **Silver Shop** or **Fabric Hall,** or take a day-long tour of all 12 houses, looking at English ceramics or learning about home life in the colonial period. Tours-by-Appointment also lets you see four buildings not open to the general public: the **Sheldon-Hawks Sled and Toy Collection,** the **Wapping Schoolhouse** of 1839, the **Frank L. Boyden** collection of carriages and buggies, and the **Museum of Architectural Fragments.** Tours are not offered Sundays, holidays, or between October 1 and 20. Half-day tours, from 9 to 12 or from 1 to 4, cost $12 a person. Full-day tours, from 9:30 to 4:30, cost $21.

8. WALKS

▪ For a delightful journey into the past, take the mile-long walk along "The Street," starting on one side and returning on the other. For an introduction to the town, first read *A Brief History of Deerfield,* for sale at Hall Tavern, next to the Information Center.

▪ Visitors to the craft center in Leverett *(see #6, Antiques and Crafts),* about 12 miles southeast of Deerfield, will enjoy an extremely vigorous walk through the nearby **Rattlesnake Gutter**—a fabulous ravine with ledges and crags leading to the 100-foot **Bourne Cliffs.** Ask at the craft center for directions.

Visitors who make the Ashfield-Shelburne-Deerfield trip *(see #4, What to See and Do)* have a choice of parks for scenic walks and picnics.

▪ The **Northfield Mountain Recreation and Environmental Center** (Northfield, about 22 miles northeast of Deerfield; phone: 659-3713) has 25 miles of cross-country trails in winter that turn into hiking trails in summer and fall. Connected with the center is the **Barton Cove Nature Area** (Route 2, Gill)—a mile-long ridge of rocky outcroppings covered with maple, hemlock, oak, and hickory.

▪ **Mount Sugarloaf State Reservation** (off Route 116, just east of Route 5) offers dramatic views of the Connecticut River winding through the valley. Further east on Route 116 are the **Conway State Forest** and the **South River State Forest.** Continuing west on Route 116, take Williamsburg Road at South Ashfield to **Chapelbrook,** a 1,128 acre reservation with streams, waterfalls, and **Pont Mountain.** The **H. O. Cook State Forest** is at the intersection of Routes 2 and 112, near **Shelburne Falls.** Nearby is the **Colrain State Forest,** 1,244 acres of woodlands with some of the oldest trees in the state.

▪ The **County Chamber of Commerce** *(see #22, For Further Information)* has a booklet with maps of all the state parks and forests.

9. BIKING

▪ The only store that rents bikes is **Northfield Bicycle Barn** (Northfield, about 16 miles northeast of Deerfield; phone: 498-2996). All speeds are available. Ask for a free biking map. A popular cycling route is along Route 47 from Hadley north, along the Connecticut River to Northfield. The northern half of the trip, particularly from **Miller's Falls** to Northfield, is the most strenuous and the most scenic.

▪ Here are two routes described in the *Greenfield Recorder,* a paper that lists many area activities:

"In the Sunderland and Deerfield area, there is a trail 14.3 miles with easy cycling with two moderately steep hills and back roads through farm land. During the ride points of interest to see are Historic Deerfield, Mount Sugarloaf State Reservation, the largest sycamore tree east of the Mississippi and Bloody Brook Monument.

"The trail begins on River Road in Deerfield, just west of the bridge that crosses the Connecticut River. After 1½ miles, turn left on Hillside Road. Bear right on North Hillside Road. This will lead you to Route 5 and you must turn right, where you will travel for three-quarters of a mile, turning left on Childs Cross Road, after a 'cow crossing' sign by a farm. At the end of this road, you will turn right on Mill Village Road. This will take you past open fields and grazing cows to historic Old Deerfield. Turn around at the end of Village Street and head south on Mill Village Road. This road leads you to Route 5. Cross it, and continue on the well-paved road on the other side of Route 5, heading toward South Deerfield. When you reach South Deerfield center, turn left on Main Street, which brings you to the base of Mount Sugarloaf. Turn left on Route 116 and your adventure is over.

"Another tour will give the rider a mixture of different roads. It is 18.3 miles and includes flat stretches, rolling hills and a few steep grades over country roads and Route 116. Interesting sites include Northampton Reservoir, an abandoned beaver dam, cascading brooks, Mount Sugarloaf and Mount Toby in profile.

"Beginning on Chestnut Plain Road in Whately center in front of the town hall. Turn right on Haydenville Road across from the town hall. As you follow the road, you will pass the Mount Esther Sugar House and as you ride down the other side of the hill, the road curves right, then left over a small bridge. Follow the signs to Haydenville and Williamsburg. After the bridge you will come to a fork in the road and will turn right and then right again on Webber Road. The route is gently hilly for 1.5 miles to West Whately, a part of Whately distinguished only by a group of houses and two forks in the road. Bear left at the first fork. A sign indicates that Conway is straight ahead on Conway Road. Go north. You will ride through 5.5 miles of woods and fields. Conway Road changes names to Whately Road. Just before the last descent into Conway center, turn right on route 116. Turn right on South Mill River Road, an obvious fork off Route 116. Turn right. Bear left by a 'camping' sign. At Whately center head south on Chestnut Plain Road, whose name changes to Pantry Road and joins Route 10 by the Dial Tone Lounge. Turn right into Bridge Road and follow it to Look Park."

10. BOATING AND FISHING

For information on boat launch areas and the best lakes and streams for fishing, contact either the **Regional Headquarters Division of Forests and Parks** (Amherst; phone: 549-1461) or the **Connecticut Valley Wildlife District** (Belchertown; phone: 323-7632). For general information, contact the **State Division of Fisheries and**

Wildlife, Leverett Saltonstall Building Government Center, 100 Cambridge Street, Boston 02202; (phone: 617/727-3151). Fishing licenses are available from the State Division of Fisheries and Wildlife (address above), from city or town clerks, and from most sporting-goods stores.

- **Northfield Mountain Recreation and Environmental Center** (phone: 659-3714 off-season, 863-9300 in-season) rents canoes and rowboats at **Bartons Cove** (Route 2, Gill) for use on the Connecticut River. This is flat-water canoeing, fine for beginners.

FISHING

- State parks with lakes for fishing include: **South River State Forest** (Conway, Route 116, about 11 miles southwest of Deerfield); **Conway State Forest** (Conway, Route 116); and **Erving State Forest,** (Route 2, Erving, about 18 miles east of Deerfield).

BOATING

- **Taylor Rentals** (369 High Street, Greenfield; phone: 773-8643) rents canoes, which you will have to transport yourself.
- **Western Massachusetts** offers the best trout fishing in the state. A comprehensive list of stocked waters is included in the *Welcome to Franklin County* booklet available from the **Franklin County Chamber of Commerce** *(see #22, For Further Information).*

11. SWIMMING

- Wear a bathing suit under your clothes, and, after a tour of houses along "The Street," follow Albany Road, behind the Civil War Monument, to the **Deerfield River.** You can swim, sun, and picnic along the river, behind the Deerfield Academy playing fields.
- **Laurel Lake** (Route 2, Erving, about 15 miles northeast of Deerfield) has a beach with supervised swimming.

12. SKIING

DOWNHILL

- The largest area in the region is **Berkshire East** (Route 2, Charlemont, about 22 miles northwest of Deerfield; phone: 339-6617). Four double-chair lifts lead to 20 trails. There is night skiing Wednesday through Saturday from 4 to 10. Lifts cost $15 weekdays, $20 weekends, $9 evenings.
- North of Springfield is the **Mount Tom Ski Area** (Route 5,

about one mile west of I-91, exit 17; phone: 536-0416). Three double-chair lifts lead to 17 trails. There is night skiing from 5 to 10. Lifts cost $7.

▪ Beginners who want to avoid crowds can go to **Berkshire Snow Basin** (Route 9, West Cummington, about 31 miles southwest of Deerfield; phone: 634-8808). Four T-bars lead to eight trails. Lifts are less expensive than elsewhere.

▪ The area closest to Deerfield (also good for families and beginners) is **Mount Mohawk** (Route 2, Shelburne, about six miles north of Deerfield; phone: 625-9048). Two T-bars lead to six trails.

▪ For information on ski conditions in the Berkshires, call 800/628-5030 out of state, and 413/499-0700 in Massachusetts.

CROSS-COUNTRY

▪ **Northfield Mountain Ski Touring Center** (Northfield, about 16 miles northeast of Deerfield; phone: 659-3713) has 25 of the most scenic and best groomed trails in New England. Some are double-tracked, so you and a friend can ski side by side. Rentals are available. At the intersection of two favorite trails is a shelter with a fire and snacks for sale. If you've never snowshoed before, here's your chance: the **Ski Shop** at the Touring Center rents snowshoes for use on five miles of trails.

▪ Is your family split between downhill and cross-country skiers? Downhillers can go to **Berkshire East** (see above) while others use the area's ungroomed cross-country trails free of charge.

▪ **Northfield Bicycle Barn and Cross-Country Ski Shop** (Northfield; phone: 498-2996) rents skis and offers lessons. A five-mile beginner's trail leads from the shop through woods and orchards. No trail fees.

▪ Only seven miles south of Berkshire East (see above) is **Stump Sprouts Ski Touring Center and Guest Lodge** (West Hawley, about 29 miles west of Deerfield; phone: 339-4265). Fifteen miles of trails, for both beginners and experts, some groomed, wind through wooded and open areas. Rentals are available.

▪ Cross-country skiing is permitted in the county's 12 state forests. Write to the **Chamber of Commerce** (see #22, For Further Information) for a booklet with maps.

13. RIDING

▪ **Mount Toby Stables** (Route 63, Leverett, about 12 miles southeast of Deerfield; phone: 549-1677) offers year-round guided trail rides through the **University of Massachusett's Conservation Forest.**

- **West Hatfield Stables** (Route 5, West Hatfield, about 13 miles south of Deerfield; phone: 247-9098) offers lessons in English and Western riding along old stagecoach trails from mid-March through November.

14. TENNIS

- The courts at Deerfield Academy are not open to the public. The nearest public courts are off High Street in **Highland Park** in a secluded residential area of south Greenfield, about three miles north of Deerfield.
- Also in Greenfield are the **Beacon Street Tennis Courts,** the **Davis Street Tennis Courts,** and the **Stoneleigh-Burnham School Tennis Courts** on Bernardston Road.
- The **Amherst Tennis Club** (Route 116, Sunderland, about 8 miles south of Deerfield, phone: 549-4545) has three indoor and two outdoor clay courts and four racquetball courts.
- **Candlelight Resort Motor Inn** (junction of Route 2 west and I-91, exit 26, five miles north of Deerfield; phone: 772-0101) has courts open to nonguests.

15. GOLF

- The closest course is at the **Mohawk Meadows Golf Club** (Deerfield, about two miles north of the historic area on Routes 5 and 10; phone: 773-9047). This is a nine-hole, par-36 course.
- **Ashfield Community Golf Club** (Ashfield, about 18 miles west of Deerfield; phone: 628-4413) has a nine-hole, par-33 course.
- **Oak Ridge Golf Club** (Gill, about 10 miles northeast of Deerfield; phone: 836-2010) has a nine-hole, par 36 course.
- **Northfield Country Club** (East Northfield, about 19 miles northeast of Deerfield; phone: 498-5341) has a nine-hole, par-36 course.
- **Cherry Hill Golf Course** (North Amherst, about 12 miles southeast of Deerfield; phone: 253-9935).
- **Candlelight Resort Motor Inn** (junction of Route 2 west and I-91, exit 26, five miles north of Deerfield; phone: 772-0101) is opening a par-3, nine-hole course this summer.

16. FOR KIDS

▪ On "The Street," the best bet for children is the **Frary House,** which has a "touch it" room. Some old-fashioned household items will give kids a sense of domestic life in the eighteenth century. In **The Wilson Printing Office,** children can see a printer at work.

▪ A trip to the **Old Burying Ground** (follow Albany Road behind The Common) is a lesson in history. Let children study the dates on the stones and ponder why so many infants, children, and young mothers are buried there. Discuss attitudes towards this world and the next, as seen through epitaphs.

▪ Discuss the Dearfield Massacre, and then see the Indian House Door in **Memorial Hall** (see #4, What to See and Do). The 1797 schoolroom here should also interest children.

▪ It will be an unusual child who will want to spend more than, say, an hour visiting the museum houses in Deerfield. There is no reason why older children can't bike up and down the mile-long street while their parents are learning about colonial needlework or Chinese porcelains. Children could also be left safely to play ball or Frisbee on the fields of **Deerfield Academy.**

▪ Children will enjoy the 90-minute river trip along the **Connecticut River** in Northfield (see #4, What to See and Do), and a bus trip to the power station inside the mountain.

17. DINING

▪ There are only a few quality restaurants in the area. The best bet is the **Deerfield Inn** (Deerfield; phone: 774-2359). The formal dining room has floral draperies and Queen Anne and Chippendale chairs. Entrées, from $9 to $14, include medallions of veal topped with a puree of mushrooms and shallots, and glazed with a Gruyère sauce; filet of scrod with wine and shallots; and baked shrimp stuffed with crab meat. Dress is optional, but ties are in keeping with the elegant setting. All major credit cards. Reservations are advised, particularly on weekends.

▪ The **Sweetheart Restaurant,** (42 South Maple Street, off Route 2, Shelburne Falls, about 13 miles northwest of Deerfield; phone: 625-2064) is a local landmark. In 1914 the Mohawk Trail (Route 2) was built from Greenfield to North Adams, past Alice Brown's door. Alice began making small hearts of maple sugar called "sweethearts." Who could drive by without stopping for his "sweetheart"? The teahouse she ran from 1916 to 1936 is today a fine French restaurant, under new management since January 1981. The dining room, which seats up to 250, overlooks the Deerfield River and the town of Shelburne Falls. Entrées, priced from $7.95 to $14.95, include filet of sole amandine, half roast duckling with Grand Marnier, breast of capon with garlic butter and rice, and rack of lamb. Favorite desserts are hazelnut chocolate mousse and frozen fruit sorbet. All major credit cards are accepted. Dress is optional. Reservations are advised on weekends.

■ For lunch, there are picnic tables behind **Hall Tavern** and dozens of picnic spots behind the historic houses on "The Street." Ask at the **Information Center** for suggestions. The **Deerfield Inn** (phone: 774-5587) sells a picnic lunch for $5 to $7 that must be ordered 24 hours in advance. The coffee shop at the inn serves inexpensive sandwiches from 11:30 to 2.

■ Visitors returning to New York can dine in Northampton (about 16 miles south of Deerfield, off I-91) at **Beardsley's Café Restaurant,** (140 Main Street; phone: 586-2699), which caters to a professional faculty crowd. The oak-paneled room with stained-glass windows is named for the father of art nouveau. Booths and tables are of solid oak. Entrées, ranging from $8.50 to $17.50, include veal tournedos; and boneless chicken stuffed with fresh chopped spinach, ricotta cheese, and herbs. Dress is casual. All major credit cards are accepted. Reservations are needed on weekends.

■ Fast food restaurants, such as **Friendly's,** are on Route 5 and 10, a few miles north of Deerfield.

18. AFTER HOURS

■ Deerfield is a house party area; weekend visitors who insist on an active nightlife will have to drive to the college towns of Northampton and Amherst, about 20 miles to the south. The bar at the **Deerfield Inn** (phone: 774-5587) is open till 1 A.M. An under-30 crowd gathers in Greenfield at **Hermes** (Mohawk Mall, the west end of Main Street; phone: 772-6300).

■ **Berkshire East** (Route 2, Charlemont; phone: 337-6617) has night skiing *(see #12, Skiing).*

■ For concerts, theater, and other local happenings, pick up a copy of the *Valley Advocate* at the **Historic Deerfield Information Center** or at any local store.

19. LODGING

■ Stay at the **Deerfield Inn** (Deerfield 01342; phone 774-5587), and you can park your car and never see it again until it's time to return home. The 101-year-old inn is located in the center of Historic

Deerfield; walk out the front door in the early morning or late afternoon, when all the crowds are gone, and you can have "The Street" to yourself. The inn was the first building the Flynts restored. Even if you don't stay here, the parlors and dining rooms are worth exploring for their eighteenth- and nineteenth-century antiques. Rooms are simply and tastefully decorated with antique furniture— Room 44 has a lovely four-poster, canopied bed—and quality reproductions. The mood is formal, yet friendly and unpretentious. In February 1979 a kitchen fire spread to the upper floors and raged for eight hours. In freezing temperatures and high winds, a brigade of students, faculty, and townspeople removed most of the antiques. The inn reopened in April 1981, as lovely as ever, and a 12-room annex was added last winter. Some visitors may want to request accommodations in the original building. Doubles with private bath cost $64 to $70. All major credit cards are accepted.

▪ **Fiske Farm** (Zerah Fiske Road, Shelburne Falls 01370, about 13 miles northwest of Deerfield; phone: 625-6375) has almost nothing in common with the Deerfield Inn. While the inn is formal and elegant, and encourages privacy, life at the Fiske Farm is family-style—laid back and homey. As Mrs. Fiske puts it, "We eat well here, but trout amandine we don't have." In the evening, guests gather around the long pine table for perhaps a roast and homegrown vegetables, and popovers with homemade jam. The six guest rooms have beautiful wide pine floors. In the downstairs room a set of kitchen steps lead to the high, canopied bed. All guests share a bathroom and a single dining room table, so don't come to Fiske Farm unless you're prepared to make new friends. During the day, Mrs. Fiske will show you through the dairy barns on her 300-acre farm, or point out the best trails to hike or cross-country ski. Rooms are $35 a person, including two meals, or $25 with breakast only. No credit cards are accepted.

▪ A real find is Mrs. Dorothy Sautter's **Highland Springs Guest House** (Route 2, Shelburne, about 9 miles northwest of Deerfield; phone: 625-2648.) Mrs. Sautter charges $12 a night per couple (!) for each of four guest rooms, one with private bath. Rooms are delightfully furnished with four-poster beds and soft, flowery wallpaper. Rooms facing away from Route 2 may be somewhat quieter. When I first met Mrs. Sautter, she was out in back, mowing a very tidy lawn bordered by flowers. "I love to work outdoors," she told me. "I think it keeps me young. I'm going to be 80 this month." Mrs. Sautter wants visitors to call first, so she can "see who you are."

▪ **Motel 6** (State Road, South Deerfield, two miles south of the historic area; phone: 665-2681) was built as a Ramada Inn, so rooms are more comfortable than one might expect. Facilities include an indoor pool. Doubles cost $23. All major credit cards are accepted.

- **Greenfield Howard Johnson Motel** (junction of Route 2 and I-91, exit 26; five miles north of Deerfield; phone: 774-2211) has an outdoor pool. Doubles cost $56 to $62.
- **Candlelight Resort Motor Inn** (208 Mohawk Trail, junction of Route 2 and I-91, five miles north of Deerfield; phone: 772-0101) is a clean, comfortable motel with swimming pool, tennis court, and par-3 golf course. Doubles cost $36 to $64.

20. EMERGENCIES

- The closest hospital to Historic Deerfield is **Farren Memorial Hospital** (Turners Falls, 4½ miles north of the historic area, on Routes 5 and 10; phone: 774-3111).
- Not much farther away is **Franklin Medical Center** (High Street, Greenfield; phone: 772-0211).

21. HOW TO GET THERE

BY CAR. *From New York:* I-91 north to exit 24, then go six miles north on Routes 5 and 10. *From Boston:* Route 2 west to I-91 south. At exit 25, turn north on Routes 5 and 10.

BY BUS. *From New York:* Greyhound (212/635-0800) has service to Greenfield, where you can get a taxi or a LINKS bus (the Franklin Regional Transit Authority; phone: 774-2262) to Deerfield. *From Boston:* Englander Coach Lines (617/423-5810), a division of Bonanza Bus Lines, goes to Greenfield, where you can get a taxi or a LINKS bus (the Franklin Regional Transit Authority; phone: 774-2262) to Deerfield.

BY PLANE. *From Boston:* Delta, Eastern, and Bar Harbor Airlines fly to Bradley Airport. Vermont Transit (413/773-9410), a division of Greyhound, has bus service from Bradley to Greenfield. From Greenfield, take a taxi or a LINKS bus (the Franklin Regional Transit Authority; phone: 774-2262) to Deerfield. *From New York:* Delta, USAir, and Bar Harbor Airlines fly to Bradley Airport (see directions from Boston).

22. FOR FURTHER INFORMATION

- **Historic Deerfield, Inc.,** Box 321, Deerfield 01342. Phone: 413/774-5581.

- **Franklin County Chamber of Commerce,** 28 Federal Street, Greenfield. Phone: 413/773-5463.

23. RECOMMENDED READING

- The **Historic Deerfield Museum Store,** across from the Deerfield Inn, has a large collection of books of local interest, including *A Brief History of Deerfield.*
- John Williams. *Redeemed Captive.* (Deerfield's most famous citizen recounts the story of his forced march to Canada with 111 other Deerfield prisoners in the great raid of 1704.)
- Mary P. Wells. *The Boy Captive of Old Deerfield.* (Children will enjoy this story of the 1704 massacre, as told through the eyes of the 10-year-old son of the village minister.)
- "Deerfield Keeps a Truce with Time," *National Geographic,* June 1969.
- Henry N. Flynt and Samuel Chamberlain. *Historic Deerfield: Houses and Interiors* (Hastings House).

Cuttyhunk Island, Massachusetts

(Area Code, 617; Zip Code, 02713)

1. DISTANCES

BY CAR AND SEAPLANE. *From New York,* 4½ hours; *from Boston,* 1½ hours; *from Providence,* 1 hour.

BY CAR AND FERRY. *From New York,* 6 hours; *from Boston,* 3 hours; *from Providence,* 2½ hours.

BY BUS AND SEAPLANE. *From New York,* 5½ hours; *from Boston,* 2 hours; *from Providence,* 1¼ hours.

BY BUS AND FERRY. *From New York,* 6¾ hours; *from Boston,* 3 hours; *from Providence,* 2½ hours.

2. MAJOR ATTRACTIONS

- An "undiscovered" island with one boardinghouse for weekend or weekly guests.
- Fresh seafood, sea breezes, dramatic views.
- Peace!

3. INTRODUCTION

There's a flurry of activity as the seaplane nudges against the dock and supplies are lifted into a pair of supermarket carts and wheeled away. Suddenly you're alone. A deer prances by. You pick up your bag and follow the road as it climbs above the harbor. Brass eagles spread their wings over the doors of clapboard and shingled homes. A life ring hangs beside a door with the words *Post Office: Cuttyhunk* printed on it. A woman in a pink Lacoste shirt drives by in a golf cart. She turns the wheel hard to avoid a dog asleep in the road, and maneuvers around him. The dog doesn't stir.

■ ■ ■

Why do so few people know about this unspoiled island only 90 minutes from downtown Boston? Closer to Times Square than either Nantucket or Martha's Vineyard, it is Everyman's dream of the perfect escape—free from commercial development or crowds. Yet the only regulars are yachtsmen who anchor here on summer weekends and row ashore for candlelit dinners of lobster or freshly harpooned swordfish.

Cuttyhunk—2½ miles by ¾ mile—lies off the southern shore of Massachusetts. It is the outermost of the 16 Elizabeth Islands, which stretch from Woods Hole westward, separating Vineyard Sound from Buzzards Bay. It's the only island in the chain with public accommodations—a boardinghouse that has been serving guests for close to 100 years.

The paved road stops at the last house above the harbor, but you can follow the path to the top of the island, 154 feet above the sea, and looking down on rolling hills and grassy meadows where mushrooms grow wild and cows and sheep once grazed.

Cuttyhunk is only fourteen miles from the mainland, but in spirit it is light years away. There are five phones on the island, all pay phones, and when service is out, as it was one summer for a week, no one can be reached except by emergency radio.

The elements still hold sway here. *The Free Gosnold News,* a mimeographed broadside, reported several summers ago:

"The severe electrical storm on August 5 caused considerable damage on Cuttyhunk. Among the damages besides the power house:

- Telephone wires knocked out and now awaiting special replacement circuits from California. No word yet as to when regular service will resume.
- Lightning hit and downed the Twichell chimney. Smoke and Tess, who were in the house, report an ear-splitting crack and impairment of electricity.
- A ball of fire went through the fish house and lightning split Don Lynch's boat antenna and knocked out his radio.
- The Schencks' refrigerator caught fire. And barefoot Ginger Thomsom suffered burned feet while she was slicing meat in the store."

Few of the forty permanent residents lock their homes unless they're going to the mainland for an extended stay.

One family left the island for good recently because the school only goes through eighth grade and they were not about to send their ninth-grade daughter to boarding school. The one-room schoolhouse was built in 1873 with a $900 appropriation. Two winters ago a teacher was imported from the mainland to instruct 4 children—two eighth-graders, a sixth-grader, and a first-grader. One of the children was his own. The number of students is down to two this year.

There are considerably more deer than children on Cuttyhunk, and some are so tame they will eat from your hand. According to local legend, the deer swam here from neighboring islands and stayed on because the islanders fed them through the winter. Several are as small as dogs. They congregate near the bakery, and some old-timers say it's a diet of bread that keeps them so small.

The baker, one of Cuttyhunk's three elected constables, told me several summers ago that the most serious crime he could remember in his eight years on the job was the theft of a generator from Mel Darr. No one ever did catch the thief, but everyone knows he came from the mainland.

Vandalism has recently become a more serious problem and Cuttyhunk has had to hire a policeman from off-island.

· ■ ■ ■

Poor Bartholomew Gosnold—the history books have been unkind to him. In 1602, eighteen years before the founding of the Plymouth Colony, he sailed from Falmouth with a company of thirty-two men, who eventually settled on Cape Cod, Martha's

Vineyard, and Cuttyhunk. His travels caused quite a stir back at the Mermaid Tavern in London and may have inspired the pilgrims to head for Plymouth, the "northern part of Virginia."

If the people of Cuttyhunk had their way, the name Bartholomew Gosnold would be written in the hearts and minds of every loyal American, alongside the names of John Smith or William Bradford. In 1903, the islanders raised a stone monument at the west end in Gosnold's honor. "We dedicate this islet," said a speaker at the ceremonies, "to Bartholomew Gosnold and his companions, who landed here, May 25th, 1602, old style, and built a fort and storehouse, the first English habitation on this continent."

In 1865, a group of New York's super-rich, mostly bankers and industrialists, decided to purchase a chunk of Cuttyhunk and build themselves an exclusive men's fishing club. It is still standing today. The striped bass that lurked among the huge boulders in the riptide between Cuttyhunk and the neighboring island of Nashawena were the best anywhere. World-record catches were made in these waters.

To join the club one had to be a millionaire at the very least. Membership was originally limited to 50, then expanded to 75. On a summer weekend it was not unusual to see a dozen of Newport's and New York's largest yachts—Rockefeller's, Mellon's, Carnegie's, and others—anchored in Cuttyhunk harbor.

The men, of course, never fished from boats. Twenty-six wooden platforms were built around the island, extending over rocks into deep water. The platforms had rope handrails strung through iron rings on stanchions welded into the rock. Seats were fixed at the ends to accommodate the fisherman and his chummer (hence the word "chum"), a local boy who baited hooks with choice pieces of lobster tail.

Old-timers say that William Wood, a Roman Catholic, built the Avalon Club when the Cuttyhunk Club refused him admission. The caretakers of the Wood estate deny this.

In any case, Wood eventually bought out the Cuttyhunk Club and today his family and their descendants own about two-thirds of the island. What will happen to this land only his trustees know for sure, but it's unlikely that it will ever be parceled out into quarter-acre plots.

A book on the history of Cuttyhunk has preserved this memento from a lost age:

July 23, 1903

CUTTYHUNK

William Woodhill returned to the island Saturday. He is much improved in health. Sunday was his 77th birthday. The menu of the birthday dinner given to him at the club was as follows:

Grapefruit

Green Turtle Soup   Sherry

Olives, Salted Almonds, Radishes

Boiled Striped Bass   Supreme Sauce

Haut Sauterne

Cucumbers   Boiled Onions

Potatoes

Rareripes   Sweetbread Cutlets

Sliced Tomatoes

Spring Lamb   Champagne

Spring Chicken

Peas, Beets, String Beans, Potato Balls

Chow Chow   Gherkins

Roman Punch

Baked Ham   Champagne Sauce

Lobster Salad

Squash Pie   Custard Pudding

Blackberry Pie

Vanilla and Coffee Ice Cream   Pineapple Ice

Ginger   Nut Cake   Fruit

Watermelon

Nuts and Raisins

Coffee   Cigars   Liquors

• • •

Today the summer population swells to nearly 600. Fanned by old money, most of the summer people seem comfortable just being themselves. Everything about them is understated yet instantly recognizable, from last year's Bass Weejuns to old Eddie Bauer sailor shirts, with perhaps a fishhook embedded in the sleeve. Nothing splashy. No gold chains. The only gold chains belong to powerboat people who cluster around the harbor. Old-timers and summer residents are equally happy to see them go.

The powerboat crowd is one of several modest concessions that Cuttyhunk has made to the 1980s. The weekend trade has also spawned several modest gift shops and a waterfront shack selling ice and seafood. Suddenly no one can do without a golf cart. No one had one 20 years ago; today there are more than 60.

Not much change, surely, given the development on Cape Cod or Block Island.

What may save Cuttyhunk is the fact that there is virtually no land for sale. Houses are passed down from one generation to the next and seldom reach the market. How many visitors can a five-passenger seaplane bring in one day? The New Bedford ferry, built in 1916 to carry supplies to William Wood's winter house, has room for only 49 passengers.

While waiting for the ferry to return me to the mainland, a summer resident came up and wished me luck with this book. "Tell everyone how wonderful it is here," he said, squinting into the sun, "but tell it in a way that attracts the good people, and frightens the others away."

I told him I would try. I want to go back to Cuttyhunk myself.

4. WHAT TO SEE AND DO

Swimming, sailing, sunbathing, fishing, walking, eating, sleeping—these are the main activities on Cuttyhunk Island. You can also:

- Take a five-minute walk to the bakery for a chocolate-chip cookie or a bowl of clam chowder.
- Say hello to the swans in the freshwater pond at the west end.
- Visit the old graveyard and speculate on life here in the nineteenth century. Find the memorial stones to two brave islanders, Captain Tim Akin and Isaiah Tilton, who drowned trying to rescue the crew of the brig *Aquatic*, which went down off Pig's Reef in 1893. No one on the ship was lost. Also memorialized here is Captain George Stetson, who drowned when his square-rigger was wrecked on the south side of the island in the 1890s. His crew was taken off in lifeboats, but the good captain refused to leave his sinking ship.
- Get a license from the Town Clerk and dig for hors d'oeuvres—quahogs or hard-shelled clams—at the west end. You can walk into the water and feel the clams with your feet; they feel like stones, and sometimes that's exactly what you'll find.
- Buy lunch at the town store or at the bakery and enjoy a picnic at the west end.
- Bird watch. Many birds make their home here, including war-

blers, swallows, meadowlarks, redwinged blackbirds, thrushes, gulls, terns, and sandpipers.

- Most New England flowers grow here. Identify them. Make a bouquet for someone. Make one for yourself and put it in a glass beside your bed. (But don't pick the heather!)
- Visit the **Cuttyhunk Historical Society,** which has exhibits in summer at the Cuttyhunk School.
- At night, wander down to the dock. Decide which powerboat or yacht you would like to own. There are no "Keep Out" signs. The mood is that of a campfire in the wilderness, where all visitors are friends.

8. WALKS

- The easiest, most popular walk takes all of 10 minutes—but what a breathtaking view! At the Four Corners, facing away from the harbor, turn right and follow the paved road to the top of the hill. The road and stone wall were built by William Wood to lead to a house he hoped to build for his son. But the navy took over the high points of the island to search for submarines during World War II, and Wood's son died during the War. From the summit you can see deer springing through a forest of dwarf poplar, sumac, and wild cherry. Dinghies thread their way through the harbor, among the swaying masts. The white cliffs at **Gay Head** rise from the waves like the cliffs of Dover. Come early and watch the sun rise; come back later, turn 180 degrees, and watch the sun set.
- For a longer walk, about one hour round trip, follow the path to the west end of the island. You can dig for hard-shelled clams here or wander along the top of 25-foot cliffs and listen to the sea pounding against the shore. The cliffs can be dangerous; never try to slide or climb down them. To reach the shoreline, follow the path on top till it descends to a beach and then walk back beneath the cliffs.
- Go beachcombing on the seaward side of the island, particularly after rough weather.
- Adventurous souls can follow the shoreline around the entire island. Be prepared to get wet.
- The deer have made hundreds of trails through the island that are fun to explore. If you walk through high grasses, however, wear long pants and long-sleeved shirts to discourage the ticks. Shake your clothes out well as soon as you take them off. Chances of an allergic reaction to tick bites are slim, but should you develop red, doughnut-shaped rashes on your skin, take antibiotics immediately *(see #20, Emergencies).*

- For a more ambitious walk with a spectacular view that overlooks the entire west end of the island, hike to **Bunker Hill.** Ask any year-round resident for directions.

10. BOATING AND FISHING

- **The Cuttyhunk Yacht Club** will rent small sailboats—Bullseyes, Lasers, and Turnabouts—to weekend guests at both lodging houses.
- **Don Lynch** (Box 173; phone: 996-9293 or 996-9215) will take you to the mainland or nearby Martha's Vineyard in a 22-foot bass boat. He also takes groups fishing for bass, bluefish, and bonita from Memorial Day to November 1. (Bass fishing is best in early spring and fall—from the end of May until late June, and from mid-September to November 1.) Other guides can be located through the Allen House.
- At the west end of the island, fish off the rocks for bass, bluefish, or tautog (a big, stupid—but very tasty—bottom fish).

11. SWIMMING

- The most popular swimming spots are **Church's Beach, Jetty Beach,** and **Barges Beach.** Islanders also like to swim out to a spit of land across from the jetty where the ferry comes in. Beware the jellyfish and the Portuguese men-of-war in the West End pond!

16. FOR KIDS

- *Toby Tyler*—the story of a runaway who joins a circus—is typical of the movie fare on Saturday nights during summer at 7:30. The cost is "a 75¢ donation from every child, adult or dog."

17. DINING

The **Allen House** (phone: 996-9292) has a lively weekend crowd of yachtspeople who anchor in the harbor and row ashore for fresh seafood dinners served on linen tablecloths with candlelight and flowers. Prices are in the $7 to $13 range for entrées. The Allen House features lobster, swordfish, and other basic seafood dishes. Sirloin steak is always available, too. Visa and Mastercard are accepted.
- **Dorothy and Seth Garfield** run a harborfront raw bar serving shrimp, local Belon oysters, and littleneck clams.

- The **Bakery,** run by Tyler Leonard, has a new addition and now serves three basic meals.

18. AFTER HOURS

There is no organized nightlife on Cuttyhunk. By 10 P.M. the Allen House has closed for the night. A pleasant way to end a day is to turn right at the Four Corners (facing away from the harbor) and enjoy an easy, 10-minute walk to the pillbox on top of the hill. On moonless nights you will need a flashlight. On bright, clear nights the lights on sailboats in the harbor flicker like stars. When there's a moon to steer by, take your shoes and socks off and wander along **Church's Beach.**

19. LODGING

Unless you're sleeping on a boat, there is only one place to stay on Cuttyhunk, the **Allen House** (phone: 996-9292). One of the Allen House owners comes from South Carolina; his partner is a textile manufacturer from Tennessee. These off-islanders have fancied things up a bit (to the alarm of some old-timers), introducing such amenities as tablecloths and printed menus. The gift shop sells Cuttyhunk T-shirts and jelly beans in mason jars tied with red ribbons. Rooms are clean and comfortable, with a simple, honest charm.

There are three cottages with private bath that make sense for families with children. Furnishings, however, are more basic than in the thirteen rooms with shared bath in the main house. Doubles in July and August, with no meals, are $60. Doubles in June, September, and October cost $45 per person with breakfast.

20. EMERGENCIES

No doctor lives on the island, but members of the fire department are trained in first aid. For medical emergencies ask the hotel personnel or any year-round resident to put you in touch with **Susan Lynch, A. P. Tilton,** or a town fireman. They have direct radio contact with the Coast Guard, which can come by boat or helicopter. Visitors with allergies should bring their own medicines.

Doctors have been visiting during summer months to study the tick problem. If you develop any red, doughnut-shaped rashes, ask the doctors for antibiotics. The postmistress has necessary information.

21. HOW TO GET THERE

BY CAR. *From New York:* I-95 north to Providence, then I-195 east to the Downtown New Bedford exit. If you're going by ferry, follow signs to the harbor. If you're going by plane, take Route 18 south to Route 6 east (toward Fairhaven). Take the first right after the bridge to the Coast Guard Auxiliary at 80 Middle Street. *From Providence:* I-195 east to the Downtown New Bedford exit. Follow directions above. *From Boston:* I-93 to Route 24 south. Take Route 140 to Downtown New Bedford. Follow directions above.

BY BUS. It is a five-minute taxi ride, costing under $3.50, from the bus terminal to the ferry or the seaplane. *From New York:* Greyhound (212/635-0800) to New Bedford. *From Providence:* Bonanza Bus Lines (401/751-8800) to New Bedford. *From Boston:* Medeiros Bus Co. (617/993-5040) to New Bedford.

BY FERRY. From mid-June to mid-September the *Alert* sails from New Bedford on Monday to Friday at 10 A.M., and departs from Cuttyhunk at 3 P.M. On weekends from Memorial to Columbus Day the ferry leaves New Bedford at 9 A.M. The number of trips depends on the need; be sure to call ahead. On weekdays from mid-September to mid-June the ferry leaves New Bedford only on Tuesdays and Fridays at 10 A.M. and departs from Cuttyhunk at 2 P.M. The trip takes ninety minutes. The round-trip fare is $10. Since the ferry holds only forty-nine passengers, it's advisable to pay in advance by mail. Prepaid reservations will be honored up to thirty minutes before sailing time. Contact: Cuttyhunk Boat Lines, P. O. Box 225, Fairhaven, MA 02719. Phone: 992-1432.

BY TAXI. The Yellow Cab Co. in New Bedford can be reached at 999-5213.

BY SEAPLANE. The ten-minute flight costs $16 per person (for a minimum of three people). Contact: Island Air Service, 80 Middle Street, Fairhaven. Phone: 994-1231. OR 524 Snipatnuit Road, Rochester, MA 02770. Phone: 763-2065.

22. FOR FURTHER INFORMATION

- The **Allen House**, Cuttyhunk, MA 02713. Phone: 617/996-

9292. Off-season: Steve and Jan Anderson, 16 Westport Road, Worcester, MA 01605; phone: 617/853-8913.

23. RECOMMENDED READING

- *The Story of Cuttyhunk* by Louise T. Haskell (for sale in the town store).

Index

DINING AND LODGING GUIDE

381

MORE TRAVEL BOOKS FROM DUTTON

Bed & Breakfast USA
Guaranteed Rates in All 50 States Plus Canada
by Betty Rundback and Nancy Kramer
$7.95 paperback
ISBN: 0-525-48144-3

The Discount Guide for Travelers Over 55
Save Hundreds of Dollars on Hotels, Sightseeing, and
Transportation in the U.S., Canada, and Abroad
by Caroline and Walter Weintz
$6.95 paperback
ISBN: 0-525-48169-9

World Guide for the Jewish Traveler
Covers Jewish Communities and Sights of Interest in 100
Countries and Regions
by Warren Freedman
$8.95 paperback
ISBN: 0-525-48095-1

Available at bookstores or from E. P. Dutton. To order from Dutton, list titles and ISBN numbers. Send a check or money order for the retail price plus appropriate sales tax and 10% for postage and handling to Dept. CW, E. P. Dutton, 2 Park Avenue, New York, NY 10016. New York residents must add sales tax. Allow up to six weeks for delivery.